Tender Care and
Early Learning

INFANT ROOM

PCC

INFANT ROOM

age

Tender Care and Early Learning

Supporting Infants and Toddlers in Early Childhood Settings

2nd Edition

Jacalyn Post, Mary Hohmann,
and Ann S. Epstein, PhD

HighScope
PRESS ®

Ypsilanti, Michigan

Published by

HighScope® Press

A division of the

HighScope Educational Research Foundation

600 North River Street

Ypsilanti, Michigan 48198-2898

734.485.2000, FAX 734.485.0704

Orders: 800.40.PRESS; Fax: 800.442.4FAX; www.highscope.org

E-mail: *press@highscope.org*

Editors: Marcella Weiner, Marge Senninger

Cover design, text design, production: Judy Seling of Seling Design

Photography:

All photos are by Bob Foran, Ann Arbor, MI, with the following exceptions:

Jan Levanger Dowling & Terri C. Mitchell — 258

Gary Easter — 115

Greg Fox — 4 (bottom left), 6, 16, 26, 28, 29, 36, 39, 45, 52, 61, 63, 65, 79, 96, 108, 118, 155, 163, 167, 177, 181 (top), 194 (left), 195, 206, 213, 220 (bottom left), 221, 249, 279, 290, 295, 304 (bottom), 308, 336, 342 (bottom right), 349, 354, 357, 389, 398

HighScope staff — 10, 54, 92, 135, 157, 197, 229, 230, 239, 289, 301, 327, 342 (top right), 368 (top), 375, 384, 395 (bottom right), 402, 408

Mary Hohmann —342 (top left)

Julie Morrison — 71, 75

Library of Congress Cataloging-in-Publication Data

Post, Jacalyn, 1951-

  Tender care and early learning : supporting infants and toddlers in child care settings / Jacalyn Post, Mary Hohmann, and Ann S. Epstein, PhD. -- 2nd ed.

      p. cm.

  ISBN 978-1-57379-583-8 (soft cover : alk. paper) 1. Day care centers--Handbooks, manuals, etc. 2. Infants--Care--Handbooks, manuals, etc. 3. Toddlers--Care--Handbooks, manuals. etc. 4. Early childhood education--Handbooks, manuals, etc. 5. Child development. I. Hohmann, Mary. II. Epstein, Ann S. III. Title.

  HQ778.5.P67 2011

  362.71'2--dc22

2010051225

Printed in the United States of America

10 9 8 7 6 5 4 3

To our very youngest children,

their parents, families,

and caregivers

Contents

Chapter 5: Establishing Schedules and Routines 281

Acknowledgments

We appreciate all the dedicated early childhood professionals who responded to our initial questionnaire, invited us to their sites, and shared their ideas with us during training:

Kay Albrecht, HeartsHome Early Learning Centers, Inc., Houston, Texas

Cathy Albro, The Creative Learning Center, Grand Rapids, Michigan

Beth Apley, Ravenswood Hospital Child Care Center, Chicago, Illinois

Donna Barrett, The Boys and Girls Club Day Care Center, Yarmouth, Nova Scotia

Frances Beck, Debbie School, Miami, Florida

Ann Brown, Kalamazoo Learning Village, Kalamazoo, Michigan

Jill Claridge, Child Study Center, Ft. Worth, Texas

Cyndi Conard, Educational Service Unit 3, Omaha, Nebraska

Sophie Cordoba, Easter Seal Society, Miami, Florida

Nanette Elrod, Corner Cottage Child Care Center, Ann Arbor, Michigan

Debra Dennisuk, Webster School Detroit Even Start Program, Detroit, Michigan

Irene Desverguna, Easter Seal Society, Miami, Florida

Daniel DeVito, ARC, Miami, Florida

Carole Fox Abbott, FDLRS/South, Miami, Florida

Pepper Goodrich, Parents and Toddlers Program of the Cherry Creek School System, Aurora, Colorado

Marian Houk, ACCA Child Development Center, Annandale, Virginia

George Kelley, Peabody Child and Family Center of Georgia College, Milledgeville, Georgia

Carrie Keys, COPE North, Miami, Florida

David Langley, First Step Day Care, Ann Arbor, Michigan

Betty Lisowski, Point Park Children's School, Pittsburgh, Pennsylvania

Constance Melville, Oberlin Child Development Center, Oberlin, Ohio

Ann Murphy, Kennebec Valley Community Action Program, The Madison Baby Bulldog Center, Waterville, Maine

Jenny Orth, South Madison Day Care Child Development, Inc., Madison, Wisconsin

Linda Peavy, Belleville Playland, Belleville, Florida

Kathy Spitzley, Good Times Family Day Care Center, Holland, Michigan

June Spriggs, First Step Day Care, Ann Arbor, Michigan

Terri Strong, Creative Learning Preschool and Child Care Center, Madison, Wisconsin

Maryann Swann, Maryland School for the Deaf, Columbia, Maryland

Patricia Travis, Washtenaw Community College Children's Center, Ann Arbor, Michigan

Joy Vickers, Project TIPP #2, Miami, Florida

Thanks to you, your staff, your children, and their parents!

We would also like to thank the directors and staff of Gretchen's House, our HighScope partner in Ann Arbor, Michigan, who graciously welcomed us to their centers so that we could photograph the children and teachers actively learning with the HighScope Infant-Toddler Curriculum: Laura Griswold, Gretchen's House Dhu Varren; Nan Mastie,

Gretchen's House Stadium; and Julie Morrison, Gretchen's House Mt. Pleasant. A special thanks goes to Erica Hill, Chosen Ones Christian Home Child Care, Warren, Michigan, for opening up her home to us so that we could capture in photos how a family child care provider successfully implements the HighScope Curriculum in a home setting.

We would like to thank our HighScope colleague Shannon Lockhart for her ongoing work on the development of the infant-toddler training and curriculum materials that contributed to this book and her assistance with the selection and captioning of the photos in this new edition. Shannon and Julie Hoelscher carefully reviewed and gave detailed feedback on the manuscript, based on their experience training diverse caregivers around the country and abroad to implement the HighScope Infant-Toddler Curriculum.

We also appreciate the ongoing support and feedback we received from our other past and present early childhood colleagues at HighScope and in the field: Lorna Aaronson, Cathy Calamari, Bonnie Czekanski, Linda Dubay, Betsy Evans, Michelle Graves, Philip Hawkins, Charles Hohmann, Beth Marshall, Jeanne Montie, Polly Neill, Pat Olmsted, Larry Schweinhart, Kathy Spitzley, Sue Terdan, Rachel Underwood, Rosemary Waldron, the late David Weikart, Julie Wigton, Connie Williams, and Diane Woodard. Thanks to you all!

Finally, we owe a special thanks to the book's talented production team. Our editor Marcella Weiner provided a thorough and thoughtful review of the manuscript. Her concern for the subject matter and getting things "just right" for infants and toddlers and those who care for them matched ours. We also value the efforts of Nancy Brickman for additional editorial work; Katie Bruckner for helping to prepare the manuscript; Judy Seling for designing the book; and Bob Foran, Gregory Fox, and the HighScope staff for the wonderful photographs that accompany the text. We extend our thanks and appreciation to all.

In this book, we present strategies for child care settings that promote a tender approach to early learning.

Introduction: The HighScope Infant-Toddler Curriculum

Two principles are central to the HighScope Curriculum. The first is that children construct their understanding of the world from their active involvement with people, materials, and ideas. The second principle…is that the role of adults who teach and care for children is to support children's construction of their own understanding of the world.

— Powell (1991, p. 26)

Since the 1960s, early childhood professionals around the nation have been using the HighScope Curriculum with preschool children (three- and four-year-olds) (Epstein, 2007; Hohmann, Weikart, & Epstein, 2008). Although HighScope's work with infants and toddlers (ages birth to three) also began in the 1960s, questions about how to support active learning with very young children multiplied in the 1990s. Searching for and finding answers to these questions resulted in the first edition of this book, *Tender Care and Early Learning: Supporting Infants and Toddlers in Child Care Settings* (Post & Hohmann, 2000). That book represented what we knew to date about implementing the HighScope Infant-Toddler Curriculum in child care settings.

In the decade since the publication of *Tender Care and Early Learning*, the field's knowledge about the earliest years of life has grown enormously. Discoveries in brain research, for example, empirically support what caregivers and teachers intuitively sensed about the role of early experience in later development. Systematic program evaluations have provided new insights into how the quality of care can affect young children's social-emotional growth and intellectual progress. In addition, group care for infants and toddlers has become a fact of life in today's world, in which increasing numbers of employed parents must find out-of-home care for their young children.

This second edition of *Tender Care and Early Learning* updates the theoretical and research information on infant and toddler development. Since the first book was written, HighScope itself has actively contributed to the ongoing transformation of the field as a whole. Our early childhood specialists now deliver a systematic and comprehensive course of training workshops for caregivers and supervisors, observe in and consult with a wide variety of program settings, and train others to use the validated child and program assessment tools we have developed. We publish print and audiovisual materials to support the implementation of high-quality programs in the United States and abroad.

In sum, the HighScope Infant-Toddler Curriculum has reaffirmed its core principles while simultaneously refining its content as a result of this engagement. We have learned a great deal by reflecting on our interactions with home visitors and with the many practitioners who are effectively nurturing and educating infants and toddlers in centers and family child care homes. (See the Appendix for a historical overview of HighScope and its work with infants and toddlers.)

This book captures the lessons learned by researchers and practitioners everywhere and from HighScope's direct involvement in the growing and vital field of infant and toddler programs.

Principles Guiding the HighScope Infant-Toddler Curriculum

The HighScope infant-toddler wheel of learning (p. 3) graphically represents the major ideas that guide the HighScope

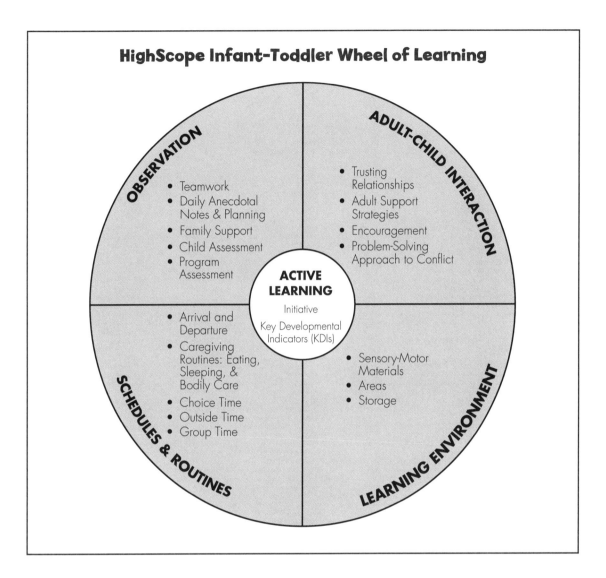

HighScope Infant-Toddler Wheel of Learning

OBSERVATION

- Teamwork
- Daily Anecdotal Notes & Planning
- Family Support
- Child Assessment
- Program Assessment

ADULT-CHILD INTERACTION

- Trusting Relationships
- Adult Support Strategies
- Encouragement
- Problem-Solving Approach to Conflict

ACTIVE LEARNING

Initiative

Key Developmental Indicators (KDIs)

- Arrival and Departure
- Caregiving Routines: Eating, Sleeping, & Bodily Care
- Choice Time
- Outside Time
- Group Time

- Sensory-Motor Materials
- Areas
- Storage

SCHEDULES & ROUTINES

LEARNING ENVIRONMENT

Infant-Toddler Curriculum: active learning for children; warm, supportive adult-child interaction; a welcoming, child-oriented learning environment; schedules and routines that flow with the children; daily child observation that guides caregivers' interactions with children, caregivers' teamwork, caregiver-parent partnerships, and program planning; and ongoing and valid assessment of children and programs to ensure that program goals to support early learning and deliver high-quality services are being met.

Active learning

Infants and toddlers are active learners from birth. Through their ongoing relationships with people and their explorations of the materials in their immediate world, they figure out how to move at will; how to hold and act on objects; and how to communicate and interact with parents,

In HighScope infant-toddler programs, active learning flows from children's trusting relationships with adults. Tender care and support for early learning are provided by adult teamwork, an engaging environment, and child-centered schedules and routines.

family members, peers, and caregivers. As active learners, infants and toddlers watch, reach for, and grasp people and materials that particularly attract their attention. They choose objects and people to play with and explore, initiate actions that particularly interest them, and respond to various events in their environment. Through their own unique combination of gestures, facial expressions, noises, and (eventually) words, they communicate their feelings and ideas. Throughout their explorations, they rely on parents and caregivers to attend to, support, and build on their actions, choices, and ways of communicating.

When surrounded by adults — parents, other family members, teachers — who understand the very young child's need to explore and thus build understanding, infants and toddlers develop a sense of trust in themselves and others that enables them to become curious, autonomous learners. They *initiate* their own "voyages of discovery" off the blanket and into the next room, driven by the desire to see what interesting people and things might lie around the corner. Even the most adventurous active learners, however, return from time to time to "home base," that trusting and trusted adult, to assure themselves that comfort and safety are well within their reach.

The *key developmental indicators (KDIs)* represent what infants and toddlers discover in their daily learning adventures. Individual **approaches to learning** begin to emerge as they encounter and

solve problems in play *(Maybe I can reach that rattle if I roll over onto my stomach)*. Children's **social and emotional development** proceeds as they gain a sense of self (a realization that they are separate from others) and form relationships *(This is my mom; Sara is my friend)*. In the area of **physical development and health**, young children move their bodies for sheer pleasure and also to serve their purposes *(I can crawl to that other baby)*. Initiating and responding to verbal interactions and exploring picture books are early signs of emerging abilities in **communication, language, and literacy.**

Cognitive development involves exploration to discover how the world works. For example, children signal their understanding of the concept "more" (with words, gestures, or sign language), discover similarities and differences between objects *(These roll away; those do not)*, and observe cause and effect *(When I poke the bubble, it bursts)*.

In the **creative arts**, children work with building and collage materials, begin to engage in pretend play, and sway to different types of music.

Active learning is the axle on which the HighScope wheel of learning turns. In active learning settings, adults support children's initiatives and desire to explore with all their senses. They understand that children's self-motivated explorations, supported by knowledgeable caregivers, lead to meaningful learning experiences in all the content areas that are key to healthy human growth and development.

Developing trusting relationships with adults is critical for young children at child care settings.

Adult-child interaction

Infants and toddlers are explorers. To gather the strength and courage they need to go forth each day, they rely on the support of their parents and teachers. Their interactions with trusted adults at home and away from home provide the emotional fuel infants and toddlers need to puzzle out the mysteries of the social and physical world.

Because *trusting relationships* are so important, programs strive to ensure that each infant or toddler in a child care center or home has the same primary caregiver or teacher throughout enrollment, whether that be for six months or three years. (See

"Caregivers and Teachers" on p. 7 for a discussion of the terms used in this book.) In settings with multiple caregivers, each one is the "primary" for only a small group of children, and the staff form a stable team that provides long-term continuity of care for children and families.

Caregivers strive to form positive, reciprocal relationships with children — relationships in which *encouragement* is the key. They cuddle, hold, play, and talk with children in a warm, unhurried, give-and-take manner. They establish a psychologically safe environment, where children's initiatives are regarded as purposeful rather than naughty or bothersome for adults.

Guided by practical theories of child development, teachers and caregivers attempt to see things from the child's point of view, encourage rather than thwart children's efforts and communications, take cues from children rather than impose their own ideas, and assume a *problem-solving approach* to children's interpersonal conflicts rather than punish children or solve their problems for them.

Very young children are just formulating a sense of themselves and an understanding of what the rest of the world is all about. As they are doing so, interactions with parents, teachers, and other significant adults influence the lifelong conclusions children draw from their experiences. For example, if parents' and caregivers' interactions are supportive, this shapes children's perceptions of themselves as capable, trusted, and trustworthy human beings. If teachers share their excitement in discovery, children see their environment as an interesting place in which learning is inherently rewarding. Therefore, positive, consistent, ongoing *adult support* is critical in satisfying a child's need to actively explore and construct a personal understanding of the world.

Learning environment

Providing an active learning environment for infants and toddlers encourages their need to look, listen, wiggle, roll, crawl, climb, rock, bounce, rest, eat, make noise, grasp or mouth or drop things, and be messy from time to time. In a HighScope infant-toddler program, the physical space is safe, flexible, and child oriented to provide comfort and variety and to accommodate children's changing developmental needs and interests. It includes a wide variety of *sensory-motor materials* infants and toddlers can reach, explore, and play with in their own way at their own pace. The *storage* of these materials is consistent, personalized, and accessible so that infants and toddlers can reach or get to the materials they see and want to explore. The space and materials are organized into play and care *areas* that serve the needs of infants and toddlers. The diapering area, for example, may be located next

Caregivers and Teachers

The terms *caregiver* and *teacher* are used interchangeably throughout this book to emphasize two very important roles played by the adults who work with very young children. The primary role of adults who spend time with infants and toddlers is that of caregiver. It is essential that adults establish strong and secure relationships through the everyday caregiving routines and interactions they provide. However, all those who care for infants and toddlers inevitably educate them as well.

For example, effective caregivers converse with both nonverbal and verbal infants and toddlers, thereby laying the foundation for early language and literacy development. As they rock and sing to very young children, adults support their physical development and expose them to the arts. When adults ask children if they want "more" juice or "another" block or sheet of paper, they are providing early mathematical experiences in concepts about quantity. In all these ways, effective teachers engage children in the joys of mastering a wide variety of knowledge and skills. However, they always do so within the context of a warm and supportive environment in which they provide young children with nurturing care and trusting relationships.

Early learning is thus comprehensive and integrated. When we care for very young children, we inspire and encourage them to learn. When we teach very young children, we show that we care about their overall well-being. Caregiving and teaching cannot be separated. Infants and toddlers depend on us to provide and be consistent in carrying out both these roles.

to a window that looks out onto a flower box or a bird feeder. The toddler block area includes a good supply of small and large blocks for satisfying stacking and balancing experiences. The learning environment, in short, is secure and inviting. Within its boundaries, infants and toddlers are free to move about, explore materials, exercise creativity, and solve problems.

Schedules and routines

In an active learning infant-toddler setting, schedules (the daily sequence of events such as *choice time, lunch, outside time*) and routines (caregiving interactions during *eating, sleeping,* and *bodily care*) are anchored, for each child, around a primary caregiver. Having this caregiver as a "home base" provides the very young child with a sense of security while away from home. Following children's cues and initiatives, caregivers, in partnership with parents, establish center schedules and routines that are consistent in order and interaction style so children can anticipate what happens next, yet flexible enough to accommodate children's individual rhythms and temperaments.

The schedules and routines are repetitive enough to enable children to explore, practice, and gain confidence in their developing skills, yet they allow children to move smoothly, at their own pace, from one interesting experience to another. Caregivers plan flexible, child-centered *group times.* They also work with parents to make *arrival* and *departure* leisurely and comforting. Children make choices about materials and actions throughout the day, and adults support and encourage children's initiatives during each time period and routine interaction. Altogether, caregivers design schedules and routines around children's needs and interests to give children a sense of control and belonging.

Observation

Child observation is an essential component of the HighScope Infant-Toddler Curriculum, since knowledge of individual children shapes not only the interactions caregivers have with children and parents but also the learning environment and the schedules and routines at the center. To observe and learn as much as possible from children, adults in infant-toddler centers rely on *teamwork.* Caregivers work as partners with parents to provide continuity of care between home and center.

Primary caregivers work together in teams for mutual support throughout the day; together, they provide *family support;* make decisions about space, materials, schedules, routines, and daily responsibilities; and discuss and plan around their daily observations of children. As they work "on the floor" with children, they collect *daily anecdotal notes.* At *daily team-planning time,* they discuss their observations of what individual children did and said that day, and they use these observations to guide their own behavior in supporting children the next day. They also exchange child observations with parents, both to celebrate children's actions and development and to nurture a partnership with families, so children can be supported consistently at home and at the center.

The ongoing assessment of children and programs helps caregivers meet their goals for early learning through the delivery of high-quality services. Not only do *child assessment* and *program assessment* allow caregivers to determine what is happening with the children and families they serve, they also let them take stock of how well the program is operating and what steps they can take to improve caregiving practices and overall program management.

Caregivers and teachers often know instinctively when children are progressing and when they need extra support. Likewise, they may have an inner sense of their own and their colleagues' strengths and areas in need of improvement. However, systematic assessment helps to confirm and elaborate their impressions. Sometimes it even offers surprises and inspires caregivers and teachers to think in new ways about the development of individual children, the dynamics of the group, relationships with parents and coworkers, and their own professional advancement.

To permit the systematic assessment of children's progress and program implementation, respectively, HighScope has developed and validated two instruments: the Child Observation Record (COR) for Infants and Toddlers and the Infant-Toddler Program Quality Assessment (PQA). Using these tools will help

programs create an active learning environment in which young children and their caregivers can learn and flourish.

These guiding principles — active learning, supportive adult-child interaction, a child-oriented learning environment, schedules and routines that flow with the children, daily child observation to guide teamwork among staff and parents, and ongoing child and program assessment — keep the HighScope infant-toddler wheel of learning turning. They also serve as a framework for this book, which elaborates on each of these six principles so caregivers in infant-toddler child care settings can put into practice the HighScope Infant-Toddler Curriculum.

Research-Based Curriculum

All HighScope Infant-Toddler Curriculum materials and services are grounded in a profound respect for practitioners and parents and the primacy of their bond with the children in their care. These adults play a vital role as teachers in the broadest sense of that term. The curriculum and training model further reflect the constructivist theories pioneered by psychologist Jean Piaget (1952), the importance of scaffolding derived from the work of Lev Vygotsky (1934/1986), and the results of current cognitive-developmental research (e.g., Goswami, 2002; National Research Council, 2000; Smith, 2002).

Emerging findings about early brain development also support the active learning approach that is central to the

Providing infants with sensory experiences helps optimize the brain circuits that develop at that time.

curriculum's theory and practice (e.g., National Scientific Council on the Developing Child, 2004, 2007; Rushton, 2001; Shore, 2003; Zero to Three and the Ounce of Prevention Fund, 2000).

For example, *Starting Smart: How Early Experiences Affect Brain Development* (Zero to Three and the Ounce of Prevention Fund, 2000) describes how the trillions of neural connections babies are born with are selectively strengthened or pruned away in the early months and years of life. This process allows the developing child to keep and enhance the pathways that serve a useful purpose while eliminating those that are unnecessary or redundant. Because the brain becomes less "plastic" or changeable over time, it is important for the environment to provide infants and toddlers with key early experiences before critical "windows of opportunity" close. Language development offers a good illustration of this principle. The number and variety of words that children hear by the time they reach age three is a significant predictor of later literacy development (Hart & Risley, 1999).

Early environments and experiences have an exceptionally strong influence on the architecture and functioning of the brain. Different brain circuits mature at different points in development. Newborns need "basic sensory, social, and emotional experiences…for optimizing the architecture of low-level circuits" (National Scientific Council on the Developing Child, 2007, p. 4). The critical period for the low-level circuits responsible for sight and hearing, for example, ends early. By contrast, "more sophisticated kinds of experiences are critical for shaping higher-level circuits," including the circuits that process communication signals (such as language and the emotions in facial expressions), and end much later in development (p. 4).

Because both the timing and content of early experiences are important, those responsible for the care and education of very young children should neither underestimate nor overestimate what their brains are capable of processing. In keeping with the latest knowledge derived from theory, research, and practice, the content of the HighScope Infant-Toddler Curriculum is therefore organized around six areas that frame the timely and appropriate experiences that promote learning in all domains of development. These six content areas are **approaches to learning**; **social and emotional development**; **physical development and health**; **communication, language, and literacy**; **cognitive development**; and **creative arts**.

The KDIs in each content area reflect the physical, cognitive, affective, and social changes that occur during these early and critical years of human growth. (See Chapter 1 for a list of the KDIs in each of the content areas.)

How This Book Is Organized

This second edition of *Tender Care and Early Learning* starts in the middle of the infant-toddler wheel of learning, with active learning. The remaining chapters in this book then turn to each of the outer sections of the wheel and the overarching role of assessment:

Chapter 1, "Active Learning and Key Developmental Indicators," describes how infants and toddlers learn through action and social relationships and introduces the KDIs as a way of seeing, understanding, supporting, and building on the broad range of things they learn about.

Chapter 2, "The Caregiving Team and Their Partnership With Parents," focuses on the elements of effective caregiving teams and caregiver-parent partnerships and describes strategies for working together to support infants' and toddlers' growth and development.

Chapter 3, "Supportive Adult-Child Interactions," discusses the role of the primary caregiver, continuity of care, and specific adult-child interaction strategies teachers and caregivers can use to nurture and support active learners.

Chapter 4, "Arranging and Equipping the Learning Environment," provides general guidelines for organizing active learning environments and specific strategies for selecting materials and arranging spaces to support the exploration and play of infants and toddlers.

Chapter 5, "Establishing Schedules and Routines," defines child-centered schedules and caregiving routines and discusses specific caregiver roles during each part of the day.

Chapter 6, "Child and Program Assessment," describes validated assessment tools for monitoring children's developmental progress and establishing and maintaining high-quality infant and toddler programs.

What's an Infant? What's a Toddler?

The terms *young infants, older infants, young toddlers,* and *older toddlers,* without exact ages specified, will be used throughout this book. In general, we focus on children's actions and behaviors rather than on their ages, because we realize that human development occurs sequentially but at highly individual rates (e.g., babies usually learn to roll over before they learn to sit by themselves, but some begin to sit unaided at 6 months, whereas others do so at 10 or 11 months).

In our shorthand for children at various developmental stages, "young infants" means babies who are not yet sitting by themselves (they may range in age from birth to 9 or 10 months); "older infants" can sit unaided and are learning to creep, crawl, pull themselves up to stand, and cruise upright from place to place by holding on to props (they may range in age from 5 months to 18 months); "young toddlers" can toddle and walk unaided, with both hands free for exploration; "older toddlers" are more sure on their feet, more skilled with their hands, and more adept at verbal communication ("toddlers," as a group, range in age from 12 months to 3 years, with "younger toddlers" generally ranging from 12 to 24 months, and "older toddlers" ranging from 24 to 36 months).

~

This second edition of *Tender Care and Early Learning* draws together High-Scope's experiences with infants, toddlers, and parents over the past 30 years and the current experience of HighScope trainers and caregivers as they provide an active learning environment for infants and toddlers in a range of program settings, from small to large and from serving mixed-age groups (infants and toddlers together) to serving groups separated by age (e.g., young infants together, older infants together, young toddlers together, older toddlers together). See "What's an Infant? What's a Toddler?" on page 12.

In this book, we present strategies for out-of-home care that promote a tender approach to early learning. It is an approach that focuses on children's strengths; builds healthy relationships between parent and child, caregiver and child, center and family, and children themselves; and supports the growth and development of very young children, their families, and their caregivers.

Tender Care and Early Learning strives to embed the practical experience in a framework based on current theory and research in infant and toddler development. It is our hope that this blend of field-based and academic knowledge proves both friendly and useful to caregivers and teachers who provide day-to-day care and education to very young children and their families in diverse home- and center-based settings.

1

Active Learning and Key Developmental Indicators

*We must recommit ourselves to a collective vision of a society
with the knowledge and the will to support all infants and toddlers
in reaching their full potential....This is not about pushing policies
and programs that work for older children down to the crib but
designing a developmentally appropriate system that supports very
young children in ways that science tells us are effective.*

— Melmed (2009, p. 60)

In a HighScope child care setting, it is important to have teachers and caregivers who lovingly, consistently, and creatively support children's natural desire to be active learners. Creating an active learning environment for infants and toddlers means consciously considering all their needs — their social and emotional needs for security and companionship; their physical needs for nourishment, bodily care, rest, movement, and safety; their cognitive needs for opportunities to make choices, explore interesting materials, and try out a range of challenging experiences; and their sociolinguistic needs to communicate their desires and discoveries to responsive caregivers and peers. What caregivers and teachers offer to infants and toddlers in their program settings speaks eloquently of the interactions and experiences they understand to be essential for supporting children as they develop into healthy, secure, creative people.

An understanding of HighScope's active learning approach guides the decisions infant-toddler caregivers make about every major aspect of their work — observing and planning for children, interacting with children and families, arranging and equipping the learning environment, establishing schedules and routines, and assessing early development and program quality. To establish the framework for the HighScope Infant-Toddler Curriculum, this chapter describes the key developmental indicators — the social and cognitive knowledge and skills — that young children acquire through meaningful experiences with people and materials.

Active Learning: How Infants and Toddlers Learn

Babies, like all young children, learn by actively exploring their environment — what HighScope calls *active learning*. According to French and Murphy (2005), active learning in infants and toddlers is "the process by which they explore the world either through: observing (gazing at their hand), listening, touching (stroking

This sensory-motor learner bends intently over her bucket. At close range, she can smell the sand, see it shift as she stirs, and feel and hear the scraping sound of the spoon.

an arm or bottle), reaching, grasping, mouthing, letting go, moving their bodies (kicking, turning, crawling, pulling themselves up on furniture, walking), smelling, tasting, or making things happen with objects around them (putting things in and out of boxes, stacking blocks, rolling a ball)" (p. 29).

An active learning environment builds trust, autonomy, and initiative in young children. To ensure that infants and toddlers enjoy these benefits and flourish in their program settings, HighScope has five ingredients of active learning that serve as practical guidelines for caregivers:

1. **Materials**: There are abundant, age-appropriate materials the child can use in a variety of ways. Learning grows directly out of the child's direct actions on the materials.

2. **Manipulation**: The child has opportunities to explore (with all the senses), manipulate, combine, and transform the chosen materials.

3. **Choice**: The child chooses what to do. Since learning results from the child's attempts to pursue personal interests and goals, the opportunity to choose activities and materials is essential.

4. **Child communication, language, and thought**: The child communicates his or her needs, feelings, discoveries, and ideas through motions, gestures, facial expressions, sounds, sign language, and words. Adults value, attend to, and encourage the child's communications and language in a give-and-take manner.

5. **Adult scaffolding**: Adults establish and maintain trusting relationships with each child in their care. Adults recognize and encourage each child's intentions, actions, interactions, communications, explorations, problem solving, and creativity.

Based on child development theory and experience with infants and toddlers, HighScope developed the following propositions[1] that guide our work with very young children and, in broad strokes, describe the elements of active learning:

- Infants and toddlers *learn with their whole body and with all their senses.*

- Infants and toddlers *learn because they want to.*

- Infants and toddlers *communicate what they know.*

- Infants and toddlers *learn within the context of trusting relationships.*

Infants and toddlers learn with their whole body and with all their senses

Infants and toddlers gather information with their every action — by gazing at the face of a parent or teacher, playing with their hands, stroking a bottle, tipping a cup, fingering a caregiver's clothing, chewing on a book or toy, crumbling crackers,

---

[1] These propositions, presented here in a slightly altered form, originally appeared in *Home Teaching With Mothers and Infants* (Lambie, Bond, & Weikart, 1974).

splashing water, kicking off a blanket, crying when another child cries, or carrying around a baby doll. By coordinating taste, touch, smell, sight, sound, feelings, and action, they are able to build knowledge. Developmental psychologist Jean Piaget (1952, 1966) used the term *sensory-motor* to characterize this direct, physical

This infant is learning by doing — figuring out how to move her whole body up the stairs so she can reach her caregiver.

approach to learning: *Sensory* refers to the way that infants and toddlers gather information about the world through all their senses; *motor* refers to the way they learn through physical action.

Ongoing brain research confirms the appropriateness of Piaget's term. An infant's brain develops in "waves, with different parts of the brain becoming active 'construction sites' at different times and with different degrees of intensity" (Shore, 2003, p. 39). The part of the brain that controls sensory-motor functions is very active in an infant's first few months of life, which makes an infant's exposure to visual and auditory stimuli so important at this time. Later, in the latter part of an infant's first year, the part of the brain that is associated with emotion and the ability to think and plan becomes the active construction site. This is the time (typically at about eight months old) when a child begins to self-regulate and form stronger attachments to his or her primary caregivers.

Infants and toddlers, then, learn by doing because their young brains are particularly primed to link action with perception (Meltzoff, Kuhl, Movellan, & Sejnowski, 2009). In the beginning of their lives, children's discoveries about themselves and their immediate environment come through action — through waving their arms, watching their hands, kicking, turning over, reaching out, grasping, poking, smelling, listening, touching, mouthing, tasting, crawling, and pulling themselves up. Before they can talk, it is also through action that they express what they discover and feel to attentive adults — by crying, wiggling, stiffening, turning away, making faces, clinging, cuddling, cooing, sucking, and looking. Their active engagement with attentive and responsive adults and with interesting and challenging materials provides them with a base of experience for interpreting their world.

Not only do infants' actions affect what and how the brain learns, they also affect how the brain itself is built. As neuroscientists Adrienne Tierney and Charles Nelson (2009) write, "the effects of experience go beyond the simple modulation of plasticity. In fact, experience shapes the structure of the brain" (p. 12).

The National Scientific Council on the Developing Child (2007) also emphasizes how early experiences affect the architecture of the brain:

> *Just as a master carpenter modifies the blueprint for a house to adapt to the needs of its setting and the people who will live in it, experience adjusts the genetic plan for the brain and shapes the architecture of its neural circuits according to the needs and distinctive environment of the individual. (p. 2)*

Young children's healthy and stimulating experiences help wire their brains to operate at maximum capacity. Conversely, early adverse conditions create a stressful electrochemical environment that can lead to brain structures of impaired capability with negative lifelong effects. Thus, "the exceptionally strong influence of early experience on brain architecture makes the early years of life a period of both great opportunity and great vulnerability for brain development" (p. 1). Author and curriculum developer Pam Schiller (2008) emphasizes that to take advantage of these critical "windows of opportunity," programs for infants and toddlers need to build on the lessons from brain research and provide experiences that explicitly support language, motor, social, emotional, and cognitive growth and development. (See "The Role of Experience in Early Brain Development" on p. 20.)

It is equally important to emphasize that "experience" is not something passive that children merely receive from the environment and the adults in it. Tierney and Nelson (2009) emphasize that "by experience, we do not mean events and circumstances that simply happen in an individual's life; rather, we define experience as the interaction between the individual and her environment" (p. 13). Young children, according to Tierney and Nelson, are active agents in shaping their experience. As an example, they note that a child who responds happily when sung to by a parent or teacher may elicit more singing. This results in more experiences with songs, which can affect the child's language development and the brain processes underlying it. For optimal development, then, infants and toddlers need to draw out the resources in their environment as much as parents and teachers need to create an environment that reaches out to them.

The Role of Experience in Early Brain Development

Brain development results from a dynamic interaction of genetics, environment, and experience (Meltzoff et al., 2009; Tierney & Nelson, 2009).

Genetics provide the basic plan by determining how nerve cells are formed and how they interconnect within and across neural circuits. Infants are born with different temperaments, which appear to have a biological, and perhaps a genetic, foundation.

The *environment* in which the brain develops, beginning with the prenatal period, can have a significant effect on the brain's structure. A healthy environment — adequate nutrition, the absence of toxins, and the physical and mental health of the expectant mother — allows the child's genetic plan to be fully expressed. Conversely, an unhealthy environment can impede the growth of, and interconnections among, brain cells.

Experience refers to the interactions between the child and the environment, beginning prenatally as the fetus responds to conditions in the womb and growing in importance after birth. Early experience affects the structure of the low-level brain circuits that mature at this stage, such as those responsible for sight and hearing. Once the child is born, experience plays a critical role in shaping the structure of higher-level neural circuits, such as those responsible for language development and establishing and maintaining social relationships. In sum, healthy and stimulating experiences in the early years allow a child's genetic makeup to reach its full potential, while adverse conditions can impair brain structure.

For most neural circuits, environment and experience have their greatest influence just as the circuit is beginning to mature. This period of maximum influence is called the "sensitive period" for that circuit. Experience can still continue to modify most brain structures — claims that the "window of opportunity" closes by age three are unfounded — but the effects are more limited the older we get. Because of this time sensitivity, early experiences and their influence on forming neural networks have a profound effect on later learning.

This influence does *not* mean that specific types of stimulation have a matching and measurable impact on brain development. For example, listening to Mozart, while pleasurable, will not make an infant a musical or mathematical genius (the now-disproved "Mozart Effect"). Nor will using flash cards produce an early reader. However, the significance of timing does mean that young children need a variety of developmentally appropriate experiences that their brains *are* wired to process in these critical early years.

Active involvement with people and materials, in interactions and activities that engage all their senses, create an optimal environment in which a young child's genetic capacity can flourish.

Very young children's pressing need to act and learn from experiences in their immediate environment takes the form of direct contact using the tools at their disposal — eyes, nose, ears, mouth, hands, and feet. They watch people or pets or objects move, closely examine patterns of light and shade, feel the textures and temperatures of things with their hands and feet, still themselves to listen to a voice or song, and put nearly everything they can grasp into their mouths. Young children, in fact, cannot resist touching and exploring anything or anyone with sensory-motor appeal. They are fascinated with every-day household objects — pots, lids, keys, boxes, spoons — and natural materials — stones, sticks, leaves, dirt. They especially like to explore soft and cuddly items, easy-to-grasp objects, squishy or messy materials, things they can set in motion, objects they can pull themselves up onto and climb, materials that make noise, and other people!

In their care setting, infants also treat adults as something to explore. Pediatrician and child psychiatrist Daniel Siegel (1999) notes that an invested and caring adult who provides attention and interacts with words, songs, touches, and smiles is a child's best toy. To infants and toddlers, she is every bit as interesting as many other items and playthings and generally more responsive! That is why infants study their caregiver's face, listen for and

A small container filled with easy-to-grasp objects that make noises encourages this infant to explore, learn, and make his own discoveries.

respond to the sound of her voice, know how she smells, and settle into the comfort of her arms and body.[2] Toddlers use adults to lean and relax against or to steady themselves as they maneuver into a sitting or standing position. A teacher's shoelaces, hair, jewelry, glasses, and clothes provide

---

[2] Because women predominate as infant-toddler teachers and caregivers in both center- and home-based programs, throughout this book we use "she" and "her" to refer to teachers and caregivers unless a specific example requires otherwise. However, we acknowledge the dedicated and growing number of men in the field.

a variety of textures and colors they stroke and clutch.

Increased mobility brings new learning experiences. When babies learn to sit unaided, they find they have greater freedom to see, reach, and handle objects. Mobile infants, whenever they can manage to do so, crawl, pull themselves up, and climb onto any inviting surface. Toddlers enjoy the balance, uprightness, pace, and freedom of walking, running, and climbing to new heights. They also use their new powers of locomotion to move materials from place to place. They pull and push wagons and wheeled toys and drag chairs or large containers to a more desirable spot. They might try to push and tug a large tub of blocks, find it does not move, empty all the blocks out, and try again. Mobile infants and toddlers mean mobile materials and playthings!

As infants and toddlers interact with people and act on materials, they construct a basic store of knowledge about what people and things are like, what they do, and how they respond to certain actions. What may begin as random movement — waving a wooden spoon and accidently hitting it against a cardboard box — leads to a fascinating discovery and is repeated deliberately again and again. Through these repetitions, children gain a sense of purpose and mastery; they enjoy feeling with their whole body the stiffness of the wooden spoon, for example, and the sturdy resistance of the box. Later on, gaining this experiential knowledge will lead them to try even more complex action

sequences, like stirring with a spoon and stacking boxes. For infants and toddlers, learning through action involves encountering and solving infant-and-toddler-sized problems (*What made that noise? How can I make it again?*) and, in the process, forming their ideas about what things and people do and how they respond to one's actions.

Caregivers who base their programs on the principles of active learning understand and support infants' and toddlers' sensory, whole-body approach to learning. They respect and accommodate children's ongoing need for space, materials, and exploration time. Because infants and toddlers can be expected to grasp and hold things and put toys and other objects in their mouths, caregivers provide playthings that are safe and too large to swallow and design play areas that ensure both comfort and safety. Anticipating drool and stickiness, caregivers routinely sanitize the materials children come in contact with. They encourage children's curiosity and mobility; respect their need to crawl, walk, run, and carry or move articles from place to place; and establish safe and spacious environments where these things can happen.

Infants and toddlers learn because they *want* to

Juan, a young infant, grasps his pacifier and puts it in his mouth, then takes it out to look at it and turn it around a bit, and finally puts it back in his mouth.

~

Marian, a toddler, sorts through the basket of pictures until she finds the one with two puppies and, looking at it, says "Dog, dog."

~

Deidre, an older infant, pushes her caregiver's hand away, takes off her own bib, and hands it to the caregiver.

~

Charlie, a toddler, uses the wooden mallet from the play dough shelf to pound the floor.

As young as they are, infants and toddlers are powerfully self-motivated to explore and learn — at their own pace, through their own means. Learning develops from their intrinsically motivated activity. No one has to tell them to learn or prod them into action. Their own choices and desire for autonomy and initiative take care of that! In fact, in extensive home observations of children 12–15 months old and 24–27 months old, researchers found that more than 80 percent of the children's experience was self-initiated (White, Kaban, Marmor, & Shapiro, 1972). Early childhood researcher J. Ronald Lally (2009) puts it this way:

> *What is now known is that babies come into care with their own learning agenda — their own curriculum. Armed with an inborn motivation to learn and explore, they are on a constant quest for knowledge, learning from what they see, hear, feel, taste, and touch. And they do this without the need for prompting. They have a holistic stance toward learning, with social, emotional, intellectual, language, and physical lessons often coming from the same experience.* (p. 47)

Even the youngest infants make simple choices and decisions all day long — choices about what to look at; whether to reach for the shell, the rattle, or ribbon; whether to stick with the wooden spoon or go for the ball; when to drink from the bottle or just stop and gaze; whether to watch the shadows on the wall beside the crib, call out for someone's attention, or coo at the stuffed bear; and when to stop playing and go to sleep.

As the infant grows into toddlerhood, the choices and decisions become increasingly complex — whether to climb into a lap or settle into the big pillow with a book, what child to play beside, how to flatten the play dough, how to fit all the toy animals into a purse, how to eat a cracker, what comfort item (stuffed animal, blanket, book) to take to naptime, what to use to wipe up a spill, and how to reach out-of-the-way objects. Infants and toddlers indicate the people or materials or experiences they prefer, decide what they will explore, and figure out how to solve problems and accomplish meaningful tasks. By making infant-and-toddler-sized choices and decisions, they gain a sense of self-control and efficacy — *I am somebody who can do things!* (as opposed to somebody to whom things are done).

In a supportive environment with appropriate opportunities and interactions, very young children act with increasing autonomy and independence. They become curious about peers and other adults. In the spirit of adventure and exploration, they roll, crawl, and eventually walk on their own to discover the unknown in the social and physical world beyond parent and caregiver. They open and close doors; play simple hiding games; hunt for hidden toys, people, or pets; seek out playmates; climb up and down stairs; look at books with peers; and fill and empty shelves, boxes, bags, and baskets. Sometimes their daring evokes feelings of delight and mastery — an infant crawls behind the couch and finds a ball, or two toddlers stand at the window watching older children play outside in the yard. Other times their adventures scare them — the ball behind the couch tastes odd, a dog barks at the children outside — and they hurry back to the parent or caregiver for comfort and reassurance. For that reason, at the same time that infants and toddlers are independent and curious, they also depend on strong social ties with the primary adults in their lives to affirm their autonomy.

Psychologist and human development specialist Erik Erikson (1950/1963) observed that in the course of his or her adventures, a toddler needs adult support rather than criticism, restraint, or shaming: "As his environment encourages him to 'stand on his own feet,' it must protect him against meaningless and arbitrary experiences of shame and of early doubt" (p. 252). Autonomous young learners rely on dependable social relationships. In fact, "it is now understood that…relationships and experiences with trusted caregivers are the base for all learning" (Lally, 2009, p. 48). (See the discussion on trusting relationships on p. 28.)

Over time, very young children in active learning environments develop the desire and capacity to act with persistence and to have an impact on people and things. A toddler, for example, decides

During choice time, this toddler chooses to explore his favorite board book from the book area.

to carry a favorite truck around all day through mealtimes, naps, and outside time. Three toddlers decide to bang on the mounds of sand that are formed as their caregiver tips out the sand she has packed in some pails. Whatever the caregiver had in mind, she respects the children's initiative as they smash what she might have thought of as sand cakes. "All gone!" she says as the children smash the sand mounds. "More!" they cry, and the mound-making-and-smashing game is on.

When children's initiatives are arbitrarily and frequently thwarted — "Don't touch that!" "Take your hands out of your mouth!" "Stop banging!" "Sit still!" "Come away from there!" — children begin to doubt their own capacity to shape and order their day-to-day existence. By contrast, "when children feel they can count on important, loved people to provide comfort, they have a strong foundation of confidence that allows them to explore their surroundings" (Hyson, 1994, p. 98). With adult support for their initiatives, infants and toddlers — and children of all ages — enjoy the risks and satisfactions of creative learning and social discourse.

In practical terms, this means that a child care setting supports young children's development if it is stocked with a variety of safe, appropriate, challenging, and accessible materials for children's exploration. In such a setting, caregivers support children's preferences and attend to their language of action and gesture. For example, when infant Halley crawls away from her caregiver to the tub of balls, her caregiver interprets Halley's actions to mean *I really want to play with the balls right now.* Rather than attempt to direct children to learn specified things at certain times, caregivers support and build on children's *self-motivated* choices and learning initiatives.

Infants and toddlers communicate what they know

Human beings are social creatures from birth. Early childhood specialists Betty and M. Kori Bardige (2008) write that "babies come into the world primed to communicate with adults, who are primed to communicate with them. Their survival and well-being depend on their ability to connect with their caregivers" (p. 4). Even before the onset of spoken language, babies communicate and represent their needs and experiences (Vallotton, 2008). Infants begin intentional communication as early as 6 months of age, and, by 10 months, typically developing infants have a repertoire of communicative behaviors that include vocalizations and gestures such as pointing and showing. By 12 months they are even intentional about using gestures to influence others' mental states, for example, to change the mood of a caregiver from one of disapproval or distress into a smile (Tomasello, Carpenter, & Liszkowski, 2007).

Infants and toddlers eagerly seek direct contact with parents, other family members, and caregivers and use a variety of strategies to convey their desires. In the beginning, babies cry — for nourishment,

Through sounds, expressions, gestures, and actions, these infants learn communication skills while establishing relationships with each other and their caregivers.

comfort, security, and sleep. As people respond to them, they communicate — for the pleasure of engaging in and prolonging face-to-face exchanges. They gaze and smile at their parents and caregivers. They frown and make funny faces when the water or juice in their bottle tastes different or when they hear a new noise. They move their hands, arms, and legs in excitement, happiness, or contentment. They coo at favorite people, pets, and playthings. They begin to babble and repeat the vowel and consonant sounds they hear

in conversation. Gradually, their babbling takes on the inflections and cadences of human speech as they attempt to join the give and take of social conversations. Interestingly, hearing impaired infants or the children of deaf parents who are exposed to sign language from birth also begin to "babble" with their fingers before their gestures take on the shapes of conventional signs (Buckley, Bird, & Sacks, 2006).

When an infant or toddler does begin to talk, early language is streamlined and economical: "Ba" for *I see my bottle,* "Me do" for *I'll do it myself,* "Out" for *Let's go outside,* "Dog-dog" for *This is a picture of a dog.* Young children hear and understand language long before they can produce it themselves in its standard grammatical form. In the meantime, they string together sounds, gestures, and words in a fashion that makes sense to them.

When normally hearing young children learn baby sign language at the same time they hear spoken language, they combine simple gestures and words. Access to this dual communication system in turn further facilitates the development of their oral language skills (Goodwyn, Acredolo, & Brown, 2000). See "Using Sign Language to Communicate With Infants and Toddlers" on pages 152–153 in Chapter 3.

By communicating what they feel and discover to receptive and responsive adults, infants and toddlers enter into the sustaining social life of the community, where they connect with other people, test their ideas, and gain feedback about their actions or feelings or perceptions.

By carefully listening and giving the child time to talk, this caregiver is then able to engage the child in a meaningful two-way conversation.

Therefore, caregivers in active learning settings pay particular attention to children's actions, sounds, expressions, gestures, and words. They watch and listen carefully to children and give them sufficient room in a conversation to express themselves in their own particular fashion. They enable children both to hear language (and "see" sign language) and to participate as active partners in communication.

Infants and toddlers *want* to communicate, connect, and convey meaning.

The more they are respectfully supported in these desires, the better communicators they become. Children's later facility with speaking, listening, reading, and writing has its roots in the very early partnerships they form with supportive parents and caregivers who take time to talk and listen to them with care. Such adults understand that infants and toddlers "talk" in their own way and *need* to talk, even before they ever use proper words.

Infants and toddlers learn within the context of trusting relationships

To learn and grow, children need the kind of emotionally rich environment that Erikson (1950/1963) described as supporting *trust* rather than mistrust. The bedrock of healthy human development is "trust born of care," as Erikson puts it (p. 250). "The infant's first social achievement, then, is his willingness to let the mother out of sight without undue anxiety or rage, because she has become an inner certainty as well as an outer predictability" (p. 247).

Children involved in trusting relationships seem to know at some deep level that caregivers will support them through new challenges and accomplishments.

Children who form mutual, affirmative relationships with parents and caregivers draw upon these relationships for the courage they need to explore the world beyond these nurturing adults.

While infants and toddlers are powerfully self-motivated to learn with their whole body and all their senses and to communicate what they know, they depend on the affirmation and warmth of trusting relationships to be able to do so. Parents and caregivers must "be able to represent to the child a deep, almost somatic [bodily] conviction that there is a meaning to what they are doing" (p. 249).

When parents and caregivers, through their actions, convey a deep-seated belief in children's intrinsic worth, children develop an empowering sense of trust, human connection, and eagerness to explore the world. Caregivers, therefore, play a very important role in influencing how the children they care for see their world and how they feel about themselves and others (Lally, 2009).

As self-motivated social creatures, infants play an active role in shaping the trusting relationships they depend on. Observing mothers and infants in Uganda, developmental psychologist Mary Ainsworth (1963) was struck by "the extent to which the infant himself takes the initiative in seeking an interaction. From at least two months of age onwards, and increasingly through the first year of life, these infants were not so much passive and recipient as active in seeking interaction" (p. 203). Psychiatrist Daniel Stern (1985) called this interactive process *attunement*.

Through deeply felt, finely tuned reciprocal interactions, the parent or caregiver matches the child's emotions and level of interest to convey her sense of what the child is feeling. For example, the baby coos and smiles at the caring adult, and the caring adult smiles and coos back to the baby and strokes the baby's cheek. This sensitive response to the child's bid for attention gives the child the feeling of being known, understood, attended to, and cared for. The child learns to trust that the caring adult will respond. At the same time, the child trusts her- or himself to elicit a satisfactory response from the adult. In this manner, a child gains confidence: *When I cry, someone hears and comforts me. When I feel hungry, I can get someone to feed me, and I feel better.*

Children involved in trusting relationships seem to know at some deep level that parents and teachers will support them through new challenges and accomplishments — *Look! I can sit up all by myself!* — and provide comfort and contact when the going gets rough — *Help! I hear a scary noise!* They learn, writes developmental psychologist Jillian Rodd (1996), "that the world in which they live is a safe and friendly place and that the people who care for them can be trusted to meet their needs promptly, responsively and consistently. If infants learn that they are valued, cared for and respected as significant members of the group, they will have a strong foundation from which to confidently explore and learn about the world" (p. 21).

This mother's warm embrace lets her son know that he is understood and loved.

Without trusting relationships, children can lose the will to live. Psychoanalyst Rene Spitz (1945) and animal-learning theorist Harry Harlow (1958) found that human infants and monkeys raised without close physical contact and loving attention fail to develop normally and may even die, although their needs for food, shelter, and bodily care are adequately supplied.

More recently, brain research has documented similar effects on babies of depressed mothers (Shore, 2003) and on infants and toddlers raised in large groups in understaffed eastern European orphanages (Talbot, 1998). Maps of the electrical activity of the brain reveal that emotional stress can impede healthy brain activity, and under extreme conditions of prolonged physical or emotional distress, the brain shuts down altogether. Without the fuel of trusting relationships, children may be overwhelmed with fear, sadness, or grief and become increasingly passive and unable to signal for help. Having "learned" that others are unresponsive to their attempts to communicate and connect, they withdraw from the world and "fail to thrive."

By contrast, trusting relationships promote physical development and emotional health. Further, one trusting relationship leads to another:

> *An infant who has at least one secure attachment will be more likely to develop secure relationships with other people in the world, such as grandparents, other familiar adults and children, and care and educational professionals. An infant's relationships with other people, such as early childhood professionals, are not considered to threaten the mother-child bond but rather [thought] to contribute to the infant's developing sense of trust in the world and the people in it. (Rodd, 1996, p. 30)*

Active learning, then, takes place within an intensely social context in which trusting relationships are essential.

In fact, collaborative research between brain scientists and cognitive psychologists reveals that social cues help to highlight what and when babies learn (Meltzoff et al., 2009). Studies show that early learning occurs more readily when it is introduced by a person rather than an inanimate object. Moreover, social interactions — most notably imitation, shared attention, and empathy — facilitate a young child's cognitive understanding. Based on the cumulative research of the past few decades, developmental psychologists and mental health professionals now know that effective early care settings blend teaching and caring, with emotional support and facilitation of learning happening simultaneously (Hauser-Cram, Warfield, Shonkoff, & Krauss, 2001). Put another way, "learning and loving are not so far apart as we once thought they were" (Lally, 2009, p. 48).

Given the absolute necessity of trusting relationships for learning and development, how do caregivers build and sustain such relationships with the children in their care? In a national study of early child care and attachment, psychologist Margaret T. Owen (1996) described the kinds of behaviors shown by caring adults involved in trusting relationships with very young children:

- *Sensitivity to the child's nondistress:* The caregiver takes interest in the child's play.

- *Positive regard:* The caregiver enjoys the child's actions and explorations.

- *Lack of negativity:* The caregiver communicates warmth and respect.

Because these children feel safe with their caregiver, they are able to focus on and learn about the world around them.

- *Shared emotions:* The caregiver acknowledges the child's feelings, from delight to frustration.

- *Positive physical contact:* The caregiver has warm, physical interactions with the child, including cuddling, hugging, holding, stroking, lap-holding.

- *Attentive responsiveness:* The caregiver responds readily to the child's signals and approaches, communication and talk; gives the child her full attention.

- *Stimulation:* The caregiver talks with the child, tells the child what will happen next, encourages the child's problem solving, reads to the child.

These trust-building behaviors and lively social exchanges, discussed further in Chapter 3, shape the way caregivers interact with infants and toddlers throughout the day.

The need to form and maintain trusting relationships with the infants and toddlers in her care shapes every aspect of the teacher's role and guides the decisions a program makes about staffing. Because trusting relationships are so vital, programs make every effort to ensure that caregivers work in teams, with each team member responsible for a small group of children who remain in her care from one year to the next as long as they are enrolled in the program setting. The continuity of care that arises from this arrangement supports the growth of trusting relationships between child and caregiver, between caregiver and families, and between caregivers themselves. For specific continuity-of-care strategies and how they support infant and toddler development, see Chapters 2 and 3.

Key Developmental Indicators: What Infants and Toddlers Learn

When all the elements of active learning are in place — materials to explore bodily, with all the senses; opportunities to make choices; opportunities to communicate discoveries and feelings; and the ongoing, responsive support of trusted adults — what do infants and toddlers actually learn? To answer this question, caregivers and parents in HighScope settings turn to a set of guidelines called *key developmental indicators (KDIs),* which frame the content of early learning and development (see "HighScope Infant-Toddler Key Developmental Indicators" on p. 33).

Based on child observation, the High-Scope KDIs for infants and toddlers provide a composite picture of what very young children do and what knowledge and abilities emerge from their actions. The six content areas that organize the KDIs parallel the dimensions of school readiness identified by the National Education Goals Panel (Kagan, Moore, & Bredekamp, 1995) and are also widely used as the basis for infant-toddler and preschool learning standards throughout the early childhood community. These six areas are **approaches to learning;** **social and emotional development;** **physical development and health;** **communication, language, and literacy;** **cognitive development;** and **creative arts.** Within these six content areas there are 42 KDIs that are appropriate and essential for infant and toddler learning.

The KDIs also provide the basis for the Child Observation Record (COR) for Infants and Toddlers, an assessment tool for use in infant-toddler programs (High-Scope Educational Research Foundation, 2002a).[3] A description of the KDIs and how teachers and caregivers use them follows. For more information on HighScope resources that support early learning of the KDIs in each content area, visit the High-Scope online store at www.highscope.org.

Approaches to learning

Approaches to learning refers to how children go about acquiring knowledge and skills. Infants and toddlers approach

---

[3] The Infant-Toddler COR is based on the categories used in the key experiences, a precursor to the KDIs. However, with minor changes in organization or wording, the KDIs described here are comparable to items in the COR.

HighScope Infant-Toddler Key Developmental Indicators

A. Approaches to Learning

1. **Initiative:** Children express initiative.
2. **Problem solving:** Children solve problems encountered in exploration and play.
3. **Self-help:** Children do things for themselves.

B. Social and Emotional Development

4. **Distinguishing self and others:** Children distinguish themselves from others.
5. **Attachment:** Children form an attachment to a primary caregiver.
6. **Relationships with adults:** Children build relationships with other adults.
7. **Relationships with peers:** Children build relationships with peers.
8. **Emotions:** Children express emotions.
9. **Empathy:** Children show empathy toward the feelings and needs of others.
10. **Playing with others:** Children play with others.
11. **Group participation:** Children participate in group routines.

C. Physical Development and Health

12. **Moving parts of the body:** Children move parts of the body (turning head, grasping, kicking).
13. **Moving the whole body:** Children move the whole body (rolling, crawling, cruising, walking, running, balancing).
14. **Moving with objects:** Children move with objects.
15. **Steady beat:** Children feel and experience steady beat.

D. Communication, Language, and Literacy

16. **Listening and responding:** Children listen and respond.
17. **Nonverbal communication:** Children communicate nonverbally.
18. **Two-way communication:** Children participate in two-way communication.
19. **Speaking:** Children speak.
20. **Exploring print:** Children explore picture books and magazines.
21. **Enjoying language:** Children enjoy stories, rhymes, and songs.

E. Cognitive Development

22. **Exploring objects:** Children explore objects with their hands, feet, mouth, eyes, ears, and nose.
23. **Object permanence:** Children discover object permanence.
24. **Exploring same and different:** Children explore and notice how things are the same or different.
25. **Exploring more:** Children experience "more."
26. **One-to-one correspondence:** Children experience one-to-one correspondence.
27. **Number:** Children experience the number of things.
28. **Locating objects:** Children explore and notice the location of objects.
29. **Filling and emptying:** Children fill and empty, put in and take out.
30. **Taking apart and putting together:** Children take things apart and fit them together.
31. **Seeing from different viewpoints:** Children observe people and things from various perspectives.
32. **Anticipating events:** Children anticipate familiar events.
33. **Time intervals:** Children notice the beginning and ending of time intervals.
34. **Speed:** Children experience "fast" and "slow."
35. **Cause and effect:** Children repeat an action to make something happen again, experience cause and effect.

F. Creative Arts

36. **Imitating and pretending:** Children imitate and pretend.
37. **Exploring art materials:** Children explore building and art materials.
38. **Identifying visual images:** Children respond to and identify pictures and photographs.
39. **Listening to music:** Children listen to music.
40. **Responding to music:** Children respond to music.
41. **Sounds:** Children explore and imitate sounds.
42. **Vocal pitch:** Children explore vocal pitch sounds.

learning in different ways, and each child brings a unique set of attitudes, habits, and preferences to his or her explorations. Caregivers must consider this individuality, along with the developmental trends of the entire group, to support early learning.

Infants and toddlers have an entire world to learn about. How they go about this process depends in part on innate temperamental differences (Chess & Thomas, 1996). Equally important is

This toddler is doing something for herself as well as expressing initiative — by adding applesauce to her cornflakes!

whether and how the adults who teach and care for them encourage their exploratory behavior. For example, to what extent do adults welcome children's independence and curiosity? How safe and inviting do they make their homes and child care settings? Culture also influences how young children express their innate motivation to learn. For example, does a culture value personal initiative or group cohesion? Does it regard shyness as a sign of academic competence or depression and withdrawal (Carlson, Feng, & Harwood, 2004)?

The combined interaction of past and present "nature" (biology and temperament) and "nurture" (interactive experiences) in turn determines how young children are likely to approach learning in the future. The attitudes and behaviors they establish early on will affect their learning throughout their school years and into adulthood. A supportive active learning setting enables infants and toddlers to develop constructive approaches to learning. In such settings, adults share children's excitement about their own discoveries and initiatives as children explore and solve problems with increasing understanding and flexibility. In the process, children develop traits associated with "executive function," the higher-order abilities that will eventually allow them to successfully organize and complete tasks (Diamond, 2006). With adult support, infants and toddlers begin to construct an image of themselves as capable people who can both influence and respond to their immediate world, as demonstrated in the following KDIs.

1. **Initiative**: *Children express initiative.* For example, over the course of her development, Makiko turns toward or away from her caregiver or an object; initiates or avoids physical contact with a caregiver or child; selects or rejects a particular toy or object to explore; moves with persistence until reaching a chosen person or object; says "No!" to some choices or proposals from others; and expresses her choice or intention in words ("Me, kitty!" "Uppy, uppy!" "Me do it!").

2. **Problem solving**: *Children solve problems encountered in exploration and play.* For example, over the course of her development, Kelly moves her eyes, head, or hand to better see or touch a desired object; repeats an action to make something happen again; moves herself or an object to find someone or something that has disappeared from sight; makes varied attempts to solve a simple problem; and verbally identifies a problem before attempting to solve it ("Wagon stuck!").

3. **Self-help**: *Children do things for themselves.* For example, over the course of his development, Dante cries to express a need; holds his bottle or a clean diaper to assist in feeding or diapering; uses his fingers for eating; attempts a simple self-help task, such as drinking from a cup or putting on an article of clothing; and does some part or all of a task, such as washing his hands, using the toilet or potty, or dressing.

Social and emotional development

Social-emotional development begins at birth and continues into adulthood. By observing how they orient themselves to see or hear, we know that babies are interested in one another from as early as two months of age. Young infants get excited by the sight of other babies and, given the opportunity, stare avidly at one another. In the middle of the first year of life, infants monitor the emotional expressions of significant others and change their behavior accordingly (e.g., approaching a smiling caregiver or turning away from one who is frowning). These early signs of *social referencing* are a precursor of the empathy that appears soon after in toddlerhood and have their roots in both genetic factors (the social dispositions infants are born with) and environmental experiences (children's first social encounters with the world) (Emde, 1998).

Attachments to parents and other caregivers determine how young children see and feel about themselves (see the section on trusting relationships, p. 28). Their early self-image, in turn, determines how they approach learning and human relationships throughout their school years and the rest of their lives. In other words, children's inner emotional well-being affects their outward-directed social selves. Early childhood researchers Lilian Katz and

A key factor in a young's child social-emotional development is attachment to the adults who care for him or her.

that affect how they approach and deal with interpersonal and educational experiences. Toddlers' expanding use of language helps them express their wishes to others. They struggle with the competition between the "me" of their personal desires and the wish to be part of the "we" of the group. While very young children still focus primarily on their own needs, they are also increasingly sensitive to the needs and feelings of others. In fact, research shows infants and toddlers are more capable of empathy than scientists originally thought (Zahn-Waxler, Radke-Yarrow, Wagner, & Chapman, 1992).

In recent years, an emphasis on academic learning has overtaken a recognition of the importance of social and emotional development in young children. Fortunately, this imbalance is being corrected by landmark reports (such as *From Neurons to Neighborhoods* [National Research Council, 2000]) and position statements from organizations such as the American Academy of Pediatrics (AAP; Ginsburg, 2007). The AAP advises its members that "as parents choose child care and early education programs for their children, pediatricians can reinforce the importance of choosing settings that offer more than 'academic preparedness.' They should be guided to also pay attention to the social and emotional development needs of the children" (p. 188).

Diane McClellan (1997) note that "socially competent young children are those who engage in satisfying interactions and activities with adults and peers and through such interactions further improve their own competence" (p. 1).

Social-emotional growth in the early years affects, and is affected by, virtually every other aspect of children's development. Infants are born with innate temperaments and individual dispositions

The importance of play is also undergoing a revival, led by such groups as the Alliance for Childhood (Miller &

Almon, 2009), who decry its disappearance from early childhood settings in favor of instruction time. While this trend is more pronounced in preschool than in infant-toddler settings, the emphasis on ever-earlier stimulation to teach children letters and numbers is a cause for alarm. As psychologists Edward Zigler and Sandra Bishop-Josef (2009) point out, "the recent attack on play contradicts sound developmental theory" (p. 8).

Through playful interactions with adults and peers, children practice and extend the limits of their abilities, thereby developing a wide range of cognitive skills. As they master new tasks and initiate and respond to overtures with others, they gain a sense of themselves as social beings. In these ways, play promotes the social-emotional skills that underlie and facilitate learning across all developmental domains.

The first step in social and emotional development is differentiating oneself from others, that is, knowing that there is a "me" apart from "you" and "we." An infant or toddler, through actions with objects and interactions with trusted caregivers, gradually begins to understand that he or she exists as a separate and individual being — *There's me and not me, my hand and Mommy's hand, my skin and the diaper, my foot kicking the squeaker toy, me crying and other babies crying.* With this physical self-awareness comes a child's sense of him- or herself as an independent actor and initiator — *I can do it,* and, later, *I can do it myself!*

Infants and toddlers learn how human beings act and treat one another through their day-to-day interactions with parents, other family members, caregivers, peers, and other adults. When they grow up surrounded by parents and caregivers who care for them in a warm, respectful manner, children learn to trust themselves and others, to be curious, and to explore new learning challenges and adventures. These early social relationships influence their approach to people in later life. Infants and toddlers who are treated well, for example, see themselves and others as "friend-worthy"; they remember and build on their affirming social experiences as they make friends throughout their school years and in adult life — even as they form relationships with their own children.

Infants and toddlers express their sense of themselves and their understanding of social relationships through the following KDIs:

4. **Distinguishing self and others:** *Children distinguish themselves from others.* For example, over the course of his development, Alec puts his own fingers, thumb, or toes in his mouth; smiles, coos, babbles at, or touches his image in a mirror; plays with his own hands and feet; claims something or someone as "mine"; and spontaneously identifies himself in a photograph or mirror.

5. **Attachment:** *Children form an attachment to a primary caregiver.* For example, over the course of his development, Ricardo snuggles and

cuddles in his caregiver's arms; gazes at the caregiver and exchanges smiles, tongue-clicks, coos, strokes, and pats with her; seeks the comfort of her lap or touch; engages with her in playful give and take; and summons her by name or tells her what's on his mind ("Mimi! Read book!").

6. **Relationships with adults**: *Children build relationships with other adults.* For example, over the course of her development, Tamara, in the presence of a trusted teacher, responds to the sounds or gestures of another adult; plays peekaboo or simple games with another adult; initiates contact with another adult; and brings her toy to or starts a conversation with another adult.

7. **Relationships with peers**: *Children build relationships with peers.* For example, over the course of his development, Nathan watches another child; exchanges sounds or gestures with a peer; physically seeks the company of a peer; pats, hugs, or brings his toy to a peer; and addresses a peer by name or talks to a peer.

8. **Emotions**: *Children express emotions.* For example, over the course of her development, Emily cries, smiles, frowns, wiggles all over with pleasure; stiffens or turns away from something or someone; laughs at, clings to, pushes away, or hugs someone or something; shows pleasure at being able to make something

work or complete an activity or solve a problem; shows frustration with a problem; and names her emotion ("I sad!").

9. **Empathy**: *Children show empathy toward the feelings and needs of others.* For example, over the course of his development, Leon smiles when his caregiver smiles or tenses when the caregiver tenses; cries at hearing another child cry; seeks comforting (by sucking his thumb or seeking a caregiver's attention) when another child is in distress; brings a comfort item (blanket, stuffed animal) to a child who is in distress; hugs Rochelle who is crying because her mom has left; and talks about an emotion displayed by another child ("Baby cry").

10. **Playing with others**: *Children play with others.* For example, over the course of her development, Olivia watches another child play; shows pleasure in playing peekaboo, "This little piggy...," and other simple social games; seeks the company of a peer and plays alongside; plays hide-and-find the teddy bear; chases or is chased by another person; and watches and joins the play of another child by engaging in similar actions or using similar materials.

11. **Group participation**: *Children participate in group routines.* For example, over the course of his development, Jesse kicks his legs at a mobile above his head while his caregiver changes

In this child care home, toddlers have the opportunity to make friends with children of different ages.

his diaper; squeezes and pats play dough at choice time; eats lunch at a low table with other toddlers and puts his dish in a tub when he is finished; and sways and claps his hands to the music at group time.

Physical development and health

For sensory-motor infants and toddlers, physical movement plays a major role in all learning:

Babies learn through movement. As they move their arms, legs, and other body parts and encounter the world through touching and being touched, babies become more aware of how their bodies move and feel. They soon discover that they can change what they see, hear, or feel through their own actions — how delightful to kick, to see the mobile move, and be able to do it again! (Zero to Three, 2009, p. 55)

Physical development and health are considered dimensions of school readiness because of the strong associations found between maternal and child health and subsequent school performance (Kagan et al., 1995). Factors such as prenatal care and early nutrition affect brain development, which affects every other area of growth and learning. Maintaining good health and developing physical skills have many benefits for very young children. Using their bodies to create effects — at first by accident and later with intention — is both gratifying and instructive. Through their actions, infants and toddlers learn what their bodies are capable of. They also explore simple laws of physics (e.g., *If I let go of something I'm holding, it falls down*). As they maneuver themselves and objects through space, they develop an understanding of the spatial relationships that underlie basic principles of geometry (see Cognitive development on p. 46).

The proposition that young children need to be "taught" to develop physically may seem odd. We assume this type of growth happens on its own, provided children have adequate nutrition and ample room to move in a safe environment. However, there is more to physical development than natural maturation. Professor Stephen Sanders (2002), a leader in the development of early childhood movement curricula, notes that "movement programs enhance play, and play provides children with the opportunity to practice movement skills in a variety of contexts. Play alone, however, is not a substitute for helping children develop physical skills....Some structuring of physical activity is necessary to help children maximize their movement experiences" (p. 31).

Research shows that young children who develop appropriate large- and fine-motor skills, such as balance and hand-eye coordination, do better in school than those who are less physically adept (Pica, 1997). Connecting movement to sound — for example, moving to the steady beat of music — may be related to the sense of "timing" — the tempo or natural flow of words — observed in fluent readers (Weikart, 2000). Physically competent children are also more likely to be socially accepted and given further opportunities to hone their skills through interactions, such as movement games.

By contrast, a lack of physical skills can lead to a general lack of confidence and may make children less willing to undertake academic and social challenges. Even toddlers and preschoolers are sensitive to "clumsiness" in peers and may reject them (Sanders, 2002). The degree to which individuals accept and care for their bodies and respect and appreciate their physical capabilities, thus, begins in infancy and has implications for self-esteem and overall functioning throughout their lives. Parents and teachers play a critical role in starting young children on a path that follows a healthy rather than problematic trajectory.

Children's emerging sense of themselves as independent actors and doers is strongly connected to their ability to control their motions, communicate through the language of gesture and action, handle objects with ease, and move at will from place to place. The importance of providing infants and toddlers with safe and ample space in which to exercise their inherent desire to move cannot be overstated. When infants and toddlers have the space and freedom to move without constraint (e.g., not confined in seats, swings, cribs, and stationary play centers), they can learn their own physical strengths and limits and practice movement patterns until mastery propels them to the next physical challenge — *I'm really good at standing up and holding on. Now I'm going to try it without any hands!*

Because movement is so central to sensory-motor learning, a young child's success exploring the physical world sets the stage for later explorations with people, objects, actions, and ideas. Here are the KDIs teachers will see infants and toddlers mastering as they explore with their bodies:

12. **Moving parts of the body**: *Children move parts of the body (turning head, grasping, kicking).* For example, over the course of his development, Juan lies on his back and turns his head, waves his arms, reaches or grasps or kicks; holds an object with his hands and feet; holds an object and passes it from one hand to another; rolls or throws a ball toward an object or person; kicks a ball; and uses small objects with precise coordination (pulls up a zipper, strings large wooden beads).

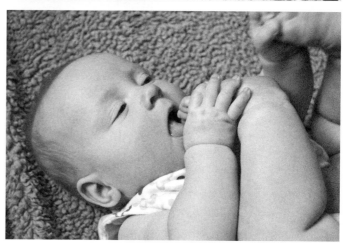

This young infant is moving parts of her body: First, she lifts her legs; then grabs her feet; and, finally, tastes her toes!

Young children gain phonological awareness (recognizing the sounds of language) by repeatedly hearing familiar nursery rhymes. Phonological awareness is important for later literacy development.

13. **Moving the whole body:** *Children move the whole body (rolling, crawling, cruising, walking, running, balancing).* For example, over the course of her development, Allison wiggles and squirms; rolls over; sits up unassisted; creeps, crawls, scoots, and pulls up to a standing position; cruises by holding on to furniture and pulling herself along; balances and walks unassisted; and runs, walks down stairs, and climbs down a climber by herself.

14. **Moving with objects:** *Children move with objects.* For example, over the course of his development, Lukas sets an object in motion by kicking or batting; shakes, bangs, drops, and rolls things; moves an object along while creeping, crawling, scooting, or cruising; carries, pushes, or pulls an object while walking unassisted; and propels himself on a wheeled toy.

15. **Steady beat:** *Children feel and experience steady beat.* For example, over the course of her development, Fiona

steadily shakes a rattle; pounds on the table with a spoon; bounces on her bottom while her caregiver sings a song; and pats or sways to the steady beat of a familiar chant.

Communication, language, and literacy

Infants communicate with movement and sound from birth. Parents, family members, caregivers, and teachers cuddle, coo, and play with infants and also talk, sing, and read to them. Within this interactive social milieu, infants and toddlers learn to talk and lay the foundation for learning to read.

According to the National Reading Panel (2000), successful literacy development depends on four factors: *comprehension* (deriving meaning from action, speech, and text), *phonological awareness* (recognizing the sounds of language), *alphabetic knowledge* (understanding the relationship between letters and their sounds), and *concepts about print* (knowing how books and other printed materials work). Early childhood specialist Rebecca Parlakian (2004) admits that "when one imagines an infant or toddler, it is often difficult to conceptualize what early literacy 'looks like' for such young children" (p. 37). Observing their behavior can help us to understand.

In infants and toddlers, communication, language, and literacy are intertwined. Emerging literacy skills depend on language, and language, in turn, is driven by the child's need to communicate. Speaking, reading aloud, and

singing to infants and toddlers stimulates their *comprehension* of and use of language. Although children, on average, begin to speak at around 18 months, they understand what people are saying to them long before that (Bardige, 2009). The more language addressed directly to them they hear, the more words they understand and use themselves when they do talk.

Studies repeatedly demonstrate the importance of a child's oral language — especially the number and variety of vocabulary words he or she knows — in learning how to read. Researchers Betty Hart and Todd Risley (1999) found that the more parents talked with their children, the more rapidly their children's vocabulary grew; the larger a child's vocabulary at kindergarten entry, the better his or her literacy skills later in school. Of particular value was "non-business" talk, that is, conversations that were not specifically aimed at getting a child to "do" something.

The first words babies typically learn to say are nouns (e.g., "ma" or "da"). Recent studies by neuroscientists at Carnegie Mellon University on how the brain encodes nouns offers some provocative findings on one of the ways infants may be hard-wired to acquire such vocabulary (Just, Cherkassky, Aryal, & Mitchell, 2010). The research team discovered that the adult brain's "dictionary" organizes nouns using three fundamental human factors: how you physically interact with it, how it is related to eating, and how it is related to shelter. Given that infants learn about the world through action and often explore things by putting them in their mouths, one might speculate that mouthing objects contributes to early language acquisition at the neural level. Research is needed to confirm this connection between these early learning behaviors and the formation of the brain structures needed for language, but it is an intriguing hypothesis for neuropsychologists to investigate.

In addition to developing vocabulary, participating in conversation also promotes *phonological awareness,* that is, recognition of the distinct sounds of language, the smallest of which is the phoneme (e.g., the /b/ sound in the word *ball* or the /p/ sound in the word *lip*). As infants and toddlers engage in conversation (using the gestures, sounds, and words at their disposal), they hear the sounds that make up their home language. In fact, when they hear lots of words and begin to use some themselves, they mentally organize these words based on their initial sound. For example, they store all the words that start with the /b/ sound together, all the words that start with the /c/ sound together, and so forth. This mental lexicon helps them call forth the word "dog" when they see the family dog and "da" when they see daddy (Walley, 1993). As they hear nursery rhymes over and over and begin to join in saying them, infants and toddlers hear and repeat words that rhyme like *cat* and *hat* that end in the same /at/ sound.

Later on, infants and toddlers who have heard lots of language and stored lots of words by sound are more likely to gain phonological awareness rapidly and with greater ease than children who have heard so few words from birth to school age that they have had not needed to sort them by sound into a mental dictionary. Because phonemes are represented by the letters of the alphabet, an awareness of phonemes is key to understanding the *alphabetic principle,* which is the idea that words are made of letters and each letter or letter combination has its own sound. This understanding of letter-sound relationships is the foundation of learning how to read. Research shows phonemic awareness and alphabetic knowledge predict whether a child will learn to read during the first two years of school (National Reading Panel, 2000).

The last factor that determines later reading success is *print knowledge,* recognizing the many uses of printed words and how print works (e.g., in English, print is read from top to bottom and left to right, books are read front to back, etc.). For infants and toddlers, print knowledge begins with exploring books and seeing print used in everyday activities (e.g., parents writing a grocery list). Toddlers also begin to incorporate other print props (such as newspapers and writing tools) in their play.

Recognizing environmental print on signs, labels, household products, and play items further contributes to a young child's emerging literacy skills. Toddlers, for example, can read familiar symbols and logos on restaurant signs or supermarket shelves. Infants and toddlers establish these foundations for later literacy when they handle books, look at and recognize pictures in books, connect pictures and stories, are read to, and pretend to read books themselves (Schickedanz, 1999).

Social beings from birth, babies want to connect with other human beings to create a context of meaning and belonging. This motivation fuels the development of language and literacy skills. Infants and toddlers communicate their feelings and desires through an increasingly complex system of cries, motions, gestures, and sounds and are acutely attuned to the body language and the warm, gentle voices of parents and caregivers. Infants and toddlers listen and respond to the organized sounds of language. They initiate social interaction with trusted caregivers and peers and, in the process, construct a set of useful ideas: that communication is a give-and-take process; that you don't need words to convey and understand safety, acceptance, approval, and respect; that there are lots of ways to make your point; and that trusted people are interested in what you have to communicate and say.

In short, infants and toddlers, like all human beings, are "meaning makers" (Wells, 1986). They weave gesturing, making sounds, speaking, watching, and listening into a two-way communication system that draws them into the social community and enables them to participate as contributing members. Evidence that they are learning to communicate is shown by their engaging in the KDIs described here:

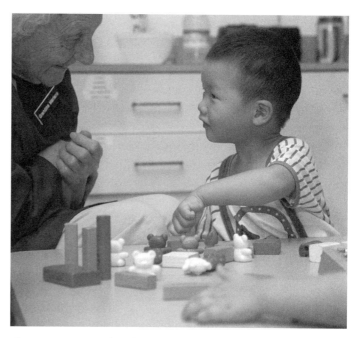

Conversations with infants and toddlers are often nonverbal. This toddler and his caregiver communicate their mutual interest and regard through their closeness, expressions, and gestures.

16. **Listening and responding:** *Children listen and respond.* For example, over the course of his development, Mario turns toward a voice; establishes eye contact and smiles in response to a caregiver's voice; imitates a vocal sound or gesture; turns around when his name is spoken; and acts on a request or a statement (e.g., goes to the coat rack when the caregiver says, "It's outside time!").

17. **Nonverbal communication:** *Children communicate nonverbally.* For example, over the course of her development, Katelynn watches, initiates physical contact with, or points to a person, animal, or object; shows

an object to a caregiver or child; and guides a caregiver to an object, a place, or another person.

18. **Two-way communication:** *Children participate in two-way communication.* For example, over the course of his development, Taylor looks directly at a person's face and coos or smiles; takes turns exchanging sounds or gestures with another person; uses babbling and words to participate in a conversation-like exchange with another person; uses words to make a request or ask a question; and sustains a verbal interchange with another person by taking turns talking.

19. **Speaking:** *Children speak.* For example, over the course of her development, Zongping makes cooing sounds; babbles; gestures by signing; uses a word or phrase to refer to a person, animal, object, or action; and utters simple sentences.

20. **Exploring print:** *Children explore picture books and magazines.* For example, over the course of his development, Matthew gazes at a picture book; touches, grasps, or mouths a book; turns the pages of a book; and points to or names what is pictured in a book.

21. **Enjoying language:** *Children enjoy stories, rhymes, and songs.* For example, over the course of her development, Luan becomes still, vocalizes, or bounces upon hearing a story, rhyme, or song or upon being rocked or patted to the steady beat of a rhyme or song; participates in pat-a-cake or a similar word game, fingerplay, or singing game; asks to hear a story, song, or rhyme; and sings or joins in on a story, song, or rhyme.

Cognitive development

Early cognitive development encompasses many areas of learning. Young children explore objects to discover their basic physical properties and investigate concepts that will later form the foundations of mathematical thinking in quantity, space, and time. Each of these areas of cognitive development, and their associated KDIs, are described below.

Exploration

Everything in the world is new for infants and toddlers. Driven by what child psychologist Selma Fraiberg (1959) called an intense hunger for sensory experience, infants and toddlers explore objects to find out what they are and what they do. Beginning with haphazard batting and kicking at things, they gradually expand their exploratory actions and organize their findings into basic working concepts: *That tastes good. This is too cold. That noise scares me. This blanket feels soft. Grass tickles my feet. Spoons make noise. Balls roll away. I can bang with a spoon, and I can bang with a rattle. I can carry stones in a bucket. The wagon moves, and the couch stays still. My blanket feels good in my mouth, and sand feels terrible in my mouth.* Because their daily lives are caught up in exploration and discovery, infants and toddlers are like amateur scientists. In *The Scientist in the Crib,* authors Alison Gopnik, Andrew Meltzoff, and Patricia Kuhl (2001) refer to the infant as "the most powerful learning machine in the universe" (p. 1).

As infants and toddlers explore objects to discover their characteristics and how they behave, we can observe the following KDIs:

22. **Exploring objects:** *Children explore objects with their hands, feet, mouth, eyes, ears, and nose.* For example, over the course of his development, Aidan looks at objects and listens to things that make noise; reaches for and grasps objects; bats at, kicks at, holds, mouths, tastes, pats, waves, turns, drops, and carries objects; uses two objects together, one in each hand; and uses an object as a tool to complete a task (shoveling sand into a bucket, pounding dough with a mallet).

23. **Object permanence:** *Children discover object permanence.* For example, over the course of her development, Autumn turns toward a familiar object or person; visually follows an object as it drops, rolls, or moves away; searches for a hidden object; and initiates hiding and peekaboo games.

24. **Exploring same and different:** *Children explore and notice how things are the same or different.* For example, over the course of his development,

Touching and mouthing are common ways for babies to explore and learn about objects.

Marwan shows preference for low rather than high voices, slow rather than fast music, or one pacifier rather than another; repeats a satisfying action or sound; selects like things from a group of toys or materials (all the long-handled objects) to mouth and explore; selects like objects to use for some purpose (filling a bag with just plastic animals or just pine cones); uses the same word to name similar objects (e.g., calls all four-legged animals "dogs"); and gathers two or more similar objects from a variety of objects.

Quantity

The early explorations of infants and toddlers also lay the foundation for later discoveries about mathematics. Educational researcher Herbert Ginsburg and his colleagues were amazed at how much of very young children's spontaneous play involves mathematical activities and thinking (Ginsburg, Inoue, & Seo, 1999). Professor Art Baroody (2000) describes how young children build mathematical knowledge from their daily activities and the lessons they derive from them — watching the level of juice in the cup go up when more is "added" and go down when each sip is "taken away," seeing if the tower will still stand when "one more" block is added.

Although the National Council of Teachers of Mathematics (NCTM, 2000) has issued learning standards for children beginning in prekindergarten, mathematics knowledge and skills are rooted even earlier in a child's development. For example, there is evidence that rudimentary ideas about quantity, such as concepts of *oneness* (a single unit or quantity of one) and *invariance* (a quantity stays the same unless it is added to or subtracted from),

appear in preverbal infants based on their direct experiences with these concepts (Brannon, 2002). Objects come singly or in groups of various sizes; materials come in various quantities. If there is a single object, or a little bit of something, there can also be "more!" Thus, young children have a sense of quantity when they point to the table and say "mo" for more grapes at snacktime. They experience the number of things when they count "One, doh, twee" while placing beans into a bottle one at a time. In these direct experiences with quantity, we see the following KDIs:

25. **Exploring more:** *Children experience "more."* For example, over the course of her development, Tierney prolongs exchanging smiles, coos, or gestures with someone; handles one object after another from a group of objects; selects one object (to put into her mouth or into a container), then another, and another; asks for "more" of something (cereal, juice, blocks); and gathers or hoards a number or quantity of something (filling her pockets with several small animals, pouring more and more sand into a bucket).

26. **One-to-one correspondence:** *Children experience one-to-one correspondence.* For example, over the course of his development, Daimon puts his thumb or pacifier into his mouth; holds one object in each hand; attempts to put on a hat, or to put a sock or shoe on each foot, or to put a mitten on each hand; and puts a toy person in each toy car or in each toy bed.

This young child is exploring one-to-one correspondence by putting one marker cap on each finger.

27. **Number**: *Children experience the number of things.* For example, over the course of her development, Shannon prolongs her gaze at a small collection of objects when the number of objects changes (from one ball to two or from three wooden spoons to two); anticipates seeing or finding the one, two, or three things that have recently disappeared (continues to search for the other shoe after finding one); and says a number name while pointing to each of several objects ("One, two, twee" or "One, two, seben") or in reference to objects ("Two doggies!").

Space

Young children are also laying the foundation for geometry when they explore shapes and space. They learn the properties of basic shapes (sides, corners, curves) by playing with wooden or felt circles, triangles, and rectangles. Seeing that the small wooden block fits inside the small plastic container — but the big wooden block doesn't — is the beginning of discovering rules about spatial relationships. Raising their hands to a caregiver and saying "Up!" shows young children have a preliminary sense of direction. Looking on

Climbing up steps on this play structure gives this young toddler a whole new view of her learning environment.

the shelf for their favorite book is evidence of a simple cognitive map in their heads with one or two familiar locations.

In their active learning journeys, infants and toddlers also gain direct bodily awareness of space. Babies inhabit the space immediately around them. With increasing activity and mobility, their sense of space expands as they learn to navigate on their own from one interesting place to another. They experience proximity (nestling in a caregiver's arms), separation (crawling across the room to the steps they want to climb), and enclosure (climbing into a sturdy box). They learn to orient themselves and objects in space so things are easier to see or handle. They attempt to solve the spatial problems they encounter in exploration and play: *I got into this box. Now I have to get out!* Through their own actions, and by actively exploring materials, young children thus begin to develop an understanding of the spatial concepts in these KDIs:

28. **Locating objects**: *Children explore and notice the location of objects.* For example, over the course of his

development, Steen watches a moving object; moves closer to a desired object; moves one object to gain access to another; locates a desired object for exploration or play; and retrieves an object he has not seen for a while (remembering and getting a sweater from his tub or personal storage area).

29. **Filling and emptying:** *Children fill and empty, put in and take out.* For example, over the course of his development, Jonathan drinks from a bottle; knocks over a cup of water or a tin of large wooden beads; takes toys off a shelf or out of a cupboard; dumps toys out of a can, box, or basket; puts objects into a box, bag, purse, or wagon; fills a cup with water; and fills and empties a container of sand, corks, and rocks.

30. **Taking apart and putting together:** *Children take things apart and fit them together.* For example, over the course of her development, Latrisha grasps and pulls on objects; waves, shakes, and bangs objects; opens books and doors; takes the tops off boxes; takes off an article of her clothing and attempts to put it back on; fits shapes into shape sorters, corks into bottles, and large pegs into pegboard holes; and puts together simple puzzles.

31. **Seeing from different viewpoints:** *Children observe people and things from various perspectives.* For example, over the course of her development, Charity observes people and things from a caregiver's arms, from the floor, from the couch, or while lying on her back, front, or side; observes as she sits on the floor or grass or on a pillow, chair, or carton; observes as she crawls across the floor or grass, under the table, into a carton, or up a ramp; and watches people and things from an upright position, from perches she has climbed onto, while swinging on a swing, or while bent over to look backward between her legs.

Time

Finally, over the course of repeated routines and explorations with materials, very young children begin to develop concepts about time. For infants and toddlers, time is now, this moment, the present. In a baby's sensory-motor experience, observed psychologist John Philips (1969), "time is limited to that which encompasses a single event, such as moving a hand from leg to face, feeling the nipple and beginning to suck, or hearing a sound and seeing its source" (p. 20). Babies' internal sensations shape what happens in the present. For example, hunger signals eating and drowsiness signals sleeping. Gradually, children learn to anticipate immediate events from external cues: The sound of running water signals bath time, the sound of Daddy's voice signals play time, and the jingling of keys means going somewhere in the car. Some older toddlers can begin to anticipate and express what they are going to do next: "Balls!" (Play with balls.) "Go ducks!" (Go see the ducks.) As infants and toddlers tangle with basic notions of time, the following KDIs emerge:

32. **Anticipating events:** *Children antici-pate familiar events.* For example, over the course of her development, Leila brightens, becomes still, or turns at hearing a familiar voice or sound; per-forms a particular action at the sight of a particular person or object (smack-ing her lips upon seeing food or a spoon or crying upon seeing Mom or a caregiver put on a coat); sees a famil-iar sight and says what will happen next (saying "Eat, eat!" upon seeing the lunch trays arrive); puts herself in position for the next event (going to the window and looking for Mom at the end of the day); and describes her immediate intentions in words ("Wash hands," "Play trucks").

33. **Time intervals:** *Children notice the beginning and ending of time inter-vals.* For example, over the course of his development, Abdul turns away at the end of a feeding; stops an action to attend to an interesting sound, smell, action, or sensation; uses words to indicate the end of an event ("Down!" "All gone!"); and uses a word to indicate a past event (looking out the window, remembering a dog from the day before, and saying "Doggy").

34. **Speed:** *Children experience "fast" and "slow."* For example, over the course of her development, Lydia rolls, bounces, rocks, bangs, and shakes things at vari-ous rates of speed and crawls, cruises,

This child is experiencing speed. She is going down the slide faster, with a helpful push from a friend.

walks, and climbs at various rates of speed.

35. **Cause and effect:** *Children repeat an action to make something happen again, experience cause and effect.* For example, over the course of his devel-opment, Giles learns to suck; watches an object after accidentally setting it in motion; repeats a simple action to make it happen again; and repeats a simple sequence of actions to make something happen again (stacking several blocks, knocking them down, retrieving them, and beginning again).

Creative arts

From their ongoing sensory-motor explo-rations, infants and toddlers accumulate a critical body of direct experience. They begin to understand, for example, what a blanket is, how it feels, and how to wrap it around themselves for warmth and comfort, and they discover that it contin-ues to exist even when they cannot see it. Gradually, with repeated blanket experi-ences, they begin to form a mental image of a blanket, that is, to see a blanket in their mind's eye when no actual blanket is in sight. This process of beginning to internalize, or mentally picture, something is the child's first experience with what is called *representation.*

The ability to represent allows the child to change a concrete experience into another form, to transform it. Written language is one type of transformation; that is, experiences can be represented in words. The creative arts are another form of representation because they allow us to transform experiences and ideas from one realm into another through painting, music, movement and dance, and dramatic role play.

Early development in the creative arts follows several trajectories. In their book *Supporting Young Artists,* Ann S. Epstein and Eli Trimis (2002) describe these devel-opmental progressions:

- *From accidental or spontaneous repre-sentation to intentional representation* For example, the younger child makes a noise and decides it sounds like a dog. The older child pretends to be a

dog and deliberately makes a "bark-ing" sound.

- *From simple to elaborated models* For example, the younger child lis-tens to music and creates a one-step movement. The older child creates a movement with two steps, in sequence.

- *From random actions to relationships* For example, the younger child makes marks on the page. The older child makes lines or shapes and considers how they "go together" on the page.

Engaging in extensive sensory-motor experience — acting on objects with their whole body and all their senses and repeating these actions at will — enables very young children to experience rep-resentation in many forms — to imitate the actions of others, interpret pictures and photographs of actions and objects they have experienced, and begin to use actions and materials to show or represent something they know about their world. Infants and toddlers build on their direct experiences and experiment with the beginnings of creative representation in the following KDIs:

36. **Imitating and pretending**: *Children imitate and pretend.* For example, over the course of his develop-ment, Nicholas watches and listens to another person; imitates the sounds, facial expressions, or gestures of other people; tries to imitate another person who is eating with a spoon or drink-ing from a cup; repeats the sounds or actions of another person, an animal,

This toddler paints his hand as well as his caregiver's hand while exploring finger paints.

or an object; and uses one or more objects to stand for something else (uses a basket for a "hat" or some blocks for "pieces of toast").

37. **Exploring art materials:** *Children explore building and art materials.* For example, over the course of her development, Mai Lee explores her own hands; reaches for and explores blocks, clay, dough, and paper; makes marks and scribbles; stacks several blocks; squeezes clay or dough; and labels an object she has built, made,

or drawn (paints some blotches and lines on a paper, looks at them, and says "Doggie!").

38. **Identifying visual images:** *Children respond to and identify pictures and photographs.* For example, over the course of his development, Tristan gazes or babbles at a picture or photograph; gestures, points to, or makes the sound of a familiar person, animal, or object in a picture or photograph; selects a picture or photograph to hold or carry; and talks about a person, animal, or object in a picture or photograph.

39. **Listening to music:** *Children listen to music.* For example, over the course of his development, Eli turns his head toward music; looks to see where the sound is coming from when his teacher begins to sing; and points toward the music player to indicate to his caregiver that he wants her to play music.

40. **Responding to music:** *Children respond to music.* For example, over the course of her development, Tia sways or bounces in response to music; stands unassisted and moves her body to music; moves from one foot to the other; and pats, walks, turns, and jumps to music.

41. **Sounds:** *Children explore and imitate sounds.* For example, over the course of his development, Rocco plays with the sounds of his voice as he babbles and coos; plays a game with his caregiver

in which he initiates and then tries to copy the sounds she makes; and imitates the sounds made by his peers.

42. **Vocal pitch:** *Children explore vocal pitch sounds.* For example, over the course of her development, Sheri plays at sliding her voice up and down the scale; attempts to pitch her voice higher or lower to match the sounds of others; and joins in singing the melody of a simple song she has heard several times.

How Adults Use the KDIs to Support Early Learning

Teachers and caregivers can best know, understand, and support each child in their care through close attention, observation, and both physical and verbal interaction. The KDIs guide adults in this effort by broadly defining the actions and learning of sensory-motor children as they build an understanding of their world through direct experiences with people, objects, and daily routines.

The KDIs help caregivers organize, interpret, and act on what they see children doing. When Samantha, a young toddler, unties one of her caregiver's shoes and giggles, her caregiver, Ida, thinks of KDI 5. *Attachment: Children form an attachment to a primary caregiver* (under social and emotional development) and thus interprets Samantha's action as a bid for a relationship. Ida knows from her observations of children and from her understanding of child development that

playful teasing is one way toddlers typically interact with trusted adults.

To let Samantha know that she will play the game Samantha has initiated and to encourage KDI 18. *Two-way communication: Children participate in two-way communication* (under communication, language, and literacy), Ida says to Samantha, in mock surprise, "Oh, dear, what happened to my shoe?" Taking this as her cue to continue, Samantha immediately unties Ida's other shoe. "Oh, dear," says Ida, taking her turn in the exchange, "what happened to my other shoe?" After Ida ties her shoes, Samantha starts the game again. In this fashion, Samantha learns both to trust herself to initiate interactions with her caregiver and to trust her caregiver to respond to her actions as playful rather than naughty.

The KDIs help caregivers to understand children's development and thus make decisions about what to do the next day, based on what they observed children doing today: "At lunchtime, I noticed Elron exploring and mushing his mashed potatoes with his hands," Ida says to Marta, her teammate. Ida is thinking about KDI 22. *Exploring objects: Children explore objects with their hands, feet, mouth, eyes, ears, and nose* (under cognitive development). "So," she asks Marta, "to extend Elron's mushing of gooey things with his hands, what do you think about using clay tomorrow at group time?"

The KDIs help caregivers to select materials and equipment to add to the play space and to think of interactions

Active Learning and the KDIs: A Summary

Five Ingredients of Active Learning

Materials: There are a variety of materials infants and toddlers can use in many ways.

❑ Children explore and play with materials rich in sensory appeal:

  ❑ Everyday household objects

  ❑ Natural and found materials

  ❑ Soft, cuddly materials

  ❑ Easy-to-handle materials

  ❑ Squishy, messy materials

  ❑ Materials children can set in motion

  ❑ Materials children can pull themselves up on

  ❑ Materials children can make noise with

❑ Children have access to people.

❑ Children have a safe place to explore and play with materials.

❑ Children have time to explore and play with materials.

❑ Children have access to materials throughout the day.

❑ Children have access to materials over long periods of time.

Manipulation: Infants and toddlers use their whole bodies and all of their senses to manipulate materials freely.

❑ Children explore materials with all of their senses (eyes, hands, feet, mouths, ears).

❑ Children experiment with materials to find out what they do, return to favorite materials and people, and repeat satisfying actions.

❑ Children use their whole bodies to reach, grasp, roll, sit, crawl, walk, climb, carry from place to place, and so forth.

❑ Children use materials to imitate actions.

Choice: Infants and toddlers choose what to do.

❑ Children make choices and decisions all day long.

❑ Children express preferences for people, materials, and experiences.

❑ Children follow their own intentions and initiatives.

❑ Children decide how to explore and what to do with materials.

❑ Child use materials to do things for themselves.

Child communication, language, and thought: Infants and toddlers communicate and use language about what they need, discover, know, and do.

❑ Children communicate their needs, feelings, discoveries, and ideas in their own individual ways and at their own pace.

❑ Children initiate contact with caregivers.

❑ Children express feelings and communicate about discoveries to receptive and responsive caregivers.

❑ Children string together sounds, gestures, and words in a fashion that makes sense to them.

❑ Children communicate through sign language.

Adult scaffolding: Infants and toddlers learn within the context of trusting relationships.

❑ Caregivers take interest in children's play.

❑ Caregivers enjoy children's actions and explorations.

❑ Caregivers communicate warmth and respect.

❑ Caregivers acknowledge children's feelings, from delight to frustration.

❑ Caregivers provide positive physical contact, including cuddling, hugging, holding, stroking, and lap-holding.

❑ Caregivers give each child their full attention and respond readily to the child's signals and approaches, communication, and talk.

❑ Caregivers talk with children, tell children what will happen next, encourage children's problem solving, and read to children.

Active Learning and the KDIs: A Summary

KDIs: The Content Infants and Toddlers Learn

Caregivers are familiar with the key developmental indicators (KDIs) in these areas:

❑ **Approaches to learning:** Children show initiative in solving problems, doing things for themselves, and learning about their world.

❑ **Social and emotional development:** Children express their feelings, differentiate themselves from others, and form relationships with adults and peers.

❑ **Physical development and health:** Children explore the movements their bodies are capable of making and use their bodies to learn about the world.

❑ **Communication, language, and literacy:** Children communicate with gestures, sounds, and words to establish human connections and explore printed materials.

❑ **Cognitive development:** Children develop early ideas about quantity and number, navigate their environment, discover the attributes of objects, and develop ideas about time from the sequence of their daily activities.

❑ **Creative arts:** Children exercise curiosity and creativity by exploring art materials, pretending, and engaging with the sounds of music.

How caregivers use the KDIs

❑ Caregivers are familiar with the KDIs related to approaches to learning; social and emotional development; physical development and health; communication, language, and literacy; cognitive development; and creative arts.

❑ Caregivers observe children and interpret their actions in light of the KDIs.

❑ Caregivers use the KDIs to guide their interactions with children, to plan for activities that support children's learning and development, and to guide their selection of materials for children.

and experiences that might support and build on children's actions, interests, and need for repetition during each part of the day.

Finally, the KDIs help caregivers to track children's growth and development, share and interpret children's actions to parents, and work together with parents to devise common strategies for supporting children's development — in approaches to learning; social and emotional development; physical development and health; communication, language, and literacy; cognitive development; and creative arts — at home and in their care setting. For more about using the KDIs to enhance teamwork on behalf of children and to assess and scaffold their learning, see Chapters 2 and 6, respectively.

2
The Caregiving Team and Their Partnership With Parents

A solid relationship with parents allows a caregiver to feel comfortable bonding with their child. Relationships with parents that are friendly and reciprocal make caregivers more likely to delight in children's progress, remember details to share about the day, think about the children after hours, and remain connected to the family beyond the child care years....A child and caregiver are more likely to form strong ties when the child's parents value that relationship.

— Baker & Manfredi/Petitt (2004, p. 17)

Active learning, adult support, a safe and inviting environment, child-centered schedules and routines — what draws these elements together and makes them work? *The focused, collaborative efforts of the adults in children's lives!* Children learn how to play with each other, communicate, empathize, and resolve conflicts by observing how adults relate to each other. The relationships among the adults in a child's life are "as important as the relationships between a child and those adults….Children's emotional safety and sense of well-being are deeply affected by the adult relationships around them" (Keyser, 2006, p. 1).

Throughout each day, the adults who are part of a caregiving team work together to observe and support the children in their program. The caregiving team also works in partnership with parents, exchanging child observations and providing consistency between children's at-home and away-from-home experiences. Caregivers, parents, administrators, and community members form even wider partnerships to advocate for children and to secure the resources needed for high-quality child care settings. The cooperation of all these adults is needed to create safe, secure active learning environments for very young children.

In the infant-toddler program setting, the goal is to build strong, supportive relationships between caregiver and child, between caregiver and parents, and among caregivers themselves; these relationships can then support the vital relationship between parent and child. This chapter focuses on all these relationships in discussing the dynamics of the caregiving team and the caregiver-parent partnership.

The Caregiving Team

Just as early development is optimized when children grow up in stable homes, infants and toddlers thrive when they remain with the same primary caregiver for the duration of their stay in out-of-home settings. This stable arrangement allows children and families to form trusting relationships with the caregiver, eliminates painful and confusing transitions from caregiver to caregiver for children, and promotes a sense of well-being and belonging for everyone involved. To provide their children with consistent and continuous care and to provide mutual support, a pair of primary caregivers (sometimes three primary caregivers) work together in a team.[1] Caregivers may choose to form teams in a variety of ways, depending on what makes the most sense for their particular setting and circumstances.

Continuity of care

For the infant or toddler who is to spend an extended period (perhaps three years) in the same program setting, it is important that his or her caregiving team be *a team that remains together for that time,* insofar

---

[1] A caregiver in a family child care home often works alone, but the caregiver might form a team with another family member, another family child care provider, or a hired assistant.

as it is humanly possible. The practice of keeping teams together for an extended period provides continuity of care for the children involved, continuity for parents, and continuity for the caregivers.

Programs that have put team continuity into practice find that stable, consistent caregiving teams — compared with ones that change from day to day, month to month, or year to year — are more conducive to forming strong trusting relationships that allow infants and toddlers to thrive and grow in their parents' absence (Smith, Goldhaber, & Cooper-Ellis, 1998). Over a three-year period, for example, the children, families, and caregivers involved in a particular caregiving team have time to know and become invested in one another. Continuity of caregivers gives children the stability and courage they need to explore challenges and form new relationships with peers and other adults.

At the same time, caregivers themselves benefit from taking part in sustained teamwork. They usually learn one another's interests and strengths and develop a rapport that allows them to share the pleasures of their work as well as support one another in meeting the unavoidable physical, emotional, and intellectual challenges involved in child care. Authors Amy Baker and Lynn Manfredi/Petitt (2004) note that when caregivers enjoy good relationships with one another, children receive better care. Teachers share information and help to make one another more conscious of the needs of individual children and the group as a whole. They also serve as

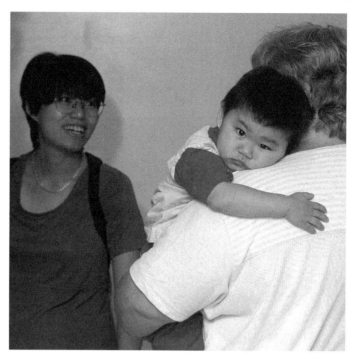

Continuity of care helps children form strong, trusting relationships and thrive in their parents' absence.

positive role models of adult interaction: "When caregivers' own relationships are positive, they set a moral tone and teach children about responsibility, mutual respect, integrity, and human values in the way children learn best — through experience" (p. 2).

Caregivers can also establish relationships across teams. When one caregiving team shares space, observations, concerns, and insights with other caregiving teams, the teams come to rely on one another for support and advice instead of walling themselves off in the infant room or the toddler room. When this *teamwork between teams* occurs, the center acts like a community. Caregivers, for example, are on the lookout for natural and found materials for their own and one another's children. They each open their doors to curious children from other rooms who wish to peek in on and even visit the children next door or down the hall. They may meet together as a larger group of four or six from time to time for daily team planning as time and schedules permit.

Caregivers who get along within and across teams impart an overall positive feeling to the entire organization. They enjoy coming to work, which improves staff retention. Instead of worrying about relationships with coworkers, they are better able to focus their energies on the children. They all become knowledgeable about the whole range of infant-toddler behavior and can act as a resource for any parent connected with the center. Cohesive caregiving teams are also more likely to include families in the workplace community. Parents know that whichever caregiver they talk to about their child, they will receive informed answers and support for their concerns.

Of course, there will be unavoidable departures of children or staff in even the best of programs. So establishing working conditions that encourage staff retention and providing program quality to ensure stability of the child population must go hand in hand with planning for team continuity. Both working conditions and program quality depend on staff having ongoing administrative support and opportunities for training and professional development. Good caregiver-director

relationships benefit both. Not only do caregivers feel appreciated and supported but directors do as well and, perhaps most important, the children get better care (Baker & Manfredi/Petitt, 2004).

A new program hiring new staff can establish caregiver continuity from the outset. An ongoing program, however, may need time to shift from the practice of moving infants and toddlers from room to room with a different caregiving team in each room. The administration and staff will need opportunities for discussion and problem solving, a strong commitment to providing continuity of care for children and families, and a firm belief in each caregiver's ability to observe children and support them through all of their infant-toddler stages.

While caregivers who are used to caring only for infants, for example, may initially miss the security of working with one, familiar age group, they generally enjoy their deepening relationships with children and parents as they make the shift to working with their children at older ages as well. Further, by staying with children as they mature, caregivers witness the same continuum of infant-toddler development that parents do. Instead of focusing on just the timetable and milestones within a narrow band of that continuum, they come to see early child development as encompassing a broad range of individual differences. See Chapter 3 for staffing and facility options that allow children and/or caregiving teams to remain together from year to year.

Team planning

To provide a program of quality, one that serves children and families as effectively as possible, *daily team planning* is essential. Meeting together for between 20 and 30 minutes each day, the members of the caregiving team discuss, interpret, and plan around child observations, using the ingredients of active learning and the KDIs as a guiding framework. Together, based on their knowledge of child development, caregivers build a common understanding of their children as sensory-motor learners and social beings and devise strategies to support their strengths, interests, and emerging abilities.

Team planning not only is a time when adults share information about children's development but also is a time when caregivers themselves can grow professionally. Reflection is an essential component of this growth process, as caregivers think about their own beliefs and practices and use their insights to solve any practical problems that have arisen.

Child development professor Robert Weigand (2007) says the personal nature of reflection means it can only occur when caregivers feel safe in their work environment. Discussing his own efforts, Weigand observes, "Re-experiencing emotionally significant interactions with children provided an opportunity to carefully examine the emotions, thoughts, and intentions that accompanied and motivated my behavior....Talking about my work in a relationship characterized by a sense of security promoted [a] careful and deeper

During team planning, caregivers discuss, interpret, and plan around child observations using the ingredients of active learning and the key developmental indicators as a guide.

exploration of my emotions and behaviors" (p. 19).

Although it may be a tall order for infant-toddler caregiving teams, finding a half hour daily for team planning can be done. It takes determination, creative scheduling, and administrative support. Here are several strategies that teams have found to work:

- Set aside as daily planning time the first 20 to 30 minutes after children have settled down for afternoon naps.

- In programs with younger children who nap at various times, plan during the time of day when the fewest children are awake. In some such programs, the center director plays with the non-nappers or hires an aide to do so while the caregiving team plans.

- Try meeting together during a 20- to 30-minute segment of morning or afternoon outside time. Replace the primary caregivers with administrative staff, early childhood education students (if your program is associated with a college or university), or an aide hired specifically to cover for teams during daily planning time.

- Plan a daily schedule for caregivers that includes 20 to 30 minutes for planning either before the children's arrival or after their departure each day.

There may be no *ideal* time for daily team planning in infant-toddler programs, where children rely on the constant presence of their primary caregivers even when other competent adults are standing in for them. Nevertheless, it is important for caregiving teams and administrators to work together to designate and schedule such a time. In the long run, team members are more effective caregivers when they take time together each day to think about what they are observing in children, how to support them, how to support one another, and how to solve problems as they arise.

Caregivers' Strategies for Collaboration

As they work together with children throughout the day, talk with parents, and meet together for their daily planning, the two (or three) caregivers who form a team try to support one another, draw on their respective strengths, and turn their understanding of children and child development into practical ideas to try. The following strategies help them carry out this role:

- Practice open communication.

- Make joint decisions about program issues.

- Observe children, discuss child observations, and plan ways to support individual children.

Practice open communication

Open communication involves speaking in an honest, straightforward manner. Psychologist Virginia Satir (1988) calls this process *leveling*. When you level with others, you strive to communicate what you mean as clearly as possible.

Caregivers strive to communicate as clearly as possible.

Your emotions, physical posture, facial expressions, and tone of voice match what you are saying. When you are upset, for example, you look upset and say so when asked. ("I'm upset," Kim says to her teammate, Yvonne, "because, when there weren't enough shovels to go around at group time, Carlos bit Tanner to get his shovel. He's *never* done that before!") This contrasts with the confusing practice of looking upset, acting upset, but saying otherwise or refusing to talk about what is troubling you. An example would be Kim saying "Nothing's wrong! Everything's okay!" at the same time that she was acting very upset about the biting incident.

Practicing open communication, or leveling, calls for recognizing and avoiding confusing conversational habits. Satir identifies four such behaviors — *placating, blaming, computing,* and *distracting.*[2] The following descriptions of these negative behaviors may help team members assess their own conversational styles.

Placating involves soothing or reducing another person's anger by yielding to that person's ideas or demands. When you placate, you agree with others, no matter what you really think or feel, so they will not get angry with you. Physically, you

---

[2]Satir's work has been elaborated by organizational psychologists to include eight behavioral coping patterns: congruent, placating, blaming, loving/hating, narcissistic, infatuated, irrelevant, and super-reasonable (McLendon & Weinberg, 1996).

may assume a posture that suggests humility as you apologize or admit responsibility for what has gone wrong, effectively closing the subject and preventing constructive discussion from taking place. For example, if Yvonne were to reply to Kim as a placater, Yvonne might say, "I'm really sorry about the biting, Kim. It's all my fault. If I had set out enough shovels, maybe it wouldn't have happened. Don't be upset, okay? I'll try to do better tomorrow!" This would have cut off open discussion in which the team members might have, together, agreed to ensure that group-time materials were always ready and in sufficient supply. They might also have gone on to discuss how to best handle biting situations.

Blaming involves accusing, holding the other person responsible, or criticizing that person. When you blame, you may assume what appears to others to be a fairly aggressive posture. You may cut a person down, talk in a loud voice, ask questions but not wait for answers, or make "you" statements that deflect the conversation from the real issue at hand. For example, if Yvonne were to act as a blamer in responding to Kim, she might say, "You get upset too easily, Kim! You'll get grey hair before your time if you get this upset when one toddler bites another one." Kim herself might have, but didn't, act as blamer in making her original statement. She didn't say to Yvonne, for example, "This kind of thing [biting] always happens because *you* don't think ahead about what we will need for group time!"

Computing involves speaking in an unfeeling way, using big words so people will think you know a lot and be afraid to prolong a discussion with you. When you compute in responding to someone who is upset, for example, you may talk at length in a calm and reasonable tone, sitting stiffly, with your hands and face still. If Yvonne were to respond in this manner to Kim, she might say, "Well, Kim, Carlos clearly needs to learn to delay gratification. I'm not surprised at his regressive behavior, since he comes from a dysfunctional family." Once again, Kim's chances of having an extended discussion with Yvonne could have been thwarted by this mechanical response delivered with a superior air.

Distracting is sidetracking the conversation by bringing up a totally irrelevant issue to avoid an uncomfortable subject. Physically, you may show your discomfort by nervously moving your arms or legs, repeatedly standing up and sitting down, or fiddling with a pen or pencil. If Yvonne were to respond as a distractor to Kim, she might jump up and say, "I just remembered, we're out of diapers for Bobby. I'd better call his mom. She's such a nice person. I really like talking with her. I think she knows my neighbor, the one with the grape arbor."

When team members make a habit of placating, blaming, computing, or distracting, the dialogue of teamwork becomes very difficult. By contrast, although it may seem scary at first, leveling brings great relief. People share their real thoughts and feelings, take turns speaking and listening, and respectfully give their full attention to others as they speak. They speak honestly but also address one another with respect instead of hurling guilt-inducing personal assaults. The urge to "let it all hang out" is tempered by a stronger desire for civility. Each person participates in a give-and-take manner in the focused discussion that further unfolds with each contribution. As levelers, team members find themselves relying on one another's strengths and differences to cocreate the strategies they need to support their particular children in their particular setting. At the same time, they practice among themselves the same honest, straightforward exchanges they have with the children in their care.

Following is an excerpt from Kim and Yvonne's conversation about biting, in which both speak as levelers:

Kim: *I'm upset because, when there weren't enough shovels to go around at group time, Carlos bit Tanner to get his shovel. He's* never *done that before!*

Yvonne: *Biting is upsetting to see, especially when you weren't expecting it. We could probably have avoided that incident by better planning on our part — making sure that at the start there's enough for everyone at group time.*

Kim: *I know that toddlers bite — sometimes even when there are enough shovels — and Carlos is very active. I'm glad that he knows what he wants, but it's not okay for him to hurt another child. There have to be some limits.*

Yvonne: *Right. I guess, to a toddler like Carlos, who's just beginning to talk, biting seems to be a good way to get a point across quickly. But even if biting is just an attempt to say something in a hurry, we don't want children biting other children. Kim, since you're obviously so upset now, how did you stay so calm at the time? How did you deal with the situation?*

Kim: *Well, I could see that the bite didn't break the skin. I tried to be calm and matter-of-fact so the children wouldn't get any more upset than they already were. I stroked Tanner's bitten arm, telling Carlos "Be gentle with Tanner. He doesn't like to be bitten." Then I stroked Carlos's arm as well and said to him, "Be gentle." Then I said, "Carlos, it looks like you want Tanner's shovel, but he doesn't want to give it up."*

Yvonne: *Oh, I wondered what you said, because I saw Tanner take another shovel off the shelf and give it to Carlos. That seemed to end the whole episode.*

Kim: *It did. Carlos wanted Tanner's shovel, but he was satisfied with the one from the shelf. I do think I have to watch Carlos in a new way, though, so biting doesn't become a habit.*

Yvonne: *Well, I guess that by helping Carlos identify the problem — he wanted Tanner's shovel — you gave both children the opportunity to come up with a satisfactory alternative to biting.*

Even as levelers, team members like Kim and Yvonne do not always agree. They learn, however, to examine their differences and do joint problem solving.

For example, when two levelers discover differences, they try to remain calm and patient with each other and acknowledge the strong feelings involved. They are ready, as early childhood educator Katie Gerecke (1998) has pointed out, to listen carefully to each other's ideas and concerns, state their own beliefs clearly, look for areas of agreement, brainstorm for solutions, and choose one to try. After trying their ideas, they reflect on how well they worked.

Here is an excerpt from a conversation between Kim and Yvonne in which they attempt to talk openly about their different opinions on what position they should place nonmobile infants in at choice time.

Kim: *Today I put Mallory in the infant seat at choice time to protect her from Jamal and Jai. They're really getting good at crawling, and Jamal almost crawled right over her head when she was lying on the floor yesterday!*

Yvonne: *Hey, I thought we weren't going to restrict babies to infant seats for choice time! I think* not *putting Jamal and Jai in those things at choice time was what led to their crawling.*

Kim: *Well, look at us! We're getting a little worked up here! I guess we both have pretty strong feelings about where infants should be!*

Yvonne: (Laughs) *Yeah, I guess we do! Okay, let's talk about this. You want Mallory to be safe, right?*

Kim: *Yes, and I think that now that Jai and Jamal are crawling, she's safer when sitting in the infant seat than when lying on the floor.*

Yvonne: *I want her to be safe, too, but I also want her to have a chance to get ready for crawling. Right now, she needs to be able to move her arms and legs so she can work up to rolling over. She can't do this in an infant seat.*

Kim: *Well, I want her to be safe, but I don't want to restrict her, either. Maybe I could put Mallory back on the floor and put the big pillows around her — not too close, but as sort of a speed bump for our two creeper-crawlers.*

Yvonne: *That might work. She could still move freely, but the pillows would create a safety barrier around her.*

Kim: *Let's try that tomorrow.*

(Several days later.)

Kim: *Well, the pillows seem to be working for Mallory.*

Yvonne: *Yes, Jamal and Jai do try to climb over them, but the pillows slow them down so you or I can get there soon enough to make sure they don't crawl on top of her!*

Make joint decisions about program issues

It is important for caregivers to discuss and reach agreement on the issues that underlie working well together. Team members need to sort out and deal with their individual concerns about space and materials, schedules and routines, and roles and responsibilities, so their interactions with children and families can reflect their ease

Team members share their real thoughts and feelings, take turns speaking and listening, and respectfully give their full attention to one another.

with one another rather than unresolved tensions. By wrestling with these issues, the caregiving team lays the groundwork for a welcoming early childhood environment. The following are examples of the kinds of questions that infant-toddler caregiving teams need to address and work out together.

Space and materials

- How will we arrange (or rearrange) our indoor and outdoor space to promote active learning?

- How might the arrangement of this space work better for nonmobile

infants? For mobile infants? For young toddlers? For older toddlers?

- What might we do to make this space more comfortable and inviting for children and adults?

- What materials might we add, eliminate, or supplement to support children's interests and sensory-motor development?

- Are there any physical changes we can make to the indoor and outdoor space to enhance children's opportunities for movement? For sensory exploration? For social interaction?

- Whose help and support do we need to make these changes?

Schedules and routines

- How will we organize our overall daily schedule? How can we make sure it is predictable (so everyone knows what happens next) yet flexible enough to accommodate individual children and their care routines?

- To what extent are we incorporating all the ingredients of active learning and adult support into each part of the day?

- What might make it possible for us to give our full attention to each child during feedings, mealtimes, and bodily care routines?

- What choices do our children have at mealtime and naptime?

- What roles do we assume at choice time and outside time?

- What are our children doing at group time?

- What can we do to make arrivals and departures smoother for children and parents?

Roles and responsibilities

- How will we divide up our daily tasks? (Who washes eating utensils and bedding? Restocks supplies? Cleans toys and equipment? Takes out and puts away play materials? Feeds the fish and waters the plants?)

- How do we keep track of what needs to be done each day and by whom?

- What daily records do we keep and for what purpose?

- What are our respective roles during team planning?

- How do we record our observations and plans?

- How do we support one another throughout the day as we work together with our children?

- How do we communicate with one another while maintaining our focus on the children?

- How do we relay important information to all families (such as changes in policies or schedules)? How do we decide who will and when and how to share information about specific child(ren) with their parents?

As caregivers work together over time, they construct their own responses to these and similar questions. While each team comes up with its own strategies to try, every team relies on open communication, patience with its team members, and a belief in its ability to solve problems and seek out support from administrators and others as needed.

Observe children, discuss child observations, and plan ways to support individual children

At the heart of the teamwork process lie three questions team members return to daily:

- What did we see children doing today?

- What do their actions tell us about them?

- How can we provide materials and interact with children to support their play and learning tomorrow?

These questions prompt the caregiving team to examine children's actions, interpret them in terms of child development, and plan follow-up support strategies. Overall, the team reflects on the nature and implications of each child's actions and communications.

Observe children throughout the day

As infants and toddlers continually grow and develop through their day-to-day active learning, their caregivers attempt to see who they are and what they are doing, so they can be present and ready with individual support. This is why caregivers are careful observers as they interact with children during their mealtimes; their bodily care routines; their naptime routines; and during their exploration and play with materials and peers at choice time, outside time, and group times. Caregivers take note of a wide range of behaviors: how children move, how they express themselves, what materials interest them, what causes them frustration, how they attempt to solve problems, and which other children they enjoy being with.

Because so much happens in a child care setting on any given day, infant-toddler teachers and caregivers have devised a number of ways of reminding themselves of all the interesting things they

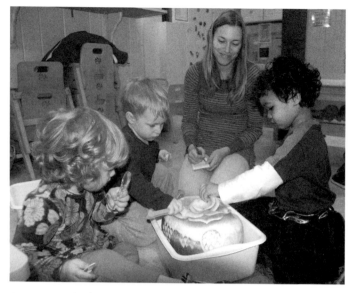

Using a pad of sticky notes, this teacher writes anecdotes as she observes the children explore a watermelon that her co-caregiver cut up for them.

have seen and heard. They bring these reminders to team planning for discussion. Some ideas for remembering these observations follow. The ideas may work for your team, or they may suggest to you other self-reminder strategies to try:

- Carry in your pocket a pen or pencil along with index cards or a pad of sticky notes. When you observe something concerning a child, jot down the date; the child's name; and key words, drawings, or symbols that will help you at team planning to reconstruct what you saw, for example: Jamal, ramp, pillows, babble → Mallory. Pocket-sized, handheld electronic devices offer another similar option for jotting down short notes that can be elaborated on later.

- Place spiral notepads or clipboards supplied with paper and a pencil in strategic places around the room(s). When making an observation, jot the child's name and key words on the notepad or clipboard nearest you.

- Keep a camera handy. Take photos of actions you want to remember, and bring them to team planning.

- As you log routine entries about a child's feedings, diaper changes, and naps, jot down key words to remind you of any unique or striking actions you saw and want to share. These brief, personal notes will help you reconstruct your observations later in the day, when you have a chance to record them in more detail and decide with your teammate what they mean and what to do about them. If you don't want to write directly on the child's log sheet, keep nearby a pad of sticky notes to write on, and attach these to the log sheet.

- At a convenient level where caregivers can write on it, tape a blank piece of paper or tack a dry-erase board to the wall for jotting down notes on each child, or keep a recording device handy. When you see actions you want to remember for a particular child (e.g., what you saw a child say or do), jot key words on that child's paper or record a brief statement.

As you observe children, watch and listen carefully, with an open mind, and stick with the facts. You want to see and hear as much as you possibly can without making snap judgments or jumping too quickly to conclusions. For example, you might note that "Liam banged his spoon on the table" rather than that "Liam deliberately annoyed everyone at the table by banging his spoon."

Discuss, interpret, and record child observations, using the KDIs as a guide

Each caregiver arrives at team planning with a head full of child observations and some quickly jotted notes or photos to refresh her memory. As team members review the day, they share their observations, and by using the KDIs as objective referents, they figure out what the observations might mean. They then record the observations, for example, by writing short anecdotes under the relevant KDI categories on a form. The notes staff record on each child's form serve to chart growth and development and can be shared with parents and other caregivers as needed. Following is a portion of Kim and Yvonne's team-planning meeting that illustrates this process:

Discuss

Kim: (Looking at the note she made to herself that reads "Jamal, ramp, pillows, babble → Mallory") *I was struck by something that happened between Jamal and Mallory today. I put Mallory on a blanket on the floor at choice time and put the big pillows around her so she'd have lots of room to move. Jamal was crawling up and down the carpeted ramp, as he has been doing for the past couple of days. At one* point, he seemed to pause and catch sight of Mallory inside her pillow barricade. He crawled down the ramp and headed straight for her. It looked like he really made a choice to go see her!

Yvonne: *Well, you know, they did spend a lot of time on the floor next to each other before Jamal learned to crawl.*

Kim: *Yes, they did, and I'm wondering if maybe he misses her. Anyway, he crawled up to one of the pillows, and then he crawled onto and over it. I was close to both of them, but this time I didn't try to stop him, because it seemed that he really wanted to make some kind of connection with Mallory.*

Yvonne: *You were probably ready to prevent him from hurting her!*

Kim: *Yes, I was, but what was really interesting was that once she saw him struggling to get over the pillow, Mallory started to wiggle all over and smile and coo as though she was really happy to see him! When Jamal did get over the pillow into Mallory's little space, he just sat next to her and waved his arms and babbled back to her. He seemed happy to see her too!*

Yvonne: *So they had what looked like a conversation?*

Kim: *Yeah! Sort of like two long-lost pals! They both wiggled and vocalized. I thought Jamal might try to pat her or something, but he didn't. And then after a bit, Mallory turned away, and eventually Jamal crawled back over the pillow and back to the ramp.*

Interpret

Yvonne: *So what do you think was going on here?*

Kim: *Well, let's see.* (To help them interpret Jamal's actions objectively in terms of child development, she turns to a list of the infant-toddler KDIs and studies them. Yvonne moves closer so she too can see the list.) *First, I'm looking at the category of social and emotional development. The KDIs* relationships with peers *and* emotions *might help us interpret Jamal's actions. Jamal wanted to get close to Mallory. He was pleased to see her. When he "talked" to her, he used his whole body.*

Yvonne: *Yes, and even though Mallory is so young, she also showed pleasure at seeing Jamal by the way she wiggled, smiled, and cooed at him! So there seems to be some kind of social relationship between the*

During their team planning, caregivers use their anecdotal notes to discuss what they observed children doing and how they can plan to support them the next day.

two, maybe one that started before either of them could crawl.

Kim: (Turning back to the KDIs list) *I guess, looking under the communication, language, and literacy category, we could interpret their actions as* nonverbal communication *because they did seem to be having a little conversation. They looked at each other and wiggled and babbled. I'd even say Jamal spoke the word "baby" when he said "Bebebe." This went on till Mallory turned away.*

Yvonne: *Yes, and under the KDI category approaches to learning, they both expressed* initiative. *Jamal decided to climb down the ramp and over the pillow to get to Mallory, and Mallory turned away when she decided she had had enough social exchange!*

Kim: *The other thing that strikes me as I look at the cognitive development KDI category is that I could see that Jamal was really* seeing from different viewpoints. *He actually saw Mallory from the top of the ramp, and then he remembered where she was even when she was hidden behind the pillow! That seems like quite an accomplishment, evidence Jamal has discovered* object permanence, *another KDI indicator in the cognitive development category.*

Yvonne: *Yes, and he had to climb over the pillow to see her again! I'm beginning to see that he was actually* problem solving *too — going back to the approaches to learning category. So his mind was as busy as his body!*

Record

Kim: *Okay, so I'm going to record this on Jamal's observation form under what?* (Pause.) *I think under social and emotional development* (relationships with peers), *since that's what first struck me,* (pause) *and then I'll also make a note under cognitive development.* (Kim writes the following in the social and emotional development column of Jamal's form: "12/15 At CT [choice time], J. [Jamal] crawled up the ramp, looked down at Mallory surrounded by pillows on the floor, crawled down the ramp and over a pillow, and sat on the floor next to her. He looked at her, waved his arms, and babbled at her, 'Oooweee, bebebe....' Mallory smiled, wiggled, and cooed back to him." In the cognitive development column of Jamal's form, Kim writes: "12/15 [See 12/15 anecdote under social and emotional development related to seeing from different viewpoints]").

Before we continue with Kim and Yvonne's plans for the next day, a word about recording child observations. The most useful anecdotes paint a picture that is clear to people who did not witness the original event. Effective anecdotes include the following characteristics:

- *Context:* Include the date (12/15; also be sure to indicate the *year* at the top of the sheet on which you record anecdotes), each child's name (Jamal, Mallory), the time of day (choice time), and where the action occurred (the ramp, on the floor next to Mallory).

- *Actions and sounds or words:* Describe what the child did and said (e.g., "crawled up the ramp," "looked down from the ramp at Mallory," "Oooweee, bebebe…").

- *Facts:* Include objective details rather than general or subjective statements (e.g., "He looked at her, waved his arms, and babbled at her, 'Oooweee, bebebe…' Mallory smiled, wiggled, and cooed back to him," rather than "They were glad to see each other").

To keep track of each child's development, Kim and Yvonne use a form to record the anecdotes from their child observations, keeping one such form for each child. On the form, they organize the anecdotes according to the six KDI categories — **approaches to learning**; **social and emotional development**; **physical development and health**; **communication, language, and literacy**; **cognitive development**; and **creative arts**. For a sample of this system of recording and organizing child observations, see "Child Observations" (pp. 76–77), which illustrates how Kim and Yvonne have recorded their observations of Jamal. (For a discussion of the parts of the daily schedule referred to on the form, see Chapter 5.)

Plan ways to support individual children

After discussing child observations and using the KDIs as a guide for interpreting and recording them, members of the caregiving team ask themselves, "So, what do we do tomorrow based on what we

After writing anecdotes describing how Lela chose and then picture-read the book to herself, Marta transferred her notes to Lela's observation form under communication, language, and literacy.

have learned about our children today?" To illustrate this step of the teamwork process, let's return to the conversation between Yvonne and Kim:

Yvonne: *So, what are these two babies telling us? How can we support them tomorrow?*

Kim: *Hmm…* (Both team members pause to think.)

Child Observations

Child: Jamal   Year: 2011   Observers: Kim and Yvonne   J = Jamal, CT = choice time, OT = outside time, GT = group time, A = arrival

Approaches to Learning	Social & Emotional Development	Physical Development & Health	Communication, Language, & Literacy	Cognitive Development	Creative Arts
8/22 J reached for and grasped a dry diaper during diapering. 10/1 Waking from nap, J cried. When Kim stroked his arms and legs and asked him what was troubling him, J grabbed his foot and put his toes in his mouth. When Kim said, "You've got your toesies in your mouth," he looked up at her with a slight smile.	8/15 At A, J cried when his mom gave him to Kim. Kim gave him back to his mom, and he stopped crying. She talked to him, held him for 10 minutes, then said, "I'm going to give you to Kim now." Kim held him the same way his mom held him. He looked sad but did not cry. 8/20 J snuggled in Kim's arms and gazed at her intently while he drank his bottle.	8/19 Lying on his back at CT, J kicked his legs vigorously. 10/12 At CT on the floor, J rolled over from his back to his front! 11/2 Lying on his back at CT, J held a short-handled spoon with both hands, let go with one hand, waved it around, then reached over and held it in his other hand.	8/17 Hearing his dad's voice at the end of the day, J cooed and wiggled all over. 9/14 During diapering, J made a lip-smacking noise. Kim repeated it, then J repeated it, and so on, for several rounds. 10/20 Waking from nap, J looked at and babbled to his stuffed bear, "Bebooo, bebooo…"	8/25 Waking from nap, J lay on his back and watched his hands move above his head. 10/8 At CT, J banged a rubber duck on the floor, making it squeak. He repeated his action, making high-pitched noises. 11/20 At GT, J patted his hand in a dishpan filled with water.	9/1 At OT, J stilled when the toddlers next door shook bells. 9/11 At CT, J crumpled a piece of blue kraft paper and made a blowing noise. 11/4 At CT, J babbled "Bebebebe…" at a bear in a board book then chewed on that page.

Child Observations (cont.)

Child: Jamal   Year: 2011   Observers: Kim and Yvonne   J = Jamal, CT = choice time, OT = outside time, GT = group time, A = arrival

Approaches to Learning	Social & Emotional Development	Physical Development & Health	Communication, Language, & Literacy	Cognitive Development	Creative Arts
12/10 J picked up banana pieces and fed himself. After smooshing some pieces, he licked banana off his fingers.	9/6 J watched himself in the mirror during CT. He smiled at his reflection when Kim said, "There's Jamal!" 9/9 At CT, J watched Mallory, who was lying on the next blanket. 12/15 At CT, J crawled up the ramp, looked down at Mallory surrounded by pillows on the floor, crawled down the ramp and over a pillow, and sat on the floor next to her. He looked at her, waved his arms, and babbled at her, "Oooweee, bebebe..." Mallory smiled, wiggled, and cooed back to him.	11/10 At CT, J got himself into a sitting position!		12/15 (See 12/15 anecdote under Social and Emotional Development related to seeing from different viewpoints.)	

Yvonne: *Well, I'm thinking about the cognitive development category. Maybe we could provide both of them with more chances to see things from different vantage points. What if we put Mallory on the mattress instead of surrounding her with pillows? Then she'd still be free to move, but she'd be able to see other children better, and Jamal could see her better, since no pillows would be blocking his view. She'd still be protected, because the mattress would act as a speed bump to slow down anyone crawling toward her. If Jamal crawls up there with her, he'd be up off the floor too, seeing things from a little different perspective.*

Kim: *That might work. We'd still have to be close by watching. And we could put the mattress in the corner so Jamal could approach it from only two, not all four, sides. This idea might lead to even more interaction between them.*

Yvonne: *Yes, and for Jamal, I'm looking at the physical development and health category and trying to think of other things he might climb or crawl onto. I could put out a couple of large hollow wooden blocks tomorrow and see if he climbs onto them.*

Kim: *How about using the small packing cartons too? If we stuffed them with newspaper for extra support and sealed them up, they'd be sturdy enough to climb on or sit on.*

Yvonne: *Great! And here's another idea — we could bring out the rocking boat and turn it step-side-up. If Jamal's ready for*

steps, he'll try them; if he's not, he won't — but Jai might. Jai's mom said he's been trying out steps at home.

Kim: *It just occurred to me that the changing table might provide Jamal or Jai with another perspective! Maybe for Jamal, especially, we could take some time during diapering for him to sit on the changing table and just look around at the rest of room. We could try describing what he seems to be looking at. It might work, it might not. We could try it and see.*

Yvonne: *Okay! Now, what about social and emotional development? What can we do to further the friendship that seems to be forming between Mallory and Jamal?*

Kim: *Well, we could try putting Mallory down on the floor near Jamal or move the mattress she's on so it's closer to where Jamal is playing. I mean, if Jamal is climbing on ramps and boxes, we could put Mallory closer to him than she was today, but of course not so close that she's in danger.*

Yvonne: *And the other way around — we could move Jamal closer to her by putting his toy basket on the floor a bit closer — even quite close — to Mallory, since they're used to being on neighboring blankets.*

Kim: *Now that Jamal's crawling, Mallory can't always be near him, or vice versa. So sometimes we could try putting Bobby and Mallory closer together on the floor or mattress — since Bobby isn't crawling yet. This might allow Bobby and Mallory to keep each other company the way Mallory and Jamal did before he learned to crawl.*

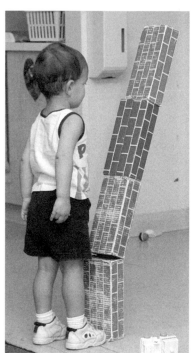

Kent's caregivers wrote this anecdote on his observation form during team planning: "7/7 At choice time in the block area, Kent stacked three cardboard brick blocks end to end. When he added a fourth block, the stack toppled, so he began all over again!" They recorded this anecdote under cognitive development, with KDI 30. Taking apart and putting together *in mind.*

Yvonne: *That might work. But I think we need to continue respecting babies' preferences when they seem to be seeking each other out or withdrawing. I just think we need to be sensitive to both situations.*

Kim: *I agree!*

Yvonne: *Now, let's figure out which of these ideas we can work into tomorrow's plan.*

The chart on page 81 is a summary of Kim and Yvonne's discussion of their observations of Jamal and Mallory. After discussing the possible support strategies in this chart, Kim and Yvonne decide how they can include some (but not all) of them in their plan for the next day. To

see how they record their ideas, see "Sample Evolving Daily Planning Form" on page 82. (For a discussion of the parts of the daily schedule referred to on the form, see Chapter 5.) As Kim and Yvonne go on to discuss observations of other children, they will generate other ideas and strategies to record on this daily planning sheet. (For further support strategies based on infant-toddler observations, see *What's Next? Planning Strategies and Activities Around Infant-Toddler COR Observations* [HighScope, 2004].)

During the daily process of team planning, it is important for caregivers to (1) record their anecdotes from child observations and (2) record their plans for the next day. Kim and Yvonne, for example, take turns at this: One day, Kim records the observations on the children's individual forms while Yvonne records ideas for the next day on the planning sheet; the next day, they switch tasks. The recordkeeping can be done by hand (e.g., using a notebook with dividers) or on the computer or online (e.g., with a subfolder or file for each child). (For HighScope computerized and/or online recordkeeping options, visit eTools at www.highscope. org.)

At various times, Kim and Yvonne personally add to the record any anecdotes they have not had time to discuss on a given day. They both refer to this growing collection of anecdotes when they are talking to parents, preparing parent reports, and assessing children's growth and development using the Infant-Toddler COR (HighScope, 2002a).

During team planning, one team member records child observations while the other records ideas they will try the next day.

Summary of Kim and Yvonne's Discussion

Observation	Related KDIs	Possible Support Strategies
12/15 At CT [choice time], Jamal crawled up the ramp, looked down at Mallory surrounded by pillows on the floor, crawled down the ramp and over a pillow, and sat on the floor next to her. He looked at her, waved his arms, and babbled at her, "Oooweee, bebebe…" Mallory smiled, wiggled, and cooed back to him.	**B. Social & Emotional Development** 7. Relationships with peers 8. Emotions **A. Approaches to Learning** 1. Initiative 2. Problem solving **D. Communication, Language, & Literacy** 17. Nonverbal communication 19. Speaking **E. Cognitive Development** 23. Object permanence 31. Seeing from different viewpoints **C. Physical Development & Health** 13. Moving the whole body	**B. Social & Emotional Development** • Put Mallory closer to Jamal. • Put Jamal's toy basket close to Mallory. • Put Bobby close to Mallory. • Respect children's preferences for approaching and withdrawing. **E. Cognitive Development** • Put Mallory on the mattress, in a corner. • Add things for Jamal to climb on: large hollow blocks, packing cartons, step-side-up rocking boat. • Give Jamal time to sit on the changing table and look around.

The Caregiver-Parent Partnership

The importance of the caregiver-relationship is shown by its prominence in virtually all state and professional early childhood program standards. For example, the Early Head Start Performance Standards (Administration for Children, Youth, and Families, Head Start Bureau, 1999), the accreditation workbook of the National Association for Family Child Care (2005), and the National Association for the Education of Young Children (NAEYC; 2007) accreditation criteria all stress the importance of caregivers communicating with parents to establish and maintain program quality. Program assessment measures, such as the Infant-Toddler Program Quality Assessment (HighScope,

Sample Evolving Daily Planning Form

Caregivers: *Kim and Yvonne*	Date: *Tuesday, 12/16*
A.M.	**P.M.**

Arrival

Choice Time *Put Mallory on mattress in corner. Put Jamal's toy basket closer to Mallory.*	*Put out large hollow blocks and turn rocking boat step-side-up for Jamal.*

Group Time
Content (KDI):

Earlier	Middle	Later

Easy to join:
Content (KDI):

Outside Time
Try putting Bobby and Mallory on blankets near each other.

Bodily Care
After diaper change, see if Jamal wants to sit on the changing table and look around.

Meals

Naps

Departure

To Remember
Gather, stuff, and seal packing boxes for Jamal to climb on (for next week).

Key Developmental Indicators (KDIs):
APP Approaches to Learning
SE Social and Emotional Development
PHY Physical Development and Health

CLL Communication, Language, and Literacy
CD Cognitive Development
CA Creative Arts

2011) and the Infant/Toddler Environment Rating Scale (Harms, Cryer, & Clifford, 2006), include items for rating the nature of family-staff relationships.

Relationships between providers and parents affect a child's attachment to both. When parents have confidence in the caregiver and the setting, the child senses this and is more likely to feel confident in turn. Likewise, a caregiver should show her respect for the child's parents, recognizing they are the most important people in this child's life (Honig, 2002).

As an added benefit, caregivers and parents are also psychologically rewarded by their mutually satisfying associations with one another. A good relationship with parents is part of a caregiver's compensation package and can help reduce burnout in a field where staff turnover is estimated at 30 percent for caregivers and 40 percent for directors (Center for the Child Care Workforce, 2001). This, in turn, results in a more stable caregiving situation for children and reduced stress for parents.

Caregivers like Yvonne and Kim form partnerships with the parents of their infants and toddlers. These partnerships are characterized by mutual trust and respect and include an ongoing conversational give and take about the growth and development of the children in whom all of them have a common, abiding interest. Because infants and toddlers cannot yet speak clearly for themselves — *Hey, let me sleep! I had a rough night last night. My new teeth were driving me crazy!* — caregivers and parents have no alternative but

to share what they know about the non-verbal but communicative children in their care. By paying close attention to each other and participating in joint activities, caregivers and parents use a teamwork approach to creating a supportive environment for their children. This relationship between parents and their child's caregiver takes time to develop. Although the caregiver may have a great deal of expertise, she should not "presume to know more than the parent before doing the work of relationship building…gathering information, testing strategies, and observation over time" (Griffin, 1998, pp. 26–27).

While caregiver-parent partnerships take time and effort to establish and sustain, everyone involved benefits. Together, parents and caregivers collect, exchange, and interpret specific information about the child's ever-changing actions, feelings, preferences, interests, and abilities. They learn from each other what does and does not work with the particular child at the center of their relationship. New parents gain confidence in their parenting skills, and experienced parents receive support as they adapt to new stages of parenthood. Caregivers grow in their ability to attune themselves to each child. Both parents and caregivers are reassured by their mutual efforts to smooth the transition between home and center, and parents and caregivers with differing beliefs about childrearing, care, and early learning often expand their perception of the possible. The child, in turn, sensing the comfortable bond between parent and caregiver,

A caring, trusting relationship between a caregiver and parent helps ensure a smooth transition at pickup time, which makes for a happy baby, a happy caregiver, and a happy mom!

reflects their ease with each other in his or her behavior — a happy parent makes the baby happy; a happy baby makes the parent happy. Further, the parent-caregiver "team" serves as a strong advocate for the child in other settings, as needed.

Guidelines for Effective Caregiver-Parent Partnerships

Partnerships can take many forms in business and personal relationships. The parent-caregiver partnership has elements of both. It is a *business arrangement* in which one person pays for the services

of the other; it is also a *personal association* cemented by mutual concern for the well-being of the young child they are both responsible for. In describing the characteristics of this unique and important partnership, parent educator and program director Janis Keyser (2006) writes that

> *A partnership is a relationship between equals.... This doesn't mean that both partners bring exactly the same thing to the partnership; it means that each is respected for his or her unique contribution. In a partnership, people are interested in discovering the other person's perspective, engaging in two-way*

communication, consulting with each other on important decisions, and respecting and working through differences of opinion. (p. 4)

For caregivers, following these basic guidelines can contribute to the success of the caregiver-parent partnership:

- Recognize role separation.
- Practice open communication.
- Focus on parents' strengths.
- Use a problem-solving approach to conflict.

Recognize role separation

Caregivers can best support active learning when they recognize the difference between supporting parents and competing with them. The overriding goal is to provide a warm, secure, interesting environment for the children parents entrust to them. Caregivers make a conscious effort not to compete with parents for children's love and attention, and they do not try to glorify their own child care abilities. Rather, they respect the primacy of the parent-child bond and see themselves as mature, knowledgeable adults whom children can trust and rely on in the absence of their parents.

Understanding their separate roles allows caregivers and parents to work together without stepping on each other's toes. While the child is at the heart of the caregiver-parent relationship, the parent's and the caregiver's respective roles relative to the child are different and

complementary. Parents, in general, love their children passionately. Their emotions play a large part in guiding their interactions with their offspring. Caregivers, as professionals, take great interest in the well-being of the individual children in their care. They tend to think very carefully about how they interact with them. In a sense, one might say that parents feel first and think later, whereas caregivers think first and then feel. Early childhood educators Janet Gonzalez-Mena and Dianne Widmeyer Eyer (1993) write that

Parents operate (and should operate) from the gut level, reacting emotionally rather than responding reasonably. Of course, parents should also use their heads, should be objective now and then....Caregivers should also be human...but they should mostly be fairly objective and thoughtful in goals and reactions....The point is balance. The balance swings more to feelings and spontaneity in the parenting role and more to thoughtfulness, objectivity, and planning in the caregiver role. (pp. 221–222)

Fortunately, children need both passionate adults and thoughtful adults, or as psychologist Urie Bronfenbrenner (1985) distinguished them, *irrational* and *rational* adults:

You [as a child] need both kinds of involvement: rational and irrational. First, you need somebody who thinks you're the most wonderful creature

Parents, in general, love their children passionately. Their emotions play a large part in guiding their interactions with their offspring.

in the world…who's that crazy about you….You also need somebody who is not irrational about you; who values you as a child but considers you no more wonderful than another child. Such a person works for your development in a fair, rational manner. If you don't have somebody like that in your life, it is very difficult to become a full human being. Another problem is that the same person can't play both roles, because a person really can't be crazy and fair at the same time. (pp. 47–48)

Parents and caregivers, then, are not in competition. Rather, they play quite different roles in relation to the child, roles the child relies on them to carry out in their own particular ways in a consistent and dependable manner. Moreover, it is important for caregivers and parents alike to be aware of one of the significant findings of an ongoing large-scale research study of early child care (beginning in infancy) involving 1,300 children in nine states. This study, which began in 1991, is being conducted by the National Institute of Child Health and Human Development (NICHD); its early reports concluded that mother-child attachment and interactions were not affected by the amount of time children from birth to age three spent in child care (NICHD Early Child Care Research Network, 1997, 1999).[3] While children are forming new relationships with their caregivers and peers, their primary relationship with their parents remains firmly intact.

Practice open communication

Another key to a successful caregiver-parent partnership is open communication — the same approach members of the caregiving team use with one another. During caregiver-parent interchanges, the caregiver always makes an effort to *level* (i.e., to communicate what she means as clearly as possible), so her emotions, physical posture, facial expression, and tone of voice match what she is saying to the parent. She clearly states her thoughts and feelings in a kind and thoughtful manner. The caregiver and parent engage in two-way conversation, meaning they take turns listening and speaking and respectfully give each other their full attention. Open communication provides a set of ground rules that guides conversations about the range of care and early learning issues caregivers and parents together face.

As open communicators, caregivers refrain from *computing* with parents, that is, displaying their child development expertise at the expense of parents' self-confidence. Regardless of how much they know about infants and toddlers, caregivers have a sense of humility about their role. They understand that supporting parents in their complex and long-term role is more effective than teaching or correcting them. They realize that parents know more

---

[3]For a complete summary of the NICHD Early Child Care Research Network's research methodology and findings and a current list of publications, visit the NICHD website (www.nichd.nih.gov).

than anyone else does about their own child. Most important, they know that their daily interactions with a particular child end after two or three years, whereas the parent-child bond is lifelong.

When caregivers model and practice open communication, parents can relax, knowing they are leaving their children with people they can trust. This encourages parents "to resolve differences rather than hide them, question themselves, or rail against their circumstances" (Baker & Manfredi/Petitt, 2004, p. 21). Caregivers and parents rely on one another to solve problems and solutions arise more easily when the doors of communication remain open.

The child is at the center of the parent-caregiver relationship. The parents and caregiver, therefore, have the same goal — to provide the best possible care for the child.

Focus on parents' strengths

While open communication with parents may take considerable thought and effort, it is greatly aided by a caregiver's willingness to focus on parents' strengths rather than on any perceived faults or social barriers. Again, it is important to remember that the child is at the center of the parent-caregiver relationship and to make the assumption that both parents and caregivers have the same goal — to provide the best possible care and education for the child. On a personal level, caregivers interacting with those seeking child care today may find themselves presented with a wide range of adults: parents in professional occupations, parents with marginal employment, teen parents, single parents, parents with disabilities, retired grandparents, foster parents, and nannies. Children may come from families representing a variety of faiths, cultures, home languages, and political beliefs. Each adult — parent and caregiver — brings who he or she is and what he or she knows to the unfolding saga of a child's care and education.

Therefore, it makes sense for caregivers to let go of any negative impressions or stereotypes they may have. They acknowledge their negative impressions in their own mind (*Uh-oh. I'm feeling angry at this 15-year-old for having a baby!*) and then allow themselves to *meet parents as they are* rather than to shut them out because they do not fit their image of what parents ought to be (*All right, this mom is here with her baby in my program. Her child deserves the best from both of us, and together, we can provide it!*). Instead of setting up barriers between themselves and the diverse families they may encounter, it is more productive and useful to the child for caregivers to seek out and build a partnership based on parents' strengths and dreams (*This mom is young, energetic, very involved with her child, and committed to finishing school. Maybe her determination will open doors*).

Use a problem-solving approach to conflict

Finally, given the diversity of family experiences and childrearing practices within our communities, it is important to realize that parents and caregivers are bound to disagree from time to time. When they do, caregivers can turn to a problem-solving approach to conflict. The steps they use with adults are related to the problem-solving steps they use with children. (See "Steps in Resolving Conflicts With Adults," p. 90.) Here is a brief example of how this process unfolds:

At the end of the day, Lacie,[4] Marlee's mom, arrives to find her baby Marlee sitting on the floor next to a basket of rattles and household items. She is holding and mouthing the cardboard tube from a roll of paper towels. Lacie takes the tube away from Marlee and offers her a rattle. Refusing the substitute, Marlee begins to cry. Lacie picks her up, approaches Kerra, Marlee's caregiver, and says, "Why are you
giving my baby trash to play with?"

As Kerra calmly rises from the floor where she has been sitting with the children, she realizes that Lacie's question makes her feel both dismayed and defensive. But, setting these feelings aside, she also realizes the question is a sign of Lacie's strong, single-minded devotion to Marlee. She gives Lacie her full attention. (**This was Step 1: Approach calmly.**)

"I can see you're upset, Lacie," Kerra says, touching Lacie lightly on the arm. "Of course I am!" Lacie replies heatedly. As Marlee begins to cry harder, Lacie pats her to soothe her and then asks in a calmer voice, "Why do you let my baby play with throwaways?" Marlee's crying subsides as her mom becomes calmer. (**This was Step 2: Acknowledge adults' feelings.**)

"Can you tell me what bothers you about the paper towel tube?" Kerra asks. Thinking for a moment as she rocks and pats Marlee, Lacie explains, "Well, it's not a real toy, it's not colorful, it's used — and you can't wash it. Besides, my mom would kill me if she saw her granddaughter playing with junk!" With this last remark, she laughs a little. "Yeah," responds Kerra, "my mom had the same reaction when she saw my kids playing with wooden spoons and empty cereal boxes! I told her that I gave them household things to play with because they're easy for babies to grasp and handle, and they give them the opportunity for some exploration. Plastic rattles

---

[4]Caregivers and parents may address one another by first name or by title (e.g., Mrs., Ms., Mr.). Parents may also have different expectations for how they want their children to refer to their caregivers. Caregivers should clarify this with parents at the time of enrollment and use whatever term(s) of address are agreed upon.

Steps in Resolving Conflicts With Adults

1. **Approach calmly.**

   Calm yourself, mentally acknowledging your own feelings.

   Prepare yourself to listen.

   Use a calm voice and gentle body language.

2. **Acknowledge adults' feelings.**

   "You look really upset." "I can see you have very strong feelings about…"

3. **Exchange information.**

   Take turns describing the details of the problem situation and your specific needs.

   Use "I" statements rather than "you" statements.

   Listen attentively as the other person speaks. Remember, this is a dialogue, not a debate.

4. **Look at the problem from the other person's viewpoint.**

   "What is this person showing or telling me through actions or words about…?"

   "How do my needs relate to this person's needs?"

5. **Restate the problem.**

   "So the problem is…"

6. **Generate ideas for solutions, and choose one together.**

   "What can we do to solve this problem?"

   Together, brainstorm to come up with ideas for solutions.

   Select an idea and codesign a strategy to try.

7. **Be prepared to follow up.**

   Take turns describing how the strategy is working.

   If necessary, make adjustments together or return to Step 6.

are smooth, but wooden spoons feel a bit rougher, and cardboard boxes and tubes crinkle and crumple and give when a baby squeezes them. Children can learn a lot through their senses when they play with different kinds of materials." (This was Step 3: Exchange information.)

"And what did your mom say to that?" Lacie asks. "Well," continues Kerra, "she said she still preferred 'real toys' for her grandchildren, but she also began to watch the children more and see just how *much they gravitated toward everyday things like wrapping paper, shoelaces, and measuring spoons. She'd rather they play with the rattles and real toys she gave them — and they do sometimes — but, seeing how much they liked the pots and pans and butter tubs, she stopped trying to take them away." "Yeah," says Lacie, "well I guess Marlee does like the cardboard tube, maybe because it's so light and 'squeezey.' I remember now that I used to like to use a tube like that as a horn, and it would*

drive my mom crazy to bear me blowing through it!" Laughing, Kerra replies, "I still like to do that!" (This was Step 4: Look at the problem from the other person's viewpoint.)

"Okay, let's see," Kerra says. "The problem seems to be...what? (She pauses to think.) You're concerned about Marlee playing with towel tubes because they're not real or colorful toys, they can't be washed, and they look junky. I am concerned about providing children with materials that offer them a variety of qualities to explore. And Marlee seems to like the towel tube because it is light and squeezey." *"And she cried when I took it away," adds Lacie. "Well, she does choose things that interest her," comments Kerra.* (This was Step 5: Restate the problem.)

"So," continues Kerra, "what can we do about this problem?" Both women think for a bit. "Let's just brainstorm some ideas and then decide together what might work," says Kerra. "Okay," says Lacie. Together, they discuss the following ideas:

- *Don't offer any towel tubes to children.*

- *Offer towel tubes, but replace them after a child has handled them.*

- *Continue to offer towel tubes along with other conventional toys and household items.*

- *Replace towel tubes with other tube-like things that are light and squeezable, perhaps plastic tubing.*

- *Offer colored cardboard tubes that are a bit sturdier and look nicer (like the*

ones from a local recycling agency). Check to make sure dyes are nontoxic.

Both Lacie and Kerra are interested in the last idea. They decide to focus on it, and as they discuss it further, they come up with this strategy to try: For younger children like Marlee, who still put everything in their mouth, replace the towel tubes with sturdier, more colorful cardboard tubes. These are just as easy to grasp but do not deteriorate as readily as the towel tubes when wet. Provide older children with both the towel tubes and the colorful cardboard tubes. Replace all tubes daily. (This was Step 6: Generate ideas for solutions, and choose one together.)

Later that month, as they talk about how the new cardboard tubes are working, Lacie asks about the possibility of bringing up the topic of using household materials as playthings at a meeting for parents and grandparents so her mom could hear from Kerra about why Marlee and other children like to play with everyday household things as well as regular baby toys. "I've talked with my mom, but it would help if she heard it from you!" says Lacie. "Yes, I'd like to do that," says Kerra. She talks with her team member about the idea, and they decide to include this topic in their next parent (and grandparent) meeting. (This was Step 7: Be prepared to follow up.)

As you engage in problem solving with parents (and other adults in your program), it is important to be aware of likely outcomes. Gonzalez-Mena (1992, p. 4) described four typical outcomes to anticipate:

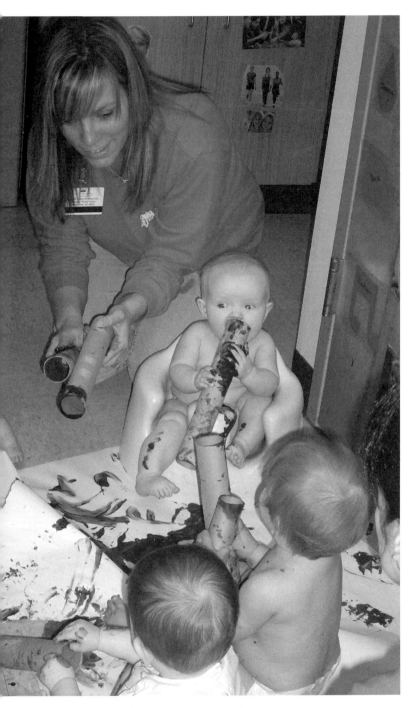

Sensory-motor learning can look quite messy to parents. Sensitive caregivers listen to parents' concerns, share information about early learning, and discuss and agree on options together.

- *"Resolution through understanding and negotiation. Both parties see the other's perspective; both parties compromise."* This is what happened between Lacie and Kerra: They eliminated towel tubes for young infants and replaced them with sturdier, more colorful cardboard tubes; they also provided the sturdier tubes, along with towel tubes, for the older children.

- *"Resolution through caregiver education. The caregiver sees the parent's perspective; the caregiver changes."* This kind of resolution would have occurred had Kerra and Lacie agreed to simply remove the towel tubes, the first idea on their list.

- *"Resolution through parent education. The parent sees the caregiver's perspective; the parent changes."* A resolution of this sort would have occurred had Kerra and Lacie agreed to carry out the third idea on their list — continuing to offer towel tubes along with other conventional toys and household items.

- *"No resolution…[at best, this can mean that] each has a view of the other's perspective; each is sensitive and respectful but unable, because of differing values and beliefs, to change his or her stance."* For example, Kerra might have continued to offer towel tubes to all children while making an effort not to offer them in Marlee's collection of playthings. Lacie, though still disliking the idea of seeing children playing with "junk," might have ceased

Cultural Variations in Beliefs and Practices Affecting Children

Our observations of and interactions with young children and their families inevitably reflect our personal biases. We see their behavior through the eyes of the culture(s) we grew up with and live in today, yet we are often unaware of how our attitudes and actions are shaped by our experiences. For optimum social-emotional development, children need synchronicity or agreement — not necessarily sameness, but compatibility — between home and school. Therefore, understanding our own cultural background, and its relationship to those of our children's families, can help us address their social-emotional needs more consistently and effectively.

Areas in which culture can affect how we interact with children and their parents, as well as with colleagues from different backgrounds, include the following issues:

- *Personal space* — Cultures vary on how close to sit or stand when communicating.

- *Smiling* — Others may only do it to convey happiness, but we misinterpret their lack of smiling as unfriendliness.

- *Eye contact* — Some show respect by making eye contact, and others, by looking away when you talk to them.

- *Touch* — Touch can be interpreted as a sign of warmth and friendliness, insult, or even danger.

- *Silence* — Silence may or may not be comfortable; it can be seen as a sign of respect or of disregard for others.

- *Time concepts* — Punctuality may (or may not) be important; getting to the point may be appreciated or seen as rude.

- *Gender roles* — Cultures differ on whether and what roles are assigned to men and women; parents may feel uncomfortable, or may even feel disrespected, if they are asked to assume a nontraditional role.

- *Autonomy* — Some cultures value autonomy and independence; others deemphasize the individual and focus primarily on the welfare of the group.

- *Adult authority* — Some cultures encourage children to question adults as intellectually and emotionally healthy; others see such challenges as disrespectful and want teachers to act as "authority" figures with children.

As a result of these differences, especially as applied to early care and education, contentious areas for early childhood programs are often *eating* (foods and feeding), *sleeping, attachment and separation, autonomy versus independence, learning through play, choice, talking versus silence* (signs of respect), and *guidance and discipline*. We often do not become aware of how culture affects our practices in these social and emotional domains until we encounter opposition from parents or coworkers: "We become conscious of our systems when they bump up against ones that are different, and we notice that we have a reaction" (Gonzalez-Mena, 2008, p. 3).

The best way, therefore, to make our programs welcoming to all children, regardless of their background, is to evaluate how our own cultural values affect our behavior in the classroom.

— Adapted from *Me, You, Us: Social-Emotional Learning in Preschool* (Epstein, 2009)

complaining, because her own child was usually not playing with towel tubes.

While another outcome is also possible — no resolution and no mutual respect for each other's views — this situation creates a tension between parent and caregiver that is bound to affect the child. Had this happened between Kerra and Lacie, Kerra might well have resorted to "resolution through caregiver education" and removed all the paper towel tubes. For the sake of her ongoing relationship with Lacie, she might have bowed to Lacie's wishes, reasoning that the children will not be seriously harmed by the removal of this one type of plaything when they have such a wide range of other interesting materials to explore and play with. She might also have reasoned that in the long run, Lacie, once she begins to trust that Kerra hears her, will in turn be more willing to trust and hear Kerra. As Abbey Griffin (1998) observed, "Negotiating conflicts can be very useful in building relationships.... However, effective negotiation requires a readiness to exchange the habit of being 'nice' for the challenge of honest dialog" (p. 29).

Differences in home and center beliefs and practices regarding young children are inevitable, especially as our culture becomes more diverse. (For more on potential areas of disagreement, and how examining our own beliefs can help us deal with them, see "Cultural Variations in Beliefs and Practices Affecting Children"

on p. 93.) Whatever the outcome of any occasional disagreement, the caregiver-parent partnership will remain intact if caregivers make a consistent effort to acknowledge the caregiver/parent role difference, communicate openly, focus on parents' strengths, and take a problem-solving approach to conflict. Following these guidelines helps both caregivers and parents to keep an eye on their common goal — to provide a consistently supportive environment for children at home and at the center.

Caregivers' Strategies for Engaging Parents as Partners

Caregivers establish partnerships with parents because they value and respect parents as the major contributors to children's health and well-being. They recognize that their own effectiveness as caregivers and early educators and the ongoing vitality of the center both hinge on whether there is successful teamwork between parent and caregiver. The following strategies help caregivers engage parents as partners and center participants:

- Create a welcoming environment for families.

- Establish a family-centered enrollment process.

- Exchange child observations, but leave the "firsts" to parents.

- Encourage parents to participate in the center.

Create a welcoming environment for families

One way caregivers can prepare the physical setting for caregiver-parent collaboration is to set up a family-oriented space or room somewhere between the center's entrance and the children's rooms. It can be furnished comfortably (e.g., with chairs, tables, coat hooks, coffee and tea, a microwave, and access to a bathroom). This transitional area resembles a café where parents can easily meet and mingle; sit down with their children, other parents, and caregivers or staff members; nurse an infant; eat a quick lunch; or simply collect themselves before leaving. Having a space like this (in addition to or in place of the reception area described in Chapter 4) encourages parents to take their time as they enter and leave and to look forward to the center as an enjoyable place for their children *and* themselves.

Caregivers, and the rest of the center staff, can make mental preparations for parents, as well. Before they meet a single family member, they might review their own professional commitment to the guidelines for building effective partnerships with parents (see pp. 84–85). Then, from the first contact with parents, caregivers should genuinely welcome them to their center. They should consistently approach parents and family members in a friendly, respectful, nonjudgmental manner and take the time to introduce parents to one another. When parents are upset, caregivers should make every effort to remain calm, empathic, and thoughtful. In short, this means seeing parents not as competitors or irritants, but as co-players in the drama of childrearing. Thus, with a welcoming attitude and readiness to listen and converse, caregivers will be able to draw parents into the communal heart of the center.

Establish a family-centered enrollment process

Parents typically experience strong emotions over leaving their baby or toddler in someone else's care for a substantial part of the day. They see this as shattering the round-the-clock intimacy they have established at home with their child. Experienced caregivers anticipate parents' feelings and consider them to be a routine part of the enrollment process. It is important to realize, however, that to the parent who is feeling sad, guilty, fearful, or anxious, these emotions are anything *but* routine — they may, in fact, be overwhelming! At the same time, the young child may also feel anxious and upset. With no sense of time, an infant or toddler has no way of knowing, initially, that his or her parent will actually return, and so the child may feel abandoned.

Even the youngest infants can pick up on their parents' anxiety and experience this stress themselves (Maxted et al., 2005). Some infants enter child care at the age of 6 weeks, while others begin at 3 months (after a parent has taken his or her 12 weeks of job-protected leave under the Family Medical Leave Act). This is a very vulnerable time for both parents and infants; parents are often sleep deprived

Transitions from home to center can be very difficult for parents and children. Clockwise, beginning at the upper left, this toddler is happy when her mom stays to play with the ball with her but distressed when she leaves. She is comforted by her primary caregiver and with her favorite "blankie." Once calm, she is continued to be comforted by a friend. She then eases into the morning activities with her friend.

and overwhelmed with the responsibilities of a new baby and young babies can sense their parents' emotions (Griffin, 1998).

A family-centered enrollment process acknowledges parents' and children's sorrows and fears and their manner of coping with them. While these feelings cannot be eliminated, caregivers can provide families with the time and support they need to regain their emotional balance and to incorporate the life of the center into their daily routine. To avoid unnecessarily abrupt and painful transitions from home to center, caregivers follow these steps to guide the enrollment process in a sustained and gradual way: (1) recall personal transitions; (2) organize enrollment materials; (3) host visits to the center; (4) make a home visit, if possible; and (5) support and learn from the parent-child pair through a series of settling-in visits to the center.

Recall personal transitions

The enrollment process begins before caregivers ever see a parent, with their own recollections of the separations and transitions they have experienced. It's helpful for caregivers to take time to remember how they felt, for example, at some time when they were aware of being all by themselves, without a parent, sibling, or family member. Perhaps it was their first time being cared for by a new babysitter, their first day in school, or a first overnight stay away from home. If the caregivers are parents, they can recall how they felt when they left their own child (or children) in someone else's care or when their child moved out of the house to live somewhere else.

Caregivers can share with their team members some stories about these personal experiences, the feelings they had at the time, and the support they received or wish they had received during these times. Sometimes well-meaning individuals minimize or dismiss another person's anxiety, hoping it will help that person's negative feelings dissipate, when acknowledging concerns actually allows an individual to get past them more easily. When caregivers have shared their experiences, and what they did and did not find helpful, they should remember that the parents and children they will be welcoming into their center will come to them with similar stories and feelings. Using their own memories to remind themselves to acknowledge their feelings and provide the calm support and reassurance that they, from their own experience, know might help parents through this transition. A caregiver's goal, after all, is to create pleasant memories for the children who are making their transition from home to a center.

Organize enrollment materials

One way to reassure anxious parents is to provide them with clear information about the program. To facilitate the enrollment process, parents should receive a packet, file, or booklet containing all the information and permission forms, policies, and descriptive statements pertinent to the program (the forms should include any that the state legally requires parents to sign). Providing such materials to parents in this way reassures them that the caregivers are responsible and organized and lets them know from the outset what policies and educational ideas guide the center's approach to children's care and early learning. In general, parent enrollment materials might include the center's own parent-friendly versions of the following:

- *Information and permission forms* requesting family data (parent/guardian names, addresses, phone numbers; child's name and birth date); a record of child's immunizations, allergies, illnesses, medications, and insurance; a list of emergency phone numbers/contacts and people other than parent(s) who are permitted to pick up the child with appropriate notification; signed release forms (for outings, on-site photographs or videotaping, administering medications); current information about the child's eating, sleeping, and toileting habits, favorite play and comfort items, and the child's daily routine before and after child care

- *A list of center policies* regarding tuition, fees, and payment schedules; center hours, attendance, arrival and departure times, sign-in and sign-out procedures, and policies for children who are ill; staffing, primary caregivers, caregiving teams, continuity of care, group size, staff-child ratios, and staff schedules

- *A list of parent/center responsibilities* regarding provision of diapers, nursing, bottles and formula, food, medications, clean clothes, and bedding

- *Procedures for maintaining home-center communication* including parent bulletin boards, parent meetings, newsletters (mailed, e-mailed, and/or online), website, informal contact at arrival and departure, formal parent-teacher conferences, and telephone and e-mail contact

- *A center calendar* including, for example, holidays, staff training days, staff vacations, parent meetings, and family potlucks and outings

- *A program overview* including, for example, statements about active learning, supportive adult-child interactions, space and materials for active learners, the overall daily schedule, and individualized caregiving routines as well as statements describing, for example, the center's approach to inclusion of comfort items and other reminders of home for children, daily outdoor play, learning to use the toilet, and using a problem-solving approach to conflict (among toddlers, among adults)

- *A list of the enrollment-process steps* including initial center visit, review of enrollment materials, decision to enroll, possible home visit, and parent-child settling-in visits

Centers can include a few photos of the program with these explanatory materials (some programs prepare a short DVD), especially pictures of children actively engaging with materials and adults and children sharing warm interactions. Centers should make sure that the ethnic and cultural diversity of the families in the program is represented in these visual and audiovisual snapshots. Parents may also ask to talk to other families in the program before deciding whether to enroll their own children; centers should make a list of current families who are willing to speak to prospective families about their experiences.

Based on these materials, a center's director may draw up an agreement or contract for parents to sign and may also translate materials into languages other than English, depending on the linguistic background of the families in the community. Note, however, that the purpose of these materials is not to overwhelm parents with paperwork, but to let them know up front that the care and learning community they and their child are joining takes its responsibilities to children and families very seriously and that the health, well-being, and active engagement of their child is the caregivers' first priority.

Host visits to the center

On their first visit, parents come to see what a program looks and feels like and to talk with caregivers about their child. It is important for caregivers to give parents a tour of the setting so they can see and talk with them about where children eat, sleep, and have their diapers changed;

where mothers can nurse their infants; where children play with materials, climb, and explore both indoors and outdoors; how caregivers organize and store diapers, bottles, and medicines; how caregiving teams interact with children; and how caregivers keep track of children's individual schedules and regularly record their observations of each child.

It is also important to set aside time during this visit for caregivers to talk with parents about their own concerns, desires, and goals for their child and to find out what they are looking for in a center and how the center can support and work toward these goals. Caregivers will also want to review the materials in the parent packet, answer any immediate questions about them, and encourage parents to read them at home and to call with any further questions they might have.

Once it becomes clear that parents have decided to enroll their child in a program (whether on this visit or on a follow-up enrollment visit), caregivers should take time to talk with parents about the transition process itself and encourage parents to talk about their own early transitions, while sharing their own transition experiences and feelings. The idea is not to alarm parents or to scare them away, but to gently guide them through the process of leaving their child at the center. Caregivers can explain that the reason they are asking them to make a series of settling-in visits with their child is to deal as effectively as possible with the feelings they may encounter. Although these

Before enrollment, visiting the center together helps children and parents to get a sense of how it might feel to spend some or all of the day there.

visits may take some planning on everyone's part, they go a long way toward easing both parent and child into center participation.

Children benefit when they are included in the visit-planning process. Ask parents to talk with their children ahead of time about visiting the center together, just as they would talk about an upcoming visit from Grandma or a trip to the store. An enthusiastic, straightforward statement, such as "Tomorrow we're going to the Tall Trees Center to play with some other children,"

lets the child know that a new adventure is imminent. Even though the child may not be able to understand the parent's words, he or she can pick up on a parent's positive attitude and confidence. Suggest that on the day before the visit, parents may wish to walk or drive by the center with their child and say something like "Here's Tall Trees Center where you'll be playing with the other children." This gives the child a glimpse of the center before the actual visit and allows parent and child to gradually approach the idea of going to the center. (This is similar to an adult, on the day before a job interview, going to the interview site to find out where it is and how long it takes to get there.)

When parents do make the first visit to the center with their child, they should bring a diaper bag packed with diapers, a change of clothes, some food the child normally eats, and the child's favorite comfort items to comfort and reassure the child in the new setting and help the caregiver learn what the child likes and is accustomed to.

Caregivers should introduce prospective parents to others whose children are enrolled at the center and encourage them to talk to other parents who have indicated their willingness to do so. (Having supplied these names as part of the enrollment packet spares parents who might feel embarrassed to ask for them directly.) This gives prospective parents the opportunity to ask questions they might be hesitant to ask a caregiver and to find out about the program from another parent's perspective. Some "veteran" parents may not only volunteer to answer questions during enrollment but may even be willing to be "buddies" to new parents to support them through the settling-in process.

Make a home visit, if possible

While not always easy or even possible to schedule around conflicting work and family demands, a getting-acquainted visit to the child's home at this time helps to ease the transition from home to center for everyone involved. Parents and children feel more at ease on their own turf, and caregivers see for themselves what the child is used to and what feels like home to the child. Also, the child sees the parent and caregiver together in a familiar setting.

Ideally, these home visits should occur at a time when the child is awake. While these visits do not have to be lengthy, they need to be long enough to begin to discover what the child likes to do — where he or she likes to explore, play, eat, sleep, and so forth. For example, caregiver Kim, on a visit to infant Bobby's family home, is told by Bobby's mom that "Bobby never stays covered when he sleeps, so I always make sure he sleeps in something warm." Mom shows Kim one of Bobby's blanket sleepers and agrees to send one along with Bobby for naps at the center.

As early childhood specialist Barbara Tizard and her colleagues (1983) observed about their experiences with home visits,

> *This informal contact at home made it very easy to relate to both children and parents when we later met them at [the center]. We do not think that home visits should be regarded as a way of finding out about a family's "problems" — [caregivers] are not social workers. The visits should rather be seen as an opportunity for gaining and giving useful positive information, and laying the basis of a friendly relationship between caregiver, parent, and child. (p. 130)*

During this settling-in visit, the mother provides her child with reassurance and words of comfort.

Support and learn from the parent-child pair through settling-in visits to the center

If, over a period of several weeks, the parent and child make a series of visits to the center together, parents can use these visits to continue the process of teaching caregivers about their child. The caregiver can watch the parent to learn how the child is accustomed to being held, fed, changed, and put to sleep. Caregiver Kim, for example, sees that Bobby's mom gently strokes his back or arm as she holds him, so when Kim receives the baby from his mom, she repeats this familiar, soothing gesture. The caregiver watches the child and also gathers information from the parent to learn about the child's temperament and his likes and dislikes: "Bobby's pretty easygoing most of the time," his mom tells Kim, "but he likes to be bathed by hand, not with a washcloth! That's one thing he's particular about."

The caregiver, in turn, shares her child observations with the parent: "Look," says Kim to Bobby's mom, "Bobby rolls over with no trouble at all. He looks very comfortable on his blanket on the floor." Bobby, in the meantime, sees his mom and Kim together, senses their ease with each other, and is free to turn his attention to the materials and children who have caught his eye.

On a very practical note, these visits are also an ideal time to take photographs of the parent and child together. The child can look at these later on, for reassurance when the parent is away, and the photos can be put on the bulletin board with photos of other center families.

The first time the parent does leave the child with the caregiver, the parent may simply go down the hallway to chat with another parent in the "café." Though the child and the parent may both feel some anxiety, by this time they both feel fairly comfortable with the caregiver, the setting, and the routine. This familiarity gives them a confidence and reassurance that helps counter their sadness at parting. Following this series of parent-child visits, when parents finally do leave the child at the center, they will still feel a wrench but perhaps one that is more manageable than if they had dropped off their child and left on the very first visit.

The number of settling-in visits varies from family to family. Some families may adjust to center life in less than two weeks. Others may take somewhat longer before they feel ready to leave their child at the center. Still others may skip the visits altogether because of circumstances beyond their control, including restricted work schedules or other demands at home. It is therefore important to communicate to parents that the center encourages — but does not require — these visits, nor does the center want to make parents feel guilty if they are unable to manage them. One thing we know for certain, however, is that these visits ease the transition from home to center for children, parents, and caregivers. They also build the trusting relationships on which the child's ongoing well-being and learning depend.

Exchange child observations, but leave the "firsts" to parents

At the outset, caregivers solicit information and observations from parents so they can plan how to ease the child's transition into the program and make the child's experience as consistent with home as possible. Caregivers meet with parents to discuss what arrivals and departures will be like, when and how caregiving routines should take place, what the child's preferences are for the pace and content of play activities, and so on. Throughout the course of the family's involvement with the program, parents and teachers meet periodically to update this information based on the child's development, changes in parental needs and preferences, and joint observations about what is and is not working for everyone involved. (For the kinds of information caregivers might elicit from parents, see "Developing an Infant Care Plan Based on Parent Input" on pp. 106–107.)

Once children are enrolled, caregivers continue to build their relationships with parents by exchanging daily child observations. As we have noted, caregivers attentively watch and listen to children throughout the day, and during their daily planning, they discuss and interpret these observations and use them to plan for the next day. (See again the observations caregivers recorded for Jamal on pp. 76–77). Consequently, caregivers have a wealth of stories and child observations to share with parents: "Today, at choice time, Bobby held on to the red wool ball. He waved it around and even held it with his feet!" Hearing these stories helps parents picture and participate vicariously in the child's life at the center.

At the same time, parents alone know what their children do and feel from the time they leave the center until they return the next day, the next Monday, or after a vacation, so caregivers need to have parents fill in their knowledge gaps. ("Bobby is sitting up now, all by himself!" Bobby's mom tells Kim one morning. "We didn't believe it. One minute he was lying on his back as usual, and the next time I looked, he had gotten himself into a sitting position!") Parents and caregivers rely on each other to stay attuned to the child and to provide care that is as consistent as possible between home and center. (Another morning, Bobby's mom tells Kim, "Bobby just started eating bananas this weekend. He really likes them, so I'm leaving some bananas for him today.") Parents also take great comfort in learning about their children's relationships with other children — for example, how Jovan offered a piece of his clay to Yomena, or how Kayla started up a game of peekaboo with Jared by hiding behind and peeking around the wall of the climber.

Note that in the previous paragraph, Bobby's mom reports a "first" to Bobby's caregiver: *Bobby's first time sitting up by himself.* Reporting major milestones like this should belong to parents. Therefore, caregivers should make a point of *not* sharing the ones they observe at the center — a child's first independent step or first word, for example. By keeping these

Mollie spends most of choice time playing with a doll and trying to put the doll in and out of the stroller. When her dad comes to pick her up, Mollie's caregiver shares with him what Mollie did that afternoon. Mollie listens intently to her caregiver and then shows her dad how she played with the doll and stroller.

observations to themselves, caregivers grant these momentous occasions to parents and family members. If a child takes a first step at the center, he or she will take another step at home the same day or the next. Unless a parent specifically asks the caregiver whether she has observed some specific development, she should wait until she hears about its occurrence from parents and then share her subsequent observations: "Hey," Kim greets Jamal's mom at the end of the day, "Jamal took some steps all by himself today, just as you saw him do last night at home!"

Caregivers should try to relate some child observations in each of their interactions with a child's parents at the beginning of the day, when the parent drops off the child (e.g., "Yesterday, Queen crawled up and down the rocking-boat steps, so I'm going to watch to see if she returns to them today") and when the child is picked up at the end of the day (e.g., "Nikki spent a long time this morning looking at herself in the mirror"). If it is permitted at a parent's place of employment, call the parent at work to relate a story about his or her child: "Remember when you told me this morning that Bobby was babbling at the cat?" Kim says to Bobby's mom over the phone. "Well, listen — he's babbling to Mallory!" She holds the phone near Bobby so his mom can hear his conversation with Mallory.

As caregivers record child observations at team planning or during the day, they write an anecdote on a file card and put it in the child's tub or cubby for the parent to read and take along at the end of the day. Some centers have journals that travel to home and back with the child each day. Others have established e-mail connections or secure websites for this type of exchange. Both caregivers and parents record their brief observations in this journal on a regular basis. For example, Jamal's mom writes, "Jamal stayed up late last night playing with his cousin. He may be cranky today." Yvonne writes back, "Jamal fell asleep at lunch time today and took an extra long nap. At outside time he crawled in and out of a large carton, full of energy once again!"

Journals can also include photographs of children as well as children's own marks and scribbles. (Digital photo files can be easily uploaded via e-mail or websites.) For example, one day, older toddler Megan, who was used to hearing her mom say "I'm putting this in your journal for Ellie" and then seeing her mom and her caregiver trade the journal back and forth, brought over to her mom a strand of yarn she was playing with. She laid it on the journal page her mom was writing on and said "Li Li" — her name for Ellie, her caregiver. Her mom taped the yarn to the page and wrote, "Megan was playing with this and wanted me to put it in the journal for you."

Caregivers should share child observations during parent conferences and home visits, when they might want to give parents a selection of the anecdotes they have collected. These anecdotes will provide a basis for discussing the child's physical,

Developing an Infant Care Plan Based on Parent Input

Complete the following form with information from parents to help plan each child's daily schedule and determine the type and pace of activities the child enjoys. Revise it together periodically to keep the information current.

Child's name: _____   Date of birth: _____

Completed by: _____   Date: _____

Arrival

What strategies and routines make you and your child most comfortable during the transition from home to center? How can we work together to support each other and your child at this time of day?

_____

_____

Sleeping

How does your child indicate sleepiness?

_____

_____

What helps your child fall asleep?

_____

_____

What position does your child sleep in? Is your child used to sleeping in a quiet setting or with some noise?

_____

_____

How does your child wake up? How can we support your child in the transition from sleeping to waking?

_____

_____

Being awake and playing

Where does your child prefer to play?

_____

_____

What kinds of things is your child most interested in exploring at this time?

_____

_____

How does your child like you to play with him or her?

_____

_____

Strategies for supporting physical, social, cognitive, and emotional growth during play:

_____

_____

Feeding and eating

How do you prepare your child's formula?

_____

_____

What temperature does your child prefer the formula or breast milk? How do you heat the bottle?

_____

_____

What, if any, solid foods is your child eating? How do you prepare them (e.g., amount, consistency, temperature)?

_____

_____

How does your child eat solid foods? (From a spoon, with fingers? Fast, slow?) Where does your child prefer to sit when eating?

_____

_____

What are some your child's favorite foods? Dislikes? Food allergies?

_____

_____

Bodily care

What kind of diapers does your child prefer? [*Note:* In some programs, there might not be a choice due to licensing regulations or environmental policies.]

_____

_____

What kind of clothing is your child most comfortable in?

_____

_____

Departure

What strategies and routines make you and your child most comfortable during the transition from center to home? How can we work together to support each other and your child at this time of day?

_____

_____

Your child's daily routine

On a typical day at home, what is your child's schedule? Please write it in the space below. For example, when does your child typically wake up, eat, nap, and play? Knowing this will help us anticipate your child's schedule at the center.

_____

_____

_____

_____

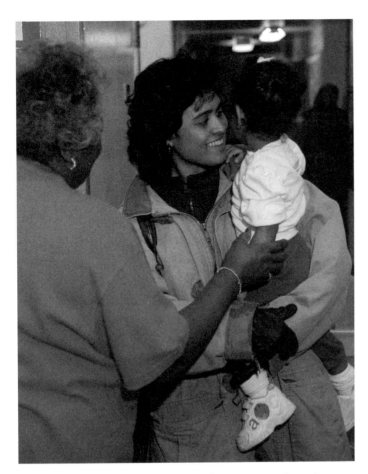

Caregivers work in partnership with parents, exchanging child observations and striving to provide consistency between children's at-home and away-from-home experiences.

social, emotional, language, and cognitive development; they will also be a way of sharing an appreciation of the child's interests and strengths.

Encourage parents to participate in the center

Once parents have spent some time in the center getting their child settled in, they themselves will most likely feel at home in the setting and comfortable with their decision to enroll their child. Parents' participation in the center need not end there.

The benefits of developing ongoing parent involvement in a program are many: Parents and caregivers can strengthen the trust and respect they have for each other and grow together in their ability to provide consistent care and education for children. Parents are able to see and appreciate their children's abilities to interact with peers. Children can feel reassured because they see their parents as being deeply connected to both home and center. "Experienced" parents can support "new" parents by giving them a parent's perspective on a program. Parents are able to form a network to support one another as they go through the various surprises and stages of parenthood; being part of such a network can help parents to work through some of the issues that inevitably arise in child care programs ("That child is biting my child!" "I don't want my child to play with her food like So-and-So does!"). Parents with real ties to the center are often willing to offer their time, energy, and resources to assist the center by, for example, donating supplies or helping to make physical improvements. They are also more willing to advocate for the center and for early childhood issues in the larger community.

Experience has shown that, as well as producing all these benefits, parent participation in the life of the center can also raise certain issues. Children may behave differently when their parents are present; for example, they may become more clingy, stubborn, or energetic. Children may not wish to share their parents with other children. Parents may discipline or interact with children in a manner inconsistent with a program's philosophy of promoting children's sensory-motor learning, providing adult support of child choices, and using a problem-solving approach to conflict. Parents may require attention that pulls a caregiver away from the children in her care. Caregivers may face parent questions they cannot answer or requests they cannot meet.

Although these or similar issues will arise from time to time, they are not reason enough to avoid parent participation. Rather, it is important to acknowledge any potential thorny issues; to talk as a team about ways others have worked through them; and to remain calm when any such issue does arise, because after all, it's another opportunity for adults to do some collaborative problem solving!

With the benefits and issues of parent participation in mind, here are a number of options for participation that an infant-toddler center may wish to offer parents:

- *Join their child at the center* — This might include spending 20–30 minutes with their child at the beginning or end of the day — changing a diaper, nursing, feeding a bottle, playing with toys, or reading a storybook; spending time at noon eating lunch with their child; playing outside with their child at outdoor time; joining group time or offering a group-time experience, such as singing, playing a musical instrument, exploring clay, telling a story, cooking with older toddlers; accompanying their child on an outing or special event; if the parents is a student, joining her child at the center between her own classes.

- *Attend parent-caregiver meetings* — This might include workshops and discussions led by parents, caregivers, or guest speakers and designed around topics raised by parents or around child development issues; family and center potlucks, picnics, and outings to local events or celebrations; parent-caregiver conferences; home visits. (Visit www.highscope.org for additional resources for and about parents.)

- *Participate in center-related service projects* — This might include fundraising events; gardening, grounds improvement, or materials procurement (collecting natural/household items for play or making curtains, blankets, pillows, bibs, smocks, play dough, blocks); updating children's photo albums; repairing toys/equipment; providing technical assistance with computers, accounting, the parent library, the toy-lending library; serving on the center advisory board, the preschool or kindergarten liaison committee, the community relationships committee, the welcoming committee.

- *Read or write (print or online)* — This might include reading or contributing to their child's home-center journal; center newsletter articles, notices, and reminders; parent bulletin boards about family and center events, parenting and child development topics, recreational opportunities, upcoming community events; books and articles in the parent library; sharing photos of children, families, and staff during daily activities or special events (posted online or on the center bulletin board).

However caregivers encourage parents to participate in their center, the relationships that result from these shared experiences strengthen the vital three-way bond between child, parent, and caregiver. As Baker and Manfredi/Petitt (2004) emphasize, "Experience tells us that children thrive when the adults who care for them also care about one another....Adult relationships directly and profoundly affect children's lives" (p. 1).

Overall, thoughtful caregiving teams and caregiver-parent partnerships create a strong framework of support for infants and toddlers in child care settings. Working closely together, these key adults observe, interact with, and plan for children in ways that interweave the elements of successful HighScope infant-toddler programs — active learning and KDIs, supportive adult-child interactions, safe and inviting environments for sensory-motor exploration and play, child-centered daily schedules and caregiving routines, and observationally based program and child assessment. In such programs, our very youngest children have the opportunity to thrive — they can depend on their caregivers and families for the tender care and early learning that will help sustain them through the rest of their lives.

When a parent participates with the child in what he is doing at the center, the child comes to see his parent as being connected to both home and center.

Caregiving Teamwork and Parent Partnership: A Summary

The Caregiving Team

- ❑ Remains together from one year to the next.
- ❑ Meets for daily team planning.
- ❑ Practices open communication.
- ❑ Makes joint decisions about:
  - ❑ Space and materials
  - ❑ Schedules and routines
  - ❑ Roles and responsibilities
- ❑ Observes children throughout the day.
- ❑ Discusses, interprets, and records child observations, using the KDIs as a guide.
- ❑ Plans ways to support individual children.

The Caregiver-Parent Partnership

- ❑ Caregivers follow certain guidelines in working with parents:
  - ❑ Recognize role separation.
  - ❑ Practice open communication.
  - ❑ Focus on parents' strengths.
  - ❑ Use a problem-solving approach to conflict.
- ❑ Caregivers create a welcoming environment for families.
  - ❑ Establish room or space for families.
  - ❑ Approach families in a friendly, respectful manner.

- ❑ Caregivers establish a family-centered enrollment process.
  - ❑ They recall their own transitions.
  - ❑ They organize enrollment materials, including information and permission forms, center policies, parent/center responsibilities, procedures for maintaining home-center communication, center calendar, program overview, and a list of enrollment-process steps.
  - ❑ They host visits to the center.
  - ❑ They make a home visit, if possible.
  - ❑ They support and learn from the parent-child pair through settling-in visits.
- ❑ Caregivers exchange observations but leave "firsts" to parents.
- ❑ Caregivers encourage parents to participate in the center.
  - ❑ Parents join their child at the center.
  - ❑ Parents attend parent-caregiver meetings.
  - ❑ Parents participate in center-related projects.
  - ❑ Parents read or write (print or online) center-related materials.

3

Supportive Adult-Child Interactions

The strength of attachment is such that the treatment and acceptance we grow up expecting from others corresponds to what we got from our own attachment figures. We tend to go through life feeling the way our attachment persons made us feel — be that happy or depressed, loved or neglected, at peace or in turmoil.

— Honig (2002, p. 5)

What do infants and toddlers in early childhood settings need from their caregivers? In every interaction, these very young children need to be treated with great care and respect from a consistent primary caregiver. Only then can they form the trusting human relationships that allow them to develop curiosity, courage, initiative, empathy, a sense of self, and a feeling of belonging to a friendly social community. Early attachments help determine our lifelong worldview — when young children develop secure attachments, they are more likely to become secure people who are better prepared emotionally to handle difficult situations in their lives and more accepting of other people's shortcomings (Honig, 2002).

Nurturing Attachment in Infants and Toddlers

Psychoanalyst John Bowlby (1988) defined attachment as "any form of behavior that results in a person attaining or maintaining proximity to some other clearly identified individual who is conceived of as better able to cope with the world. It is most obvious whenever the person is frightened, fatigued or sick, and is assuaged by comforting and caregiving" (pp. 26–27). Bowlby stressed that attachment is an essential human need that is present throughout our lives.

Most work by Bowlby (1969/1982, 1973, 1980) and other attachment researchers focuses on the critical period from infancy to early toddlerhood and the four stages of attachment development. (See "Bowlby's Stages of Attachment," p. 117.) In this context, pediatric psychiatrist Diane Benoit (2004) defines attachment as the part of the child-caregiver relationship that makes the child feel safe, secure, and protected. While caregivers may also be responsible for playing, feeding, limit-setting, or teaching, attachment is where "the child uses the primary caregiver as a secure base from which to explore and, when necessary, as a haven of safety and a source of comfort" (p. 542).[1] The quality of attachment that an infant forms is largely determined by how the adult responds when the child's attachment system is activated, for example, when the child is frightened, hurt, or ill. Depending on the nature of this attachment, infants feel secure enough to venture forth and explore their world, or they may be fearful and insecure about how their initiatives with people, actions, and objects will be received. (See "Why Trust and Attachment Are Important for Infants and Toddlers," pp. 122–123.)

Beginning at about six months of age, infants come to anticipate certain responses from their caregivers based on their daily interactions with them. Mary Ainsworth and her colleagues (Ainsworth, Blehar, Waters, & Wall, 1978), pioneers in defining and measuring attachment behavior, identified four patterns that result from the nature of these interactions:

---

[1] Attachment is not the same as "bonding," an idea put forth by Klaus and Kennell (1976), which says that skin-to-skin contact between a newborn and parent immediately after birth is essential for healthy psychological development. Studies do not confirm the concept of bonding, whereas attachment theory has been substantiated by decades of research (Jacobsen, Edelstein, & Hofmann, 1994; Waters & Cummings, 2000).

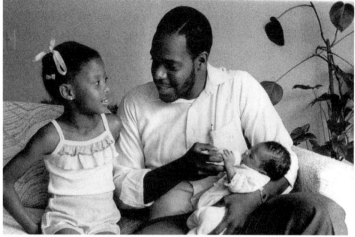

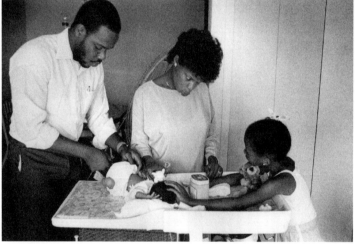

When all goes well, a child has the same supportive family throughout childhood, and the family grows together over the years. Infant-toddler programs strive to provide children with similar continuity of care.

Continuity of Care

Continuity of care means having the same primary caregiver or caregiving team every day over a long period of time, preferably for the entire duration of the child's enrollment in the program.

In programs with maximum continuity of care, caregivers and children "age" together. The children also benefit from staying with the same group of peers instead of having to transition into an "older" group when they reach a given age.

- *Secure* attachment results when the caregiver consistently responds to the infant's distress in sensitive and loving ways, such as picking up and comforting a crying infant. Secure infants seek proximity and maintain contact with the caregiver until they feel secure again.

- *Avoidant* attachment results when the caregiver consistently responds to the infant's distress in insensitive or rejecting ways, such as ignoring, ridiculing, or becoming annoyed. This type of attachment is considered *insecure.* Avoidant infants learn to ignore the caregiver in times of need and often develop adjustment problems later in life.

- *Resistant* attachment results when the caregiver responds to the infant in inconsistent ways. Sometimes the caregiver ignores the infant, and other times the caregiver gets involved but

perhaps in a negative way, such as expecting the infant to worry about the caregiver's own needs or adding to the infant's distress (e.g., making a loud, scary noise even louder). Resistant infants display extreme negative emotion, perhaps hoping the caregiver cannot possibly ignore them. However, they also run the risk of a negative response. This type of attachment is also said to be *insecure* and places infants at risk for social and emotional maladjustment.

- *Disorganized* attachment results when caregivers display disordered or atypical behavior, such as physical aggression or sexual abuse toward the infant. The aberrant behavior is not limited to times when the infant is distressed. Such caregivers are often the product of childhood trauma themselves, and infants reared in these circumstances are at very high risk for developing severe behavioral problems (van IJzendoorn, Schuengel, & Baker-mans-Kranenburg, 1999).

Attachment is measured with the Strange Situation, a 20-minute laboratory procedure in which the behavior of children aged 6–20 months toward their primary caregiver is observed after two brief separations (Ainsworth et al., 1978). Securely attached infants (about 55 percent of the general population) greet the returning caregiver, allow themselves to be comforted, and return to play. Avoidant/insecure infants (23 percent) fail to greet or even ignore the returning caregiver

Bowlby's Stages of Attachment

Psychoanalyst John Bowlby (1969/1982) was the first to apply theories of animal imprinting to the attachment between infants and their primary caregivers. Bowlby believed that infants, like other species, are born with a built-in set of behaviors that keep a parent nearby to provide protection from danger and support as the infant masters the environment (Waters & Cummings, 2000). While initially designed for safety and competence, attachment over time is characterized by true bonds of affection, supported by the child's emerging emotional and cognitive capabilities and the adult's sensitive responses. Attachment develops in four phases:

1. **Preattachment**
   - Typically occurs from birth to 6 weeks.
   - Child cries, gazes into adult's eyes, smiles, and grasps to communicate.
   - Child recognizes caregiver's smell, voice, and face.
   - Child does not mind being left with an unfamiliar adult.

2. **Attachment in the making**
   - Typically occurs from 6 weeks to 6–8 months.
   - Child does not protest when separated from primary caregiver and continues to react in a friendly way to a stranger.
   - Child responds more strongly to caregiver than to a stranger.
   - Child learns her behavior will elicit a response.

3. **Clear-cut attachment**
   - Typically occurs from 6–8 months to 18 months–2 years.
   - Child displays separation anxiety, becoming upset when caregiver leaves (not all show separation anxiety). Older infants and toddlers try to maintain the caregiver's presence (e.g., cling).
   - Separation anxiety may actually increase between 6 and 15 months with the understanding that caregiver continues to exist although out of sight.
   - Child prefers caregiver to others.
   - Child uses caregiver as a secure base from which to explore.

4. **Formation of reciprocal relationship**
   - Typically occurs from 18 months–2 years; is ongoing.
   - With growing representation (the ability to hold mental images) and language skills, the child understands the comings and goings of caregiver and can predict her return.
   - Separation protest declines. The child negotiates with caregiver, using requests and persuasion to alter her behavior. Child and adult act more like partners.

Children use the secure attachments they form with their primary caregivers at home as the basis for forming attachments with other significant adults in their child care setting. The creation and development of these out-of-home relationships is facilitated when children have a designated primary caregiver they can relate to in the out-of-home setting. *Continuity of care* in child care programs is thus a critical factor in helping them adjust to the separation from parents and being able to thrive in their group-care arrangements.

A young child attains secure attachment with her caregiver when the caregiver consistently responds to the child's distress in sensitive and loving ways.

and remain focused on toys. Resistant/insecure infants (8 percent) are extremely distressed by the separation and cannot be soothed by the reunion, displaying a great deal of anger toward the caregiver. Based on a scoring system developed by Main and Solomon (1986), disorganized infants (nearly 15 percent) show bizarre or contradictory behavior, such as alternately playing and freezing, and display fear in the parent's presence. They are trapped because their source of comfort can also be a source of pain.

Most infants and toddlers are remarkably resilient in forming attachments that are in tune with their needs and temperaments, while also adapting to the nature of their caregivers (Waters & Cummings,

2000). Child psychiatrist Stanley Greenspan (1997) emphasizes the following points about the normal development of attachment in young children:

- *Forming an attachment takes time.* Infants get to know the response patterns of their primary caregivers over a period of months. As their own behaviors change (e.g., an infant becomes a mobile and curious toddler), children discover how the caregiver in turn responds to their changing needs.

- *Parent-child bonds form at different rates for different parent-child pairs.* Both child and caregiver bring their distinct needs, personalities and temperaments, and circumstances (family composition, health status, and so on) to the attachment situation.

- *Clear-cut attachment is generally evident by the time the child is three years old.* While this varies somewhat depending on the child's experiences with separation (e.g., whether the child has been in group-care settings or experienced home care only), most children show stable attachment patterns by preschool (Speltz, Greenberg, & DeKlyen, 1990).

- *Attachment is primarily a social behavior.* It refers to how young children relate to the primary caregiver throughout the day as a source of comfort and reassurance. Attachment is not based on providing food or meeting other basic needs (though these may play a

role) but deals more broadly with how the caregiver protects the child from danger (*safety*) and allows the child to explore and achieve mastery over the environment (*competence*).

- *A child's attachment is generally directed toward a mother (or a mother figure) and lasts a lifetime.* The basic sense of security (trust) or insecurity (mistrust) that is established with the primary caregiver during the early years forms a core part of the child's identity and endures throughout a person's life (Erikson, 1950/1963).

- *Through the attachment process, the child constructs an internal working model of how human relationships operate.* This model serves as the child's guide for future relationships (Bretherton & Munholland, 2008). Longitudinal research shows that attachment affects the development of social relationships through school and beyond (Jacobsen et al., 1994).

When placed in a child care setting, securely attached young children generally manage to handle the normal stress of separation from a parent (Sroufe, 1988). However, the adjustment may not be instantaneous. It requires the support of responsive adults who should be aware of several things to simultaneously support the attachment between the child and parent while fostering the development of an attachment between the child and the primary caregiver in the early childhood setting:

This child is upset because his parent has just left. His caregiver responds by acknowledging his feelings and offering him comfort.

- Protest and despair are a child's normal, healthy responses to separation from the parent[2] to whom the child is strongly attached.

- In typical (i.e., nonresidential) child care settings, a child's separation from the parent is temporary — the parent comes back at the end of the day. Caregivers will most often see children responding to separation from the parent by protesting.

- As a child protests a parent's leaving, it is important for caregivers to calmly acknowledge the child's feelings of anger and grief and to offer comfort and contact as long as the child needs it rather than to tell the child to stop crying or to ignore or punish the child for misbehaving.

- The child protests because she or he does not want the cherished parent to leave. While a caregiver cannot be the parent, a caregiver can become a consistent, responsive, dependable, trusted parent-substitute for the child while the parent is absent.

- A child who has not formed a strong attachment to a parent (because the parent is depressed or unavailable) and is left in the care of an ever-changing cast of caregivers may give up trying to find a responsive person to whom to become attached and becomes emotionally detached. This puts the child's future relationships in jeopardy.

- The child's attachment to the parent and need for a responsive, trusted caregiver in the parent's absence provides the rationale for primary care-giving and continuity of care in child care settings.

Infants and toddlers who experience adults' daily, ongoing support and respect are free from undue stress. This

---

[2]In this book, we use "parent" to refer to whatever parent figure a child may have, whether it be a parent, grandparent, foster parent, or an adult sibling.

allows them to devote their energy to the all-important work of sensory-motor exploration, through which they construct an understanding of their social and physical world. They also have the opportunity to form healthy working ideas about themselves and others: *I am a good person. People are generally trustworthy and pleasant to be with. The world is full of interesting possibilities. With help from trusted friends, I can meet life's challenges.*

Treating children well so they can grow and learn is the primary aim of teachers and caregivers in an active learning setting. Alison Gopnik (2009), a leading researcher on cognitive development in infants, points out that unlike older children, "babies aren't trying to learn one particular skill or set of facts; instead they are drawn to anything new, unexpected, or informative. Babies are designed to explore and they should be encouraged to do so" (p. WK10). Therefore, the role of the teacher in infant-toddler care settings is "neither babysitter nor trainer but rather a caring facilitator of the child's journey toward emotional, cognitive, language, physical, and social competence" (Lally, 2009, p. 48).

How caregivers go about this task may vary from person to person and from setting to setting. In general, though, caregivers use four broad strategies for building and sustaining supportive, respectful relationships with the infants and toddlers in their care by:

- Establishing policies that promote continuity of care
- Creating a climate of trust for children
- Forming partnerships with children
- Supporting children's intentions

Establishing Policies That Promote Continuity of Care

Psychologist Stanley Greenspan (1997) says that consistent, nurturing relationships with primary caregivers are the cornerstone of emotional and intellectual competence. It is essential that young children have these stable connections with both parents and child care staff, for it is through these strong sets of bonds that they later develop the human traits of empathy and compassion.

When all goes well, a child has the same supportive parents (or parent) throughout childhood. The child and parent(s) grow together and come to know one another's interests and interaction styles as the days, months, and years unfold. Infant and toddler development proceeds most smoothly when directors and caregivers replicate the continuity of care represented by the stable, ongoing parent-child relationship. At home, for example, infants and toddlers typically do not exchange one parent for a new parent every six to eight months; at the center, therefore, they should not be expected to exchange one caregiver for a new caregiver every couple of months. The disruption of having numerous caregivers over a short period of time can cause young children undue stress and confusion.

Why Trust and Attachment Are Important for Infants & Toddlers

Trust and attachment support resilience.

"A young child's experience of an encouraging, supportive, and co-operative mother, and a little later father, gives him a sense of worth, a belief in the helpfulness of others, and a favourable model on which to build future relationships. Furthermore, by enabling him to explore his environment with confidence and to deal with it effectively, such experience also promotes his competence. Thenceforward, provided family relationships continue favourable, not only do these early patterns of thought, feeling and behavior persist, but personality becomes increasingly structured to operate in moderately controlled and resilient ways, and increasingly capable of continuing so despite adverse circumstances."

— John Bowlby
(1969/1982, p. 378)

Trust and attachment counteract fear and mistrust.

"Erikson's first stage of emotional development is the development of babies' and infants' trust or mistrust in the people and world in which they live. Caring adults, such as parents and early childhood professionals, have a responsibility in their relationship with infants to teach them that the world in which they live is a safe and friendly place and that the people who care for them can be trusted to meet their needs promptly, responsively and consistently. If infants learn that they are valued, cared for and respected as significant members of the group, they will have a strong foundation from which to confidently explore and learn about the world as well as for establishing and maintaining relationships. On the other hand, if infants learn from lack of, insensitive or inconsistent adult responsivity to their needs that they are not important in their environment, they may feel insecure, rejected and mistrustful of people and the world. Such infants will not have a secure base from which to learn and make relationships.

Infants who have developed a sense of trust are more likely to meet adult expectations about behaviour because, at some unconscious and fundamental level, they comprehend that the adults in their world have their best interests and well being at heart. Infants who have developed a basic sense of mistrust become suspicious about their world and the adults in it. Such infants are more likely to act in ways which perpetuate mistrust and consequently result in unsatisfying relationships between adult and child. Unless infants develop a basic sense of trust, they are not psychologically ready or competent to meet the demands of the second stage of emotional development."

— Jillian Rodd
(1996, pp. 21–22)

Why Trust and Attachment Are Important for Infants & Toddlers (cont.)

Trust and attachment build confidence.

"It is the luck of most babies to be held well most of the time. On this they build confidence in a friendly world, but, more important, because of being held well enough they are able to make the grade in their very rapid emotional growth. The basis of personality is being laid down well if the baby is held well enough. Babies do not remember being held well enough — what they remember is the traumatic experience of not being held well enough."

> — Donald Woods Winnicott
> (1987, pp. 62–63)

Trust and attachment promote curiosity.

"An intimate trusting relationship [with a primary caregiver] is the prerequisite for children's healthy separation and individuation. Only after they get 'refueled' during the unhurried times spent with their caregiver will they be willing to let go of the caregiver and explore the environment."

> — Magda Gerber
> (1981, p. 84)

Trust and attachment underlie self-regulation.

"The biological foundations for the development of self-regulation in brain maturation and temperament do not mean that the quality of care is unimportant. Indeed, children's interactions with parents, child care providers, and other people create an environment of relationships in which brain development unfolds and temperamental individuality is expressed. In the early years, a developmental transition occurs from adults serving as external managers…to young children gradually assuming their own responsibility for self-regulation, with adults providing a supportive context for this growth. Developmental research indicates that warm, responsive care that provides developmentally appropriate structure is an important contributor to the early growth of self-regulatory competence."

> — Ross A. Thompson
> (2009, p. 36)

Adult behaviors that promote trusting relationships:

- Sensitivity to child's non-distress (takes interest in the child's play)
- Positive regard (enjoys child's explorations)
- Lack of negativity (communicates warmly)
- Shared emotions (acknowledges child's delight and tears)
- Positive physical contact (cuddling, holding, stroking, lap sitting)
- Responds to child's communication and talk
- Helps child do things
- Talks and reads to child
- Gives child full attention

> — Margaret T. Owen
> (1996, November)

A child care setting that is organized in a way that provides continuity of care benefits everyone involved — children, caregivers, and families. Children form trusting relationships with the primary caregivers who are with them day after day, from one year to the next. Being surrounded by known and trusted people enables children to explore the novelties and challenges that promote their growth. At the same time, caregivers come to know "their" children and accumulate a growing store of very useful, specific knowledge about each one of them as they change from creeper-crawlers to cruisers to walkers, for example, or from nonverbal communicators to cooers and babblers to talkers. Families have the opportunity to form trusting relationships with their children's primary caregivers — caregivers and parents come to know each other, form common expectations, and learn to communicate effectively about the children who draw them together.

The following specific strategies for promoting continuity of care are easiest to implement for a new center where no other staffing policies and expectations yet exist. For an established center, however, these strategies might be implemented gradually over a year or so, with small volunteer groups of existing staff or newly hired staff. (See "Incremental Steps Toward Continuity of Care," p. 125.) In either case, implementing continuity of care is greatly aided when a program has in place the factors that promote low staff-turnover — administrative support and professional working conditions for caregivers, including appropriate salaries and benefits.[3]

Anchor each child's day around a primary caregiver

Infants and toddlers feel at ease when they are surrounded by interesting materials and familiar supportive adults. To ensure that each child develops a close, reliable, affectionate relationship that will sustain him or her while away from home, it is important to assign each child to a *primary caregiver* for the duration of enrollment in the program. According to Honig (2002), "Young children are quite conservative about changes in their lives. Long, leisurely years of getting to know one another increases the chance for a baby to develop a secure infant-caregiver attachment and for the caregiver to have strong bonds with the child" (p. 23).

Having such a stable relationship with a primary caregiver reduces the considerable stress on infants and toddlers if they would have had, instead, to adjust to an ever-changing stream of caregivers. It also helps to provide the trust and predictability that enable children to live through the inevitable challenges necessary for growth

---

[3]Low staff-turnover was cited as one explanation for the long-term positive effects of early child care reported by the Abecedarian Project (Campbell, Helms, Sparling, & Ramey, 1998). Teachers in the project received ongoing training and were compensated at rates higher than is typical in this low-paying field. Other workplace research also supports the importance of training in reducing staff turnover and improving the quality of child care programs (Bloom & Sheerer, 1992).

Incremental Steps Toward Continuity of Care

In established programs, altering staff schedules or rethinking how the facilities are used can be a challenge. Providing continuity of care also requires a mental shift on the part of caregivers, who may be attached to working with a particular age group and resist "moving up" as children get older. These logistical and psychological barriers explain why more child care settings "talk" about continuity of care rather than actually make the necessary changes.

Several resources describe a series of steps that enable programs to incrementally establish and put into practice policies for continuity of care. For example, program consultant Linda Signer (1995) and authors Amy Baker and Lynn Manfredi/Petitt (2004) offer the following ideas:

- Have staff reflect on the pros and cons of continuity of care for children and for themselves.

- Make transition plans as a team; consider including parents in the planning.

- Train caregivers to work with different age groups and/or in multiage settings.

- Have one member of a team move up with the older children while the other member, who is an "expert" in the younger age range, stays behind.

- Expand the length of time children stay together with a caregiver team. For example, have a group of infants remain together until age two instead of moving to another caregiver team upon reaching age one.

- Hire new staff with the expectation of continuity, for example, with the expectation that they will work with the same small group of children for three years.

- Purchase toys and equipment adaptable for children of a wide age range.

- Focus on teamwork and trust building among staff.

- Educate parents about the importance of continuity of care; train and support caregivers in their communications with parents.

and development and underlies their ability to become an active member of society (Falk, 1979).

Emerging research also shows that attachment is critical to brain development. Researchers at the University of Georgia report that the development of higher-level thinking skills is affected by early relationships. Insecure attachments limit the young child's ability to move from being dominated by the midbrain's emotional center, which manages trust and impulse control, to using the forebrain's executive center, which is responsible for abstract thought and reasoning (Bales & Campbell, 2002). Because of this link to the brain's impulse control center, attachment is also related to the development of self-regulation. The child's ability to manage emotions and behaviors depends on the security of attachments and the quality of care received (Shore, 2003).

Further, attachments influence the young child's predisposition to explore his or her universe. Secure attachments increase the child's confidence to venture forth because he or she knows that the adult will be there as a hub when the child needs to touch base. Children without this secure grounding are more fearful and less willing to discover what the world holds. Attachment relationships, thus, "serve as guides for and interpreters of emotions, perceptions, and behaviors in all future relationships" (Honig, 2002, p. 4).

At home, a loving and consistent parent is the young child's critical attachment figure. In a program setting, the primary caregiver is the child's anchor, the person on whom the child can rely for reassurance, guidance, and basic care. She is attuned to the child's personal cues, interests, and strengths. She knows, for example, that Maria's diaper-changing routine includes cuddling and playing This Little Piggy…; she knows that Demetrius says "de" when he wants a drink; she knows that Jennifer says "beboo" when she means peekaboo and that she rubs her eyes when she is tired, naps fitfully when she's teething, can find and retrieve the "blankie" she left in the chair, and needs more lap time when she is coming down with a cold.

The primary caregiver plays a major role in the child's life at the center but is not the child's exclusive caregiver, just as a child is occasionally cared for by someone other than a parent at home. Because of illness, vacations, parent meetings, conferences, or other unavoidable circumstances,

she may need to be absent from the center from time to time. Therefore, she shares that child's caregiving (and thus forms a team) with one or two secondary caregivers. Each child, then, interacts daily with one primary caregiver and one (or two) secondary caregivers, all of whom know the child and provide consistent care and support. The secondary caregiver is crucial to the child, so that he or she will not feel abandoned when the child's primary caregiver is not there (Lally, 1995).

Another way to provide a fallback but consistent and secure attachment is to establish a permanent substitute who can fill in when a primary or secondary caregiver is gone. The substitute is *not* in place of the primary or secondary caregiver but is part of the consistent caregiving team on a daily basis. The substitute is regularly involved in planning and caring for the children, allowing staff to take breaks, filling in during vacations or staff illnesses, and so on. Because the substitute is part of the regular flow of the program day, the children do not experience any disruption in the routine or the people they are used to having care for them.

Create small groups of children who share a caregiver team

Each caregiver takes primary responsibility for two, three, or four children. (The actual number is usually related to the ages of children and to the minimal standards set forth by the state or federal licensing requirements, accreditation standards, and available funding.) For example, the joint recommendation of the AAP, American

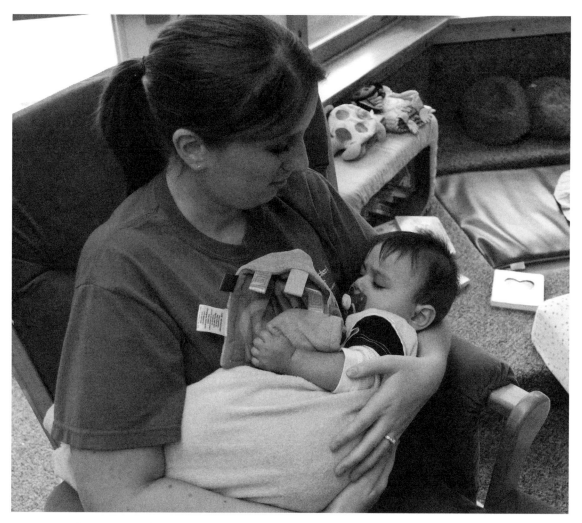

Over time, this caregiver has come to know that this infant likes to hold on to his favorite toy and be rocked while he falls asleep.

Public Health Association, and National Resource Center for Health and Safety in Child Care is a 1:3 adult-child ratio with a maximum group size of 6 for children birth to 12 months; 1:4 ratio with group size of 8 for children 13–30 months; and 1:5 ratio with group size of 10 for children 31–35 months (AAP, American Public Health Association, & National Resource Center for Health and Safety in Child Care, 2002).

Zero to Three (2008) and NAEYC (2007) offer similar guidelines, with ratios up to 1:4 and group sizes of 12 for older toddlers.

To create a team, the primary caregiver and her children join with one (or, at most, two) other primary caregivers and their children, and the adult team members act as secondary caregivers for one another's children. Working with a small group of children allows caregivers and children to establish trusting relationships and a sense of belonging. The team approach enables the caregiver to have personal contact with the children in her care; the caregiver "(1) is able to see the infant's cues from afar, (2) makes eye contact and provides emotional support from a distance, and (3) is available if the child needs to return for emotional refueling" (Lally, 1995, p. 65).

Keep children and caregivers together from year to year

When an infant or toddler enrolls in the center, the child joins a small group (or cluster) of one, two, or three other children under the care of one primary caregiver. This adult-child cluster, together with a second (and possibly third) adult-child cluster, remains together from year to year. Depending on how the center is organized, this might mean all moving together from one room to another room each year, or all remaining together in the same room year after year, until the children leave the program. Also, children within each cluster may be close in age, or they may range in age. In either case, children remain with their primary caregiver as long as they are enrolled at the center.

The following are three options (see pp. 130–132) for providing continuity of care through staffing patterns and/or the use of space in the program facilities. Bear in mind that these options are illustrative examples, not a definitive list or strict guidelines. Your program may have a room for nonmobile infants, a room for mobile infants/young toddlers, and a room

for older toddlers, for example, rather than having the three rooms described in Option 1. Also four, rather than three, toddlers may be assigned to each primary caregiver in your program.

The teamwork arrangement of Option 1 (see p. 130) tailors each room to roughly a single age group; it also promotes a sense of community and collaboration among the three caregiver teams as they move in and out of rooms they have all "lived in" for a year at a time.

A variation on Option 2 (see p. 131) is an arrangement in which a small center (perhaps a family child care home) or each room of a larger, multiroom center has a stable, ongoing caregiver team that stays in one place and works with the same, *multiage* group of children from year to year. As a toddler in this program leaves for preschool, a new infant fills the vacancy. When a child of less-than-preschool age leaves the program, he or she is replaced with a child of similar age, when possible, to preserve the multiage mix.

Of the options described here, Option 3 (see p. 132) is the most problematic teamwork arrangement, because having nine infants and toddlers in one space may create more commotion than some children can comfortably tolerate. However, the arrangement can work reasonably well when used with a lot of thought and care. For example, if the two toddler groups (younger and older) alternate their choice times and outside times, there will be only six children and two caregivers indoors for a large part of the time. The challenge is in providing the youngest infants with the safe, quiet space they need. The payoff is in seeing the strong, caring relationships younger and older children often form with one another when they are in daily contact.

All three of these options (and the variation of Option 2) can be adapted to an extended-hours program by doubling the number of staff (so each child has two primary caregivers — one in the morning, one in the afternoon) and having half of the staff work the first part of the day and half of them work the second part of the day, with an overlap of an hour or so in the middle of the day. So the pair of caregivers in the Option 1 infant room, for example, might work from 6:30 a.m. until 1:00 p.m., and another pair of caregivers might replace them for the afternoon, working from 11:30 a.m. to 6:00 p.m. During the overlap time, while children nap, both caregiver teams have a chance to meet together as a foursome to share child observations and plan for the following afternoon or morning.

One strategy for providing consistent all-day care is for caregivers to work 10-hour shifts, with each caregiver working four days a week. A permanent floater, who works across two classrooms, fills in on the uncovered days of four caregivers (i.e., two in each room). This provides children with a familiar and stable set of secondary caregivers, and no changes in caregivers on any one day. This strategy and a sample two-week staffing schedule are presented on page 133.

Arrange caregivers' schedules around children's needs

Children in group care are often content to spend time with various caregivers or on their own, exploring materials, sharing mealtimes, and interacting with peers. However, for regular reassurance and when things go wrong, these children often want the comfort that their primary caregiver can offer. Only *she* will provide consolation when they are tired, hungry, hurt, or ill. Therefore, it is important to schedule caregivers so they are present when their primary care children arrive and/or depart, eat, and go to sleep, and so they are at least "on call" when one of their children becomes sick or injured.

For example, in the "Sample Daily Schedules for an Infant-Toddler Program" on pages 292–293 of Chapter 5, caregivers Yvonne and Leanne are present at the beginning of each day for children's arrivals (Yvonne alone for the earliest children), caregivers Kim and Yvonne are present at the end of each day for children's departures (Kim alone for the latest departures), and Yvonne and Kim are present for breakfast and for the transition from outside to lunch to naps; during naps, all three caregivers are available to meet together for 20 to 30 minutes of daily team planning. Consistent greetings and good-byes, mealtimes, and transitions with the same caregivers each day, as shown in this example, help to build a sense of trust and security for children and their families.

Option 1: Multiroom With Looping
(three 2-person teams, 3 rooms, 3-year looping)

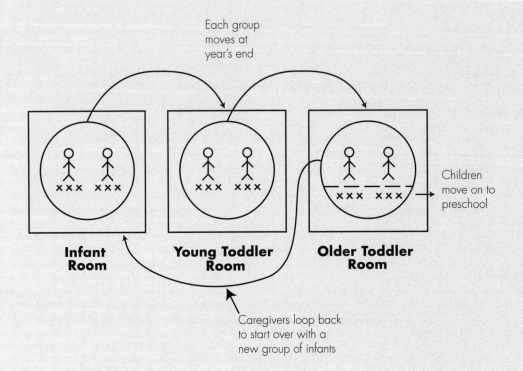

Each group moves at year's end

Children move on to preschool

Caregivers loop back to start over with a new group of infants

Infant Room

Young Toddler Room

Older Toddler Room

This center has an "infant room," a "young toddler room," and an "older toddler room." Each room has a two-caregiver team with six young children of about the same age. Each year, as the children in a given room grow older, they and their caregivers move on to the next room (e.g., the former young toddlers move on to the older toddler room with their two primary caregivers). At the same time, children who have been in the older toddler room move on to preschool, and their caregiver team then loops back to the infant room to begin caring for an incoming group of infants.

Option 2: Multiroom Without Looping

(three 2-person teams, 3 rooms, each team stays in the same room for their children's 3-year cycle)

ROOM 1

ROOM 2

ROOM 3

Year 1:   6 infants
(Infant Room)

Year 2:   Children become
young toddlers
(Young Toddler
Room)

Year 3:   Children become
older toddlers
(Older Toddler Room)

Year 4:   Start over with infants,
in same room
(Infant Room)

etc.

Year 1:   6 young toddlers
(Young Toddler
Room)

Year 2:   Children become
older toddlers
(Older Toddler
Room)

Year 3:   Start over with
infants, in same
room (Infant Room)

etc.

Year 1:   6 older toddlers
(Older Toddler
Room)

Year 2:   Start over with
infants, in same
room (Infant Room)

etc.

This center has, at any given time, three separate rooms — one for infants, one for young toddlers, and one for older toddlers — but the two-person caregiver team in each room stays in place with their six (possibly up to eight) children from year to year. Thus, as their children grow from infants to young toddlers and then to older toddlers, the caregivers arrange and adapt their room to support children's developing abilities, and the room changes in designation from one year to the next: It is the center's "infant room" one year, its "young toddler room" the next, and its "older toddler room" the next.

A variation on this option is to have children of multiple ages in each room who stay together with the caregiving team and one another for the program's duration. When an older toddler moves to preschool, that child is replaced by an infant. If a child leaves midprogram for another reason, that child is replaced by another child of approximately the same age.

Option 3: Shared, Subdivided Space With Looping

(one 3-person team, shared space with separate areas for 3 different ages, 3-year looping)

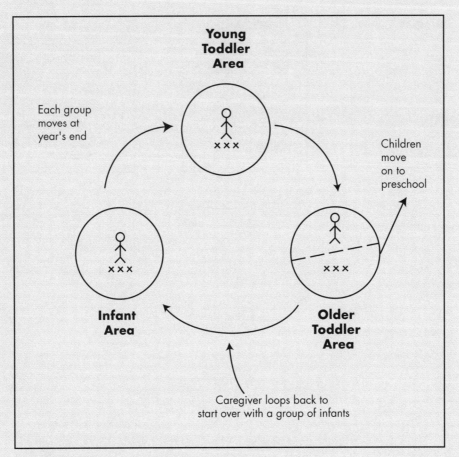

Each group moves at year's end

Young Toddler Area

Children move on to preschool

Infant Area

Older Toddler Area

Caregiver loops back to start over with a group of infants

This center has one large space that is subdivided into three areas, each adapted for a different age group. (Additional kitchen and diapering/bathroom facilities are available to be shared by all three age groups. Also, the age-adapted play areas are situated so children may see and even at times interact with those in other age groups.) A team of three primary caregivers rotates in using the three age-adapted areas. One cares for her three infants in the "infant area"; another cares for her three young toddlers in the "young toddler area"; and another cares for her three older toddlers in the "older toddler area." Each caregiver moves along to the "next-age" area with her children as they reach that age. The caregiver whose children move on to preschool loops back to begin with an incoming group of infants in the area adapted for infants.

How to Provide Consistent All-Day Care

(multiroom with longer caregiver shifts and a permanent caregiver-floater)

Week 1

	Monday	Tuesday	Wednesday	Thursday	Friday
Team A (Room 1)					
Caregiver 1	10 hours		10 hours	10 hours	10 hours
Caregiver 2	10 hours	10 hours		10 hours	10 hours
Team B (Room 2)					
Caregiver 3	10 hours	10 hours	10 hours		10 hours
Caregiver 4	10 hours	10 hours	10 hours	10 hours	
Caregiver — Floater		10 hours (for Caregiver 1)	10 hours (for Caregiver 2)	10 hours (for Caregiver 3)	10 hours (for Caregiver 4)

Week 2

	Monday	Tuesday	Wednesday	Thursday	Friday
Team A (Room 1)					
Caregiver 1	10 hours	10 hours	10 hours		10 hours
Caregiver 2	10 hours	10 hours	10 hours	10 hours	
Team B (Room 2)					
Caregiver 3	10 hours		10 hours	10 hours	10 hours
Caregiver 4	10 hours	10 hours		10 hours	10 hours
Caregiver — Floater		10 hours (for Caregiver 3)	10 hours (for Caregiver 4)	10 hours (for Caregiver 1)	10 hours (for Caregiver 2)

By creating longer caregiver shifts over fewer days, programs can provide their infants and toddlers with consistent caregivers throughout the day. For example, each caregiver works a 10-hour day for four days per week. A permanent caregiver floater, working across two rooms (four caregivers), fills in on each of the caregivers' uncovered days. This provides children with a familiar set of secondary caregivers, and no changes in caregivers on any one day. Also, by alternating weeks, each caregiving team will take turns having three 10-hour days consecutively. (*Note:* To provide an easier transition from the weekend, it is beneficial for both primary caregiving teams to begin the week with their primary children. This can be accomplished if the day off for the caregiver floater is on Mondays.)

Tell children and parents about caregiver absences and returns

Caregivers are, of course, absent from time to time because of illness, emergencies, vacations, or attendance at conferences and training. On these occasions, it is important to inform even the youngest children. When Yvonne, for example, was out with the flu, Kim told each child and parent as they arrived, "Yvonne's not feeling well, so she won't be here today. Kelly (the center's permanent substitute caregiver) will be here all day in her place. She and I will take care of you." (Even infants are comforted by the reassuring tone of such statements.) Children and families need to know very clearly who is caring for children in the absence of their primary caregiver.

Staff at one active learning infant-toddler program use photos and a pocket chart to let children and parents know who will be at the center each day and who will not. A box containing photos of individual children and caregivers is located in the entrance area. As each child or caregiver arrives for the day, that person's photo is taken from the box and placed in a pocket on the "in" side of the chart so all can see who is in that day. (Toddlers enjoy placing their own pictures in the pockets.) The "out" side of the pocket chart is draped with a transparent scarf. When a child or caregiver is absent, his or her photo is placed in an "out" pocket, under the scarf. The children soon learn that the "out" people (under the scarf) will not be at the center that day. They also learn that, as in the game of peekaboo, the absent people *will* come back!

Have primary caregivers record observations of their children

To better focus on her small group of children, each primary caregiver records daily brief anecdotal observations of her individual children. These observations then serve as a basis for the caregiver team's daily planning and for conversations with parents. In one active learning center for infants and toddlers, for example, each primary caregiver records brief anecdotal observations related to the infant-toddler KDIs. Parents eagerly read these observations each day to find out what their child has been doing at the center. (See "Interesting Things Your Child Did Today!" on p. 136.) Parents, in turn, also write brief observations about their child in the morning as they sign in. This fills in caregivers about what the child has been doing at home. (See "Sample Section of Parent Sign-In Sheet" on p. 137.)

Creating a Climate of Trust for Children

Social intelligence — a child's knowledge and skills about how to interact with others — develops in accordance with how the child is welcomed by the world and how the world, in turn, responds to the child's initiatives. Emotional sharing — interpersonal give and take that responds to needs and moods — is central to guaranteeing that these earliest social experiences are positive. A sensitive caregiver promotes a baby's sense of effectiveness as a social partner; when a caregiver, for example, reciprocates an

As she assists these two toddlers in resolving their disagreement, this caregiver kneels down on their level, acknowledges their feelings, and helps each child communicate her wants and find a solution to the problem.

infant's coo or babble, the infant can see the caregiver as someone who is *like him* as well as *with him,* in that moment (Markova & Legerstee, 2008). The caregiver knows how to engage in this verbal game the infant has initiated (hence, she is *like him*), and she is also picking up on his mood of playfulness (hence, she is *with him*).

Caregivers use the principles of active learning to help infants and toddlers develop a positive and secure understanding about the social world. They treat children in ways that help them to

Interesting Things Your Child Did Today!

Child's Name: *Jamila G.*   **Date:** *5/28*

Approaches to Learning

- *At choice time, Jamila figured out a way to get the big rubber ball into the climber. She tried to fit it through the ladder rungs, but it was too big, so she rolled it up the slide.*

Social and Emotional Development

- *When Jamila saw Coty crying during choice time, she brought him his "blankie."*

Physical Development and Health

- *Jamila fit corks through the small openings of some plastic pop bottles.*

Communication, Language, and Literacy

- *Each time Jamila put another ball inside the climber, she said, "Aw gone!"*

Cognitive Development

- *Jamila put one cork in each of several small yogurt containers.*

- *At choice time, after naptime, Jamila found the baby doll in the cradle that she used that morning and said "Up, up."*

- *After lunch, Jamila anticipated diaper change by getting a diaper from her cubby and giving it to Yvonne, her caregiver.*

Creative Arts

- *Jamila used large arm movements to make scribbles with a marker on a big piece of white paper while listening to classical music.*

- *Jamila wiggled her bottom while listening to a story about a dog wagging its tail.*

- *After fitting corks in a bottle, Jamila shook the bottle to listen to the sound they made.*

Note: This sample and sample section of the parent sign-in sheet (p. 137) show the type of observations caregivers and parents might write. The number and length of observations may vary depending on the time they each have available, but written notes offer another way, in addition to talking, to share information.

Sample Section of Parent Sign-In Sheet

Child's Name: *Jamila G.*   **Date:** *5/29*

Reporter's Name: *Marta S.*   **Relationship to Child:** *Mother*

Let me tell you about my child!

- *Jamila wanted me to hold her in the grocery store, didn't want to sit in the cart as usual. She also fell asleep early last night, so she may be coming down with something. This morning she ate fine, though.*

- *In the car on the way here, Jamila spotted 4 "doggies." One was a cat, but I didn't correct her!*

---

develop a sense of trust in their caregivers and in themselves. They use the following strategies, which spell out what it means to treat children with great care and respect. Regardless of the organization or scheduling options used in a setting, these strategies in themselves will help to promote continuity of care when they are put to use by everyone, including caregivers and all the other adults (administrative, clerical, and support staff) who interact with children throughout the day.

Touch, hold, speak to, and play with children in a warm, unhurried manner

Caregivers interact with infants and toddlers in very physical ways, knowing that holding, touching, cuddling, hugging, rocking, singing, speaking kindly, and being within sight and reach are essential to very young children, who experience everyone and everything in sensory and active ways. While infants and toddlers may not understand *all* of what adults say to them, they comprehend body language immediately and thoroughly.

In her book *Essential Touch,* program administrator and teacher-educator Frances Carlson (2006) explains why touch is necessary in every aspect of a young child's life:

> *The physical benefits of touch begin as soon as we are born. Newborns who experience skin-to-skin contact with their mothers soon after birth cry less, sleep longer, and have longer periods of quiet alertness, which is when learning most often occurs....Conversely, without adequate touch, infants may fail to thrive or may even die. (p. 6)*

Touch supports and sustains healthy brain development in the early months of life. Through intricate neurochemical mechanisms, touch can stimulate or suppress the release of powerful hormones that affect a variety of bodily functions including emotions, behavior, growth, and thinking. For example, touch can raise the level of oxytocin, which protects the body from the damage caused by stress. It also increases serotonin and dopamine, the two "feel good" brain chemicals that help to balance mood and control movement, memory, and attention. Conversely, touch lowers the level of the stress hormone cortisol which, at high levels, can damage the hippocampus, the part of the brain that controls memory and cognition (Carlson, 2006).

Because so much information in the early years is communicated through physical contact, caregivers strive to carry out every adult-child interaction — a game of peekaboo, a trip to the bathroom, a look out the window, a temper tantrum — in a warm, unhurried manner. No matter what

This caregiver shows genuine concern for this distressed infant and comforts her, while the other infant in her care sleeps peacefully (and blissfully unaware) in her other arm.

is happening, they want children to feel, hear, and see that they are loved and cared for. Caregivers try to match their pace to the pace of the infant or toddler they are engaged with, responding to the child's actions and cues at the tempo set by the child. This gives caregivers an opportunity to understand and respect what the child is doing and communicating. The child, in turn, experiences being seen, heard, and understood.

Take pleasure in interactions with children

Caregivers of infants and toddlers tend to genuinely enjoy and appreciate the unique characteristics of very young children — their energy and curiosity, their rapid spurts of growth, their physicality, their unique means of communicating. Interactions with these children can be as varied and diverse as the children themselves, and caregivers find themselves tailoring their interaction styles to fit individual children. Since children of this age are too self-involved to be treated as a group, caregivers enjoy the challenge of engaging in one-to-one interactions with them even when they have more than one child to feed, read to, or pull in a wagon at one time. In dealing with each child, caregivers exhibit authenticity, an essential human quality psychologist Carl Rogers (1983) defined as "a transparent realness… a willingness to be a person, to be and live the feelings and thoughts of the moment. When this realness includes a prizing, a caring, a trust, a respect for the learner, the climate for learning is enhanced"

(p. 133). Further, since infants and toddlers learn through sensory-motor exploration and play, caregivers, in their own manner, are genuinely playful with children, rather than being stern or demanding.

Respond supportively to children's needs and attention-getting signals

Caregivers strive to give infants and toddlers their undivided attention during each interaction. This practice allows them to notice and attend to each child's needs and unique attention-getting signals.

Whether they express themselves nonverbally or in words, infants and toddlers in active learning settings know they can count on caregivers to answer their calls of distress. Instead of viewing a child's distress as an annoyance or interruption, caregivers, even when they are engaged with another child, show a genuine concern for the distressed child through eye contact, verbal reassurance, or some more direct action, such as holding, rocking, hugging, or touching. They acknowledge children's feelings and ask even the youngest children what is troubling them ("You're crying hard, Lissa. I can see you're upset. What's the trouble?"). Even when a child cannot yet answer in words, he or she is reassured by the caregiver's presence, calm voice, and focused attention. Eventually, infants and toddlers learn how to give better cues to their caregiver and the caregiver learns how to interpret these cues (Gerber, 1979). In this scenario, Arun's cue consists of wanting to be close to his caregiver:

After his mom leaves, Arun clings to his caregiver's leg. "It's sad when mommy leaves for work," she says to Arun as she bends down and encircles him with her arm. "Would you like to cuddle, Arun?" she asks gently. When he nods yes, she picks him up. "Rock," Arun says, pointing to the rocking chair. He spends a good while on his caregiver's lap, looking at books and watching the other children. Instead of trying to push Arun away or brush off his concerns, his caregiver provides the extra comfort he needs.

When she leaves the rocking chair to greet another child, Kara, and later to change Kara's diaper, she invites Arun along with her. Throughout these interactions, Arun clings to his caregiver's leg, and she strokes his head when she has a free hand. When she completes Kara's diaper change and Kara has returned to her play, she lifts up Arun and holds him on one hip while she makes an entry on Kara's diapering log. By midmorning, after a nap, Arun feels ready to leave his caregiver and venture off on his own to play at the sand table.

By responding supportively in this manner, and acknowledging the validity of his feelings, Arun's caregiver gives him a sense of hope and significance. "A fussy infant," observed infant and toddler specialist Peter Mangione (1990), "may turn out to be a hungry infant. A caregiver's prompt response will satisfy much more than hunger. As the caregiver finds out what the child needs, the child learns that someone is there for him or her. In other words, the child is learning basic trust" (p. 11).

Give children time to interact and respond in their own way

Each infant or toddler has a unique way of acting or interacting and does so on his or her own timetable. An older infant, Michelle, for example, initiates a game of scarf peekaboo with her caregiver. Natalie, an infant of about the same age, watches the game with apparent interest but does not join in, even when the caregiver offers her a scarf. Her caregiver, however, accepts Natalie's response, realizing, that Natalie *has,* in a sense, joined the game simply by choosing to watch it. Sometimes in our zeal to emphasize the importance of young children actively handling materials, we forget that they also learn through quiet observation — we recognize the "motor" but overlook the "sensory" aspects of sensory-motor development.

In their landmark resource on developmentally appropriate practices for infants and toddlers, editors and authors Carol Copple and Sue Bredekamp (2009) remind us that manipulating objects (touch) is only one of the ways young children acquire knowledge and experience. They also learn through the unmediated use of other senses, notably sight, sound, taste, and smell.

Caregivers also understand that infants and toddlers, craving repetition, often spend a long time repeating an enjoyable action — banging a spoon, turning the pages of a board book, opening and closing the door of the toy oven, filling and emptying a basket of shells. Therefore, caregivers might play endless games of peekaboo with

Children sometimes learn through quiet observation, as the toddler in the background is doing. He is interested in the ball play but chooses to watch from a safe distance where he can observe but not feel that he has to participate unless or until he is ready.

children or willingly look at their favorite books or read their favorite stories again and again, because they understand that with child-initiated repetition comes understanding and mastery. Sensitive caregivers are also alert to those times when they need to hang back and not be overly eager to jump in and join the young child's play. An adult's repeated interruptions to an infant's play can contribute to an infant developing a shorter attention span (Copple & Bredekamp, 2009).

Judith Leipzig (1996), a professor at Bank Street College of Education, points out the many cognitive and social advantages that accrue to young children when teachers learn to watch and wait:

> *It is important for adults to recognize when not to interrupt as a baby crawls in and out of a box on the floor repeatedly, or a toddler concentrates for a full five minutes on sponging off an already clean table. Children need time to process their experience, so if they continue to look absorbed, we can know they are still working on learning and integrating information. They also need time to gain a sense of completion of the task. When possible, a teacher should think about whether that baby really needs her diaper changed this very minute, if it's absolutely necessary*

Even the youngest children begin "socializing" with their peers through simple gestures that say "I know you are here."

to go to the store right now, or if the adult can honor the child's absorption for a little while longer. (p. 31)

Support children's relationships with peers and other adults

Infants and toddlers thrive on supportive relationships, and with each relationship, their world to explore expands. Caregivers, therefore, help children form and sustain relationships with peers and with other adults at the center. For example, a caregiver might acknowledge one toddler's preference for another: "Tejas and Emily, I see you like to sit together at lunch!" Or a caregiver might think of ways to provide ongoing opportunities for a particular child to interact with a peer as the two children's interest in each other emerges and develops. Over several days, for example, a caregiver observes that four-month-old Anil looks in another infant's direction every time that infant Raina cries, coos, or makes a noise, so today the caregiver places Anil on a blanket next to Raina. Both babies look at each other, wiggle, and coo with pleasure.

It may seem surprising that children this young directly interact with one another, but in fact there is ample evidence that peer sociability emerges quite early (Epstein, 2009). Infants orient toward peers by two months of age, make simple gestures by three to four months, and direct smiles and vocalizations by six months to try to get the attention of others. By 9–12 months, babies begin to imitate one another. This imitation is the beginning of infant play, as though they are saying "I know what you're doing, so let's do it together!" (National Research Council, 2000).

Summarizing the early development of peer relationships, Epstein (2009) notes that sequential actions with peers (one child's behavior follows or imitates another's) appear in the first year of life. This is followed by parallel play (children playing alongside one another) in the second year and cooperative or reciprocal play (children interacting around a shared play theme) in the third year. As early as age two, children show peer preferences (indicate who they would rather play with) and begin to form friendships (a voluntary, two-way, positive bond). Friendships are unique — even toddlers adjust their style of play to each friend. The more two children play together, the greater the complexity and compatibility of the play. By supporting these early peer relationships, then, caregivers are helping to promote the social-emotional, language, and cognitive development of young children.

Relationships with adults in addition to the primary caregiver are equally important in early development. Therefore, primary caregivers resist the temptation to lure "their" children away from playing and interacting with other caregivers. While they may feel a twinge of jealousy, primary caregivers acknowledge this feeling and then set it aside in favor of the child's need to explore and connect with other trusted adults. It is important for a primary caregiver to remember that her caregiving role is not an exclusive one. It is meant to guarantee continuity of care rather than to limit children to one trusting relationship at the center.

When a child shows preference for relating to a program director, volunteer, or student teacher whose participation with a caregiver's cluster of children is intermittent or unpredictable, it is important that the caregiver acknowledge the child's sense of sorrow and loss when that person is not present and provide an opportunity for the child and his or her parents to say good-bye on that person's last day at the center. At the same time, whenever possible, directors may want to schedule ancillary caregivers so their participation with the children is regular and ongoing.

In one setting, for example, the director arranged for a foster grandparent to spend the same four hours of the day with the same cluster of children four days a week, instead of having her switch from one cluster of children to another on a daily basis. Another child care center that was connected to a college arranged to have two student teachers work with the same cluster of children for two semesters instead of having one student with the cluster for one semester and then another student with them for the next semester. The same center also relegated some other early education students to the observation room (instead of having them in the classroom on the floor with children) to complete the observations they needed to make as part of a course requirement. This plan avoided the development of temporary relationships that would be quickly broken.

Forming Partnerships With Children

Adult-child relationships are a major component of program quality, and high-quality care is a consistent and positive predictor of children's later development. Ongoing longitudinal studies by the NICHD Early Care Research Network (2002, 2003), Belsky et al. (2007), and McCartney et al. (2010) show that infants and toddlers who receive sensitive and responsive child care have fewer behavioral problems in preschool and beyond. The quality of child care in the first three years of life is also significantly associated with subsequent language development, cognition, and school readiness.

How caregivers interact with children establishes a program's emotional tone and forms the social matrix within which the child's emerging abilities unfold. Caregivers and children share many kinds of interactions. Even though caregivers are the experienced senior members in these interactions, they strive to structure their relationships with infants and toddlers as *partnerships*. This means making every effort to create a sense of shared control with children so that children are free to initiate ideas as well as to try out and adapt others' ideas to fit their own needs. Following are some practices caregivers can use to establish partnerships and share control with infants and toddlers.

By age two, toddlers engage in parallel play — they play next *to each other but not necessarily* with *each other.*

Interact at the child's physical level

Very young children spend a lot of time on or close to the floor. Since communication is generally aided when the participants can see each other clearly, caregivers find themselves sometimes holding or lifting up an infant or toddler for a face-to-face exchange and sometimes lowering themselves to kneel, sit, or lie on the floor beside the child. By getting on the child's physical level as often as possible, caregivers share control. And children, in turn, are less likely to perceive adults as giants who swoop down without warning to impose a change of activity or carry them off to "faraway places."

Respect children's preferences and individual temperaments

Caregivers try to respect rather than to alter children's preferences for certain companions, foods, or activities. One day six-month-old Miguel, for example, eats all of his strained peaches. The next day he closes his mouth and turns his head away when his caregiver offers a spoonful of strained peaches. "I see you don't want these peaches today, Miguel," she says, sensing that either the taste, or the texture, or being spoon-fed isn't to Miguel's liking on this particular day. When she then puts some banana slices in front of him, Miguel picks them up and feeds fruit to himself.

Sometimes children express conflicting needs and preferences: Hanna, a toddler, wants to fall asleep at her usual naptime because she is tired; she also wants to stay awake to watch Lamar play next to her with his stuffed bear. In such cases, the caregiver strives to understand the child's internal conflict of *I'm tired but I don't want to miss anything!* She verbally acknowledges the child's dilemma ("Hanna, you want to go to sleep, but you want to watch Lamar") and offers sympathy and comfort ("It's really hard when you want to be asleep and awake at the same time, Hanna"). She strokes Hanna's arm and says, "I'm going to cover you with your blanket so you can watch Lamar until you go to sleep." While Hanna may still fight to stay awake, she does so with the sense that her real feelings have been acknowledged and accepted, rather than with the sense that now she must fight against sleep *and* her caregiver.

To accommodate the needs and rhythms of individual children, a program needs to be flexible in its overall scheduling. For example, in one center, caregivers found that although their toddlers are sleepy right before lunch, *after* lunch many children are too energized to fall asleep directly. Therefore, while several children leave the lunch table and go right to their cots, the others play vigorously about the room for a short time until, one by one, they too settle down for naps. Even then, Jacob requires less sleep and rarely naps. Instead, he plays with toys or looks at books on the floor while the caregiver team meets nearby. This child was particularly happy throughout a neighboring building's renovation. During naptime, he was glued to the window, watching the workers and their machines.

Caregivers understand that children's temperaments affect how they interact with people and materials. Decades ago, child psychiatrists Alexander Thomas and Stella Chess introduced the idea of "innate temperamental differences" (Chess & Thomas, 1996; Thomas & Chess, 1977). Although the specific definition of temperament shifts somewhat over time and researchers, there is general agreement about its properties and importance in human development. Developmental biologist Lynne Sturm (2004) says the term *temperament* refers to "early-appearing patterns of observable behavior that are presumed to be biologically based and that distinguish one child from another" (p. 5). Leading researchers Mary Rothbart and Douglas Derryberry (2000) define temperament as "constitutionally based individual differences in emotional and attentional reactivity and self-regulation, influenced over time by heredity and experience" (p.

5). Psychologist Jerome Kagan (2008) confirmed that "inhibited" and "uninhibited" behaviors — his way of characterizing temperamental differences in self-control — remain quite stable from infancy into adolescence and adulthood.

Researchers disagree on how many different aspects of temperament actually exist. Mary Rothbart and John Bates (2006) define two major dimensions: reactivity and self-regulation. *Reactivity* is how strongly children react to stimulation; they may be high reactive or low reactive. *Self-regulation* is the degree to which children can control their emotional reactions. They may be inconsolable, allow themselves to be soothed by an adult, or able to direct their own attention away from a distressing event. Children, however, may balance these two dimensions in different ways (Wachs, 2004). For example, a child may be highly reactive but also have the self-regulation to control intense feelings with adult support or through his or her own efforts.

The particular dimensions are less important than being aware that young children have different temperaments and caregivers need to respond to them accordingly. Most researchers agree that the following four dimensions best capture individual variation: *emotion, inhibition, activity,* and *sociability.* (See "Aspects of Temperament" on p. 148.) Whichever system or categories work for the caregiving team, they apply it to providing materials, pacing activities, and interacting with infants and toddlers in ways that respect children's individuality.

Because children's temperaments are a normal part of who they are, caregivers strive to adjust their interaction style to accommodate and support each child's pace and style. An energetic caregiver, for example, does not try to prod a deliberate, cautious child into action. And a quiet, deliberate caregiver does not try to slow down an energetic child. If a child finds a certain pair of socks intolerably tight, his caregiver, who may not be bothered by wearing tight socks, does not try to persuade him otherwise. Instead, she helps him to remove the irritating socks and to select a comfortable alternative.

Caregivers must also be sensitive to the cultural differences that may interact with a child's temperament. Nearly 40 percent of children in the United States are being raised in families that may espouse different socialization goals and value different "ideal" traits than those promoted among Anglo-American families (Carlson et al., 2004). For example, a particular culture may value a child's caution and desire to remain close to an adult while the caregiver sees "hesitation to explore" or "clinging behavior" as a problem. Not only might this put the child and caregiver at odds, but the parent and caregiver may be sending different messages to the child. To respect both temperament and culture, caregivers need to work with the behavior and values that the child brings to the early childhood setting. Flexibility on the part of adults models for children how to adapt their own temperament within the increasingly varied environments in which they find themselves.

Aspects of Temperament

Although researchers differ on the number and nature of separate domains of temperament, most agree that any listing should include the following four dimensions:

- *Emotionality* is the degree to which the child's predominant affect is positive and happy or negative and distressed.

- *Inhibition* is the degree to which the child approaches and adapts to new situations or people with openness, trust, and curiosity or with avoidance, discomfort, or fear.

- *Activity* is the degree to which the child's characteristic level of motion is high and energetic or low and lethargic.

- *Sociability* is the degree to which the child responds to and initiates interactions with people or ignores and turns away from others (Rothbart & Bates, 2006).

At a more specific level, researchers have identified the following temperamental differences in early infancy: fear, irritability/frustration, positive affect/approach, activity level, and attentional persistence (how long an infant stays with an activity) (Sturm, 2004). Another dimension that appears later in infancy is "effortful attention control," the child's ability to focus attention but to shift it with some degree of flexibility. It also includes "inhibitory control," the child's ability to feel an impulse and yet refrain from acting on it.

Temperament plays a major role in early development (Teglasi & Epstein, 1998). It affects how caregivers react to the child and how the child chooses and interprets experiences. It is important to recognize that temperament acts in a continuous feedback loop; temperamental differences determine both how the child deals with the world and how the world responds to the child.

Although temperament is based on genetics and biology, this does not mean quality of care is unimportant. On the contrary, says psychologist Ross Thompson (2009): "Children's interactions with parents, child care providers, and other people create an environment of relationships in which brain development unfolds and temperamental individuality is expressed" (p. 36). Adults need to be sensitive and responsive, respect emerging abilities, talk about emotions and how to manage them, and be flexible adapting the environment to children's ever-changing needs.

Whether children are naturally "easy-going," "quiet," or "always on the go" (Brazelton, 1983), caregivers in an active learning setting try to accept rather than alter the child's overall orientation toward life. For example, caregivers accept and support the child who is fairly active, tries out new foods with interest, naps at predictable times, is not easily distracted when exploring self-selected materials, and is generally happy except before and after naps. At the same time, they slow themselves down and patiently support the child who moves very deliberately and only when necessary, who tends to withdraw initially from new people and materials, likes to eat a few familiar foods, naps regularly twice a day, plays alone or watches others play, and is generally quiet and self-contained. And they also energetically support the child who is active all day long except for one 20-minute nap, enjoys some new people and not others, loudly disputes any attempt to interrupt his or her play, and is generally either very involved or very frustrated.

Follow children's lead

Another way to build partnerships with children is by following children's cues throughout the day. During play and caregiving routines, caregivers can

- *Imitate what the child is doing.* As nine-month-old Elizabeth gets her diaper changed, she blows a kiss to her caregiver, who blows one back to her.

- *Pause and wait for the child to take a turn during interactions.* Toddler Sean's caregiver Marina rolls a ball toward Sean, who is sitting opposite her on the floor. As he reaches for the ball, she waits to see what he will do with it, instead of urging him to roll it back to her or quickly rolling another ball to him.

- *Follow the child's pace and interests.* Sam, a caregiver, sets a small basket of blocks next to infant Jessica, and Jessica immediately dumps out the blocks. She then looks at Sam, crawls to the bookshelf, takes down a book, and hands it to Sam. "You want to read this book now, Jessica?" he asks. She nods affirmatively and crawls into his lap.

- *Play with the same materials the child is using.* Marnie, a caregiver, sits down next to Josh, an older toddler, who is using sponges to dab paint on a piece of newsprint. Marnie watches Josh for a few moments, then picks up a sponge, dips it in paint, and applies it to another piece of newsprint. Josh stops to watch Marnie briefly and then continues painting.

Watch and listen to children

Communication is a complex process, especially when one of the partners is just learning the ropes. Infants and toddlers rely heavily on patient listeners to understand and respond appropriately to the intent of their messages.

Caregivers in HighScope active learning settings try to be especially alert to children's nonverbal communications, because they are so easy to miss. Through careful attention, they learn that infants communicate interest, pleasure, and excitement by looking, smiling, making noises, or wiggling — and that turning away is an infant's way of saying *That's enough*. In one setting, for example, caregivers observing their children at mealtime documented the following ways that a child nonverbally communicates *I'm finished eating:* accepting the nipple without sucking, turning away from the bottle, playing with the bottle, gazing at other children, pulling the bottle out of his or her mouth, turning away from the spoon, not opening his or her mouth for the spoon, holding food in the cheeks but not swallowing it, letting food drip out of his or her mouth, dropping bits of food on the floor, leaving the table, putting the bowl on his or her head, and pulling at or removing the bib. As their children learned to talk, the caregivers documented them using words such as "all done," "no," "no more," or "bib off" to bring an end to eating.

Because learning to talk is a long-term process, developmental psychologists are increasingly exploring the potential benefits of teaching simple sign language to typically developing infants and toddlers as well as those with hearing impairments. Preliminary research documents the benefits of learning to sign at an early age not only for language and literacy development but also for cognitive, motor, and social development. For more on the effective use of baby sign language with very young children, see "Using Sign Language to Communicate With Infants and Toddlers" on pages 152–153.

Through watching and listening to all the ways that very young children communicate, caregivers also learn to fill in the context for toddler's often elliptical utterances and gestures. For example, they learn that Tommy's "Tata!" means *I see a tractor!*, Eleanor's "Me! Bag!" means *I want to carry the bag!*, and Felipe's bouncing up and down on his bottom means he wants someone to sing to him while he "dances." As early educators Elinor Goldschmied and Sonia Jackson (1994) have reminded us, "Giving full attention to a child as he tries haltingly to express himself can be difficult for a [caregiver] amidst the distractions and demands of a group, but it is essential if we aim to help a child gain command of language" (p. 110).

Communicate and converse in a give-and-take manner

In the spirit of partnership, caregivers try to converse with children in a style that does not overwhelm an infant or toddler with adult talk. They communicate and converse in a balanced, turn-taking manner, allowing enough time for the child's responses. Here is an example of how Selena, a young infant, and her caregiver communicate:

Selena: (Smiles at her caregiver.)

Caregiver: (Smiles back.) *I see a smile!* (Pauses.)

Selena: (Smiles and wiggles.)

As this young toddler paints with his unusual paintbrush, his caregiver finds a similar tool to paint with and imitates the kinds of strokes he is making.

Caregiver: (Smiles, nods her head.) *I see a smile and a wiggle!* (Pauses.)

Selena: (Smacks her lips.)

Caregiver: (Smacks *her* lips.)

Selena: (Smiles, then turns her head away.)

Caregiver: (Smiles.) *That was fun!*

Notice that the caregiver leaves room in her exchange with Selena to allow the infant to shape the direction of the dialogue. She also adopts the same pace as Selena, leaving pauses before and after responding, to match the infant's pauses. Each young child communicates at his or her own pace. A child needs time, for

Using Sign Language to Communicate With Infants & Toddlers

Sign language (or signing) is a visual-gestural system of communication used primarily by deaf and hard-of-hearing individuals. However, psychologists, educators, and parents are becoming increasingly interested in the potential of signing to enhance the language and literacy skills of hearing children who are not yet verbal or are just learning to talk. There are many simple gestures in American Sign Language (ASL) that are appropriate for infants and toddlers to learn and use.[4]

The idea behind teaching young children to sign is not to replace spoken words with sign language but, rather, to open the communication between adults and young children as well as enhance a young child's repertoire of communication skills. Because motor development precedes vocal development, children are able to control their hand gestures before they have the physiological maturity to form words with their mouths. Signing as a supplemental means of expression can help them communicate their needs and thoughts to caregivers before they can talk. This reduces frustration on the part of both children and adults.

Most young children develop their own hand signals (e.g., raising their arms when they want to be picked up), just as they develop rudimentary sounds to represent whole words (e.g., saying "ba" for blanket). However, learning standardized signs makes it more likely that children and adults can communicate accurately and efficiently, just as it is easier to understand one another when children begin to learn the language(s) spoken by their caregivers.

Studies show that learning sign language at an early age has multiple benefits for both hearing and hearing-impaired children (Johnston, Durieux-Smith, & Bloom, 2005). Most important is its contribution to the development of language and literacy skills (Goodwyn et al., 2000). When researcher Joseph Garcia (1999) investigated the use of signs as a method of communication among hearing infants and their parents, he found that babies consistently exposed to signs at six to seven months of age began to use them effectively by eight or nine months. They were therefore "speaking" earlier than most infants, who rely solely on verbal communication. Moreover, their parents correctly interpreted what they were "saying."

Signing raises communication awareness because it is a means of expression that is available and usable to even the youngest children. They gain a sense of competence through using gestures to convey needs and ideas in ways that grown-ups can understand (Volterra, Iverson, & Castrataro, 2006).

Sign language also increases a child's total vocabulary (Johnston et al., 2005). Hearing children who learn to sign are becoming bilingual and are developing a dual lexicon. As research demonstrates, the larger a child's vocabulary, the better his or her subsequent literacy skills (Hart & Risley, 1999). Preliminary studies show this relationship also holds for deaf children who learn to sign early (Buckley et al., 2006) and applies to hearing children who sign as a second language (Daniels, 2001).

[4]For signs appropriate to use with infants and toddlers, there are several online resources, including Sign2Me (http://sign2me.com) and ASLPro (www.aslpro.com).

Using Sign Language to Communicate With Infants & Toddlers (cont.)

Beyond promoting literacy, learning to sign also enhances general cognitive, physical, and social development. Because signing is a motor activity, it stimulates activity in the right brain (which is responsible for visual-spatial reasoning and long-term memory) as well as the left brain (which is responsible for processing language).

Using sign language is another way infants and toddlers can exercise fine-motor coordination. Infants learning sign language "babble" with their fingers in the same way that those learning to speak babble with their voices. Practicing and gradually refining finger movements is good preparation for drawing and writing as children get older.

Finally, sign language can serve as a communication bridge for English language learners and children with special needs. Not only does it enhance these children's language and literacy development, by allowing them to be participating members in their child care setting, signing helps to promote their social and emotional development. Communicating, whether with words and/or gestures, helps young children become part of the group and enjoy the give and take of social exchange.

For more information on using sign language effectively in child care settings, see the book and accompanying DVD *Ready, Sign, Go! Using Sign Language to Promote Preschool Learning* by HighScope early childhood specialist Kay Rush (2011).

---

example, to decide whether to respond, how to respond, and (if verbal) what words to use. Here is an exchange, for example, between young toddler Nomi and her caregiver Ann at the "waving window" as they wave good-bye to Nomi's mom.

Nomi: *Byyye!* (She waves.)

Ann: *Bye, bye.* (She waves. Nomi's mom gets into her car.)

Nomi: *Uppy! Uppy!* (Holds her arms up to her caregiver.)

Ann: (Picks up Nomi.) *Now you can see better.*

Nomi: *Ma. Bye. Ma.*

Ann: *Bye, bye, Mom.* (Mom's car disappears around the corner.)

Nomi: *Aw gone.* (Looks at Ann.) *Back?*

Ann: *Mommy's all gone. She'll come back to get you.*

Nomi: *Get me, get me, get me.*

Ann: (Begins singing.) *Your mom will come back to get you. Your mom will come back to get you. Your mom will come back to get you, at the end of the day.*

Nomi: (Rests against Ann, then squirms to get down.)

Ann: (Puts Nomi gently on the floor.)

This caregiver makes the sign for milk while talking with this baby about how she is going to make her a bottle.

Nomi: (Touching Ann's leg, looks around. Sees Laramee, another child.) *La-me, La-me!*

Ann: *There's Laramee!*

Nomi: (Heads toward Laramee.)

Make comments and acknowledgments

Caregivers who want to encourage dialogue offer children comments, observations, and acknowledgments instead of asking a lot of questions. They do so because factual comments or observations ("You're watching the rain splash against the window") and acknowledgments ("I see!" and "You did it!") leave opportunity for children to respond without actually pressuring them to respond in a certain way or at a particular pace. A question, by contrast, requires children to produce an answer that satisfies the questioner. Therefore, it is important to ask questions sparingly and to make comments, observations, and acknowledgments generously.

Another way that caregivers acknowledge young children's vocalizations and converse with them is to repeat and restate their babbles and words. For example, when Devin babbles "ba, ba, ba," his caregiver can repeat "ba, ba, ba" in a back-and-forth communication. When Gwen points and says, "ball, tree, ball tree," her caregiver might respond with, "Yes, you found a ball by the tree!" By using this strategy, caregivers support children's early language utterances while modeling sentence structure and descriptive language.

Caregivers who are tuned in to children's active learning find there is no shortage of material for adult comments and observations. They describe what children are seeing and doing: "You see your Daddy, Peter!" "You're kicking your legs!" Or they describe what they themselves are observing or doing: "I see you, Carlos, lying on your bunny blanket!" "Now, I'm pulling your shirt off over your head, Katie." They also talk with children about what will happen next: "I'm going to put your sweater on you so we can go play outside, Max." "I'm going to lift you up and take you to the changing table for a dry diaper, Abdul." With this kind of support, infants and toddlers develop the ability to communicate and talk by playing with interesting objects and with interacting adults who leave space and time in conversations for them to respond at their own pace, in their own way.

You may have noticed the factual nature of the sample comments and observations in the previous paragraph. In these and other examples, caregivers strive to speak to children about what the children are doing ("You're washing your hands

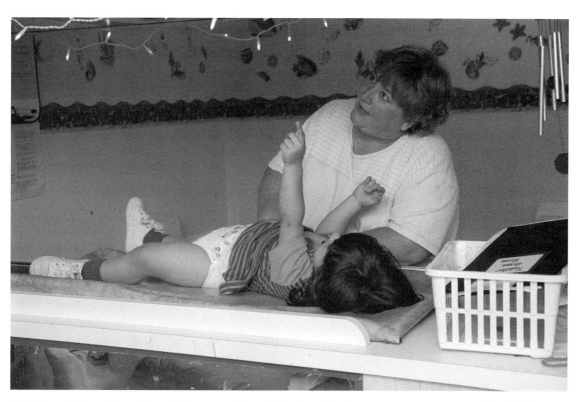

"Ook!" exclaims this toddler. "Those are shiny lights," replies the caregiver. "Yots!" says the child. "Yes, there are lots of shiny lights!" affirms her caregiver. In an active learning environment, there are many opportunities for comments and conversations.

with soap") rather than to praise their efforts ("You're doing a good job washing your hands" or "I like it when you wash your hands"). Although praising children is tempting because it seems to motivate desired behavior (like hand washing), it also can have an adverse effect by breaking down the trusting relationships that are so important to build (Kohn, 1999). For one thing, giving praise puts children in competition with one another to gain a caregiver's praise. It also undermines the self-trust children are building as they do things for themselves. With praise, for example, the child's self-perception *I can wash my hands whenever I need to* is apt to turn into *I can wash my hands to gain the love of important adults*. Children need to feel loved and respected regardless of their specific actions.

Another drawback to praise is that children come to expect it when they are "good" and may assume that when praise is not forthcoming they are "bad" and/or that the adult does not like them. Since caregivers generally do not give praise *every* time a child acts according to expectations (she may be distracted or by now take the behavior for granted), receiving no message from the adult can be interpreted as a negative one by the child. The adult does not intend to criticize or imply dislike, but that is the inadvertent effect. For the child, this inconsistency can be confusing and even discouraging.

Similarly, caregivers may think they are building self-esteem when they give compliments such as "Mona, you look pretty in that pink shirt. Pink is my favorite color!" But from Mona's perspective, it might mean the caregiver won't think she's pretty if she wears her blue shirt. What about Jason who overhears the compliment and is wearing a green shirt? He might conclude the caregiver does not think he is nice looking. Or he may worry that she dislikes him because his favorite color is different than hers. In these situations, the adult is again inadvertently sending negative messages, both to the child to whom the praise or compliment is directed and to any other children in earshot (Katz, 1993). By contrast, a simple factual statement such as "Mona, you're wearing a pink shirt today, and Jason's shirt is green" carries no such potential for mixed messages. Instead it delivers important information, namely "I see you. I notice things about you because you are important to me." In addition to such comments building a strong social bond, the vocabulary and information conveyed also contribute to children's language and cognitive development.

Look at children's actions from their viewpoint

Two people often see the same situation from differing viewpoints, depending on their individual experience, culture, problem-solving approach, and temperament. Imagine the disparity of viewpoints between two individuals who are as far apart in age and experience as an infant or toddler and an adult caregiver! Caregivers in active learning settings are keenly aware

Instead of saying "I like your painting," this caregiver describes what she sees the child do: "I see that you are making swirls with your finger and the blue paint. I wonder if I can do that too."

of this disparity and know that an infant cannot assume another person's viewpoint and that toddlers are only beginning to do so. For very young children, the world primarily revolves around themselves and the present moment. They react to how people, places, and things affect them personally.

Fifteen-month-old Misaki, for example, wants her mom to stay and play a while longer after bringing her to the center. Her caregiver understands Misaki's point of view, remains physically close to Misaki while her mother is departing, and verbally acknowledges Misaki's strong feelings of anger and sadness at her mother's departure. Throughout this difficult time, the caregiver does not assume Misaki's feelings herself or become angry at Misaki as she cries furiously after her mom leaves. Misaki accepts her caregiver's embrace and then sits in her lap. Eventually, Misaki's crying subsides as she begins to watch Ryan finger-paint; she is signaling that she is at last ready to move into the life of the child care setting.

Give children choices when they have to do something

Sometimes, an infant or toddler resists doing something that needs to be done, such as getting a diaper changed, taking a bath, or coming in from outdoors. When this happens, a caregiver can encourage the child's partnership in and control over the process by giving, in simple words, a reason for the necessary action and then giving the child a feasible choice about how he or she will participate in that action. Here is what happened one day at the end of outside time when Jack, an older toddler, was having such a good time pulling a wagon that he didn't want to go indoors for lunch:

Caregiver: *Jack, it's time to come inside for lunch!*

Jack: *No! Play!*

Caregiver: (Squats next to Jack.) *You really want to keep playing, Jack, don't you. I need you to come in now because your lunch is on the table.*

Jack: (Looks at her but makes no move toward the door.)

Caregiver: *You can pull the wagon up to the door, or you can get in the wagon and I can pull you up to the door.*

Jack: (Considers a moment, looks around the play yard, and sees no other children.)

Me pull! (He pulls the wagon, and together he and his caregiver head for the door.)

Supporting Children's Intentions

In active learning settings, caregivers are observing, interacting with, and learning about their children throughout the day — during mealtime, choice time, outside time, group time, dressing, and diapering. Here are some strategies caregivers can use to continually give as much support as possible to children's interests and ideas.

Focus on children's strengths and interests

A child progressing from infancy through toddlerhood demonstrates an amazing capacity to learn new skills within a relatively brief time. Throughout this period of rapid development, caregivers are able to best support the child's growing repertoire of actions and ideas by focusing on what the child is doing at the moment instead of looking for and commenting on what he or she is not yet able to do.

Children's strengths and interests, rather than their deficits, provide adults with positive guideposts to follow in adult-child interactions. Through their actions, children let caregivers know *Hey, this is me. This is what I like to do right now.* Tia's caregivers, for example, note that Tia is pulling herself up to stand. They provide her with low chairs and tables, sturdy boxes and blocks, and their own bodies to steady herself with as she cruises

Caregivers are able to best support a child's rapidly growing repertoire of actions and ideas by focusing on what the child is doing at the moment. This child is pouring sand from one container to another.

around the room. They watch for her first steps and are happy when they occur, but they do not pressure her or expect her to walk alone until she herself demonstrates that she is ready by taking her first unaided step. Similarly, a caregiver's observation that "Terrell is figuring out how to use both hands to hold the pitcher when pouring juice" is more supportive and informative than the observation that "Terrell cannot pour his juice without spilling it."

Caregivers also support children's continued interaction with the materials and activities they show interest in, instead of focusing on and urging children toward things they show no interest in. For example, Priya observes that one-and-a-half-year-old Jake often chooses to play at the water table and push the little plastic

Experience Versus Stimulation

"I don't think it's healthy to be *at* the child too much, to have him taste this, and smell that, and feel this, trying to enrich all aspects of his life. It's too much, it's intrusive. The normal kind of interaction that takes place in the course of routines, where there is some conversation and smiling back and forth and perhaps a little play, or in periods that are consciously devoted to play — I think that is what the infant needs in the way of stimulation. That doesn't mean the child's interest in other things shouldn't be encouraged, but he'll have that interest if he just has a chance to explore. Stimulation is something you *do* to somebody else. It's experience the child needs."

— Mary Ainsworth interviewed by Robert Karen (1990, p. 69)

boats from one end of it to the other. Based on this observation, she and her teammate discuss ways to support Jake's specific interest in water, boats, and perhaps other objects that can float in water. Focusing on boats and water, they decide to add to the water table two wooden boats and some little wooden passengers who fit into the boats. The next day, when Jake again goes to the water table, he exclaims, "Boh! Boh!" He picks up first one wooden boat and then the other and eventually pushes these new boats through the water. He shows no interest, however, in putting passengers into the boats, until another day, when he sees another child doing so.

Books are another example of when adults need to follow children's interests. Toddlers often like to look at the same picture book again and again — and again! Well-intentioned caregivers, eager to expand the child's literacy skills, may try to introduce new books, only to have the child pick the same book each time they cuddle up to read. The child may even want to look at the same one or two pages over and over again, pointing out and naming familiar pictures. Rather than urge, "Let's read something else today," supportive teachers recognize the child's need to visit a well-loved book as many times as he or she wishes. The child is getting something from the experience that the adult may not even realize — the comfort of the familiar, a new detail each time a picture is examined — but the adult appreciates and respects the child's need to do so.

When caregivers introduce new materials or experiences into the setting, they anticipate that children will warm up to and explore the new challenges on their individual terms and time schedule. Through their actions, children let caregivers know if and when they are ready to try something new. Caregivers therefore provide the materials and experiences that allow children to pursue their own interests instead of trying to stimulate or overload them with the things adults want children to be interested in. (See "Experience Versus Stimulation" on p. 160.)

In addition to supporting *what* children do, caregivers are also sensitive to *how much* children choose to interact with materials. Adults avoid the temptation to think young children, especially mobile infants and toddlers, must be constantly engaged with and stimulated by their environment. Quiet observation or even knowing when to tune out are also strengths that show the child is following his or her need to quietly absorb information or to simply slow down and replenish energy. NAEYC practice guidelines, therefore, advise that because children this age "can so easily be overstimulated, sensitive adults will ensure that a good balance is maintained in the levels of intensity of play — from active to quiet to sleep" (Copple & Bredekamp, 2009, p. 63).

Anticipate children's explorations

Caregivers providing an active learning setting understand that sensory-motor exploration drives infant-toddler growth and development. Throughout the day, therefore, they try to anticipate what their children will want to explore, so they can make appropriate preparations. For example, one caregiving team knows from experience that the first time they offer their toddlers pieces of mixed fresh fruit for lunch, most of the children will check out the new concoction, exploring it with their hands as well as their mouths. Some children will pick out only certain pieces of fruit to eat, liking the feel and taste of some fruits but not others. Some children will mash and smoosh bits of fruit, getting their hands, arms, faces, and even hair sticky. The satisfaction of this will distract some of the children from actually *eating* the fruit. The caregiving team allows for the fact that washing up children and equipment before naps will probably take a little longer than usual!

Because they value this fruit exploration as a learning experience for children, the caregivers remain calm and good-spirited about how little or how much fruit children eat or smoosh — and about the extra cleanup it creates. They also know that at another time, after the novelty wears off, children will most likely eat rather than "wear" their fruit.

Young children, especially toddlers, also explore the novelty of their environment through language. They are fascinated by words and love to learn the names of things. Caregivers, therefore, anticipate that young toddlers will constantly ask "Huh?" just as older toddlers and preschoolers put forth a litany of "Whys?" Rather than get impatient with these repeated questions, sensitive caregivers, therefore, not only take the time to supply the information young children seek but take delight in the eagerness with which they explore the world of language and ideas.

Encourage and acknowledge children's choices in exploration and play

In the course of their active learning, within the setting provided by adults, infants and toddlers make choices about what and how to explore. For example, one summer day, at outside time at a child care center, this scenario takes place:

Korina and Melody offer their eight toddlers dish tubs of blue and red (nontoxic) tempera paints and new fly swatters, thinking the children might use these to paint on large pieces of white butcher paper that hang at the children's level on the board fence surrounding the play yard. Initially, as three of the children gather around one of the paint tubs, Korina says, "Here are some big brushes for painting." The children look at her but make no move, so she takes a fly swatter, dips it in the paint, and uses it to spread paint on the paper. Two of the children then get fly swatters for themselves and begin to use them to smear paint on the paper and on the wooden fence. The third child watches awhile, then dips a fly swatter into the paint, looks at the paint-dipped fly swatter, and feels it with her free hand, thus covering her hand with paint. Eventually she tastes the paint on her hand. "How does that paint taste?" Korina asks her. "Sour," the child replies, wrinkling her nose.

In the meantime, the other five children (who also could have joined the painting if they had chosen to) have decided to engage in other pursuits: one fills a bowl with grass, sits at the toddler-sized picnic table, empties the bowl, leaves the table, fills the bowl with grass again, and so forth; another drives a big wooden truck across the play yard and back; another is busy opening and closing the doors and shutters of the little playhouse; a fourth is digging in the sand; one child "waters the grass," turning on the outdoor faucet, filling a small bucket with water, and dumping it out on the grass.

Eventually, two of the painters join caregiver Melody at the water faucet, where they become involved in rinsing the paint off themselves. "Paint!" says one child, showing her hands to Melody. "You painted your hands red and blue!" Melody says, admiring the child's hands. After the painters rinse off under the faucet, Melody offers them premoistened wipes to complete their cleanup. Later, the child who has been filling and emptying the bowl with grass carries the box of wipes to the little picnic table. She pulls the remaining few wipes out one by one and uses them to clean the table top. When the box of wipes is empty, she looks at it awhile, then takes one of the used table-cleaning wipes, stuffs it back into its box through the hole in the top, pulls it out again, and again cleans the table. Watching this process, Melody says to this child, "You really like the wipes, Angela. You figured out a way to get more!"

While preschool educators have long recognized the importance of choice in children's learning, infant and toddler programs are only now beginning to understand that offering choices also promotes physical, cognitive, and social

Caregivers provide these toddlers with nontoxic tempera paints, fly swatters, and large pieces of paper attached to a fence to explore. One child chooses to paint the paper while another child explores the paint by touch and taste.

development in the earliest months and years of life. It is common to assume that the youngest children are not capable of knowing and therefore choosing what they want. Yet, if caregivers are observant, they see that children exhibit preferences from birth on, influenced by temperament, the people and objects around them, their experiences, their culture, and other factors we do not yet know or fully understand. Recognizing the importance of child choice in motivation, self-discovery, and exploring the environment, HighScope therefore includes *choice time* — a sustained period of self-chosen exploration and play — as part of its daily routine, even for the youngest infants.

Help children achieve what they set out to do

When infants and toddlers attempt to do things they are not able to complete or accomplish, a caregiver's support can be invaluable. Through careful observation, caregivers consider when they might help children follow through on their intentions. Children may need additional materials or a caregiver suggestion to complete their task, or as in the story that follows, they may simply need a caregiver's attentive presence:

Keisha, an older infant, sits on her blanket, touching and patting a colorful cloth ball. At one point she pats it so hard that it rolls away out of sight, whereupon she looks up at Ann, her caregiver, who is sitting on the floor close by. "The ball rolled away," says Ann. Unperturbed, Keisha turns back to where she was playing with the ball, sees a small plastic bowl, and picks it up and contentedly puts it in her mouth. As Keisha explores the bowl, Ann quietly places the ball so it is again within Keisha's sight. She does this because she knows that Keisha focuses all her attention on things she can see — "out of sight, out of mind" is quite literally true for her.

Ann interprets Keisha's intention as not just wanting to play with the ball but wanting to play with anything she can see and reach. Therefore, because Keisha is now content playing with the bowl, Ann simply puts the ball within Keisha's reach (instead of distracting her by handing it to her). Keisha continues playing with the bowl for a while and then picks up a spatula. For a moment, she holds the bowl in one hand and the spatula in the other. Then she drops the bowl and uses both hands to guide the spatula to her mouth. After chewing on and playing with the spatula for quite some time, Keisha drops the spatula and again reaches for the ball that Ann retrieved.

Young toddlers often set out to do things for themselves. They enjoy the sense of independence they feel when they accomplish something "myself!" For older toddlers, it is also important to them to feel they are being helpful to others, for example, by setting the table or swiping at a spill with the sponge. The developmentally appropriate practice guidelines from NAEYC (Copple & Bredekamp, 2009) advises teachers to help toddlers feel successful in such activities by offering just enough support — by being observant (and not intrusive) but willing to offer a suggestion or two — so the toddler can take pride in the contribution he makes by cleaning up that spill or setting the table.

Give children time to solve problems they encounter with materials in exploration and play

A toddler may be struggling to fit a block into a shape sorter, or an infant may be straining to touch an out-of-reach toy. For adults, deciding whether or when to intervene in these situations can be difficult. Caregivers want to protect children from unreasonable frustration, but they also want to provide children with enough time to solve these child-sized problems on their own. If a caregiver always quickly steps in and "rescues" the infant or toddler, the child does not get a sense of being an active agent in his or her own life. Part of the equation in deciding if, when, and how to assist is knowing each child's temperament (activity level, adaptability, intensity of reaction, persistence, and so on) and current level of development. In the following scenario, Ann, a caregiver, responds differently to two different problem solvers.

Ann watches Theo, a toddler, as he tries to fit a wooden rectangular block into its slot in a shape-sorter box. He tries turning the block this way and that; he bangs the block and pushes it but to no avail. He persists with this problem without apparent frustration. Finally, he puts the block down, picks up a spoon, and easily pushes

it through the slot. He also drops some keys through the slot, along with several wooden beads. When he looks up briefly at Ann, she says, "You fit lots of things into that hole." He continues contentedly putting things into the slot.

Later that same day, Takumi, an older toddler, plays with the same shape-sorter box and bursts into tears after numerous unsuccessful attempts to fit the rectangular block through its slot. "It's really upsetting when the block won't go through the hole," Ann says stroking his back. His crying abates somewhat. "Won't go!" he says. "I wonder what would happen if you stand the block on its end," she says, knowing Takumi has often placed building blocks in this position. After a brief pause, Ann stands a block on end on top of the shape sorter, next to the slot. Takumi looks at the block in his hand and slowly, using both hands, turns it to an upright position on the shape sorter, next to Ann's block. Then, as Ann holds her block still, with both hands he slides his block into the slot. Then he pushes Ann's hand away and slides her block in as well. His whole body seems to relax with relief. He opens the lid, takes both blocks out, and puts them in again and again.

Sometimes, the problems children solve involve other people:

At snacktime, when caregiver Sonja picks up the napkins to pass out, Alex tugs at her arm and says, "Me do!" So Sonja gives Alex the napkins, saying "Alex wants to give each person a napkin today." Alex gives one napkin to Rob, two napkins to Megan, and a small pile of napkins to Kris.

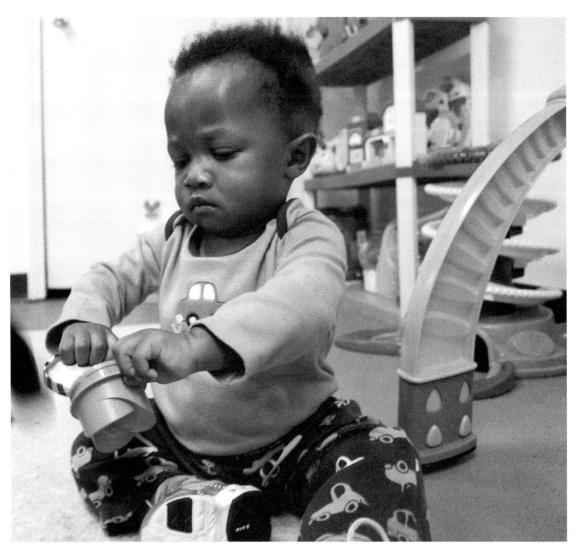

It is important to give young children the opportunity to work through problems they encounter with materials. This infant tries to fit a jar cover into an opening that is smaller than the cover.

When he sits down, he sees that he himself does not have a napkin and so takes several from Kris's pile. While this is not standard napkin-distribution procedure, Sonja notes that Alex and the rest of the children are satisfied with the results. Having encouraged Alex to try something on his own, his caregiver supports his particular solution.

Support toddlers in resolving social conflicts

For many decades, behavioral scientists assumed that infants and toddlers were too egocentric to think beyond their own subjective viewpoint. Yet recent research shows that even very young children "have a remarkably early awareness that other people have different views, feelings, preferences, interests, goals, and desires" (Thompson, 2008, p. 5). For example, we know from watching whether toddlers imitate a partner's actual behavior or do what the other person "means" to do that young children have an understanding of underlying intentions — that is, they perform the partner's intended action, not the actual act (e.g., if an adult "accidentally" drops something in the process of retrieving it, the child will successfully retrieve the object and hand it to the adult, not imitate the act of dropping it) (Goodman & Tomasello, 2008). Older toddlers learn to understand that there is a connection between emotions and fulfilled or frustrated desires. Happiness accompanies getting what you want; sadness or anger goes with being thwarted. They recognize that the relationship between wants and feelings holds for others as well as for themselves (Henderson, Gerson, & Woodward, 2008).

Of course, very young children still find it hard to "decenter" from their own desires and emotions, especially when they really want something, which is often true of whatever happens to be before them. Nevertheless, they can begin to use their emerging social understanding to take another person's perspective in their dealings with peers and adults. The assumption that toddlers are incapable of participating in resolving conflicts is thus becoming an outdated idea.

The ability to take part in social problem solving is a useful skill for toddlers, given how often they do become entangled in interpersonal conflicts. As they gain a sense of self and the accompanying idea of ownership, they begin to claim things as "Mine!" When toddler disputes lead to crying, hitting, or biting, caregivers calmly approach the toddlers in conflict, stop their hurtful actions, acknowledge the children's feelings, gather information, engage the children in describing the problem and finding a solution, and offer follow-up support. Here is an example of these problem-solving strategies in action:

Two toddlers, Kyle and Tony, both want the same blue toy racing car. As Kyle takes it out of the car box, Tony says "Mine" and tries to grab it away. "No!" says Kyle, pulling the car away from Tony and hiding it under his shirt. Tony cries and repeats "Mine, mine!" Sandy, their

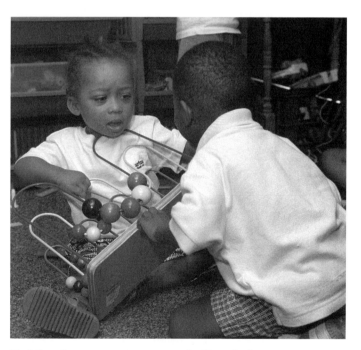

Toddlers have a growing sense of self and "their" possessions. "Mine!" this toddler says with his whole body when another child attempts to take his bead maze.

Steps in Resolving Conflicts Between Toddlers

1. **Approach calmly, stopping any hurtful actions.**
- Place yourself between the children, on their level.
- Use a calm voice and gentle touch.
- Remain neutral rather than take sides.

2. **Acknowledge children's feelings.**
- Name and describe the children's feelings: "You seem pretty upset."
- Let the children know you need to hold the object in question.

3. **Gather information.**
- With infants and younger toddlers, observe children's actions and describe the problem: "It looks like the problem is _____. Is that right?" Then look and listen for their acknowledgment.
- Ask older toddlers "what" questions: "What happened?"

4. **Restate the problem.**
- Repeat the information you have observed or heard: "So the problem is…"

5. **Ask for children's ideas for solutions, and choose one together.**
- Encourage *children* to think of a solution: "What can we do to solve this problem?"
- With infants and younger toddlers, describe choices or describe the solution they spontaneously carry out.
- Ask older toddlers for ideas and agreements.
- Check to make sure the solution is acceptable to both children.

6. **Provide follow-up support.**
- Tell the children, "You solved the problem!"
- Stay nearby to support the solution.

See the HighScope website and online store (www.highscope.org) for HighScope's conflict resolution resources that include examples and real-life filmed interactions of strategies to help prevent social conflicts and set positive and realistic expectations for resolving confilcts in child care settings.

caregiver, hearing Tony's distress but unaware of its cause, approaches the two boys calmly and sits down on the floor with one child on either side of her, an arm gently around each one.

"You seem pretty upset, Kyle," Sandy says to Kyle as she gently strokes his arm. "And Tony, you're sad and crying," she says to Tony while stroking his hand. Both

boys nod their head up and down, and Tony's crying subsides. "It looks like Kyle has something that Tony wants," Sandy says, noting the bulge under Kyle's shirt. "Is that right?" Both boys look at her and nod yes. "Kyle, what do you have under your shirt?" she asks with genuine curiosity. Kyle immediately pulls out the car. "My car!" he says, clutching it tightly in his hand.

"Mine!" says Tony, his eyes filling again with tears. "Oh, a car," says Sandy. "Let me hold it for you." She takes it carefully from Kyle, and holding it in one hand, she addresses both children: "So the problem is, you both want the car." Kyle and Tony look at Sandy and nod in agreement. "What can we do to solve this problem?" she asks them. The boys are quiet and still, taking in the situation. "You seem to be thinking very hard," Sandy comments quietly.

Eventually, Kyle turns to the car box, carefully selects a red racing car, and hands it to Tony. Tony accepts the red car with a broad smile. "Would you like to play with this red car, Tony?" Sandy asks. Tony nods yes. "So, Kyle will have the blue racing car, and Tony will have the red racing car," Sandy says. The boys nod their heads in agreement. Sandy looks at both boys clutching their cars and says, "You solved the problem!" Kyle and Tony squat down, push their cars along the rug, and make car noises. Sandy watches them for several minutes and then joins two other children at the nearby art table.

In this scenario, Sandy uses a six-step problem-solving approach to conflict (see "Steps in Resolving Conflicts Between Toddlers," p. 168). First, she *approaches calmly,* positions herself at Kyle and Tony's physical level, and establishes gentle contact with each child. She knows that her relaxed, unhurried manner and gentle touch will help reassure the children and create a positive climate for working out the problem. She remains neutral instead of blaming one child or the other for causing the problem. Her neutrality allows her

to mediate the dispute, which she could not do if she were to take sides. Her gentle touch, calm body language, and kind concern speak directly to the children of her genuine regard for their powerful feelings and the dilemma they are facing.

Sandy's first words, gentle and concerned, *acknowledge the children's feelings* ("You seem pretty upset, Kyle. And Tony, you're sad and crying"). Hearing their feelings described gives these toddlers names for their emotions. Once they get the message — through gentle touch and a voice that registers genuine concern — that an adult understands how strongly they feel, children are generally able to let go of these negative feelings. They are then free to devote their energies to thinking clearly about what to do about the problem.

When their feelings subside, Sandy *gathers information* from the children about what is happening. Since toddlers' verbal communication is still in its formative stages, Sandy does not ask Kyle and Tony a question that requires more than a single word, nod, or gesture to answer. (For example, she does not ask "What's the problem?") Instead, she describes the information she gathers from carefully observing their actions ("It looks like Kyle has something that Tony wants"). She asks the children for confirmation ("Is that right?"). And she asks Kyle a fact-finding question that he can answer with a single word or an action ("Kyle, what do you have under your shirt?"). Once Kyle reveals the car, she requests to hold it herself. This puts the disputed object in neutral hands and allows the children to focus more freely on the problem the car presents to them.

Sandy *restates the problem* for clarity ("So the problem is, you both want the car"). Then she *asks for children's ideas for solutions* ("What can we do to solve this problem?"). Toddlers are new to the problem-solving process. They take time to comprehend what might work next, and they are apt to offer some action as a solution to the problem rather than to state their solution in words. After a long moment, without saying anything, Kyle finds and gives Tony another car, which Tony accepts. Sandy sees that Tony appears to be happy, but she checks with him to make sure Kyle's solution suits him ("Would you like to play with this red car, Tony?"). Assured by Tony's nod, Sandy confirms their solution with them in words ("So, Kyle will have the blue racing car, and Tony will have the red racing car").

Notice that Sandy *provides follow-up support*. She verbally brings closure to the problem-solving process by recognizing the significance of the work the two boys did together ("You solved the problem!"). Note also that the *children* resolve the conflict, not Sandy. She interprets what has happened without making judgments or imposing her own ideas for a solution. As Kyle and Tony play with their cars, Sandy remains directly within their reach for several minutes and then goes to the art table where Kyle and Tony can still see her and gain her attention if they need it.

Most caregivers are new to this problem-solving approach to conflict. They are finding, however, that with thought and practice, they and the children get used to it, and they are finding that toddlers can be capable problem solvers. With the support of their caregivers, toddlers can develop and practice the ability to solve many of their own social conflicts. Throughout their efforts, they exercise thinking and reasoning skills, gain a sense of control over the solution or outcome of the problem, experience cooperation, and develop trust in peers and caregivers.

In its guidelines for developmentally appropriate practice, Zero to Three (2009) notes that science is constantly learning why relationships are so important in early development:

> *Group care may provide unique opportunities to support relationships and learning. Infants and toddlers develop expectations about people and themselves on the basis of how parents and others treat them. It is exceedingly important that in these first relationships, babies experience sensitive, affectionate care. When infants learn that adults meet their needs predictably and consistently, trust and emotional security develop. At the same time, infants and toddlers develop self-confidence as the adults around them help them master challenges in the world. (p. 53)*

Following the principles, policies, and practices described in this chapter, caregivers can help ensure their interactions with infants and toddlers promote young children's optimal development now and into the future.

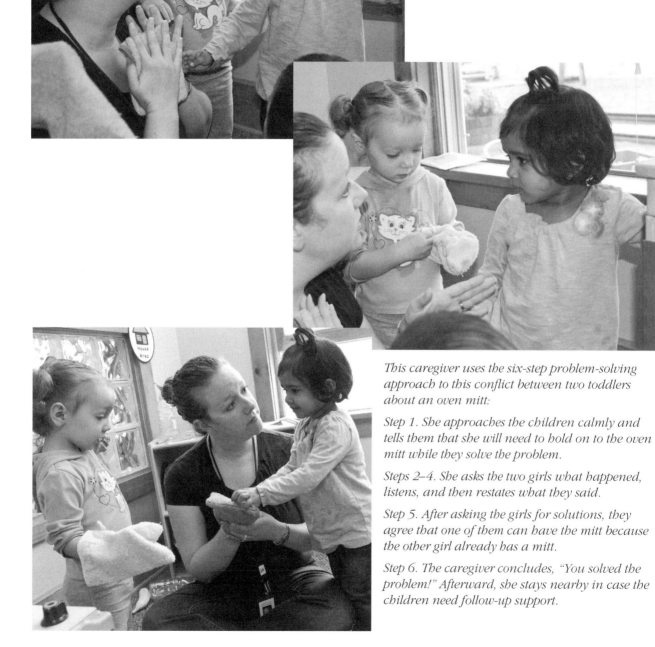

This caregiver uses the six-step problem-solving approach to this conflict between two toddlers about an oven mitt:

Step 1. She approaches the children calmly and tells them that she will need to hold on to the oven mitt while they solve the problem.

Steps 2–4. She asks the two girls what happened, listens, and then restates what they said.

Step 5. After asking the girls for solutions, they agree that one of them can have the mitt because the other girl already has a mitt.

Step 6. The caregiver concludes, *"You solved the problem!"* Afterward, she stays nearby in case the children need follow-up support.

Supportive Adult-Child Interactions: A Summary

Establishing policies that promote continuity of care

❏ Anchor each child's day around a primary caregiver.

❏ Create small groups of children who share a caregiver team.

❏ Keep children and caregivers together from year to year.

❏ Arrange caregivers' schedules around children's needs.

❏ Tell children and parents about caregiver absences and returns.

❏ Have primary caregivers record observations of their children.

Creating a climate of trust for children

❏ Touch, hold, speak to, and play with children in a warm, unhurried manner.

❏ Take pleasure in interactions with children.

❏ Respond supportively to children's needs and attention-getting signals.

❏ Give children time to interact and respond in their own way.

❏ Support children's relationships with peers and other adults.

Forming partnerships with children

❏ Interact at the child's physical level.

❏ Respect children's preferences and individual temperaments.

❏ Follow children's lead.

❏ Watch and listen to children (including using simple sign language).

❏ Communicate and converse in a give-and-take manner.

❏ Make comments and acknowledgments (including repeating and restating children's babbles and words).

❏ Look at children's actions from their viewpoint.

❏ Give children choices when they have to do something.

Supporting children's intentions

❏ Focus on children's strengths and interests.

❏ Anticipate children's explorations.

❏ Encourage and acknowledge children's choices in exploration and play.

❏ Help children achieve what they set out to do.

❏ Give children time to solve problems they encounter with materials in exploration and play.

❏ Support toddlers in resolving social conflicts.

1. Approach calmly, stopping any hurtful actions.

2. Acknowledge children's feelings.

3. Gather information.

4. Restate the problem.

5. Ask for children's ideas for solutions, and choose one together.

6. Acknowledge children's problem-solving efforts. Provide follow-up support.

In an active learning setting, caregivers take pleasure in their interactions with children.

4

Arranging and Equipping the Learning Environment

Active learning requires a spacious and inviting place

where babies and toddlers can freely pursue their personal

interests and goals. Active learning environments are

designed to provide freedom of opportunity and

choice with a consistent structured space.

— French & Murphy (2005, p. 59)

When adults enter an infant and toddler care setting, our first impressions are usually visual. Do we see a setting that is warm and inviting, with soft surfaces and gently lighting? Does it remind us of a home, rather than an institution? Do the furnishings provide comfort, and do the materials and atmosphere invite exploration? Settings should neither look too bare nor overwhelm children by bombarding them with excessive stimulation. The surroundings should appeal visually to the caregivers as well, who cannot offer tender care while working in a harsh-looking environment.

Next we observe whether the setting is functional and easy to use. Does the equipment and its layout meet the needs of very young children and the adults who care for them? Are things within easy reach so infants and toddlers need not wait to have their basic needs met? Is there an easy flow to caregiving routines and activities? Does the setting accommodate both active times of exploration and quiet times for restoration and relaxation? Does the arrangement of space and equipment allow for both social engagement and periods of solitude or one-on-one closeness?

The learning environment in an infant and toddler care setting must satisfy both of these criteria — beauty and practicality (Torelli & Durrett, 1998). Moreover, the needs of children and adult caregivers, both of whom who spend many hours a day in these settings, are equally important to consider in a center's design and layout.

"We believe that childcare centers should provide infants and toddlers with beautiful environments that support child-directed, child-initiated, and teacher-facilitated play. Childcare providers also deserve highly functional, easy-to-use, and aesthetically attractive work environments," write Louis Torelli and Charles Durrett (p. 1).

In *Caring Spaces, Learning Places,* child care advocate Jim Greenman (1988) summarized how an infant and toddler care setting should look and feel in these evocative words:

Imagine a room with light streaming in the windows, shadows dancing on the floors and walls, and a richly textured world of different shapes and sizes of furniture to climb on, over, around, and in — with places to just sit, places to snuggle. It is a room where you can sometimes make wild messes as you discover the mysteries of sensuous substances that often end up on you. It is a room with different places to be, just like your house — places that look, feel, sound, and smell different....It is NOT a room dominated by cribs, nor are you sandwiched between the glare of florescent lights and gleaming tile. It is NOT a tiny cell-like space where the day is divided into time on the crowded rug, the bounce chair, and the crib — nor is it a room filled with tables and chairs and a random assortment of toys, where activities are put out to keep the group busy. (p. 12)

A well-set-up child-centered environment promotes children's physical development, communication, cognitive skills, and social interactions.

Active Learning Environments for Infants and Toddlers

In creating an active learning environment for infants and toddlers, caregivers need to consider several practical issues:

- Given our space and resources and the children in our program, how can we arrange areas, equipment, and materials to best support children's growth and individual levels of development?

- How can we ensure that we meet all licensing requirements for the health and safety of children and staff as well as other criteria that support high-quality experiences specific to the program's funding auspices or accreditation?[1]

---

[1]Child care licensing requirements, which are the minimum standards for approved operation, vary by state and auspices. Recommendations in this chapter are guided by the criteria established by professional and administrative organizations, including the AAP, Zero to Three, Early Head Start, NAEYC, and the National Association for Family Child Care. Readers are advised to check the standards specific to the location and auspices that govern their programs as well as the facilities requirements that are consistent with the Americans With Disabilities Act.

- How can we involve families in the program?

- How can we make the setting a welcoming and responsive one, where children are encouraged to interact with materials, with adults, and with other children, and where adults are encouraged to interact with children and with one another?

If caregivers have carefully worked through these issues, the physical space they design will be one that proclaims its own purposes and provides "a world at the child's fingertips" (Greenman, 1988, p. 55). There will be a variety of places for toddlers to explore and to have different visual, auditory, motor, and sensory experiences as well as plenty of protected spaces for infants so they can observe the exciting goings-on of the room.

In a HighScope infant-toddler program, the learning environment promotes children's progress in physical development, communication, cognitive skills, and social interactions. It allows children to do what they are currently able to do yet grows with them as they grow. Such an environment neither unnecessarily restricts children from their natural inclinations to move (wiggle, roll, crawl, cruise, balance, toddle, walk, climb, and run) nor pushes children to do things before they are ready. The environment is consistent enough to give children a sense of security and mastery and yet flexible enough to accommodate children's changing needs and interests. Remove the children and the caregivers, and the learning environment

alone shows how it supports the basic development of infants and toddlers — through softness; child-sized furnishings; a variety of levels, vistas, and materials for children; and distinct areas for their eating, sleeping, bodily care, and play. Add back the children and the knowledgeable, trained adults, and you have a complete picture of an active learning setting in operation — a pleasant setting where adults observe, value, and support children's actions, choices, and ideas.

Broad Guidelines for Organizing Space and Materials

This chapter looks at arranging and equipping specific spaces for children's eating, sleeping, bodily care, and play. It expands on these three basic guidelines for setting up and maintaining infant-toddler settings:

- Build *order and flexibility* into the learning environment.

- Provide *comfort and safety* for children and adults.

- Support children's *sensory-motor approach* to learning.

Build order and flexibility into the learning environment

A well-organized room promotes young children's security, attachment, and self-assuredness (Honig, 2002). A carefully planned room that is stocked with a wide variety of materials children like to use helps ensure that they will be comfortable and busy, which also helps prevent conflicts (Lockhart, 2005b). Thoughtful equipping and arrangement of the learning environment is also essential to support children's physical and cognitive development.

While the need to explore and play remains constant throughout infancy and toddlerhood, *what* very young children want to explore and play with changes as they grow and develop. Therefore, the environment needs to provide both order and flexibility if it is to respond to children's changing interests, promote child choice, and help children gain a sense of control over their immediate world. As caregivers assess, modify, or arrange their infant-toddler setting, they consider the following ways to build order and flexibility into the learning environment.

Distinct care and play areas

It is essential that a child-care environment for infants and toddlers include *clearly designated areas* for food preparation and eating, sleeping and napping, and bodily care (diapering, dressing, and using the toilet). For health reasons, it is necessary that any area having to do with food be clearly separate from any area used for children's bodily care, that is, that there be two separate sinks for these routine tasks.[2] Organize each of these types of areas (food and bodily care) around a sink with hot running water.

It is also important to locate sleeping areas away from play areas so children can sleep undisturbed. However, at the same time, these sleeping areas, specifically cribs, should not overtake the whole room and leave little play area for infants. Once these areas are clearly defined, the rest of the space is devoted to exploration and play, and if possible, includes an inviting greeting area near the door, to help ease children's and families' arrivals and departures. This greeting area serves as a space where children, families, and caregivers converse and exchange information about the child and help the child make the transition to and from the care setting.

Play areas should include ample space for children to move about (e.g., roll over, creep, crawl, scoot and walk), to use materials, and to have social interactions but also provide some private places, where a child can be alone yet within the sight and ready care of a trusted caregiver:

> *Private spaces in the group care environment support the development of the young child's self-concept and personal identity....Instead of experiencing the stress of being in a large group all day, the infant can withdraw to a private space to rest, observe, and recharge emotionally. With access to a private space, two toddlers who are just beginning to develop a relationship can go off together. (Torelli, 1992, p. 40)*

---

[2]NAEYC (2007) program standards and accreditation criteria indicate as "emerging practice" (i.e., licensing requirements and standards are moving in this direction) that areas for sleeping, bodily care, and food preparation be separated by a solid barrier (such as a partial wall) or three feet of space from areas used by children for other purposes (criteria 5.A.08 and 9.A.01).

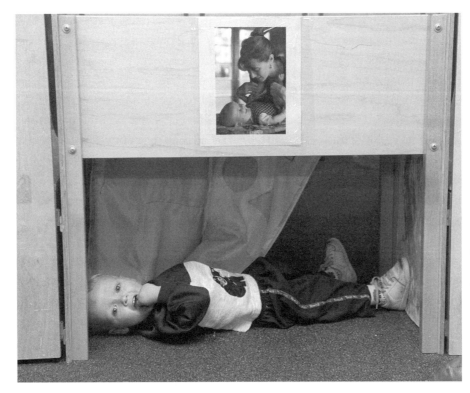

Very young children need private space — like this nook for time alone under the climber — and social space — like this sensory table that children can explore together.

One way to provide a private place is to use low shelving units and pillows, for example, to create a small space enclosed on three sides — just the right size for one child. Caregivers can also place a mattress in a corner or a cozy loft for infants to lie on; provide a box, crate, barrel, or tunnel for mobile infants and toddlers to hide in, crawl through, and sit in; cover a table or a climber with sheets or blankets to create a "tent"; set up small climbers indoors and out for children to crawl under and inside of; hang sheets to enclose the space underneath a loft to make a little house with a door just big enough for a small child; or leave some crawl space between the wall and an easy chair or couch. Greenman (1988) emphasized the importance of such provisions: "Nooks and crannies and their makeshift equivalents are not frills, but psychological necessities" (p. 149).

Likewise, NAEYC also includes "private spaces with room for one or two children" under developmentally appropriate practices for play and learning areas used by toddlers (Copple & Bredekamp, 2009, p. 97). Sometimes parental values and family culture may affect the families' view of such arrangements. For families that value independence, these private spaces make sense; for families in which children are always with adults, these private spaces may seem puzzling (Copple & Bredekamp, 2009). Depending on their background and temperament then, children may — or may not — choose to use private places. However, for those who need them on a

regular or occasional basis, they provide a reassuring escape from the hustle and bustle around them.

Of course, very young children also want to spend time with others. To support this desire, caregivers provide cooperative play equipment — small tables, rocking boats, side-by-side easels, and connecting riding toys — and arrange couches, chairs and tables, pillow groups, and small mattresses to create spaces for pairs and threesomes. Sink areas are designed to accommodate more than one child at a time so washing and cleaning up can be a social occasion too.

An open floor plan

The layout of a learning environment can have a direct affect on how the children behave in such an environment; "when there is a clear path from one interest area to another, the message is 'Come and see what else there is to do'" (Copple & Bredekamp, 2009, p. 97). It is therefore important to keep the floor plan as open and uncluttered as possible instead of using every bit of space for shelves, furniture, equipment, and toys. Early childhood licensing requirements and accreditation standards generally require 35 square feet of free space per child (or 40 square feet for children with special needs), not including kitchens, bathrooms, furnishings, and spaces used exclusively by adults (NAEYC, 2007). These requirements are based on both behavioral and health considerations, because a cramped space can make infants and toddlers more irritable and less secure and increase the likelihood of passing illnesses to one another (Aronson, 2002).

One way to achieve an open floor plan is to locate eating, sleeping, bodily care, and fixed specialized play areas (e.g., the block, book, and toy areas) along the edges of the room, leaving the middle of the room open for crawling, balancing, and walking. This allows the areas around the periphery of the room to remain fairly stable and thus familiar while the middle of the room is open to change as, for example, walkers become runners and climbers or block carriers become block arrangers and stackers. Such an open floor plan lets the caregiver easily see the children and respond to whoever needs attention; it also enables the children to look around, see what interests them, and get there easily (Lally & Stewart, 1990).

Open floor plans thus provide the advantages of freedom and safety to every age group. Mobile infants and young toddlers can test their emerging gross-motor skills through the unfettered movement of their bodies. Older toddlers can continue to develop their large-motor abilities. They can also coordinate moving their bodies and manipulating objects (push and pull toys, wheeled vehicles, low climbing equipment) without danger of bumping into things. Meanwhile, caregivers can keep track of children "by sight and sound at all times without relying on artificial monitoring devices," travel easily between individual children and groups, and have ample space to join children's play as they

maneuver within and between areas of the room (NAEYC, 2007, criterion 9.A.05).

Movable furnishings, equipment, and storage containers

Keeping built-in and heavy furnishings to a minimum and equipping shelves and platforms with casters allows caregivers to rearrange low shelves, platforms, large pillows, and mats as needed. Caregivers should remember, however, to remove any wheels or casters or, if possible, to lock them in place once they have used them to move a piece of equipment so it becomes stable. Shelves, in particular, need to be immovable and untippable for infants and toddlers who hang on to them to pull themselves up to stand.

Because children vary by age, interest, and activity level, furnishings can help create separate areas for individuals and groups to engage in either quiet or more boisterous endeavors. For example, older toddlers pursue some fairly delicate tasks, such as stacking blocks, assembling a puzzle, or spreading out on the floor to paint with brushes on a large sheet of butcher paper. One caregiver team supported their toddlers' need to be undisturbed in this kind of play by creating a "delicate work zone" in one section of the room. The area was surrounded by low, movable partitions, one of which incorporated a latched gate that older toddlers could open and close but younger toddlers could not. This provided the older toddlers with a safe, semisecluded space to work in and to access art supplies without being entirely

This toddler room has an open floor plan, which enables the children (with the help of their teacher) to create a temporary ramp to climb.

separated from the other children. Another team used similar low, hinged, movable partitions to set off a large safe area for nonmobile infants. The active toddlers played outside the infant area, but since a number of the partition panels were acrylic glass, children on opposite sides could still see each other.

Caregivers store small collections of toys and materials suitable for nonmobile infants in individual baskets, bins, or bags. For example, they can create a *treasure basket* with natural and household objects for children to explore (see "Treasure Baskets," p. 184). This allows caregivers to handily provide a range of appealing

Treasure Baskets

First conceived by Elinor Goldschmied (1989) to engage older infants and young toddlers who are beginning to sit or move on their own, a treasure basket is an open container (e.g., a box, basket, metal or wooden bowl) that contains a collection of natural and household items to play with. The items chosen for treasure baskets should vary in weight, size, texture, color, taste, temperature, and sound. These types of materials engage young children's minds longer than typical plastic materials.

Geraldine French and Patricia Murphy (2005), HighScope consultants in Ireland, describe the treasure basket this way:

> Once the baby can sit up, household objects can be collected into a basket for selecting, investigating and discovering. The Treasure Basket…is a medium-sized, low, round or oval rigid-sided basket, which contains up to one hundred natural and household objects. Objects can include: a pine cone; a lemon; a leather ball; a wooden egg; a natural sponge; a marble egg; a velvet jeweller's box; or an egg whisk. The only rules are that the objects should be non-synthetic, and that the adult should feel comfortable about what is put in. The inclusion of a lemon in the basket can offer opportunities for the baby to explore weight, smell, and texture, as well as colour. All objects should be checked for safety. The Treasure Basket offers choice and variety, and encourages exploration and independence. Babies spend as long as they want picking up each piece, feeling it, mouthing it, waving it, banging it, exploring it. (p. 64)

Treasure baskets contain natural and household objects for infants to explore using all of their senses.

items to the child who is not yet crawling, wherever he or she might be. With this kind of flexibility, it is not unusual to see a crawling child settle next to a shelf containing interesting objects to explore while a nonmobile child sits nearby playing with items selected from a basket his caregiver has placed within his reach.

Easy outdoor access

Infants and toddlers need daily play outdoors, where the opportunities for sensory-motor exploration are endless. Therefore, if possible, every indoor infant-toddler space should have access to an outdoor play area. "A trip outdoors provides a complete change of scene for infants," observed psychologist Thelma Harms (1994), "with different things to watch, and changes in temperature and air movement to experience" (p. 157). The outdoors provides a variety of surfaces (grass and wooden decks for lying, sitting, crawling, and walking; paths for wheel toys; sand for digging and making soft landings), a changing "ceiling" (the sky, clouds, branches, and leaves), softness (grass, fine ground cover, sand, blankets, and plants), and natural lighting.

Though weather is always a factor, it is important for children to experience whatever variety the local climate affords. Snow and warm light rain, for example, can be very exciting for this age group. The learning environment for infants and toddlers, therefore, should include a see-through protective covering near a door so children can observe safely the exciting

weather changes (Torelli & Durrett, 1998). Such an overhang can serve as a transition from indoor to outdoor play.

Provide comfort and safety for children and adults

To promote active learning, caregivers strive to combine the requisite physical and psychological comfort and safety for children with practicality and convenience for adults. Soft furnishings, fresh air, natural lighting, soothing colors, and pleasant sounds and smells, for example, tend to evoke a sense of well-being for infants and toddlers, who learn about the world directly, through their senses and actions. When the environment provides an array of interesting sights, textures, sounds, smells, and tastes and also warmly invites and safely supports children's active exploration of these things, children feel physically and psychologically comfortable. Protected from cramped spaces, sharp corners, toppling or falling objects, and slippery surfaces, they venture to examine their immediate sensory world. In a physically friendly setting that doesn't "bite back," children can feel pleased with their adventures and confident in themselves as adventurers. At the same time that caregivers are providing new interests and safe adventures for children, they can also include some features that children are used to, to make them feel at home in group care (see Pleasant reminders of home," pp. 193–195).

Torelli (1992) has reminded us that "a developmentally appropriate space is designed to be emotionally supportive for both children and adults" (p. 39). Thus, a psychologically comfortable environment also includes practicality and convenience — things that make the setting work for adults. NAEYC's guidelines for early care settings echo this concern for the adult: "It's important that caregivers as well as children feel comfortable. Long days in a setting that doesn't support the adults' physical comfort will add to their fatigue and stress, which is bad for children" (Copple & Bredekamp, 2009, p. 81). In addition, the equipment in an early childcare setting should be organized so caregivers don't have to unnecessarily carry and lift heavy things, which helps reduce their risk of back injuries (Aronson, 2002). As caregivers assess, set up, or modify their setting for comfort and safety, they should consider the following elements from the perspective of both children and adults.

Inviting floors, walls, and ceilings

Since infants and toddlers spend a lot of time on the floor, it is important that the floor be clean, warm, comfortable, and varied. Caregivers might cover one part of their indoor space for children with long-wearing, relatively plain, low-pile, stain-resistant carpeting. Such carpeting provides warmth, muffles ambient sound, is easy to clean, cushions falls, and provides a suitable surface for children's exploration and play and for barefoot babies' first attempts at walking.

When selecting carpet, caregivers should look for solid colors or heather tones. Carpet that is multicolored or has bold patterns or figures (animals, numbers, letters) not only is expensive but also can cause visual overload and make it difficult for children to distinguish playthings from the carpet.

While part of a room's flooring may be soft with carpeting, it is important to vary the floor surface, for example, with tile or wood around toilets, sinks, and eating areas, so that not everything is soft. Infants feel resistance with a hard floor, which helps them develop their gross-motor skills (Copple & Bredekamp, 2009). Different floor surfaces for mobile infants and toddlers also allow them to experience variations in texture and appearance as they navigate between areas. In fact, the feel and look of carpeting or tile can itself become the focus for play and exploration. Whatever the surface, however, it is important that it be in good condition, clean, and, if wood or tile, finished with wax or polish that is *nonskid*.

Walls and ceilings painted in a soft, light color (with lead-free paint that is not chipping or peeling) generally provide a more soothing atmosphere for children and adults than do walls and ceilings painted in one or more bright colors or covered with bright, busy wallpaper. Plain walls and wall coverings, such as bulletin boards and cork strips painted in soft colors, also complement rather than compete with the materials displayed on them (e.g., mirrors, wall hangings, photos, children's creations, samples of various textures). Electrical outlets need to be covered with

Light-colored walls, natural and soft lighting, carpeted floors, and comfortable seating make this space inviting and cozy.

childproof covers or installed high on the wall, well above children's reach, so children cannot poke things into them. All cords (electrical, shades, blinds, and so on) need to be out of children's reach at all times. Acoustical ceiling tiles also help to muffle ambient sound.

Soft places

Both children and adults appreciate soft places. These may include a corner of the room furnished with pillows and comforters; a mattress on the floor covered with a mattress pad and fitted sheet; and couches, easy chairs, and low, deep, cloth hammocks (hung over a carpeted surface). Air mattresses and large vinyl-covered mats and cushions in a variety of shapes and sizes can be used singly or in various combinations to build soft structures for children to explore and climb on. Outfitting the diapering and infant-dressing area with a thick, cleanable pad provides a soft surface for children to lie on during diaper and clothing changes. At higher levels, easy-to-grow house plants, sheer curtains and valances, and fabric wall hangings can be used to soften the look of corners and edges and add a pleasant texture and movement to windows, walls, and corners. (Consult a local poison control center to make sure house plants are nontoxic. Any curtains or wall hangings should comply with local fire regulations.)

Remember, too, that caregivers' laps, arms, and bodies serve as soft vantage points and places of repose for infants and toddlers. Natalie, for example, crawls over to her caregiver, climbs into her lap, and settles in to watch Mona and Chad negotiate the climber. Natalie herself is not interested in climbing, but from the safety of her caregiver's lap, she is interested in watching Mona and Chad in action.

Soft and natural lighting

Infants are especially sensitive to light. While they need light to see, they are less fussy and more comfortable in spaces lit by soft and natural light. In an infant-toddler setting, it makes sense to light the space as you would a home — with windows, window walls, skylights, and shaded lamps. Child care centers can install dimmer switches on overhead lights or, better yet, avoid them altogether in favor of sturdy wall and hanging lamps strategically placed about the space. "In planning the lighting," said Greenman (1988), "it is important to consider the plan from all angles, literally. Will there be glare in the sight lines of the children, including infants staring straight up into the ceiling?" (p. 112).

In the past, programs were advised to use incandescent rather than fluorescent lighting to seem more homelike and less institutional. However, as environmental and energy concerns mandate the use of fluorescent bulbs (regular and compact), programs can still choose those that mimic the soft lighting characteristic of incandescent bulbs ("warm" rather than "cool" fluorescent bulbs, with color temperatures in the 2700–3000K range). Using this new technology will also save on energy costs.

Purposeful sound

Infant and toddler care settings are full of different sounds to experience, create, and explore. There is the patter of children babbling and talking with caregivers and one another. Caregivers may sing a lullaby while rocking an infant to sleep or hum a soothing melody to help an overly tired toddler wind down for a nap. At group time, there are songs and chants for active little bodies to move to. Many of the objects young children like to play with make noise — beads rattle when shaken inside a box; a wooden spoon makes a satisfying noise when banged on a metal lid. Bodies can produce fascinating noises just by clapping hands and pounding feet!

Of course, in the midst of all these interesting sounds, there is also a need for quiet times and places — to nap, gaze about while drinking from a bottle, cuddle up with a book, or just take a break from the hubbub of activity. Acoustical engineers who help to design child care centers are becoming increasingly aware of the need to balance purposeful and meaningful noise, which stimulates children's senses and learning, from indoor and outdoor background noise (e.g., fan, heaters, machines, vehicles), which can actually interfere with development.

Researchers report that acoustics can have a significant effect on the speech and language development of infants and toddlers (Manlove, Frank, & Vernon-Feagans, 2001). Environmental design scientists at Cornell University, for example, noted that background noise, especially "irrelevant speech" (such as that coming from television, radio, or electronic devices), can affect a child's ability to understand language (Maxwell & Evans, n.d.). It is therefore critical that caregivers reduce unnecessary noise and instead provide sounds that will engage infants and toddlers without overwhelming them.

Sometimes, in a well-intended effort to duplicate the atmosphere of home, caregivers play background music throughout the day. They may think it is soothing or see it as an opportunity to introduce children to a variety of musical styles. While soft music may help children fall asleep, background music during play times can interfere with children's concentration. Background music may also distract the teachers, who are either entertained by it or listening to hear when it ends so they can put on the next selection. Music, therefore, should have a purpose. For example, it can be used at group times when children are singing and/or moving to music or at choice time when children

want to play instruments or march around the room. In a language-rich environment, children and caregivers supply their own music through singing, telling rhymes, tapping their feet and clapping their hands, and playing instruments, while recorded music is used for group times and at the children's request (Bardige, 2009).

Infant- and toddler-sized equipment and furnishings

Children are likely to feel they belong and have some control when the setting has furnishings and equipment that are sturdily constructed and sized especially for them. For infants and toddlers, this includes very low sinks, drinking fountains, and toilets. There should also be very low tables, chairs, stools, benches, toy shelves, and bookracks. All these furnishings need to be well balanced and sturdy enough to accommodate mobile infants who hang on to furniture to pull themselves up to stand. To an adult caregiver, infant and toddler furnishings may appear to be extremely close to the ground, and this makes sense — infants and toddlers, after all, are very short human beings!

Furnishings sized to infants and toddlers help create an environment children can often manage on their own, although adult help will still be needed. Sturdy, low, accessible toy shelves, bookracks, baskets, and bins encourage mobile children to find and use (and sometimes even return) play materials they have chosen. Child-sized furnishings and child-accessible storage also enable older toddlers to join

Toddler-sized tables and chairs and low sinks and drinking fountains help these children feel like the space belongs to them.

caregivers in cleanup routines. After meals and snacks, for example, toddlers will often help to wipe off tables and chairs that are within their reach. Even very young children enjoy helping others, as it makes them feel valued and competent. They develop a sense of community membership and begin to take ownership of the space where they spend the day.

All equipment and furnishings should meet both licensing standards and guidelines of the US Consumer Product Safety Commission (www.cpsc.gov). Generally, these equipment standards are more stringent for child care centers than they are for home-based child care (Aronson, 2002).

Adult-sized furniture

The setting, of course, also needs to have some adult-sized furniture for adults' physical comfort! A comfortable adult is also better able to meet children's needs. One of the accreditation standards of NAEYC (2007) includes that "adults have a comfortable place to sit, hold, and feed infants" (criterion 9.A.14). Adult-sized chairs and couches also serve a purpose for children by providing them with physical challenges *(How can I get myself up onto that comfortable-looking couch?)* as well as a cozy place to cuddle with a caregiver, a blanket, and a book. Simple camping chairs or bleacher chairs provide added back supports for caregivers and can easily be moved from place to place.

Having some adult-sized furniture also makes the setting look home-like. As Greenman (1988) observed, "A mixture of adult and child scale is valuable for both caring and learning and minimizes the teacher as an outsized Gulliver in a Lilliputian world" (p. 62).

Storage for belongings, extra toys, and supplies

Adequate and accessible storage space plays a big part in making infant and toddler settings workable for everyone. For their own sense of order and control, caregivers need a place to store their personal belongings. Adult-height shelving and cupboards and safety-latched closets can meet these needs as can adult-height hooks in the entrance area. If facilities permit, adult belongings may be stored in an area separate from the space that the children use. Many state standards and NAEYC (2007) also recommend that caregivers

These storage cubbies are labeled with the children's names and photos so caregivers and parents can easily store and locate children's personal items.

have a place where they can take a break from children and a separate resource area where they can plan and prepare materials (criterion 9.C.02).

Caregivers and parents also need a set of conveniently located cubbies, tubs, or storage bins — one per child — clearly labeled with each child's name and photo. These provide a storage place for extra clothing for the child, along with whatever personal items parents and the child may bring in from home — an extra pair of mittens, a special bear for naptime, spare pacifiers, clothes for the weekend away from home, and so on. (Children's medications and topical creams are stored on shelves above their reach or in the refrigerator, as needed.) Generally, the younger the child, the more space the child needs for storing personal belongings.

Most infant-toddler centers have toys and supplies that are not in use with the children at the moment. By keeping these materials in a storeroom, in a closet, or on high shelves well above the children's reach, caregivers can cut down on clutter and dedicate floor space and low shelves to children's play and the materials intended to be child accessible.

Safe, convenient adult access to appliances and everyday supplies

To keep the day running smoothly, caregivers need easy access to basic appliances (sinks, refrigerators, microwaves) and everyday supplies (bottles, diapers, wipes). In a well-designed infant and toddler setting, "the environment needs to be furnished, equipped, and organized to maximize the caregivers' time and ease of providing care: no sinks down the hall; no looking for bottles, training pants, or materials" (Greenman, 1988, p. 54). Caregivers locate clipboards, notebooks, and other information-recording materials where they can easily reach them as they care for and play and interact with the children. Items such as sticky notes or handheld electronic devices for jotting down brief observations may be stored in a pocket or clipped to a belt. (Given young children's propensity to grab eye-catching things, it is not a good idea for caregivers to hang them around their necks.) Careful placement of appliances and supplies not only reduces caregivers' steps but also enables them to focus their attention on children's actions and communications.

A welcoming entrance or greeting area

When space allows, having a defined place for parents and other family members to meet and mingle as they come and go with their children can help families feel connected to one another and to center staff, who have thought to provide this pleasant space. When establishing a greeting area, whether it be a foyer, hallway, or room, caregivers consider ways to make its decor and furnishings welcoming by including some of the following:

- Comfortable seating
- Plants
- Soft and natural lighting

- Photos of families, children at play, and staff (labeled with individuals' names)

- A bulletin board for posting parent-friendly notices and reminders to parents in the languages they speak and read

- Tables or front-facing racks with brochures, information sheets, notices of community events, coupons for child care products and child-oriented outings, and other items of interest, again using family-friendly vocabulary and language(s)

- One or more tables to gather around

- Space for strollers, diaper bags, and all the things parents and very young children routinely travel with

If space permits, having a separate area where nursing mothers can privately and comfortably breastfeed their infants also sends a welcoming message.

Pleasant reminders of home

Not everything in a child care setting should present novelty to children. Familiarity helps to create comfort and security and acts as a stable base upon which

This center's greeting area is furnished with comfortable chairs, natural lighting, area rugs and hanging plants, a bookshelf with books about parenting for reading there or borrowing, and a front-facing rack with information about the center and community events and resources.

further learning can build. Caregivers can consider ways to incorporate the following familiar materials throughout their infant-toddler setting:

Children's comfort items. Many infants and toddlers feel more at home when they can have at hand or carry around some personal comfort item, whatever it might be — a particular striped blanket, a stuffed gray dog with floppy ears, a pacifier on a green ribbon, or a blue ring-shaped teether. When children cling to these items, it is as if they are holding on to a piece of themselves, something intimately connected to home and family. They are happier with these comfort items in hand or nearby, even though *what* they choose to cling to — such as a tattered blanket — may look insignificant and even grubby to anyone but themselves! These items help children deal with their separation anxiety throughout the day or comfort them at other times of distress (e.g., when they must temporarily suspend play for a diaper change). Understanding this, caregivers permit children to hold on to or let go of these items at will.[3]

Family photos. Young children take pleasure in photos of themselves and their families. They touch, look at, and if they can talk, name the people they see as they connect the images in these pictures with the loved ones they represent. To protect photos from bending or smearing by eager fingers and hands, they should be covered with clear plastic sleeves or Con-Tact paper or laminated. Using Velcro, reusable plastic adhesive, or foam mounting tape, adults mount the pictures where children can easily see and touch them: low on walls or corkboard alongside children's play areas; on the wall alongside the diaper-changing table; on walls in the sleeping area, where children can study them as they fall asleep and wake up; on the floor, for creeping and crawling infants. Photos of children and their families can also be collected in small, easy-to-handle albums so infants and toddlers can look at them on their own and with others.

Comfort items help children soothe themselves throughout the ups and downs of daily life away from home.

---

[3]For sleeping infants in cribs, check local licensing regulations for whether these items are permitted.

Some caregivers suggest to families that children bring to the center or child care home a small photo album of their family, pets, and residence to ease the transition from home. If families do not have such photos, caregivers can consider taking some, with the family's permission, on a home visit or at the care setting, using a digital camera, cell phone, or other instant photography device. These photos should be updated periodically to capture changes that are meaningful to the child, such as the birth of a sibling, a move to a new apartment, or the change from sleeping in a crib to a bed at home. Not all families will want to display home photos, however; an alternative option is for children to bring a meaningful object from home that they can see and touch while at the center (Copple & Bredekamp, 2009).

Space for children's creations

Seeing their own creations on display can help to give very young children a sense of belonging. When they crawl or toddle over to a wall or bulletin board containing samples of their art exploration (e.g., their papers covered with marks and scribbles or streaks and blobs), they see familiar things that have emerged through their own actions. When a toddler exclaims "Mine!" while examining a personal creation mounted low on the wall of the play space, he or she refers not only to the paper filled with color, for example, but also to the space or territory it occupies. In a setting that includes examples of their creative explorations, children can see

A plastic-covered photo montage of the children mounted at floor level encourages this young toddler to crawl over and find herself.

reflections of themselves just by looking around. Displaying children's creations is another way to help them take ownership of the child care setting where they spend so many hours each week.

A floor-level focus

Since infants and toddlers spend lots of time on or near the floor, it is important to establish and maintain a warm, interesting floor-level setting. To achieve such a setting, caregivers look at their environment from the child's perspective, for example, by crawling around on the floor; lying down on their backs; and rolling over and examining what they see, feel, hear, and smell from a variety of floor-level positions around the play and care space. Caregivers then make whatever adjustments are necessary so that the surroundings present inviting sights (including clear, unobstructed sight lines), sounds, smells, textures, objects, and spaces from the very young child's vantage point.

Caregivers also consider how they can vary children's perspective and the sensory input they receive by periodically turning over nonmobile infants or repositioning them so they face in another direction. Other floor-level ideas include using clear Con-Tact paper to cover and affix pictures, photos, or other flat visual items to the floor or creating a sensory path by taping different textured items (e.g., fur, window screening, sand paper, rubber mats, vinyl tiles) to the floor.

Support children's sensory-motor approach to learning

To create an environment that holds and engages infants and toddlers, it is essential for caregivers to understand that infants and toddlers are eager to explore and learn directly using their whole body and all their senses. Early motor growth is so evident that we often overlook the corresponding changes in sensory abilities. Infants' visual perception, for example, rapidly increases in the first few months of life. By the time they are four or five months old, infants can identify familiar faces and also see shades of light and

dark (Copple & Bredekamp, 2009). Newborns orient to a parent's voice, and recent research in Germany and France reveals that even the crying patterns of two-to-five-day-old babies reflects the melodic rising and falling intonations of their native language (Mampe, Friederici, Christophe, & Wermke, 2009). Think of the faces infants make when they are introduced to new foods, as if saying, "This smells, tastes, and even feels different than anything that's gone in my mouth before!" Clearly, every sense comes into play as children engage with an expanding world of experiences.

Because very young children grow and change rapidly and individually, they need a dynamic environment with people, materials, and equipment that provide the challenges they seek when they are ready for them. At the same time they need enough consistency in their environment to allow them to return again and again to familiar things and experiences. As caregivers assess, set up, and modify their setting based on these characteristics of infants and toddlers, it is important to consider the following environmental elements that support children's sensory-motor development.

Appealing to children's senses

To support very young children's natural desire for sensory exploration, caregivers should include the following kinds of experiences and materials for exploration and play: aromatic materials and experiences; sound-producing materials and experiences; and materials to touch, mouth, taste, and look at, including a wide variety of found and natural materials so children experience more than plastic playthings (which have limited sensory appeal). The environment should also include open-ended materials; furnishings, flooring, and items with textural variety; and a variety of vistas for children's exploration and play.

Open-ended materials. Open-ended materials are objects or playthings whose use is not predetermined or narrowly limited in action or purpose; rather, children can use them in many different ways. A set of blocks, for example, is open ended because growing children can see and use them in different ways: Infants reach for, grasp, mouth, drop, and bang blocks; toddlers carry, stack, and make

A paper towel tube and a spatula are open-ended materials. They can be held; dropped; waved about; dumped in and out of a basket; and, of course, chewed on.

simple structures with blocks; preschoolers pretend and build with blocks, making increasingly complex structures, and use blocks for pretend-play props; elementary-school-aged children build elaborate designs, structures, and cityscapes of blocks and use them for tools.

A basket of large wooden beads is another example of an open-ended plaything. Infants and toddlers can do many things with the beads — handle them, hold them, mouth them, drop them, roll them, dump them out of the basket and put them back in, hide them under the basket, offer them to another child, bang them against the floor, and carry them in their hands or in a bucket or purse. A bead maze, by contrast, is less open ended. A young child can sit next to this toy and slide some attached wooden beads along a series of winding wire tracks. This device calls for a limited set of actions (sliding one or more beads along a track or spinning beads) and therefore engages a child's creativity less than the basket of beads does.

Providing infants and toddlers with a variety of open-ended materials like the set of blocks or basket of beads enables them to explore and manipulate the materials in ways that are personally meaningful and suited to their individual levels of development. It also allows them to discover and gain knowledge about the multiple properties and uses of the objects they explore. In these ways, open-ended materials are both more emotionally and intellectually satisfying to children for longer periods of time than single-purpose toys.

A many-textured environment. Another way to support infants' and toddlers' direct sensory-motor method of learning is to include in their environment a lot of different textures for tactile exploration. Caregivers can consider the following opportunities to incorporate or make use of textural variety in and around their setting:

- *Varied floor surfaces,* such as carpet, vinyl tile, and wood; outdoor walkways with small mirrors, ceramic tiles, or smooth stones embedded in them

- *Various types of movable surfaces to sit on, lie on, crawl on, play on,* such as tatami (straw) mats, blankets, pillows, comforters, fleeces, mattresses, and futons; a plastic wading pool containing sand or filled with crumpled newsprint

- *A variety of outdoor surfaces,* such as grass, fine ground covers, wooden decks and pathways, flat stone pathways, areas of sand, areas of soil, and leaf-covered areas

- *A variety of low-level wall surfaces/ coverings,* such as metal mirrors, cork, wood, butcher paper, foil, cardboard egg cartons, pegboard, glass brick, fabric, Con-Tact paper with the sticky side out

- *Various types of outdoor barriers or fences* made of such materials as board, stone, brick, chain link, rubber tile, straw bales, and tree stumps

- *A variety of fabrics used for drapery, upholstery, and pillow/mattress coverings,* such as corduroy, chenille, polished cotton, seersucker, ribbon, felt, silk, velveteen, leather, vinyl, suede, and knitted or crocheted pieces

Interesting vistas. Vision continues to develop over the first two years, as children's ability to focus and coordinate their eyes improves (Kellman & Arterberry, 2006). Visual acuity — 20/20 vision — is generally reached by age two. During this period, infants and toddlers initially look at things close-up but become increasingly able to see things at a distance (e.g., up to six feet away by the age of two months). It is therefore important to provide interesting visual experiences at a wide range of viewing distances for the rapidly changing visual abilities of infants and toddlers.

Child care settings should include lots of windows that are accessible to children for peeks into the outside world, which they usually find captivating. Infants and toddlers like to crawl or toddle over to a window or climb up to a window to see who is going by; to watch the rain come down and the trees tossing in the wind; to observe the activities of birds, butterflies, squirrels, and other local animals; and to check out passing people, trucks, cars, and buses.

To provide very young children with interesting things to see, the types of windows in the design of an infant-toddler setting may include skylights, floor-to-ceiling windows or sliding glass doors, low-level windows in walls and doors, and

a sun room or sun porch (good for plants *and* people). Staff of child care centers can also think about including child-level windows that look into other children's indoor and outdoor play spaces, allowing children to watch their peers at play. These kinds of windows "can function as an additional learning center," according to Torelli (1992, p. 40).

Even an adult-level window can be accessible to mobile infants and toddlers if a broad, sturdy platform, loft, window seat, or climber is placed in front of the window to allow children to safely climb up to stand or sit at window level. In addition, caregivers might consider locating the diapering and dressing area next to or near an adult-level window so, during washing and diapering, children can choose to look and perhaps talk about what's going on outside.

Caregivers should also think about what they might place or plant outside the windows for children's viewing and observing over time. They can, for example, add a window box planted with flowers or establish a flower bed, some flowering trees and shrubs, a meadow with grasses and flowers, or a rock garden with ferns and a small waterfall. To build some action into the scene, staff can add a windsock, wind chime, colorful and patterned flag or banner, birdbath, or bird or squirrel feeder.

An aquarium with a secure top with low-maintenance fish, aquatic frogs, aquatic plants, stones, and pebbles makes for an interesting and soothing indoor vista. Children are fascinated and soothed by the colors and motions of the fish and the plants, and caregivers find them calming too.

Providing space and materials for movement

As noted movement educator Rae Pica (1997) says, "Children were meant to move!" (p. 4). Children of all ages have a built-in need for movement, and movement in young children, in particular, is important to their development:

Early movement experiences have the potential to greatly enhance a child's self-concept because [they] are so personal and because success depends so much on one's own skills and abilities.... When such a positive atmosphere for movement exploration is established and maintained, young children may be more willing to try new things in other areas as well. (Weikart, 2000, p. 5)

For sensory-motor infants and toddlers, learning how to move, control their

In this open space, children have plenty of room to play with balls, run, jump, and use riding toys.

body, and get from one place to another are major developmental tasks that take up a good deal of their time and energy. Therefore, it is absolutely essential to include space and materials that support the movement tasks very young children are striving to master. Infants need to have freedom and room to wave their arms and kick their legs, turn themselves over, and roll. Eventually, they want to sit, scoot, crawl, pull up to stand, cruise, and walk. Once toddling, children are soon climbing, jumping, running, riding, and rocking (add to this all the tasks they perform in gaining control of arm, hand, and finger movements). To give infants and toddlers opportunities for all these kinds of movement, caregivers think about ways that their environment can provide variety in scale, multiple levels, and places for active and quiet play.

Variety in scale. We discussed previously reasons for having both child- and adult-sized furnishings. This variety in scale provides infants and toddlers with important movement experiences and allows them to relate positively to both their own close-to-the-ground world and the out-of-reach world of the taller people around them.

Caregivers can also provide variety in scale by supplying infants and toddlers with equipment, toys, and materials that vary in size. There should be cardboard boxes small enough for children's hands to put things into or carry and cartons large enough for children to get inside of; blankets sized for dolls and stuffed animals, blankets sized for infants and toddlers, and blankets large enough to drape over a small table to make a tent; and large rubber balls that are big enough to push or sit on as well as small, easy-to-handle tennis and rubber balls. Small buckets, pots, and pans are easy and fun for toddlers to carry, but large buckets, pots, and pans (like the ones adults use) give toddlers a chance to test their strength and balance. Small, light, high-impact plastic wagons are ones that new walkers can pull, but larger, heavier, wooden wagons that require more strength, balance, and walking experience to pull present a challenge to older toddlers.

Children who regularly play with one another may even discover that they can move a large object when they pull or push together. When an infant-toddler setting includes this kind of variety in scale, children have both chances to succeed and opportunities to be challenged. While they are developing physical skills, they learn important lessons about the properties of objects (size, weight) and may develop social skills as well.

Multiple levels. An environment that has multiple physical levels for young children provides them with opportunities to see and reach things above floor level, to balance and coordinate their bodies, to use their muscles to climb, and to experience safe heights. Infants enjoy the change of view afforded by multiple levels and eventually enjoy the challenge of crawling from level to level. Toddlers like to climb up to view their environment from different vantage points — an important early lesson in spatial awareness — and to sometimes feel as tall as adults or relate to adults face to face. To create a variety of levels (both indoors and out) for children, caregivers use mattresses, raised platforms, climbers of all sorts, ladders, hammocks, ramps, hills, benches, balance beams, large blocks, and carpeted steps leading to sunken play areas.

Places to suit different activity levels. Very young infants who are not yet creeping or crawling need safe floor and outdoor space where they can lie or sit to play on blankets, mats, or mattresses without being crawled over or stepped on by the more mobile infants or by toddlers. One way to create a safe play place for nonmobile infants is to provide them with their own room and outdoor area; if young infants, older infants, and toddlers share one room or outdoor area, caregivers can separate some part of the floor or outdoor space by surrounding it with low soft barriers, such as large pillows or bolsters. Low, hinged partitions made of framed acrylic glass serve the same purpose and may be more effective in the case of particularly curious toddlers. Being within this "buffered" space allows very young infants to see the activity going on around them, to see and be seen by their caregivers, and yet to play safely without being as isolated or confined as they would be if left to play in a crib or playpen.

To promote active learning, cribs should be used as comfortable places for sleeping, *not* as playpens or holding areas

for infants who are awake and interested in interacting and exploring. NAEYC guidelines for developmentally appropriate practices state succinctly that "caregivers put infants in cribs mainly to sleep, not to play" (Copple & Bredekamp, 2009, p. 81). Playpens should not be used as play areas for nonmobile infants, because they don't encourage infants to crawl and tend to isolate the children who are stuck in them, away from the caregivers and other children (Goldschmied & Jackson, 1994).

Nonsleeping children should spend limited amounts of time in highchairs, swings, bouncy seats, infant seats (e.g., a Bumbo baby seat), and stationary play centers (e.g., an ExerSaucer). These types of equipment should be used only when necessary and for a specific purpose, such as feeding an infant, providing a flat and stable surface for a messy activity (such as painting), or occupying a baby while feeding or changing another child. Time in any of these items should be limited to 5–10 minutes and never more than 75 minutes a day. Child care centers should also avoid purchasing tables with built-in seats for toddlers, because toddlers need tables and chairs that they can get in and out of by themselves.

Mobile infants need not only a large, open space for their active, noisy play but also smaller, separate spaces for their quiet, more stationary play. By providing soft quilts, mattresses, and pillows and lowered lighting in one or more corners of the room, caregivers can provide opportunities for quiet, less active pursuits, such

By placing pillows, furnishings, and toys along the perimeter of the carpeted area, caregivers leave the center of this area free for infants to rolls, crawl, and move about.

as looking at books, exploring a basket of rocks and shells, filling a tin cup with large wooden beads, or simply observing and listening to what is going on in the rest of the room. This leaves the middle of the room open for more active, noisy pursuits.

Toddlers also need their own places for active versus quiet play. For them, the corners of the room and areas along the sides of the room can serve as specific interest areas for looking at books, playing with small toys, exploring art materials, sand and water play, block play, and pretend play, while the middle of the room can serve, as it does for mobile infants, as a place for active play as they practice their emerging skills in mobility. Children's growing abilities should be driven by their bodies, not artificially enhanced by equipment.

Guidelines for Organizing Space and Materials: A Summary

Build order and flexibility into the learning environment with

- ❏ Care and play areas that are distinct
  - ❏ Food preparation and eating, napping and sleeping, bodily care
  - ❏ Places for social interaction, private places
- ❏ An open floor plan
  - ❏ Fixed, specialized areas along perimeter
  - ❏ Middle space left open for active play
- ❏ Movable furnishings, equipment, and storage containers
- ❏ Easy access to an outdoor play yard

Provide comfort and safety for children and adults with

- ❏ Clean, inviting floors, walls, and ceilings
- ❏ Soft places (pillows, couches, easy chairs, mats)
- ❏ Soft and natural lighting
- ❏ Purposeful sound

- ❏ Infant- and toddler-sized equipment and furnishings
- ❏ Adult-sized furniture
- ❏ Storage for belongings, extra toys, and supplies
  - ❏ Children's cubbies
  - ❏ Child-accessible shelves, containers
  - ❏ Adult-height shelves, cupboards, hooks
- ❏ Safe, convenient adult access to appliances and everyday supplies
- ❏ A welcoming entrance or greeting area
- ❏ Pleasant reminders of home
  - ❏ Children's comfort items
  - ❏ Family photos
- ❏ Space for children's creations
- ❏ A floor-level focus

Support children's sensory-motor approach to learning with

- ❏ Materials that appeal to children's senses
  - ❏ Things to smell, hear, touch, taste, see
  - ❏ Open-ended materials (found/natural as well as commercial)
  - ❏ A many-textured environment (indoor, outdoor surfaces; furnishings)
  - ❏ Interesting vistas (windows, skylights, aquarium)
- ❏ Space and materials for children's movement
  - ❏ Variety in scale (equipment, furnishings, playthings)
  - ❏ Multiple physical levels
  - ❏ Places to suit different activity levels
    - ❏ Active play
    - ❏ Quiet, stationary play

Applying the Guidelines to Specific Areas

The specific areas in an infant-toddler setting might include eating places and food preparation areas, sleeping and napping areas, bodily care areas, infant indoor-play spaces, toddler indoor-play spaces (including their movement area, sand and water area, book area, art area, block area, house area, and toy area), infant outdoor-play areas, and toddler outdoor-play areas. The rest of this chapter describes how the broad guidelines just presented apply to

each of those areas. (Readers should also check relevant licensing standards. For additional health and safety guidelines, refer to the manual *Healthy Young Children* edited by physician Susan Aronson [2002] and policy statements of the American Academy of Pediatrics [www.aap.org]).

Eating places and food preparation areas

Infants spend a significant amount of time each day eating, and what and where they eat affects their growth and development. Overall, infants' personal

Like bottle-feeding, beginning spoon-feeding is an intimate one-to-one interaction with the caregiver.

nutritional needs are best met in a safe, relaxed, peaceful environment in which a thoroughly familiar nurturing caregiver plays a major role. Child care standards generally stipulate that infants be fed when hungry, that food never be used as punishment, and that "feeding is not used in lieu of other forms of comfort" (NAEYC, 2007, criterion 5.B.12). (For specific health and safety information on preparing, serving, and storing food, see relevant state licensing standards and the US Department of Agriculture Child and Adult Care Food Program guidelines for child care.)

Nutritious food gives toddlers energy for exploration and growth, and a pleasant dining space supports children in eating, exploring their food, feeding themselves, and socializing. Small groups of toddlers generally enjoy sitting with their caregivers while eating and sharing observations: "Charlie, cup!" "What this?" "Marta, me, chicken!" "Big!"

Toddlers have the opportunity to socialize during mealtimes, giving them a chance to further develop their language and communication skills.

Location

In a child care setting, infants do not necessarily eat in or even near the food preparation area. Caregivers generally prepare bottles in a fixed location, but they bottle-feed infants in a variety of locations. For young infants, the bottle-feeding takes place in the arms of the primary caregiver, anywhere that the pair can find a peaceful place to settle — in a comfortable chair; on a couch; or on the floor or outside on the grass, nestled against a few pillows. Some infants are highly sensitive to their surroundings and prefer to settle with their caregiver in the same place for each feeding. Other infants are content to be held and to drink from their bottle in any comfortable location. As long as the infant is in the caregiver's arms, bottle-feeding takes place wherever it works best for each particular infant-caregiver pair.

For infants who are sitting and trying out solid foods,[4] eating generally takes place in a consistent location that is close to the food preparation area and that has an easily cleaned floor. Early on, the sitting infant might be propped up in the caregiver's lap, against a pillow, or in an infant seat while the caregiver offers food on a spoon. When infants are able to sit by themselves and are interested in picking up finger foods, guiding the spoon to their mouth, and exploring food with their hands, caregivers can provide them with very low tables. This allows children to sit on the floor or on low chairs or stools while

eating and to move away when they have had enough. Being able to get in and out of eating spaces on their own contributes to their growing sense of independence. This arrangement is also easier on adults' backs because they do not have to lift and lower children in and out of highchairs. Caregivers can also set up adult breakfast-in-bed tray tables directly on the floor, with the infants then sitting comfortably on the floor to eat from them (Gerber, 1996).

To promote movement for infants and toddlers and to support toddlers' independence, child care centers should avoid purchasing tables with built-in seats. Infants tend to be left in these seats for long periods of time, which restrains both their mobility and the chance to see their environment from different perspectives. Older infants and toddlers need tables and chairs that they can get in and out of by themselves, both to promote their emerging mobility and sense of autonomy. Some centers use small plastic molded chairs and a low, rounded table for children who are creeping, crawling, or walking. Such child-sized tables and chairs give the children to power to sit down (or get up) from the eating area (Gerber & Johnson, 1998).

For maximum convenience, it is a good idea to locate the toddlers' eating tables close to the food preparation area and running water. The toddlers' eating area needs to have an easily cleaned floor, since spills are frequent as toddlers explore their food and try to master a

---

[4]For the latest recommendation on when to begin infants on solid food, see the AAP website at www.aap.org.

variety of ways to convey it from the table to their mouth.

The bottle and food preparation area itself is conveniently located in an area with a sink (within sight of the children on the floor at play) at a distance from the changing area to prevent contamination. It also allows caregivers to warm bottles and prepare food in full view of the very young children in their care who cannot yet hold a mental image of their caregivers in mind and are therefore likely to become distressed if their caregivers "disappear" around the corner or into another room. If infants and toddlers share the same space, caregivers can locate and set up one food preparation area to serve both infants and toddlers.

Materials and equipment

A well-stocked infant food-preparation area includes, for each child, a set of bottles, a set of bibs, and a set of towels (to protect caregivers' clothing and wipe away drool), all labeled with the child's name. Personal bottles (bibs and towels) restrict the spread of germs and accommodate infants' individual formula or breast milk requirements. This area also includes the tableware for children who are beyond bottle-feeding — unbreakable (usually plastic) plates with turned-up edges, short-handled spoons, shallow bowls, and cups with spouts and weighted bottoms.

Toddlers who have graduated from spouted cups can use chunky, plastic drinking glasses that are wide enough in circumference to be held with both hands.

Additional equipment or utensils may be needed based on the individual eating habits of the children in the program, including napkins, smocks, aprons, or hand towels for children who no longer wear bibs and personally labeled bottles for toddlers who still prefer bottles to cups or who are in the process of switching from a bottle to a cup.

A refrigerator provides necessary storage for prepared bottles and food. Caregivers also need a bottle warmer (a slow cooker can substitute), a microwave oven, a sink with hot running water, a dishwasher, and cleaning supplies. Check local licensing regulations to see if specific food preparation and cleaning equipment or supplies are required or prohibited.

To minimize time spent on cleanup and maximize time with children, the eating and food preparation areas are stocked with enough bottles, spoons, bowls, utensils to last the day (alternatively, caregivers run the dishwasher periodically throughout the day). For older toddlers, who often regard cleaning up the eating area as a play opportunity, provide dishcloths, sponges, and buckets of warm soapy water along with child-sized brushes, brooms, and dustpans so they can help.

The type of furniture needed for infants' and toddlers' mealtimes has already been described in the previous paragraphs. We might add here, however, that the tables for toddlers should be big enough to seat three or four toddlers and a caregiver so they can enjoy the social interaction of eating together.

Storage

Since infants follow individualized eating schedules, caregivers need to prepare their bottles and food throughout the day. Organizing all the spoons together, all the bowls together, all the clean cloths together, for example, and making them easily accessible in one place minimizes the time that caregivers must spend away from children in food preparation tasks. Sorting food preparation items in baskets or on racks helps organize cupboards, drawers, shelves, and counter tops so caregivers can easily locate what they need. Bibs and towels can be stored in baskets or on hooks labeled with individual children's names, and unopened bottles or cans of formula should be labeled with infants' names and stored on a shelf or in a cupboard.

Caregivers store toddlers' tableware and a clean supply of their slip-on bibs (dishtowels with neck holes) in an organized fashion in cupboards or on shelves in the food preparation area, as close to the eating tables as possible. If parents provide toddler bibs, smocks, or aprons, caregivers label these items with children's names and store them in children's individual cubbies, in a bib "mailbox," or on individual hooks close to the eating tables. Food for meals or snacks from home are also labeled with the child's name and date and stored in the cupboard or refrigerator until needed.

Finally, caregivers should store cleaning supplies together, away from food supplies and out of children's reach, for example, on a high shelf or in a cupboard or closet fitted with a child-proof latch. (See p. 262 for a summary checklist of equipment and materials for the eating and food preparation area.)

Sleeping and napping areas

Although all children need sleep, sleep needs vary considerably from child to child and from month to month. Infants generally spend more time sleeping than toddlers and older children do, but even toddlers need a time and place to sleep or rest for an hour or so at least once a day. As children grow, their need for daytime sleep gradually decreases, although it continues to fluctuate for a variety of reasons, including illness, nighttime sleep patterns, special events, and changes in routine. Whatever is happening in their world, infants and toddlers depend on their caregivers to support their individual sleep schedules and to provide them with peaceful, comfortable places to sleep whenever the need arises.

Location

The location of the sleeping area varies from program to program, depending on the layout of the physical space. Caregivers set aside a separate and accessible room for sleeping, if such a room is available. In temperate climates and dry weather, the sleeping area may be outdoors on a shaded deck or screened porch. In either case, caregivers should have easy (and quick) access to the children. They also check on children frequently so as to be available when

In this center, the cribs are put in an alcove in the program's main room so that sleeping infants are separate from the main hub of activity but are easy for adults to see and check on.

children awake. If a separate room is not available, the sleeping area may be located in an alcove or a corner in the program's main room, where lights can be dimmed and noise and distractions minimized.

For health and safety reasons, caregivers should arrange cribs so that there is at least three feet between them (a requirement for infectious disease control) unless the cribs are separated by shoulder-height partitioning (Aronson, 2002). Caregivers are also advised to place cribs away from open windows, window blinds, and shade cords. Given the obvious danger, stacking cribs or bunk beds should never be used.

The AAP recommends that caregivers place infants on their backs for sleeping because this position has been found to significantly decrease the incidence of sudden infant death syndrome (SIDS). Infants, may, however, roll over and change their sleeping position without jeopardizing

Responding to Families' Values About Sleep Routines

In *Diversity in Early Care and Education: Honoring Differences*, educator and diversity expert Janet Gonzalez-Mena (2008) describes two contrasting patterns of family attitudes toward eating and sleeping. Pattern-one families favor a regular and predictable schedule, where babies are fed on a timetable and put down to sleep. Such babies often fit easily into child care programs. Pattern-two families follow the baby's natural body rhythms and ignore the clock — babies eat when they are hungry and fall asleep whenever and wherever they are tired. This pattern may clash with programs that follow a stricter schedule and regulated sleeping arrangements. For example:

> The issue of sleeping alone in a crib sometimes arises in child care. A pattern-one parent is more likely to put her baby to sleep in another room, or at least in his own crib in her room. She is most likely to regard her baby as an individual who needs to come to see himself as separate from her.
>
> A pattern-two parent may also have a crib but may not use it as much as a pattern-one parent. Some pattern-two parents never even buy a crib, preferring that their babies not sleep alone. Pattern-one and pattern-two parents may disapprove of one another. Each has strong reasons why the other is wrong.
>
> Most programs in Canada and the United States lean more toward pattern one than pattern two and are dedicated to the idea that each child needs a crib to sleep in, and there is often a licensing regulation to back up the program's policy. (p. 74)

Gonzalez-Mena describes a refugee family that enrolled their infant in a center program. The baby had never slept by himself and was terrified when put alone in a crib in a darkened room. The only place he could fall asleep was near someone, amidst the activity of the playroom. Staff members were conflicted. They wanted to honor this family's cultural pattern, but state licensing requirements got in the way. Fortunately, the program was able to persuade their state licensors to grant them a waiver in this case, so the infant was able to sleep near the play area where *he* felt calm and safe.

their health. In 2005, the AAP issued additional clarifications: They no longer recognize side sleeping as an alternative to full back sleeping, emphasize the rollover danger of adults sleeping in the same bed with infants, and consider it safe to put children to sleep with pacifiers because they fall out of children's mouths shortly after they are asleep. Studies by the US Consumer Product Safety Commission also document an association between various types of bedding materials and infant deaths. Given that new research on safe sleeping practices for young children is continually emerging, it is best to check the latest recommendations at the AAP website (www.aap.org).

Some parents may wish their children to sleep, or at least fall asleep, in their caregiver's arms or cuddled up next to another infant or older child, on the couch, on the floor, or wherever they are when sleep overtakes them. When this is the case, it is important for caregivers to listen carefully to parents and together find a sleeping place in the program setting that works for parents, children, and caregivers. If necessary, caregivers work with licensing personnel to accommodate cultural differences in where and how infants fall asleep. (See "Responding to Families' Values About Sleep Routines," p. 211.)

In settings where toddlers are in a separate room from infants, at naptime the toddler's central play area may be set up with cots to become the napping area. This arrangement works when all the toddlers within a given small group of toddlers rest at approximately the same time each day. While this approach to napping is an efficient use of space, it can be somewhat disconcerting to toddlers unless they can each nap in the same, familiar spot every day. Even then, some children may find it difficult to fall asleep when they have a full view of inviting toys and play materials; for such children, some shelves and equipment might need to be temporarily turned to the wall or covered with a sheet or drape. Cots should be located out of the pathways children and adults use going to and from the bathroom.

Equipment and materials

The sleeping equipment and materials needed for each infant generally include a cradle, basket, or crib (depending on the age and comfort needs of the infant), a firm and snugly fitting mattress, bedding (mattress pad, fitted sheet, firmly tucked-in blanket), and the infant's particular comfort items ("blankie," teddy, soft toy) from home. (See the previous discussion of SIDS and safe sleeping practices for safety recommendations.) Cribs (cradles, baskets), bedding, pacifiers, and older infants' and toddlers' comfort items are labeled to help prevent the spread of germs and to create a familiar, personalized place where each child can fall asleep and wake up comfortably. At the same time, there may be occasions when the parent-caregiver team, following the cues of the particular child or children involved, takes exception to the one-child-per-crib practice, and for example, puts siblings or twins to sleep in the same crib or sleeping space.

Young toddlers may continue for some time to nap in the cribs they slept in as infants. However, somewhere between their first and third year, most toddlers generally move from a crib to a cot. Bedding for older infants and toddlers includes a sheet to cover the cot and a blanket for the child to snuggle under, which are labeled for individual children. In addition, many older infants and toddlers prefer to nap with some personal item that gives them comfort. If center staff, rather than parents, launder soiled bedding, a washer and a dryer for this purpose need to be located somewhere in the center. Alternatively, some centers may keep a large supply of clean bedding on hand and use a laundromat or a laundry service on a regular basis.

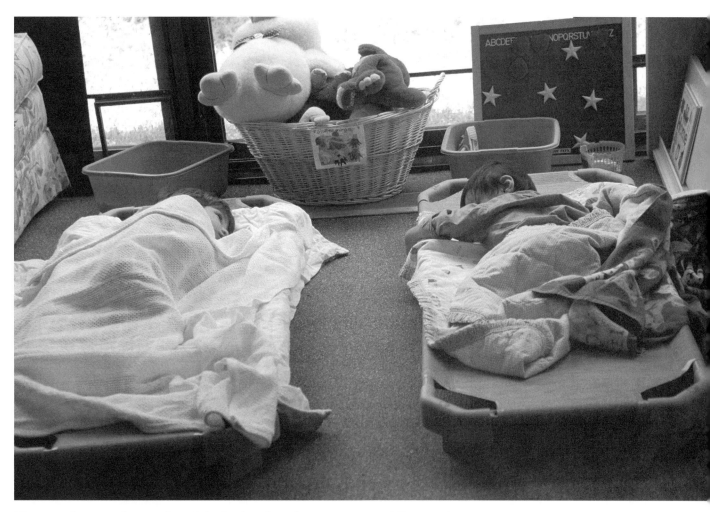

The space between the couch and the bookrack makes a cozy two-toddler napping spot.

Storage

In an adult-accessible cupboard in the sleeping area, caregivers store extra clean bedding and safe comfort items for each child. These can be on a shelf or in a basket labeled with the child's name. Soiled bedding can be placed in a closed hamper that is located in the changing area or next to the washer and dryer. Some centers keep soiled items in sealed bags until they can be put in the hamper or until they can be taken home by parents to launder and return.

If the sleeping area is not permanently set up, caregivers stack the cots, stripped of bedding, in a clean, out-of-the-way but accessible place. The bedding currently in use on cots can be folded and put on a shelf above the stored cots, or it can be folded and placed on top of each cot; in this way, when cots are stacked, one child's bedding does not come in contact with another child's. Crib bedding currently in use need not be stripped if the cribs are permanently set up. Similarly, safe comfort items can be kept in their individualized cribs or in their cubbies. (See p. 263 for a summary checklist of equipment and materials for the sleeping and napping area.)

Bodily care areas

The infant diapering and dressing area should be convenient to use and easy to keep clean. It is also important that the diapering and dressing area be inviting and interesting enough that infants willingly spend time there even though they might rather be on the floor playing and moving about.

Each toddler moves from diapers to underpants at his or her own pace. As walkers and active learners, toddlers are generally eager to take on the self-help tasks involved in their own bodily care. They rely on caregivers to set up changing

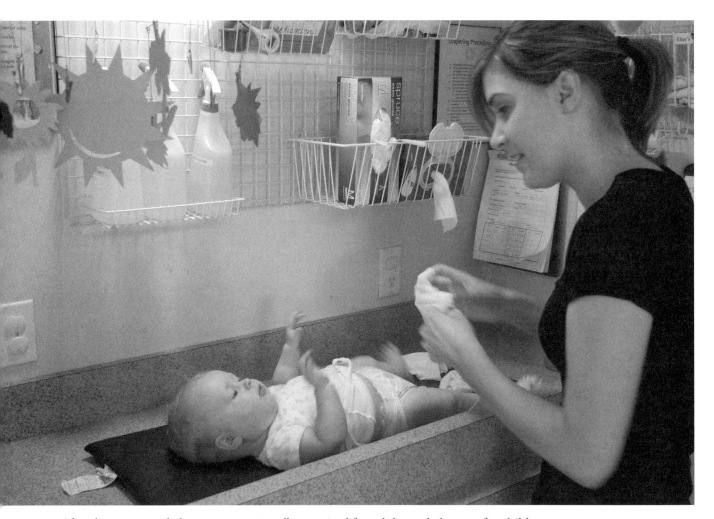

This diapering and changing area is well organized for adults and pleasant for children.

areas and toddler bathrooms in ways that allow them to exercise their developing motor abilities and growing desire to do things for themselves.

Location

For the sake of sanitation, the diapering and dressing area needs to be located next to a sink and at a distance from eating and food preparation areas in a well-ventilated space that can be easily sanitized, as licensing regulations generally prohibit the use of air-freshening sprays, chemicals, and deodorizers in areas that are used by children. To be more respectful of this intimate part of a child's routine, the diapering and dressing area needs to be away from the entrance of the room where traffic is coming and going most of the day.

In planning the location for the bodily care area, it is important to consider how caregivers will keep other children in view when using these areas so that the caregiver who is diapering or dressing an infant can provide reassurance to other children in her care. Additionally, locating the diapering and dressing area next to a window or mirror provides a view for children and caregivers to enjoy while engaged in these tasks. Mirrors also "reinforce the message that the program…promote[s] children recognizing themselves and growing their own unique personalities" (Raikes & Edwards, 2009, p. 139). Mirrors can also help very young children see what is happening and, in this way, participate in the diapering process.

Locating the toddler bathroom directly off the main toddler play area gives children the easiest access to toilets. Otherwise, they would have to wait for caregivers to take them out of the room and down the hallway to the bathroom. If the toddlers' bathroom is not directly accessible to their play space, centers should allocate space in or next to the diapering area for small portable toilets or potty chairs for toddlers to use as needed throughout the day.

When building or creating a new infant-toddler facility, program directors can consider combining the diapering area and the toddler bathroom into one room within or off the main indoor play space, making the bathroom large and dividing it from the rest of the room with low walls (around 48 inches high) so children in the main play space can easily see and be seen by caregivers as they assist children in bodily care routines.

Equipment and materials

The focal points of the diapering and dressing area are the sink and a sturdy changing table or counter about 36 inches high, with low, raised sides (to prevent the child from rolling off) and an easily cleaned soft pad. If the changing table is used for toddlers as well as infants, it should include a movable set of steps that the toddlers can climb to get themselves up to the changing table. Alternatively, centers can have a separate, climb-up changing table for toddlers; this option both supports toddlers' physical

A climb-up changing table supports toddlers' "me-do-it" spirit and saves caregivers' backs!

development and sense of control and helps prevent caregiver back strain.

Materials for this area include a supply of clean diapers and extra clean clothes and a hairbrush (as needed) for each child; creams (as needed); diaper fasteners and diaper covers (as needed), disposable wipes or soap, and a supply of individual washcloths for each child; disinfectants and cleaning supplies, such as a spray bottle of water and bleach or a roll of clean paper for covering the diaper-changing surface; disposable, protective gloves for the caregiver; closed, foot-operated containers for the soiled diapers, soiled wipes, and the used changing-table covers; and hampers and sealable bags for soiled washcloths, clothes, and (if used) cloth diapers that are on their way home or to the washing machine.

Caregivers may also stock the area with one or more containers of small toys and objects for children to hold and play with while they are being changed. These items should be washable and frequently cleaned to prevent spread of contamination from bodily waste. While cleanliness is a particular concern for the small toys kept in this area, it is important to provide a choice of objects for infants to play with to help children retain some control over diaper changing, an event about which they have little choice.

The toddlers' bathroom should include very low, toddler-sized toilets and toilet paper in dispensers children can easily reach. If the facility's toilets are too high for toddlers, caregivers can add step stools

In this child-friendly bathroom, toddlers can reach everything they need — toilet paper, faucets, soap, and towels — all by themselves. A caregiver contributed her artistic talents to make this area visually appealing to both adults and children.

or provide low, portable toilets or potty chairs, which are emptied into the full-sized toilets and disinfected after each use. A low sink or a stable set of steps leading up to the sink in the toddlers' bathroom enables children to easily reach the tap (it should be an automatic tap or a lift tap that is easy for children to use and, for safety, the hot water should be no more than 110° F). At the hand-washing sink, pump soap and a paper-towel dispenser should be mounted within toddler reach. Alternatively, caregivers can hang a set of cloth hand towels on low pegs labeled with individual children's photos, so

each child can recognize and use his or her own towel. Having a mirror over the sink allows toddlers to watch themselves as they wash and further promotes the emergence of their self-recognition and self-identity (Raikes & Edwards, 2009).

Storage

Each infant's diapers, extra clothing, and other diapering supplies should be stored in a clearly labeled container; large, resealable plastic bag; or pillowcase in cupboards or on shelves that are easily accessible to the caregiver as she stands at the changing table. These cupboards and shelves can be restocked daily, or as necessary, from some larger, less convenient storage areas. Older toddlers' supplies of extra diapers, underpants, and clothing changes can be stored in their cubbies, so the children can get these items themselves and bring them to the bathroom or diapering area as needed. Extra hand-washing soap, paper towels, toilet paper, and cleaning supplies for this area should be stored safely out of toddlers' reach. (See p. 264 for a summary checklist of equipment and materials for the diapering, dressing, and bathroom area.)

Infant play spaces

Any indoor play space intended for infants needs to be on or near the floor where infants can safely move and explore their immediate environment, still keep their caregiver in sight, and engage her attention. When their play space provides comfortable surroundings and interesting materials, this piques infants' curiosity and encourages them to interact with people and materials. It may help to think of this indoor play space as the essential laboratory where, through their senses and actions and movement, infants learn about their physical and social world.

Location

An indoor play space for infants (including those nonmobile and those mobile) may be located any place within the room or setting that meets the following criteria:

- It is physically separate from the food preparation/eating, sleeping, and diapering/dressing areas.

- It is out of the path of major traffic.

- It is large enough for three or four infants to lie, move, roll, sit, creep, crawl, or play without crowding.

With these criteria in mind, it often makes sense to locate the areas for food preparation/eating, sleeping, and diapering/dressing, and also any specialized or fixed play areas, along the edges of the room, leaving the middle of the room open for mobile children to creep, crawl, balance, and play on movable mats, ramps, and steps.

Safe space for nonmobile infants. A play space for infants who are not yet creeping or crawling may be established in a fixed location, for example, on a raised carpeted platform or a covered mattress bounded by walls, low windows, and/or cushions. Another play space may be defined by a large blanket or quilt on which an infant or a small group of infants are lying. Caregivers may change the location of this blanket play space from day to day to accommodate whatever else is going on in the room and to provide the infants on the blankets with a variety of interesting vistas. If there are also mobile infants and toddlers playing in the immediate vicinity, caregivers can encircle the nonmobile infants' play space by buffering, as described on page 202.

Safe space for mobile infants. Creepers and crawlers require more space than

This infant area includes a carpeted floor with plenty of room to lie, roll, and creep; pillows to support or buffer nonmobile infants; a cozy alone space inside of an unused fireplace; low shelves and baskets within easy reach; mirrors at eye level; and carpeted stairs for more mobile infants to crawl up and look out the window.

nonmobile infants do. Mobile infants may start out on their own low platform, mattress, or blanket and gradually work their way across the floor to the couch, the window, the fish tank, a caregiver or another child, or any object that attracts their attention. It is important to locate their play space where it is clear of such hazards as swinging or opening doors and where it can accommodate a variety of

levels and things to crawl into and behind. Again, an open central area may best serve this purpose.

Equipment and materials

As active learners, infants need a variety of open-ended materials that support their exploratory, sensory-motor approach to learning. The following types of playthings meet these criteria:

Babies take great interest in everyday materials. A metal tin, chain, pumice stone and brush, address book, and even edible flowers are easy to grasp and appealing to look at, touch, smell, listen to, or taste.

- *Pleasant reminders of home.* See pages 193–195 for a discussion of comfort items and family photographs.

- *Materials that appeal to children's senses.* This includes the general kinds of items discussed earlier, on pages 196–200. For a checklist of specific materials that appeal to children's senses, see pages 265–267. Note that many of the materials on this list appeal to more than one sense. Also, most of the materials suggested are ones that can be found at home and in nature rather than purchased from toy stores or catalogs. Commercial toys are usually (but not always) durable, colorful, safe, and washable, but they should not be the only types of things infants explore and play with. Inexpensive materials found both indoors and out often hold a special fascination for children. However, in providing either commercial or found playthings to infants (and toddlers), adults need to be alert to safety issues and potential health hazards, such as allergies. (See "Choosing Safe Materials for Infants and Toddlers" on p. 222.)

- *Materials and equipment that encourage movement.* Infants spend a lot of time rolling, maneuvering themselves into a sitting position, scooting, crawling, and pulling themselves upright. They need equipment and materials that, instead of restricting them, allow them to move in these ways on a variety of physical levels and surfaces. (See "Why Not Infant Swings,

Balloons enclosed in mesh bags and hung from the ceiling invite exploration.

Seats, Stationary Play Centers, and Walkers?" on p. 224.) Also, because infants enjoy initiating and repeating satisfying actions, they need objects and materials that readily respond to their movements rather than playthings that are self-propelled or controlled by adults. (See p. 268 for a checklist of movement-supporting materials and equipment for children at various stages.)

Choosing Safe Materials for Infants and Toddlers

Safety is a primary consideration in choosing play materials for infants and toddlers. Check toys and equipment frequently, and do minor repairs or discard toys as needed. Guidelines for choosing safe materials include:

Toys and materials

- Choose toys that can be washed many times without damage (e.g., toys that can be washed in the sink or put through the dishwasher; cloth toys that can be laundered).

- Keep toys designed specifically for older children out of the reach of younger children. Use the manufacturer's stated age for a toy as a guideline.

- Examine toys for sharp, jagged edges, or small pieces that can be easily broken off and swallowed. Pull on the heads/limbs of dolls to make sure they won't come off.

- Cover hinges and joints to prevent fingers from getting pinched or caught.

- Cut off or shorten strings on pull toys that are long enough to wrap around a child's neck.

- Bend plastic toys to test for brittleness.

- Look for the nontoxic label on painted toys.

- Look for the flame retardant label on all cloth toys.[5] Check seams for tearing and loose or weak threads.

- Remove toys hung across cribs when children begin to sit or get on their hands and knees.

- When choosing art materials, opt for wet clay; water-based paints, paste, and glue; natural dyes; and black newsprint.

- Assume all plants are toxic unless known otherwise, and check with the local poison control center.

- Ask parents about potential allergies to nontoxic plants and other natural items.

Gross-motor equipment (indoors and outdoors)

- Be sure riding toys are stable and well balanced. Provide helmets for riding toys with wheels more than 20" in diameter. Remove helmets *before* children get off so they do not catch on handles or other objects.

- Provide impact-absorbing surfaces warranted to meet the safety standards of the ASTM International (www.astm.org).

- Do not use trampolines.

Acknowledge when children play with toys and equipment in safe ways, making descriptive (not praising) comments. If children use materials in ways that could lead to injury, suggest and model proper ways to use the materials safely, and, for older toddlers, encourage them to offer safe-play solutions.

For additional information, see Aronson (2002, pp. 25–26); AAP, American Public Health Association, & National Resource Center for Health and Safety in Child Care (2002); Consumer Product Safety Commission (www.cpsc.gov); and, for outdoor areas, National Recreation and Park Association (www.nrpa.org) and National Program for Playground Safety (www.uni.edu/playground).

---

[5]Preliminary research (Herbstman et al., 2010) finds a link between prenatal exposure to the flame retardant PBDE and children's neurodevelopment. Consult the resources listed here for current information on safe flame retardants.

- *Balls*. Balls deserve special mention as toys that encourage children's movement. Wiffle balls, as well as cloth, wool, leather, rubber, and tennis balls, are wonderfully responsive infant toys. They are always poised for action and easy to set in motion. Young infants enjoy both tracking their movement and making them move. Once infants are mobile, they enjoy setting balls in motion and crawling after them as they roll across the floor. In a sense, balls serve as infant guides through space.

- *Wheeled vehicles and animals*. Like balls, simple, sturdy, easy-to-grasp toy vehicles and animals with large wheels or rollers are easy and satisfying for sitting children to set in motion. Practiced crawlers also enjoy pushing them or rolling them along under one hand as they crawl.

- *Mirrors*. An infant's reflection in a mirror responds immediately to the infant. When the infant looking into the mirror moves, the reflected baby magically moves! Infants regard their own reflections with great interest long before they begin to understand that the reflected eyes and faces and motions that hold their attention are their own. Older infants reach out to play with their reflections; they may even "converse" with them. Positioning firmly fastened, metal mirrors on the floor, walls, and closet doors and next to or over the changing table and securely mounting large mirrors low on walls in infant play spaces allows children to regard themselves and their reflective play partners from a variety of vantage points. If a low railing is near a low, wall-mounted mirror, infants can watch as they pull themselves up to a standing position.

Simple wheeled cars and trucks are easy for nonmobile infants to push and roll.

- *Soft dolls and stuffed animals*. Small, simple, soft washable dolls and stuffed animals appeal to infants for a number of reasons. The softness feels good. The toys' facial features reflect the features infants study in the faces of their parents, siblings, and caregivers. Further, as infants learn to grasp and wave these soft toys around, the blows they inadvertently deliver to themselves are gentle and sometimes even soothing. Older infants tend to converse with their dolls and stuffed animals, probably because infants associate faces with "talk."

Why Not Infant Swings, Seats, Stationary Play Centers, and Walkers?

When making decisions about equipment and materials for infants, remember that it is through whole-body movement that babies learn about what their bodies can do. Given their need to flex their limbs, turn their heads, roll over, sit, creep, crawl, and pull themselves upright, it makes sense to put infants in a safely watched, comfortably cushioned place that allows free whole-body movement — on the floor, a bolster-surrounded platform, or a grassy space — for exploration and play.

In contrast, infant swings (and other types of seats), *when used as places for play*, confine infants to one position, severely restricting many of the kinds of movement they are ready and eager for. While walkers allow infants to scoot themselves from place to place with their feet, they actually prevent children from practicing many of the motions vital to learning to walk — pulling themselves into a standing position, balancing, and bearing their own weight. Further, they physically restrict exploration, because they prevent infants from touching and grasping things on the floor. (They also permit scooting to precarious places, such as edges of steps and ramps.) NAEYC accreditation criteria explicitly exclude the use of baby walkers (NAEYC, 2007, criterion 9.C.08b).

- *Cloth and board books.* Small, sturdy, easy-to-handle cloth and board picture books provide infants with their earliest literacy experiences. At first, lying in a caregiver's arms, on the floor, or on the changing table, nonmobile infants may simply look at a picture on the cover or an open page of a book as a caregiver holds or props the book up. Infants tend to prefer simple, bright, high-contrast pictures of people, animals, and familiar objects. (Very young infants see black-and-white pictures best.) See "First Books for Infants and Toddlers" on pages 226–227.

- *Hinged doors and boxes.* Infants, when old enough to sit with both hands free, develop a fascination with doors and hinged lids they can readily open and close over and over again. Given the satisfaction this action brings, it makes sense for caregivers to provide wooden boxes or tins with hinged lids, toy cupboard doors, dollhouse doors, and small climber doors, for example, that infants can safely operate as much as they like.

- *Lightweight blocks.* Sitting infants enjoy the challenge of stacking or attempting to stack two or three lightweight blocks or cubes they can easily grasp. The sound and sight of toppling them over is equally rewarding.

- *Open containers.* Infants' initial interest in open containers centers around grasping and mouthing them. This is relatively easy to do, since empty juice cans, cottage cheese containers, butter tubs, and small wicker baskets, for example, have thin sides that are easy for infants to grasp with one hand. When an infant puts a shell or rattle into a container, it is usually accidental, and a young infant may not even be aware of the item in the container once it can no longer be seen. Gradually, however, with maturation and experience, infants remember out-of-sight objects, and they begin to fill and empty containers deliberately.

Storage

In an active learning setting, play materials for infants are stored in ways that allow children to choose what they want to explore and play with. For nonmobile infants, this means creating a portable storage system of small baskets, boxes, buckets, cloth bags, and tins, so wherever the infant is lying or sitting, the caregiver can readily supply a container of appealing sensory materials. For mobile infants, along with using the portable storage system, caregivers store toys and play materials directly on low, sturdy shelves or in baskets or clear plastic containers on shelves. Infants can then crawl over to get particular items they wish to play with.

Infant books should be stored where they are easy for creeper-crawlers or cruisers to see and reach — in plastic tubs or boxes for easy access, stood up on very low shelves, on forward-facing bookracks, or in clear, hanging pockets (available from supply catalogs). Using any of these three book-storage options may require more adult involvement, but these options allow children to see all the covers and make a choice based on what they see. (See p. 269 for a summary checklist of indoor play equipment and materials for infants.)

Where and how do toddlers play?

As babies gain their feet and turn into toddlers, their world expands. With their increasing ability to move, communicate, and engage in complex play, toddlers continue to look for the comfort and security of known people and materials but also are ready for the challenge of bigger spaces and new materials. If they share the setting with infants, toddlers need both shared play space and space of their own, where they can pursue "toddler only" activities.

Toddlers, therefore, play in appealing interest areas set up around the room but also on the floor, on the couch, at small tables, in a loft, on the grass, and in a sandbox. Caregivers set up specific toddler play spaces to reflect and encourage toddlers' increased mobility and interest in the physical and social world, their growing sense of themselves as doers, and their emerging cognitive capacities. Toddlers are beginning to explore and understand categories — how things are the same or different — and to develop a spatial sense of where things are, so having consistently located play areas stocked with accessible materials that are organized around specific types of play begins to make sense.

First Books for Infants and Toddlers

Initially, infants treat these first books as they do any other object of interest — looking at them, batting at and reaching for them, grasping the edges of pages, and mouthing the books' corners. Once infants can sit up and have both hands free, they often like to turn the pages, especially with a caregiver holding the book. During page turning, they gradually begin to pause, examine the pictures, and imitate the caregiver as she points to and talks about the objects pictured. As reading specialist Cathleen Soundy (1997) has noted, "During these early reading sessions, infants often smile, reach, point and babble. With repeated exposure, babies will pat the book, show pleasure in familiar favorites, turn the pages and jabber at the pictures….Older infants and toddlers who have been introduced early to books take great pleasure in being read to, often requesting that one book be read repeatedly during the same session" (p. 151).

Teacher, writer, and editor Mary Jalongo (2004) offers the following tips for choosing picture books that will appeal to infants and toddlers:

1. **Choose themes or subject matter that appeal to very young children,** such as learning to do things by themselves or being reassured they are loved. Young children enjoy stories about relationships with family members, playing with toys, and pets. In other words, the things that are important in the children's daily lives will also be appealing as the subject matter in books.

2. **Look for effective and imaginative language.** The text should be short with only a few words per page. Young children love rhythm and rhyme. Melodic text is also enjoyable for adults to read, which is important, since children will want a book they like to be read over and over again.

3. **If it is a storybook, the plot should be simple and direct** (no tangents). The narrative should briefly set the scene, move the action along, and build quickly to a satisfying conclusion. Even children who are just learning how books work should understand that the story has ended.

In addition to building essential language and literacy skills, reading picture books helps create a closer bond between the child and caregiver — the caregiver selects the book appropriate for the child and then, with the child in her lap or very close to her, she interacts with the child through the pictures and words in the story (Jalongo, 2004). When reading is associated with pleasurable feelings and the undivided attention of a caring adult, children will learn to like reading.

Finally, even when caregivers appreciate the importance of books in early literacy development, they sometimes worry about very young children mouthing or tearing books as they explore them. Adults therefore either do not provide any books to this age group or else offer them only damaged ones. However, there are other options. For example, infants can chew on other items while they look at books. They can also explore cloth books, which are explicitly designed for curious mouths and are easily washable. With toddlers, adults can model appropriate ways to handle and read books.

First Books for Infants and Toddlers (cont.)

When children do damage a book, the situation can be used as an opportunity for problem solving. Consider the following example between Jeremy (the toddler) and Beth (the caregiver):

Jeremy: (Throws a book at the shelf and the cover is torn off.)

Beth: *Jeremy, we have a problem. When we throw books, they get broken and we can't use them anymore.*

Jeremy: (Touches the book while Beth holds it) *Book broke.*

Beth: *Yes, the book is broken. I wonder how can we fix it.*

Jeremy: *Fix it.*

Beth: *I wonder if we can fix the book with tape?*

Jeremy: (Nods yes. He goes with Beth to the art area, and together they tape the cover back on.)

Beth: *There! We fixed the book. Jeremy, can you put it back on the shelf gently?*

Jeremy: (Carefully places the book on the shelf) *All fix!*

When caregivers model appropriate ways to handle books and enlist help managing mishandled books, young children learn to be responsible for preventing and solving problems with reading materials. These lessons can generalize to taking care of other materials in the environment.

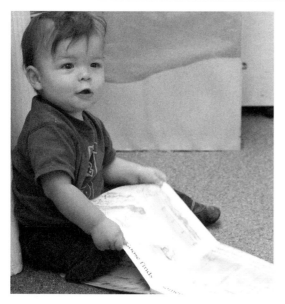

Infants treat books like they do any other object that interests them, including looking at, touching, and pulling.

Toddlers often repeat satisfying actions both to gain a sense of mastery and to challenge themselves by introducing slight variations in their play, so they rely on a consistent stock of open-ended materials and playthings they can locate on their own and play with or explore as often as they choose. Toddlers also need more play space than infants do. In fact, in the opinion of developmental psychologist Doris Bergen and her colleagues (1988), "Toddlers need more space for their size than children of any other age; they should not have to spend the entire day in one small room" (p. 202). The following sections describe some specific play areas that support toddlers' expanding interests.

The toddler movement area

The movement area should be a safe, accessible, open place where toddlers can do their first, tentative walking without bumping into people or things and, as they become increasingly sure on their feet, where they can run, climb, push, pull, rock, and ride. Large-muscle movement — walking, running, climbing, carrying — defines, in large part, how toddlers explore and construct knowledge about themselves and their world.

Location

The toddlers' indoor movement area is best located in the middle of the center's floor plan so toddlers can easily move into it from other activities. Their movement area may also extend toward the side of the room to include a sunken play area and particular pieces of equipment, such as a dowel climber (a short ladder with closely spaced rungs made of dowels) attached to a wall or a toddler loft placed against a wall. Depending on the layout of the center, caregivers might dedicate an alcove or an entire room to the toddler movement area, as long as it opens directly onto the rest of the toddler play space (for adult visibility and easy movement between areas by toddlers).

Equipment and materials

Aside from open space in which to walk and run, a toddler movement area needs things for toddlers to climb on. In the absence of appropriate climbing structures, toddlers will climb anyway — on tables, chairs, and shelves — so it is up to caregivers to provide sturdy, appropriate climbers! Toddlers also need low objects to jump off of, things to get into, balls for rolling and throwing, wheeled toys to push and pull, rocking toys, and riding toys. The riding toys should have at least four wheels widely spaced for stability, and at least some of them should not require use of a steering mechanism (although older toddlers enjoy and can generally manage steering). When sitting on the rocking or riding toys, toddlers should be able to rest their feet flat on the floor.

In addition to having recorded music that they can move to, toddlers also need a set of sturdy, high-quality musical instruments they can play while sitting down or as they move about. Though many of these materials are initially expensive, their impact on children and their durability over the years make them wise investments.

Storage

Climbers and large pieces of movement equipment should be stored in the movement area, where they are used, while riding toys and toys that can be pushed or pulled can be stored in a designated "parking" area next to a loft or along a wall and musical instruments on a low shelf or in open containers or baskets. (See p. 270 for a summary checklist of equipment and materials for the movement area.)

The toddler sand and water area

Toddlers like to muck about in sand and water, enjoying the look, sound, and

The toddler movement area needs plenty of space in which to walk, run, climb, and ride on wheeled toys.

soothing feel of sand and water and the continuous changes that occur as they pat, splash, dump, and pour. In fact, the sand and water area is one toddler play space where play with squishy, messy materials is encouraged!

Location

If possible, the sand and water area should be located on a tile floor and close to a sink to simplify cleanup and the process of adding and draining water. If a space with tile floor is not available, caregivers can prepare the area by securely fastening down a piece of nonskid waterproof floor-covering of some kind.

Equipment and materials

This area centers around a toddler-height sand and water table partially filled with sand and/or water. (If space permits, provide two tables, one for sand and the other for water.) If a center does not have a suitable table, a baby bathtub or a child's plastic wading pool placed on the floor or on a low table can be substituted. If the table, tub, or pool is some distance from the sink, caregivers can provide small buckets with handles so children can participate in adding to and draining the supply of water. For children's play with sand and water, caregivers include containers to fill and empty; things to hide

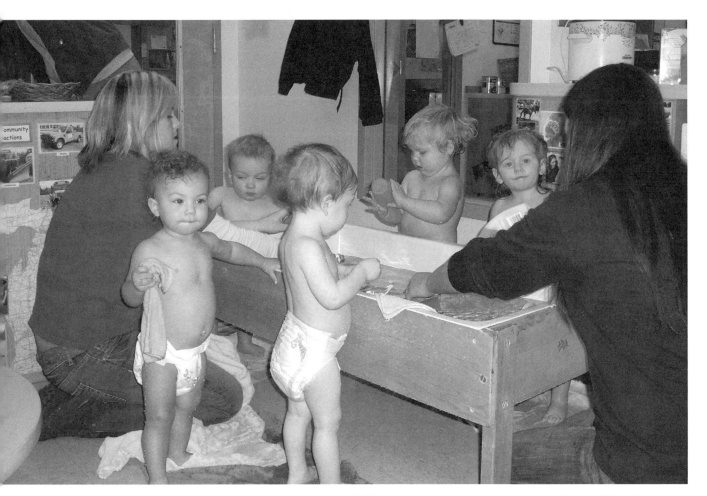

The sand and water area is very popular with young children because they can look, touch, listen, fill and empty, squeeze, splash, and get wet!

and find; things to float; things to soak and squeeze; and, for older toddlers who are beginning to pretend, rubber or plastic animal and people figures.

Storage

At the end of the day, caregivers remove all the containers and objects from the sand and water table and store them where children can easily see and reach them, for example, in baskets, plastic milk crates, or dish tubs next to the table or on a low nearby shelf. This allows children to see and feel the sand or water itself and to make choices about what materials they wish to add to their sand and water play on any given day. The sand and water table is cleaned and washed regularly, and the sand is replaced as needed. (See p. 271 for a summary checklist of materials and equipment for the sand and water area.)

The toddler book area

The book area should be a cozy place where toddlers can easily find and enjoy picture books. For toddlers, handling books, carrying them around, looking at the pictures, sitting on a caregiver's lap pointing to and "talking" about things in pictures, hearing stories, and "reading" stories are immediately pleasurable experiences that have a lasting impact. When toddlers have had these early experiences on a regular basis, it facilitates their learning to read in the elementary school years.

The joint position statement of the International Reading Association and NAEYC emphasizes this link between being read to at an early age and children's later literacy development (Neuman, Copple, & Bredekamp, 2000) as do other researchers. For example, a study by linguists Dorothy Allison and J. Allen Watson (1994) found that the earlier parents began reading aloud to their infants and toddlers, the higher the children's emergent reading levels were at the end of kindergarten. In a longitudinal study of literacy achievement, linguist Gordon Wells (1986) found that the best readers had heard approximately 6,000 stories between birth and age 5. The Committee on the Prevention of Reading Difficulties in Young Children (Snow, Burns, & Griffin, 1998) includes reading with children among its recommendations to help children learn not only the technical skills for reading and writing but also how to use these tools in their thinking and reasoning. In sum, "the single most important

activity for building these understandings and skills essential for reading success appears to be *reading aloud to children* [emphasis added]" (Neuman et al., 2000, p. 6). Thus, a pleasant, well-stocked toddler book area can make a real difference in children's lives.

Location

The toddler book area should be located in a corner or along the perimeter of the toddler play space so that major traffic patterns and active play will not interfere with book exploration and reading. Caregivers use bookshelves and other furnishings as boundaries for the area; for example, one boundary might be formed by a large open carton tipped on its side and furnished with pillows to create a comfortable "carton nook" where children can retreat with books.

Toddlers will spend some time using books in the book area, but they will also carry books about with them as they play in other areas. For example, they may "read" to baby dolls in the house area, drive books around in dump trucks, or look at books outside on the deck while sitting on a caregiver's lap.

Equipment and materials

However large or small the book area, it should be furnished comfortably. This might mean providing a carton nook, or simply a mattress or quilt and some pillows, some low easy chairs, or a couch. Children will want to sprawl or sit comfortably with a book alone, with peers, or snuggled up with a caregiver. Equipping the area with several stuffed toys and toddler-sized puppets representing familiar story characters offers the opportunity for pretending.

The book area includes a variety of books for toddlers to handle and look at.

Being read to at an early age is crucial for children's later literacy development.

Caregivers will want to have a permanent collection of books in the book area, but they should also use the local children's library for adding to and updating their collection (Neuman et al., 2000). (See "Library and Museum Visits" on p. 238.)

When selecting books, caregivers should look for board books with clear, well-drawn pictures or photographs. If text is included, it should be a simple description of what is pictured or a simple story or rhyme. An alphabet or counting book should be selected for the quality of the pictures, which will be of more interest to toddlers than the letters or numbers. Older toddlers may be interested in reading regular (nonboard) picture books (both with and without text) and some catalogs and magazines with lots of illustrations.

Along with books, caregivers include small albums of photos they have taken of the children at the center, along with a box or album of post cards depicting animals, flowers, places of interest to children, and art reproductions (which often hold interest for young children — see "Library and Museum Visits" on p. 238). Children, staff, and families can be invited to add to this picture collection.

Because it is a relatively peaceful setting, the book area is also a natural place to locate the aquarium suggested on pages 199–200. Also, caregivers who provide a computer for toddlers' use sometimes locate it in the book area, although a computer is *not necessary* in settings equipped for toddlers. As computers and other technology become more widespread in our

To encourage book exploration, a book area should be located in a cozy corner, furnished with comfortable seating.

culture and in the home, however, they are likely to find their way into child care settings as well. If a center already has a computer for toddlers (or if they share one with older children in the center), caregivers should choose toddler software that includes music activities, peekaboo games, and creative art activities rather than preacademic content like letter, number, and shape recognition. (See "Using Computers With Very Young Children" on pp. 234–235).

Storage

Caregivers store books in ways that allow toddlers to see their covers — propped in forward-facing bookracks, hanging in clear pockets, or standing up on low shelves, with overflow books stored in baskets, plastic milk crates, or tubs, rotating the toddler books between forward-facing display and tub (or basket) storage. Plastic milk crates can also be turned with the open side facing forward, making it easier for children to see what is inside.

Using Computers With Very Young Children

Very young children are increasingly being introduced to various forms of technology at home and in child care. Thirty years ago, children began watching television at age two-and-a-half. Today, children as young as six months old are exposed to various media, including computers (Anderson & Evans, 2001).

The fastest growing segment of the educational software market is for children under age five, including *lapware,* which is designed for adults to use with children ages six months to two years. The benefits of appropriate technology in preschool has been acknowledged by the field (NAEYC, 1996); however, what about children under age three? Although there is little research on the subject, opinions run high and range from strongly negative to cautiously positive.

What the opponents say

Those opposed to using computers with infants and toddlers believe it is at best a waste of time and money, and, at worst, potentially harmful. Noted child development writer David Elkind (1988) says, "The parent's lap notwithstanding, the use of computers with the very young carries many more risks than it does benefits" (p. 44). He cites as an example the unknown effects that staring at a computer screen may have on the child's vision. Educational psychologist Jane Healy (1998) warns that "the minute we introduce an artificially engaging stimulus with fast-paced visuals, startling noises, silly scenarios, and easy excitement, the brain is diverted away from its natural developmental tasks" (p. 101). Time spent with media cuts into other activities, such as active exploration of materials or experiences with other sensory input. This concern is shared by the Alliance for Childhood (Cordes & Miller, 2000), a play-advocacy group that believes early computer use can adversely affect children's physical health, social relationships, and intellectual development. Further, the AAP (2001) discourages any kind of screen time for children younger than two years and "encourage[s] more interactive activities that will promote proper brain development such as talking, playing, singing, and reading together" (p. 424).

Even the background noise of other people using electronic devices may interfere with various aspects of early development, such as speech (Anderson & Evans, 2001). Young children talk to themselves when they play, and this eventually becomes internalized *private speech.* Media, which tend to have a noticeable visual or auditory change every six seconds, may structurally interfere with this process. *Social speech* may also be affected if children are intermittently diverted from interacting with peers and adults, who may themselves be distracted.

Fast-paced media also make it difficult for young children to sustain their play at increasingly mature levels. Moreover, even if they watch and listen to electronic devices that purportedly contain educational content, there is no evidence from either physiological or behavioral measures that toddlers pay attention, understand, or apply the content to real life experiences (Richards & Cronise, 2000).

Using Computers With Very Young Children (cont.)

What the proponents say

Other educators hold more positive views toward technology. For example, the editors of *Children's Software Revue* (Buckleitner, Orr, & Wolock, 2000) contend that well-chosen software can give even very young children an educational advantage, provided it is chosen by adults who know the child well and is used in moderation. Professor Douglas Clements shares this view. In an interview with *Scholastic Early Childhood Today* ("Computers and Young Children," 1999), he stated that "children as young as one or two can sit on someone's lap and interact with the person and with what's on the screen" (p. 45). He likened the interactive experience to reading a book or playing blocks together with an adult.

"It is unlikely that this debate will be resolved any time soon," say professor Patricia Cantor (2001), "because little solid research exists about the effects, positive or negative, of lapware" (p. 2). The AAP (2001) recognizes that while a market for software aimed at infants and toddlers is growing, "little is known about the actual impact of this new technology on children's developing minds and bodies" (p. 4). The AAP has called for systematic research on the topic to evaluate the proliferation of technology aimed at this young age group.

What should caregivers do?

While the field awaits the results of such studies, what should caregivers do in the meantime? One point on which there is agreement is that lapware experiences for older toddlers should be social and interactive; very young children should not be "plunked down" alone in front of computers or other technology but should only use such devices as a shared experience with an adult. Another piece of sound advice is to choose software that is open ended, that is, programs that do not emphasize drill and memory but encourage children to experiment and be creative. A third recommendation is to limit children's time with computers in favor of hands-on experiences with real materials, physical movement, outdoor play, and so on.

In addition, caregivers can talk about this issue openly with the parents of infants and toddlers, first by educating themselves on what's popular on the market and then by talking to parents about what they use at home. Caregivers can share with parents how many of the popular "skill and drill" programs that require children to recognize letters, numbers, and colors are often not appropriate for this age group and offer some suggestions on how parents can use the computer in a more creative and interactive way with their young children (Cantor, 2001).

As parents increasingly ask about the use of computers in early care and education setting — whether they are in favor of or opposed to them — caregivers need to be able to explain the reasons behind their choices.

Because toddlers enjoy hearing the same stories over and over, caregivers save display room for children's favorite books. If infants and toddlers share the same space, it may be necessary to store any nonboard books above the reach of mobile infants. (See p. 272 for a summary checklist of equipment and materials for the book area.)

The toddler art area

The art area is where toddlers have the chance to experience and explore basic art materials, get their hands messy and sticky, and enjoy the sensation of making motions that leave a mark — smearing finger paint across a large sheet of paper, making dots and scribbles with markers, kneading and squeezing dough or clay, and crumpling and tearing paper. Through these sensory-motor experiences, children discover the essential nature of paint, paper, dough, clay, and markers. This sensory-motor understanding of the properties of basic art materials provides them with a body of experience to turn to when they reach the point of wanting to use these materials to represent their ideas, make things for play, and solve problems.

It is particularly important for caregivers to appreciate that toddlers are involved in *exploring* art materials rather than using them to make something. This means they are interested in feeling the finger paint,

Materials in this art area are clearly organized, simply labeled, and easily accessible on low shelves for toddlers to choose and explore.

hearing paper rip and crunch, squeezing dough or clay and watching it smoosh through their fingers, seeing how paint colors bleed together, sticking their fingers together with paste, and moving the brush across the paper. For toddlers, the actions of art matter more than the outcomes.

Location

The toddler art area should be located on a tile floor or on some other permanent or taped-down, easily cleaned, nonslip floor surface. Having the area close to a sink gives children and adults easy access to water for mixing paints, washing hands, and cleaning up; if possible, it should also be close to a window or skylight so children can easily see colors and materials. Since the requirements for toddlers' art and eating areas are similar, it may make sense to locate these two areas close to or overlapping each other. Alternatively, it might make sense to locate the art area around the corner from the toddler bathroom. In warm weather and temperate climates, the art area can be located outside on a deck or in a shady area and close to a water source, such as an outdoor tap with a hose connected to it (caregivers can also bring buckets of water from inside).

Equipment and materials

To protect children's clothing during any messy art activities, caregivers have children push up their sleeves and provide them with one-piece, plastic or vinyl smocks that are easy to put on. (For smocks that fasten, the buttons or Velcro pieces should be fairly large so toddlers can manipulate them.) If it is warm enough, children might simply remove their shirts before launching into messy art activities.

A table in the art area can provide children with a stable, smooth work surface. Depending on the space available, the art table may be dedicated to art activities or serve as a mealtime table as well. In either case, there should be plenty of space for children who prefer to spread out and work with art materials on the floor.

As young toddlers begin to form mental pictures of their experiences and hold in mind the attributes of objects, "they begin to represent their ideas, thoughts, and understanding of their experiences through the use of art materials" (Lockhart, 2005a, p. 2). Older toddlers are fine-tuning their movements and "their abilities to use art materials and express intentions are now more refined…and can benefit from a richly stocked art area" (p. 3). Caregivers, therefore, need to provide young children with a variety of materials so they can continue to explore their properties (such as shape, color, texture, size, and weight) and combine them in different ways, accidentally at first and intentionally later on. Basic art materials for toddlers to explore fall into these broad categories: painting and drawing materials, paper, and dough and clay (including materials toddlers can poke into and use to create textures in them).

Painting and drawing materials. Finger painting lets toddlers experience the paint directly on their palms and

Library and Museum Visits

"Regular visits to the school or public library and library card registration ensure that children's collections remain continually updated and may help children develop the habit of reading as lifelong learning. In comfortable library settings children often will pretend to read, using visual cues to remember the words of their favorite stories."

— Neuman et al. (2000, p. 7)

"Teachers and parents can take young children on field trips to nearby museums, galleries, art fairs, landscaped parks, historical monuments, and special exhibits and art demonstrations in public spaces. The Arts Education Partnership (1998) says that even toddlers can visit children's museums and child-friendly exhibits. Concerns that such experiences may be beyond young children are not supported by field testing and observation....Young children enjoy looking at art and sharing their observations with others....As more museums recognize that young children can experience and respond to art, they are expanding programs for this age group."

— Epstein & Trimis (2002, p. 93)

small, contained motions required by small sheets of paper. White paper allows them to see the color they are using and also to see what happens when primary colors overlap and combine to make secondary colors (orange, green, and violet). If finger paints are given to toddlers on paper or plastic plates or in rectangular plastic food containers, they can put their palms and fingers directly into the paint.

For brush painting, toddlers can use tempera in the primary colors and short-handled brushes or small house-painting brushes in several widths. They also need large sheets of white paper, such as butcher paper, and a flat painting surface, such as a table, the floor, or the ground. Some older toddlers may enjoy painting at free-standing or wall-mounted easels or on a wall- or fence-mounted piece of paper. Powdered tempera should be mixed with just enough water to make a fairly thick, nonrunny paint. Paints should be poured into low, flat containers that do not tip (muffin tins, cut-down yogurt containers, or tuna cans snugly arranged in a small square cake tin; baby food jars set in cut-out holes in sponges). Some toddlers prefer to use their fingers and hands instead of brushes. Others enjoy spreading paint with scrub brushes, dish-washing mops, feathers, sticks, cotton balls, or pieces of sponge. Caregivers provide a bucket for transporting painting tools to the sink to be washed — cleaning brushes and other tools is a task toddlers enjoy as much as painting!

For drawing, caregivers provide toddlers with a variety of colors in crayons

fingers, feel the way it moves across the painting surface, and clearly see their actions making a mark. Caregivers provide children with finger paints in the primary colors (red, yellow, and blue) and large sheets of white paper spread on the table, floor, or ground. They need large sheets of paper (e.g., butcher paper cut from a roll) because it is easier and more natural for toddlers to make large, sweeping arm motions rather than the

This toddler is holding a brush in one hand but prefers to use her other hand to explore the paint on paper.

(large and small), nontoxic water-based markers, large pencils, and pieces of chalk. After children have had many opportunities to mark and scribble with these on large sheets of white drawing or butcher paper, colored kraft or construction paper can be added to their drawing materials.

For squeeze-bottle drawing and painting, children use pieces of cardboard and toddler-sized plastic squeeze bottles (such as small condiment bottles) filled with what educator Karen Miller (2000) described as "salt dribbles": equal parts of flour, salt, and water (with enough drops of paint for color). Toddlers may also enjoy squeezing paint onto pieces of scrap

wood (the edges of the wood should be sanded smooth).

Paper. Children use paper not only as a painting or drawing surface but also as an art medium to explore in its own right — by crumpling, tearing, folding, and twisting it to find out how it sounds, feels, or changes shape or texture. Therefore, it is important to provide toddlers with different types of paper, such as newsprint; white paper; colored construction, kraft, and tissue paper; foil; wrapping paper; and stiff cellophane. Children can go through a lot of paper in a short time, so families can contribute paper they would otherwise put in the recycling bin.

Toddlers also like to use more unusual art materials, including dishwashing brushes (instead of paint brushes), shaving cream (instead of paint), and rocks (instead of paper)!

Dough and clay. Children use play dough and clay to knead, pull, squeeze, roll, pat, and pound. Besides poking their fingers into these materials, older toddlers also like to poke objects into them, so it makes sense to provide them with a variety of objects to use in this way, such as sticks, corks, stones, shells, beads, rubber stoppers, plastic and metal tableware, and kitchen utensils.

Storage

Though bulk art supplies are usually stored in cupboards or on shelves accessible to staff, the art materials toddlers use each day should be where they can see and reach them. For example, in one child care setting, caregivers hang toddlers' smocks in the art area on low wooden hooks (made from dowels with knobs on the ends) and store brushes together in small buckets, clear boxes, or racks. They store the daily supply of art materials on a set of low shelves in the art area, so children can choose what they want to use. If the set of shelves has wheels or casters, it is then easy for the caregivers to move the art materials outside on nice days. A low supply cart can also serve as portable shelves.

At the beginning of each day, caregivers prepare the toddlers' art shelves by setting out that day's supply of paints in the nonspill containers described earlier. Storing markers upside down with their caps inserted into holes drilled in a block of wood (this type of a holder can be made or ordered from a supply catalog) helps keep them from drying out. Play dough and clay should be stored in clear airtight containers (and checked at the end of each day to make sure the lids are back on and to replace any dried-out dough or clay). For older toddlers who can hold images in mind, caregivers might label each storage container on the art shelves with a sample item, a picture, or a photo to enable children and staff to easily return items to their designated containers.

Sheets of paper on racks can be stored in the art area. Caregivers can then stand a roll of butcher paper on an upright paper-holder and cut off strips and pieces each day or keep the roll on a horizontal paper-holder and have a long piece rolled out on the floor or taped to the wall at the beginning of each day. (See p. 273 for a summary checklist of equipment and materials for the art area.)

The toddler block area

Providing a block area gives toddlers the space and opportunity to explore and work with easy-to-handle blocks, manipulate basic shapes, and begin to construct an understanding of spatial relationships. They like to handle, carry, and balance blocks, sometimes stacking them higher and higher to see when the stack will tip over. They use blocks to make simple enclosures they can climb into or put objects and figures inside of. Older toddlers line up blocks end to end and then walk along or over the path they have made. In sum, toddler block play is a satisfying whole-body experience.

This low shelving unit, which can be moved or closed up to provide more space, holds blocks and vehicles for toddler play.

Location

The toddler block area should be located away from the book area, in a place where there is space enough for spread-out block structures and where block play can extend if necessary into the open center of the room. Toddlers are awkward and need plenty of room to maneuver both themselves and their blocks. The floor surface should be smooth and flat to allow stacking and balancing of blocks.

Equipment and materials

The block area should be stocked with large, relatively lightweight blocks that toddlers can lift or handle with two hands.

These might be large foam, plastic, or cardboard "brick" blocks that are uniform in size and easy for toddlers to stack. A set of wooden unit blocks gives toddlers satisfying experiences handling denser, heavier blocks in a variety of shapes. (The pine unit blocks are lighter; the maple ones are more durable.) This area can also include sturdy plastic or wooden vehicles for carrying and pushing blocks and sets of pretend people and animals for filling, emptying, and pretending.

Storage

Blocks and large vehicles should be stored on low shelves, where children can easily see and reach them. If shelves are not available, the large blocks and the vehicles can be stacked on the floor against a wall and the unit blocks in a basket, plastic milk crate, or sturdy clear container, with other small items stored in open baskets. (See p. 274 for a summary checklist of equipment and materials for the block area.)

The toddler house area

Here toddlers can find and explore dolls, kitchen-related items, and dress-up clothes. They can engage in a lot of filling and emptying — putting dolls in beds and strollers, emptying cupboards, and filling the toy sink with dishes and spoons. They can imitate things they see family members doing at home — talking on the phone, putting dishes on the table, turning toy sink faucets off and on, putting on shoes like Mommy's, and feeding the baby. Older toddlers may begin to pretend by using one object to stand for another, for example, using a pillow for a doll bed or a cooking pot for a hat.

Location

The toddlers' house area should be located in a corner or along the perimeter of the central, open play space. Since the play in this area often reflects what adults do at home in the kitchen, caregivers can consider establishing the toddler house area

In the house area, children explore and play with everyday household materials.

close to or across from the food preparation and eating area. It may also work to locate the house area in a cozy space under a loft.

Equipment and materials

To support children's exploration and imitative play, the house area should include familiar household materials, such as a sturdy, stable sink, stove, and refrigerator equipped with hinged doors children can open and close as often as they want; toy and/or real telephones; and a toddler-sized table and several home-like wooden or wicker chairs. Surrounded by these appliances and furniture, toddlers can enjoy exploring, combining, and filling and emptying a variety of nonbreakable real (rather than toy) dishes, small

cooking pots, and empty food containers. Caregivers can also provide a variety of real kitchen utensils (wooden spoons, rubber spatulas, scrub brushes, measuring cups and spoons) and collections of small items (corks, shells) to use for "food." (Note that the kitchen equipment and materials should reflect what children from different backgrounds in the program might find at home [wok, rice steamer, tortilla press, clay pot].)

For doll play, the house area should include soft-bodied baby dolls reflecting the racial and ethnic identities of the children in the program; simple doll clothes (e.g., that slip over a doll's head without requiring complex arm and leg insertions) with Velcro closings; baby bottles and baby blankets; and a doll bed and doll

A well-organized and easily accessible dress-up area encourages young children to imitate and pretend.

carriage or stroller large and strong enough to hold a toddler, because children will get into doll beds, carriages, and strollers themselves. Caregivers can provide sleeping mats, sleeping bags, or other similar furnishings if the children and families in their program use them at home.

Dress-up materials should be relatively simple. Toddlers are often content to wear one thing at a time and also like to use dress-up items such as purses and bags (with handles or short straps) for filling, emptying, and transporting materials. Families can also contribute old clothing and accessories for this purpose. Toddlers also like to wrap or drape themselves (as well as dolls and stuffed animals) in pieces of scrap fabric (e.g., remnants from a fabric store). A full-length mirror so children can see themselves in their dress-up attire is also a must.

If the house area is near a window, this is also a natural place to include nontoxic plants children can enjoy and help care for.

Storage

The house area materials should be stored where toddlers can easily see and reach them, for example, stacks of dishes and large open containers of utensils on low shelves; baby dolls in the doll bed or carriage; and doll accessories and dress-up clothes in baskets, plastic milk crates, or tubs. Caregivers can label storage containers with a sample object, picture, or photo to help older toddlers put toys away. To store pots and pans, for example,

caregivers in one family child care home attached large shower-curtain rings to the holes in the pan handles so that toddlers could easily slip these large rings onto wooden pegs on the wall in the house area. (See p. 275 for a summary checklist of equipment and materials for the house area.)

The toddler toy area

In their toy area, toddlers explore, manipulate, and play with small toys and collections. Here they engage in fitting things together and taking them apart, filling and emptying, and pretending. Children spend time in this area as a quiet place of play. They also take things from this area to use in other parts of the play space.

Location

The toddler toy area should be located in a corner or along the perimeter of the central, open play space. Since play in this area tends to be on the quiet side, it can be near the toddler book area, where there is sufficient comfortable floor space to spread out with toys and collections.

Equipment and materials

This area can include toys, puzzles, and other materials toddlers can fit together and take apart; graduated-size nesting toys and containers (including bowls, cups, and measuring spoons); magnetic blocks and various kinds of large interlocking blocks; a wooden pounding bench; simple off/on, open/close items; boxes with hinged

The toy area should include puzzles, toys, and natural objects, such as a collection of large shells.

lids and easy-to-work latches or locks; things toddlers can fill and empty; sets of large cubes, beads, and pegs; and figures and vehicles for pretending. Keep in mind that while it is very easy to stock this area with things made from plastic, this is also the place to include collections of a wide variety of household and natural objects of different textures, aromas, and weights.

Storage

To help toddlers find and choose what they need, these toys and other playthings should be stored on low shelves in open, easy-to-access baskets and containers.

Labeling these baskets and containers with a sample object, picture, or photo may help older toddlers put toys away on days when they have emptied all the containers. (See p. 276 for a summary checklist of equipment and materials for the toy area.)

Outdoor play yards for infants and toddlers

The outdoor play area is an important extension of the indoor exploration and play environment. Outside, infants can hear, smell, feel, or see trees, clouds, wind, warm and cool temperatures, and changes in light. Toddlers can run, throw, kick, climb, swing, or dig; they find plants, animals, and insects to examine. (See "Learning About Nature" on pp. 251–253.) Rich in sights, textures, sounds, smells, and opportunities for movement, an outdoor play yard greatly expands children's store of sensory-motor experiences.

Generally, 75 square feet of outdoor space per child is considered appropriate in early childhood licensing standards and accreditation criteria. "The outdoor space should be designed for play value and safety," says pediatric health and safety expert Dr. Susan Aronson (2002, p. 120). Since many technical issues feature in the design of a safe playground, Aronson recommends that a certified playground safety inspector review existing facilities and plans to modify or build new outdoor spaces.

A significant concern in outdoor play areas is the safety of the surfaces and equipment. Since the majority of playground injuries are due to falls, the most important safety feature is an impact-absorbent surface that meets the standards of the ASTM International (www.astm.org). The US Consumer Product Safety Commission (www.cpsc.gov) conducts tests on the shock-absorbing properties of common loose-fill surfacing material, including wood chips, shredded bark mulch, sand, pea gravel, and shredded rubber tires. Each has advantages and drawbacks, including the cost of periodic replacement due to weather-related deterioration. While commercially manufactured surface materials (also called unitary materials) may be more expensive initially to purchase and install, they require less maintenance and may save money in the long run.

In addition to protecting children from falls, outdoor play areas should guard against entrapment, tripping, and choking and avoid exposure to excessive wind and direct sunlight. They should be separated from streets, traffic, and access by unauthorized persons and be inspected daily to guarantee they are free of glass, litter, and other hazards. This is true especially for local public playgrounds used by the child care setting. For more information on the safety of outdoor areas, see Aronson (2002), accreditation criteria (NAEYC, 2007, criterion 9.B.06), and the websites of the organizations cited in the previous paragraph.

Location

To make movement from indoor to outdoor play easy and hassle-free, the play yard should be located as close to the indoor play space as possible. In stand-alone or school-based facilities, a play yard often adjoins the indoor care space. Child care centers located in apartment buildings or office complexes may have to be more creative to find a suitable outdoor play area. For example, urban centers are creating rooftop play areas with natural features (sod, raised beds) that let young children escape intrusive stimuli from the city down below. (For examples of rooftop play areas for child care centers, visit the website of the Association of Play Industries [www.api-play.org].)

A stroller ride in the neighborhood can be a supplement to regular experiences in an outdoor play yard.

Infants and toddlers generally spend more time outdoors when the indoor play space opens directly onto the play yard. If the yard is not directly accessible, caregivers will need to think about how children can safely move (or be moved) there from indoors. Infants can be transported in strollers or wagons, and toddlers will be able to walk to the yard with caregivers if it is only a short distance away. If the distance is really too far for toddlers to walk, caregivers can transport small groups of them in wagons or strollers. If one outdoor play yard serves both infants and toddlers, child care centers can separate the infants' space from that of the older children by a low barrier of canvas- or vinyl-covered cushions, a low wall or fence, or low shrubs.

In settings that share an outdoor space with preschool programs, the infant and toddler play area should be separated from that of older children. Even if use of the shared space by each group can be scheduled for different times of day, mobile infants and toddlers need play equipment geared to their specific needs, located in its own designated area. Mobile infants and young toddlers need stable, sturdy wheeled toys and vehicles to push, pull, and ride. Older toddlers need small-scale climbing equipment. Older toddlers should be able to use this equipment (e.g., swings and low slides) by themselves; that is, with adult supervision but without needing assistance to get on or off the equipment (Copple & Bredekamp, 2009).

Young children should have plenty of opportunities to explore the outdoors. This young toddler is fascinated with blades of grass she is collecting in a small bowl.

The immediate neighborhood can also be a part of the children's outdoor experience. Pushing infants in a stroller, pulling infants and toddlers in a wagon, or walking with toddlers gives them the opportunity to go places they cannot yet go on their own and to see, hear, or smell a variety of sights, sounds, and aromas. Because of the children's need to move and act on and touch things, however, it is important that stroller and wagon rides supplement rather than take the place of children's on-the-ground exploration and play in a safe outdoor play yard. During this on-the-ground exploration, it is important to ensure that any sticks, leaves, and stones that children pick up to mouth are nontoxic and too large to swallow.

Equipment and materials for infants

The playthings that support infants' indoor activity will also work outdoors. They will play outdoors with balls, rattles, and containers, for example, as long as someone brings a basket or tub of these materials outside for them to play with. There are some other things, however, that work particularly well in holding infants' interest outdoors, and they include:

- *Movement opportunities.* Something as simple as a change in terrain, such as a gentle grassy hill built into the play area, will provide mobile infants with a good deal of crawling pleasure. For other up-and-down crawling opportunities, caregivers can consider adding low, flat tree-stump rounds; a smooth log or landscape timber children can straddle; low, flat rocks; a few wooden steps; an inflated inner tube; a low wooden platform; and a canvas- or vinyl-covered mattress. A large carton, a tunnel, or a tent can provide a cozy crawl-through space. Mobile infants who are pulling themselves up to stand can do so beside a sturdy bench or wagon, the seat or bed of

which also makes a good place for banging and pushing small wheeled toys while standing and balancing. Infants *who sit well by themselves* may enjoy being pushed gently back and forth in a sturdy, safely suspended outdoor infant swing-seat. (If the caregiver pushes from the front of the swing, the caregiver and child can see and converse with each other.) Infants also enjoy the swings that are designed to accommodate two infants face to face.

- *Things that move in the wind.* Young infants lying and sitting on blankets or mats enjoy watching and listening to the fluttering and flapping of banners, streamers, hanging foil pie tins, or wind chimes. These can be tied to branches, poles, or fences.

- *Crawling surfaces.* The outdoor play area can afford a variety of crawling surfaces, such as grass, aromatic-herb ground covers (such as mint), sand, leaves, wooden decking, and pathways made of smooth flagstone, packed clay, concrete, or wood. Direct contact with each of these surfaces will tell babies that each surface has a distinct look, smell, and feel (some will feel more comfortable than others).

- *Water-play materials.* Supplying a sitting infant with a small container of water and some objects that float provides opportunities for splashing and dabbling where nobody minds if the "floor" gets wet.

Learning About Nature

For infants and toddlers, adventures in nature expose them to a world that they do not experience indoors. Many caregivers wonder how to start infants and toddlers on a path toward greater awareness and appreciation of nature. With their highly attuned senses, very young children are primed to explore and develop an affinity with the natural world. In addition, by learning how to gently handle and care for living things, children also become more sensitive to the needs of, and differences, among people. "Deep bonds can form between children or child and adult when they share experiences with nature. When children have daily opportunities to care for plants and trees, animals and insects, they practice nurturing behaviors that help them interact in kind and gently ways with people as well," says educational consultant Nancy Rosenow (2008, p. 10).

Research shows that children benefit from contact with the outdoors (e.g., fresh air, vitamin D, better eating and sleeping patterns) and may suffer health problems (e.g., obesity) and psychological fears (e.g., insect phobias) when deprived of regular interactions with nature (Kahn & Kellert, 2002). In fact, NAEYC's early childhood standards and accreditation criteria specify as an essential curriculum component that programs include "both indoor and outdoor experiences" (NAEYC, 2007, criterion 2.A.07.b) and that the facility's physical environment has a safe outdoor play area (criterion 9.B).

Unfortunately, the amount of time young children spend outdoors is decreasing, not only in urban areas and developing countries but also worldwide. For infants and toddlers, caregivers tend not to take this age group outside because it takes too much time to get them dressed and/or they are concerned about children putting "dirty" things in their mouths. To help reverse this trend, child care settings can think more broadly about outdoor spaces and children's interactions with the natural world. These changes do not require major investments of money or time. Rather, they entail a shift in attitude and can be undertaken in small, incremental steps.

Experiences with the outdoors

With varied hands-on and feet-on experiences, infants' and toddlers' interactions with and attitudes about nature can take many forms. Ideas for caregivers include the following:

- *Grow flowers and vegetables* — Where space is available, gardening can be done in a plot in the ground. For urban or rooftop areas, use planter boxes. Children will enjoy digging in the dirt, watching seeds germinate, watering flowers, and tasting vegetables they grow themselves.

- *Provide easy-to-care-for pets* — Infants and toddlers benefit from having pets in the classroom. They are fascinated watching the behavior of animals as they eat, sleep, and play. Pets also provide an opportunity for adults to model simple caregiving behaviors that children can often help with, such as providing food and water or cleaning out a tank or cage. Under careful adult supervision, children can also learn how to handle living creatures gently. Fish are the easiest pets to maintain, although guinea pigs and other small animals are also feasible.

Learning About Nature (cont.)

- *Welcome all weather* — Except for extreme conditions of heat, cold, wind, and precipitation, caregivers don't let "bad" weather stop them from taking children outdoors, even for a brief period of time every day. Provide, or ask families to provide, weatherproof jackets and footwear so children can splash through puddles; pat snow into balls; and see, hear, and smell the change in seasons.

- *Take neighborhood walks* — Young children enjoy such sensations as the warmth of the sun, caress of the wind, chattering squirrels, and chirping birds. For older toddlers, play I spy games and encourage them to look for animals or plants with familiar characteristics (e.g., squiggly worms, red flowers). To guarantee that such walks are relaxed and enjoyable, Alyson Williams (2008) of the Smithsonian Early Enrichment Center advises caregivers to allow plenty of time to get infants and toddlers dressed and loaded into strollers and wagons. (*Note:* Remember that taking walks in strollers or wagons should *not* be the only contact young children have with nature. They also need direct, hands-on contact with nature in the outdoor play area.)

- *Look out the window* — At times of day, or periods of the year, when children cannot go outside, look out the window with them. Watch and comment on the effects of the weather, for example, how the ground disappears under the snow or how the pavement turns darker in the rain. "Bend" with toddlers in the same way that plants bend in the wind. Feel the cold window pane.

- *Bring the outdoors into the classroom* — Bring leaves and snow indoors for the sand and water table. Collect twigs, pebbles, shells, fallen leaves, and other natural objects for children to feel, smell, crush, roll, put in and take out of containers, sort, and use in their pretend play.

- *Hold fears and prejudices in check* — Be careful not to communicate disgust or fear toward the natural world. Children are quick to pick up on such attitudes and adopt them as their own. Approach nature even-handedly, even if it does not come naturally at first.

- *Share the children's sense of wonder* — Rediscover the fascinations of nature along with the children. Pay attention to the buzzing of insects, the shimmering drop of sunlit dew on a leaf, the structural complexity of dried grass stalks, and the smell of the earth after a rain shower.

Learning in the outdoors

The "outdoor classroom" supports learning in many domains: "The outdoors is *not* just a place for children to release pent-up energy or discover odd bugs (although those are definitely important outdoor activities); it is a total learning environment" (Neill, 2008, p. 116). Depending on their developmental level, children playing outdoors make choices, solve problems, express feelings, imitate and pretend, make friends, build, move, sing, talk, and explore the properties of objects. Experiences with nature support scientific and aesthetic thinking, so children "appreciate beauty, express creativity, and perceive patterns and variety on sensory

Learning About Nature (cont.)

dimensions of their world and themselves" (Torquati & Barber, 2005, p. 40). When outdoor play spaces are created with attention to the needs and interests of infants and toddlers, they learn something in every content area. For example:

- *Approaches to learning* — Children choose what area of the outdoor play space to explore. They solve problems with dirt, water, wheeled toys, and buckets. They learn to put on their coats, hats, and mittens on their own.

- *Social and emotional development* — Children begin to resolve conflicts, such as who gets to use the red shovel. They share a ride on a sled, squat side by side to look at a caterpillar, and shout with glee when a worm tickles their finger.

- *Physical development and health* — Children crawl and roll on the grass, climb on a tree stump, straddle a log, run between the picnic table and the tree over and over (and over) again, and jump over (or into) a puddle. They carry their discoveries from one part of the play yard to another.

- *Communication, language, and literacy* — Children enjoy the sound of their voices yelling in the open air. They talk about the interesting things they discover on a branch or burrowing in the ground. Children are naturally curious and will continually ask why and what questions.

- *Cognitive development* — Children use all their senses to explore an object, for example, how does this dried leaf feel? Does it smell? They notice how things are the same and different and use their bodies to move

through space at different speeds. Children build with twigs, leaves, and pebbles and fill and empty pails in the sandbox. They remember where they left the riding toy and return to that location to ride it again. Children look at the same thing from different perspectives — from under the climber, behind the bush, upside down lying on their back or stomach, or swaying back and forth in the swing.

- *Creative arts* — Children mold shapes with snow and make marks in the dirt with sticks and shells. They draw with chalk on the pavement. Children pretend to be doggies and crawl on all fours. They listen to the musical sounds of insects, birds, and wind chimes. Even their own voices sound different in the open air than they do indoors.

"No matter where we live," says Rosenow (2008), "we all have a chance to enjoy the enduring beauty and goodness of nature. We must work hard to ensure that the next generation has that same opportunity" (p. 13). One group aiming for that future is the Nature Action Collaborative for Children (NACC), an international initiative of the World Forum Foundation. Membership is free, and the collaborative offers many resources and promotes the sharing of ideas. For more information, visit the NACC website at www.worldforumfoundation.org/wf/nacc.

- *Garden plants.* Gardens of any type provide infants with a wealth of sights, textures, and smells. Raised garden beds provide young infants with colors and textures to view, and they give older infants who want to reach the flowers an added incentive for pulling themselves up to stand. Plantings can include flowers (nontoxic), vegetables, herbs, grains, and grasses.

Equipment and materials for toddlers

As walkers and climbers, toddlers are eager to explore a wide range of outdoor equipment and materials, including natural features and things to climb, balance on, swing on, throw and kick, dig, push and pull, or ride.

- *Natural features.* The toddler outdoor-play area is more than a fenced-off patch of grass, although this is what caregivers may start with. Shade trees, grasses, low shrubs, and plants (all nontoxic), vegetable gardens, a hill, a very shallow water course, stepping stones, and sand invite toddlers to spend time exploring nature, picking flowers, and enjoying the rigors of outdoor play. The more the area is like a backyard and the more varied its natural features, the more toddlers and caregivers will want to be outdoors.

- *Things to climb.* A climbing structure allows toddlers to safely climb sturdy steps, ladders, or ramps. This climber may include a low-sided, toddler-height slide; alternatively, the slide may be free-standing or set into a hillside. To cushion falls, caregivers can position the climber and slide on a surface such as sand or rubber matting.

- *Things to get inside of.* Toddlers enjoy playing in cozy places (corrugated packing boxes, tunnels, tents) and underneath the low-hanging branches of trees or shrubs. Some climbers also include little "rooms" to crawl into.

- *Things to balance on.* Along with liking the challenge of steps and ramps, toddlers like to try balancing on low tree-stump rounds, flat rocks or stepping stones, planks, flat boards, and low balance beams. They also like to straddle logs.

- *Swings.* Toddlers like to use low soft-seat swings for sitting or lying on their tummies. Underneath these should be a soft surface, such as sand or rubber matting. A very low, deep, cloth hammock provides children with a type of swing they can either sit or lie on — don't forget the soft surface underneath, however, as hammocks may tip their users.

- *Sand and water.* The outside area should include a sandbox large enough for several children (and perhaps an adult) to sit in comfortably with a collection of sand toys. If possible, the sandbox should be located close to an outdoor water faucet so children can add water to their sandbox play. The sandbox should be constructed to allow drainage, covered

This play yard includes a variety of surfaces, levels, equipment, and materials for toddlers to explore.

when not in use, and cleaned of foreign matter on a regular basis (NAEYC, 2007, criterion 9.B.05).

- *Balls.* Caregivers can provide toddlers with large beach balls, 10" and 12" playground balls, small rubber balls they can hold in one hand, and tennis balls for kicking, throwing, rolling, and carrying. Some toddlers will enjoy rolling balls down the hill, slide, or ramp and through tunnels, and dropping them off the climber.

- *Riding and rocking toys.* The play yard should include sturdy rocking toys and riding toys (without steering mechanisms for younger toddlers, with steering mechanisms for older toddlers). Some older toddlers may also enjoy small (10"-wheel) tricycles. Though toddlers will use riding toys on grass, they can generally ride better on decks, paths, walkways, or sidewalks. They also enjoy ringing and tooting vehicle bells and horns.

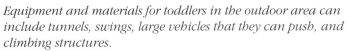

Equipment and materials for toddlers in the outdoor area can include tunnels, swings, large vehicles that they can push, and climbing structures.

- *Push and pull toys.* Toddlers take pleasure in pulling wagons; filling them with sticks, sand, or leaves; and even turning them over and spinning their wheels. They also enjoy maneuvering small, lightweight wheelbarrows, garden carts, shopping carts, or baby carriages. If it snows, the play yard should include small plastic sleds for pulling, pushing, and sliding.

- *Loose materials.* Some indoor materials are particularly fun and easy to use outdoors, for example, paints and paper, colored chalk, bubble-blowing materials, beanbags, and blankets for tents.

Storage

Whenever possible, caregivers should store all loose outdoor playthings at the play yard, in a shed or watertight storage box. Otherwise, these materials, along with riding toys, wagons, carts, strollers, and sleds can be stored as close to the yard as possible. The storage system should allow caregivers to save steps and time and to focus more on children than on moving materials. Any indoor materials that are usually used outdoors can be stored in baskets, bags, or buckets with handles; this makes it easy for caregivers to quickly sling them over their shoulder or arm, and toddlers are able to help in carrying them outdoors. Wheeled luggage is also a good option to avoid back strain and allow easy movement to and within the outdoor area. Toddlers will enjoy helping to pull a piece of luggage on wheels, and it may even become the toy or equipment of interest

itself. (See pp. 277–278 for a summary checklist of equipment and materials for the outdoor play yard).

Modifying the Learning Environment to Accommodate Children With Special Needs

Infants and toddlers with a wide range of special needs (e.g., speech and language delays, chronic illness, physical impairments, developmental disabilities) benefit from being in programs with typically developing children. Staff and children without special needs are also enriched by their daily contact with such children and their families. Infants and toddlers are particularly well suited to accepting children of different abilities and developmental levels as a matter of course. As far as they are concerned, everyone and everything is equal when it comes to learning about a world that presents new people, objects, and events on a daily — even an hourly — basis.

The primary goals of inclusion programs — those enrolling children both with and without special needs — are to allow all children to participate fully, operate as independently as possible, and reach their maximum developmental potential. The equipment and materials in the learning environment can contribute significantly toward the accomplishment of these individual and program goals. To support children as they navigate the space, caregivers need to avoid a tendency toward overprotection so infants and

Toddlers with special needs need the same opportunities for exploration and learning as their peers who do not have special needs.

toddlers with special needs will develop feelings of competence alongside their typically developing peers. This entails maintaining an ongoing and open dialogue with family members as well, concerned for their children's health and safety.

Furnishing a program that includes children with special needs presents both challenges and creative opportunities. In addition to meeting regular licensing standards, such programs must also comply with requirements in the Individuals With Disabilities Education Act (IDEA). This involves adapting policies and practices, including making various physical accommodations in the learning environment.

Modification typically involves how the space is arranged and how the equipment and materials are chosen and used in the setting. Considerations include addressing relevant health and safety precautions, promoting the young child's emerging self-sufficiency, and providing opportunities for learning on a par with children who do not have special needs.

Sometimes accommodations require only minor adjustments. Often creative problem solving and readily available supplies suffice to increase the safety, accessibility, or use of equipment and materials. Other cases entail the purchase of specialized equipment or specific assistive devices. For guidelines and suggestions on how to modify a learning environment to accommodate children with special needs in an inclusion setting, see the sidebar on page 259. Other resources include the Division for Early Childhood of the Council for Exceptional Children (www.dec-sped.org), IDEA Infant and Toddler Coordinators Association (www.IDEAinfanttoddler.org) and National Dissemination Center for Children and Youth With Disabilities (www.nichcy.org).

Creating an Infant-Toddler Active Learning Setting: Where to Start

This chapter has described setting up an environment that offers order and flexibility, provides comfort for children and adults, and supports infants' and toddlers' sensory-motor approach to learning. If caregivers feel overwhelmed thinking

Accommodating Children With Special Needs

Below are several ideas for adapting materials in an early childhood setting to accommodate children with special needs. Many of these strategies will also help typically developing infants and toddlers to operate with greater independence and use their senses in more diverse and interesting ways.

Ideas for adapting available materials

- To make brush handles and crayons easier to grip, wrap them with masking tape or slide them through a slit in a small rubber ball.

- Paste fabric shapes and other small materials onto a storybook to make it more tactile.

- Lower easels and coat hooks.

- For children with impaired vision, accompany vision-based activities with auditory options.

- For children with impaired hearing, accompany auditory-based activities with visual options.

- Prop children who cannot sit with bolsters or pillows.

- Raise or lower surface heights as needed, for example, shorten table legs or add sturdy extensions.

- Eliminate pets or plants that may aggravate respiratory problems.

Ideas for accommodating wheelchairs

- Measure traffic lanes to guarantee easy maneuverability.

- Add ramps to maximize access not only in and out of the building but also to areas children use within the building.

- Make sure wheels will not catch on the edges of rugs, tables and chairs, and other furnishings. If necessary, add padding to corners (firmly secured so children will not pull it off).

- Check table heights so wheelchairs can fit underneath. Add blocks, rubber or foam pads, or other sturdy wedges as needed. Securely fasten large trays to the arms of wheelchairs so children can use this surface to work alongside their peers.

- Position water and sand tables with ample space for wheelchairs around them.

- Explore scooter boards or other safe and appropriate options as mobility alternatives.

Possible specialized purchases

- Eating utensils with special grips or edges

- Puzzles with extra-large pieces or knobs

- Books with extra-large pictures

- Hypoallergenic art materials

- Foods that accommodate allergies or other nutritional problems

- Magnifying glasses, sound amplifiers, and other assistive devices

For information on how HighScope programs can be adapted for children with special needs, see Dowling and Mitchell (2007) and other resources on special needs listed at HighScope's online store (www.highscope.org).

about setting up or redesigning their environment for infants and toddlers, they should remember that it is a gradual, thoughtful team process. Here are some ideas caregivers can keep in mind as they work together with all the adults who share their space:

Start simply

Look at the space and resources available and the areas already established. Decide what is working, and identify just one or two things to change or modify first. Try out these new ideas, and watch to see how they affect the children and working relationships among staff before attempting further changes.

Gradually add new items or new arrangements to the setting

Without taking away any of children's old favorites, start by adding a few new materials or perhaps just reorganizing some of the ones already there. Once there are new materials for toddlers to use, add to or subtract from them gradually instead of suddenly removing one set of materials and introducing a whole new set. This same approach applies to replacing old equipment with new. Toddlers are choice-makers and rely on a predictable environment. They trust that the materials, toys, and equipment they have played with today will be there for them to play with tomorrow and the next day and the next.

Remember, most toys travel

This chapter has offered many suggestions for storage. But infant-toddler caregivers know that regardless of where things are stored and what area they are associated with, many objects and materials will move about the play space according to the needs and desires of the children. The dolls may be stored in the house area, for example, but toddlers will play with them all over the room. Some art materials, however, may be used only in the art area, where the floor is easy to clean. When materials are consistently accessible to children on a daily basis, children in a child care setting quickly learn, for example, that messy materials like paint stay in designated areas where cleanup is easy, whereas materials like blocks, books, and baby dolls can travel with them wherever they choose to play. At cleanup times things that have "traveled" can be returned to their storage places.

Provide an appropriate area and materials for *all* the children who use the play space

If nonmobile and mobile infants as well as younger and older toddlers share the same general play space, think of ways to provide, for example, a consistent art area for the interested toddlers, as well as the different kinds of play spaces that both nonmobile and mobile infants need. This may mean storing art materials in see-through drawers that toddlers can operate but infants cannot, or dedicating one ample area to nonmobile infants, another to mobile infants, and another to young toddlers and then surrounding each of these areas with low barriers so children of all ages can still see one another but learn to play and explore within their own area.

Take room-arrangement cues from the children

If toddlers are frequently building block structures that topple over into the book area, think about relocating the books or the blocks, or come up with a way to create a low barrier between the two areas. If infants are tearing picture books, place these more delicate books in pockets on a shelf that is above infant reach but within reach of toddlers. Or, as one caregiver team did, solve this problem by placing nonboard books in a toddler loft that is accessible by a short ladder. In another center, when several toddlers developed the habit of emptying

their cubbies to play "house" in them, caregivers brought in corrugated cartons for the children to play in. The children liked these cartons and quickly appropriated them as "new houses," leaving their cubbies to serve, once again, as personal storage space.

Enjoy the active learning environment

Finally, caregivers should enjoy the setting they have created — its indoor and outdoor areas, the comfort and opportunities they provide, the kinds of exploration and discovery children can engage in there. If caregivers look forward to entering their active learning environment each day, so will the children in their care!

In a well-designed learning environment, even the youngest children have plenty of places to explore and learn.

What Caregivers Need for the Eating and Food Preparation Area

Eating utensils
- ❑ Baby bottles (labeled sets for each infant)
- ❑ Plastic plates with upward-curved edges
- ❑ Plastic shallow bowls
- ❑ Plastic cups with weighted bottoms and spouted tops
- ❑ Plastic drinking glasses wide enough for toddlers to hold with both hands
- ❑ Spoons with short handles

Protective clothing
- ❑ Bibs (labeled sets for each infant)
- ❑ Towels (labeled sets for each infant)
- ❑ Slip-on bibs for toddlers
- ❑ Napkins or hand towels for toddlers not using bibs
- ❑ Smocks or aprons, as needed for toddlers

Cleaning supplies
- ❑ Dishcloths and sponges
- ❑ Disinfectants
- ❑ Detergents
- ❑ Cleaning solutions
- ❑ Broom, dustpan, mop, vacuum (depending on floor surface)
- ❑ Buckets for warm, soapy water
- ❑ Child-sized brooms, brushes, dustpans
- ❑ Wastebasket

Appliances/furnishings
- ❑ Sink with hot running water
- ❑ Refrigerator
- ❑ Dishwasher
- ❑ Microwave oven
- ❑ Bottle warmer or slow cooker
- ❑ Cupboards or shelves above children's reach
- ❑ At least one cupboard/closet with a childproof latch
- ❑ Baskets or hooks for individualized bibs, smocks, aprons

Furniture

For bottle-feeding infants
- ❑ Comfortable chair, couch, or pillows for adult holding child

For infants sitting and trying out solid food
- ❑ Pillows (e.g., Boppy pillow) or an infant seat (e.g., Bumbo baby seat) to prop the sitting child

For infants able to sit alone
- ❑ Breakfast-in-bed tray tables to seat one child or very low tables (12" high)
- ❑ Infant-sized chairs or stools (seats 5½"–6" high)

For toddlers
- ❑ Toddler-sized tables (14"–16" in height)
- ❑ Toddler-sized chairs or stools (seats 6½"–8" high)

What Caregivers Need for the Sleeping and Napping Area

Furnishings

❑ Crib, cradle, or basket (one for each infant, labeled with child's name)

❑ Crib or cot (for each toddler)

❑ Firm mattress, snugly fitting (one for each crib)

❑ Closed hamper, sealable bags for soiled bedding

Bedding (*Note:* Check AAP and local licensing regulations regarding the safety of these items.)

❑ Protective mattress pad (one for each bed)

❑ Fitted sheet (one for each bed)

❑ Blanket or quilt (one for each bed)

❑ Extra bedding for each child

Comfort items (*Note:* Check AAP and local licensing regulations regarding the safety of these items.)

❑ Items chosen by, reserved for each child (stuffed toy, pacifier, "blankie")

Appliances (optional if parents or a commercial laundry clean soiled bedding)

❑ Washer

❑ Dryer (or accessible clothesline in sunny, dry climate)

What Caregivers Need for the Diapering, Dressing, and Bathroom Area

Furnishings
- ❏ Sink
- ❏ Step stool for sink (if not toddler height)
- ❏ Mirror over sink
- ❏ Changing table or counter (about 36" high, low raised sides, cleanable soft surface)
- ❏ Set of steps for climbing to changing table (or climb-up changing table)
- ❏ Closed, foot-operated containers for soiled disposable diapers, wipes, changing-table papers
- ❏ Hampers, sealable bags (for soiled cloth diapers, clothing)
- ❏ Container of small, washable toys
- ❏ Child-accessible toilet paper dispensers
- ❏ Toddler-sized toilets or potty chairs
- ❏ Step stools for full-sized toilets, if needed
- ❏ Cupboards or shelves for adults' easy access to changing supplies

Clothing
- ❏ Diapers and diaper covers and fasteners (if used) for each child
- ❏ Underpants for each child, as needed
- ❏ Change of clothes for each child
- ❏ Container (plastic tub, bag, pillowcase) labeled for each child to store clothing items

Personal care items
- ❏ Soap suitable for children's skin
- ❏ Disposable wipes or a supply of washcloths for each child
- ❏ Hairbrush for each child, as needed
- ❏ Diaper creams (as needed, with written parental instructions)
- ❏ Hand-washing soap in pump dispenser
- ❏ Child hand towels, paper or cloth
- ❏ Toilet paper

Cleaning supplies
- ❏ Disinfectants
- ❏ Spray soaps and cleaners
- ❏ Cleaning cloths
- ❏ Roll of paper (for covering changing surface)
- ❏ Disposable gloves

Materials That Appeal to Children's Senses

Aromatic materials and experiences[6]
- ❏ Large wooden balls and boxes
- ❏ Wool, felt, and leather balls
- ❏ Sturdy rubber balls and teething rings
- ❏ Tennis balls
- ❏ Sturdily constructed small cloth bags filled with common household spices
- ❏ Wicker baskets and woven mats
- ❏ Bread dough, play dough, and clay
- ❏ Shaving cream
- ❏ Newspaper
- ❏ Flowering plants (nontoxic)
- ❏ Outdoor play where children can smell grass, dirt, leaves, bark, flowers, rain
- ❏ Smells of food being prepared and cooked
- ❏ A variety of foods to eat and smell
- ❏ Empty spice bottles (cinnamon, garlic, cloves)

Sound-producing materials and experiences
- ❏ Toy rattles, dried gourds
- ❏ Firmly sealed film cans or tins containing beans, rice, pea gravel, water
- ❏ Rain sticks
- ❏ Castanets
- ❏ Bells
- ❏ Xylophones, metallophones
- ❏ Pan lids

- ❏ Cookie tins
- ❏ Metal juice-can lids, metal and wooden spoons and bowls
- ❏ Crinkly paper
- ❏ Wind chimes, ticking clocks, chiming clocks, music boxes
- ❏ Musical recordings
- ❏ Singing
- ❏ Outdoor play and sounds
- ❏ Banners, streamers that flap in the breeze
- ❏ Sound of rain on the roof and windows
- ❏ Jumping and rolling in piles of dry leaves

Materials to touch, taste, and look at

Objects from nature
- ❏ Pine cones (closed "petals")
- ❏ Rocks
- ❏ Sturdy shells
- ❏ Sticks and twigs
- ❏ Dried gourds
- ❏ Big feathers
- ❏ Pumice stone
- ❏ Fresh avocado pits
- ❏ Natural sponge
- ❏ Pieces of loofah
- ❏ Lemons, apples
- ❏ Edible flowers

[6]Check with families regarding children's allergies to foods, scents, and fabrics.

Materials That Appeal to Children's Senses (cont.)

Objects made from natural materials
- ❏ Marble "eggs"
- ❏ Small baskets
- ❏ Bottle corks
- ❏ Small rafia mats
- ❏ Natural-bristle brushes with wooden handles (for nails, teeth, shaving, shoes, house painting, cosmetics)
- ❏ Prisms
- ❏ Stained-glass windows

Wooden objects
- ❏ Small boxes
- ❏ Small drum on wooden frame
- ❏ Rattles
- ❏ Castanets
- ❏ Clothespins (peg or pincer grip type)
- ❏ Large, strung, colored beads
- ❏ Inch cubes
- ❏ Spools
- ❏ Spoons, spatulas
- ❏ Egg cups
- ❏ Small bowls

Metal objects
- ❏ Measuring spoons
- ❏ Spoons
- ❏ Small whisks
- ❏ Keys on a chain or ring
- ❏ Small tins
- ❏ Small pot-pie tins
- ❏ Lemon squeezer
- ❏ Small funnels

- ❏ Brass curtain rings
- ❏ Garlic press
- ❏ Whistle
- ❏ Slip-on bangle bracelets
- ❏ Bottle brush
- ❏ Small metal mirrors
- ❏ Key rings linked together
- ❏ Large bells, attached to wraparound band (in musical instrument catalogs)
- ❏ Tea strainers
- ❏ Lengths of chain
- ❏ Bicycle bell
- ❏ Tea infuser
- ❏ Aluminum foil

Objects of leather, cloth, rubber, fur
- ❏ Leather purse
- ❏ Small leather bag or key case with zipper
- ❏ Leather eyeglass case
- ❏ High-bouncer balls
- ❏ Lengths of rubber tubing
- ❏ Bath/drain plugs with chains
- ❏ Velvet powder puffs
- ❏ Fur ball
- ❏ Pieces of felt in assorted colors, sizes, shapes
- ❏ Small rag dolls
- ❏ Small teddy bears
- ❏ Balls of yarn
- ❏ Potholders
- ❏ Bandanas

Materials That Appeal to Children's Senses (cont.)

Objects of leather, cloth, rubber, fur (cont.)

- ❑ Silk scarves
- ❑ Short lengths of blanket satin, lace
- ❑ Tennis balls
- ❑ Golf balls

Paper/cardboard items

- ❑ Small notebooks or note pads
- ❑ Wax paper
- ❑ Small boxes
- ❑ Paper towel/cardboard tubes
- ❑ Board books
- ❑ Post cards
- ❑ Foil paper
- ❑ Cardboard boxes

Materials and Equipment That Support Movement

When children are moving their limbs, turning themselves over, and rolling, they need
- ❏ Safe, soft spaces on the floor and ground for lying, turning over, rolling
- ❏ Interesting, graspable toys, materials, and people to reach for, hold on to, let go of

When children are sitting, they need
- ❏ Safe, comfortable places to sit on a variety of physical levels with a variety of vistas, both indoors and outdoors
- ❏ Very low tables to use while sitting on the floor
- ❏ Materials to explore, grasp, bang, and drop while sitting

When children are scooting and crawling, they need
- ❏ Safe open spaces and pathways for scooting and crawling on the floor and ground
- ❏ Ramps and steps for crawling to different levels
- ❏ Tunnels to crawl through
- ❏ Boxes or cartons and other cozy spaces to crawl into
- ❏ A variety of appealing materials and vistas to crawl toward
- ❏ Balls to crawl after

When children are cruising, they need
- ❏ Sturdy, well-anchored equipment to hold on to and lean against as they pull themselves up to stand (chairs, benches, tables, handrails, handholds)
- ❏ Sturdy push toys with long handles (to push, lean against, and help with balance)

When children are walking, riding, and rocking, they need
- ❏ Clear pathways with safe surfaces for walking both indoors and outdoors
- ❏ Ramps and steps with railings to practice walking up and down
- ❏ Wagons and sleds big enough to pull and ride in
- ❏ Rocking chairs, rocking boats, rocking horses, and low deep hammocks
- ❏ A variety of riding toys to sit on and propel by scooting with their feet

When children are climbing, jumping, and running, they need
- ❏ Safe spaces both indoors and out for climbing, jumping, running
- ❏ A variety of safe climbers, slides, steps, and ladders
- ❏ A variety of levels and padded landing areas for safe jumping
- ❏ Interesting things to run toward, around, up and down (trees, boulders, benches, bales of straw, ramps, hills)

What Caregivers Need for Infants' Indoor Play

Pleasant reminders of home
- ❏ Comfort items (favorite "teddy," "blankie," pacifier)
- ❏ Family photographs (laminated)

Materials for sensory exploration and play[7]
- ❏ Mirrors (unbreakable)
- ❏ Materials with aroma (wool, rubber, leather, cedar wood)
- ❏ Rattles, bells, sealed tins with noisy contents
- ❏ Other sound-producing materials (water, music recordings, chimes)
- ❏ Objects from nature (shells, rocks, cones, a lemon, a gourd)
- ❏ Objects made of natural materials (natural-bristle brushes, bottle corks, marble eggs)
- ❏ Wooden objects (spoons, inch cubes, clothespins, spools, large beads)
- ❏ Metal objects (keys on a chain, spoons, whisks, bangle bracelets, juice-can lids)
- ❏ Textile, leather items (scarves, powder puffs, leather eyeglass case)
- ❏ Soft dolls and stuffed animals
- ❏ Paper products (newspaper, boxes, towel tubes, food cartons)
- ❏ Open containers (juice cans, butter tubs, baskets)
- ❏ Lightweight blocks

Materials to set in motion
- ❏ Balls (cloth, fur, wool, leather, rubber, tennis balls, Wiffle balls)
- ❏ Hinged doors and boxes
- ❏ Small-wheeled vehicles and animals

Movement equipment
- ❏ Ramps
- ❏ Steps
- ❏ Climbing platform
- ❏ Mattress
- ❏ Tunnels
- ❏ Boxes
- ❏ Full-sized chair, couch for pulling up to stand
- ❏ Handrails, handholds for pulling up
- ❏ Sturdy push toys to lean against while cruising

First picture books
- ❏ Cloth books
- ❏ Board books, for example:[8]

  Blue Buggy by Janet and Allan Ahlberg

  Big Red Barn by Margaret Wise Brown

  Find the Puppy by Stephen Cartwright

  Tomie's Little Mother Goose by Tomie dePaola

  Pat the Bunny by Dorothy Kunhardt

  Dressing by Helen Oxenbury

Storage
- ❏ Portable baskets, plastic milk crates, buckets, boxes, tins, cloth or mesh bags
- ❏ Low sturdy shelves (with clear plastic storage containers)
- ❏ Forward-facing bookrack, clear hanging book pockets

[7]Check with families regarding children's allergies to foods, scents, and fabrics.
[8]Visit the HighScope website (www.highscope.org) for additional board books.

What Caregivers Need for the Toddlers' Movement Area

Things to climb on and jump off
- ❑ Steps
- ❑ Ramps
- ❑ Toddler loft
- ❑ Dowel climber
- ❑ Risers
- ❑ Sturdy wooden boxes
- ❑ Large hollow wooden blocks and planks
- ❑ Large vinyl-covered foam cubes and wedges
- ❑ Pillows and soft mats to jump onto

Things to get inside of
- ❑ Boxes, cartons
- ❑ Tunnels
- ❑ Small hollow risers that can be turned over to be boxes
- ❑ Space under toddler loft

Push and pull toys
- ❑ Wagons
- ❑ Pull toys on strings
- ❑ Push toys with long handles

Riding/rocking toys
- ❑ Rocking toys (horse, boat)
- ❑ Riding toys (to sit on, scoot with feet, no steering mechanism) for younger toddlers
- ❑ Riding toys (to sit on, scoot with feet, simple steering) for older toddlers

Balls
- ❑ Cloth and foam balls
- ❑ Tennis balls
- ❑ Rubber balls
- ❑ Wiffle balls

Simple musical instruments/recordings
- ❑ Rattles, shakers
- ❑ Bells
- ❑ Xylophone and mallet
- ❑ Metallophone and mallet
- ❑ Sturdy bongo drum or floor drum
- ❑ Tambourine
- ❑ Small, sturdy rain stick
- ❑ Musical recordings with distinct beat

What Caregivers Need for the Toddlers' Sand and Water Area

Equipment
- ❑ Sand/water table(s), toddler height
- ❑ Baby bathtub or child's wading pool (inexpensive alternatives to sand and water table)
- ❑ Baskets, tubs, plastic milk crates for storage of sand/water playthings
- ❑ Clean playground sand
- ❑ Low box/platform for shorter children
- ❑ Buckets for filling/draining water table

Things to fill and empty with
- ❑ Small plastic buckets, cups, ice cube trays
- ❑ Empty food containers (butter tubs, small milk cartons)
- ❑ Wide-mouth cloth bags
- ❑ Small plastic plant pots (one glued inside another)
- ❑ Basters and plastic squeeze bottles
- ❑ Metal shovels, scoops, spoons
- ❑ Funnels, sieves

Things to float, soak, and squeeze
- ❑ Boats
- ❑ Corks
- ❑ Ping-Pong balls
- ❑ Sponges
- ❑ Loofah
- ❑ Washcloths

Things to hide and find
- ❑ Shells
- ❑ Stones
- ❑ Feathers
- ❑ Sticks

Things to pretend with
- ❑ Rubber or plastic animal figures
- ❑ Rubber or plastic people figures

What Caregivers Need for the Toddlers' Book Area

Comfortable furnishings (some combination of the following)
- ❏ Mattress, quilt, pillows
- ❏ Low easy chairs
- ❏ Low couch
- ❏ Large carton (for book nook)
- ❏ Stuffed toys, toddler-sized puppets for representing story characters

Book storage
- ❏ Forward-facing bookrack
- ❏ Clear hanging book pockets
- ❏ Low shelf with tub(s) or basket(s) or plastic milk crate(s)

Books[9]
- ❏ Board books with clear drawings or photos and simple text if any, such as

  See the Rabbit by Janet and Allan Ahlberg

  Goodnight Moon by Margaret Wise Brown

  Bus by Chris L. Demarest

  All Fall Down by Helen Oxenbury

  I Can by Helen Oxenbury

  Shake Shake Shake by Andrea and Brian Pinkney

- ❏ Picture books, for example

  My First Mother Goose illustrated by Rosemary Wells

  Play With Me by Marie Hall Ets

  Ask Mr. Bear by Marjorie Flack

  Flower Garden by Eve Bunting

- ❏ Wordless books, for example

  The Snowman by Raymond Briggs

  Rosie's Walk by Pat Hutchins

Magazines, pictures, photos
- ❏ Small photo albums
- ❏ Post card collection
- ❏ *Babybug,* a board book magazine for infants and toddlers (www.babybugmagkids.com)
- ❏ Magazines with pictures
- ❏ Catalogs

Fish (optional)
- ❏ Aquarium or fish tank
- ❏ Pebbles, stones for the bottom
- ❏ Goldfish or other low-maintenance fish
- ❏ Fish food

[9]Visit the HighScope website at www.highscope.org for additional board and picture books, with and without words.

What Caregivers Need for the Toddlers' Art Area

Painting and drawing materials

- ❏ Finger paints (red, yellow, blue), commercial or homemade
- ❏ Nontoxic tempera paints, liquid or powder (red, yellow, blue)
- ❏ Small, stable containers for paint (muffin tins; cut-down yogurt cups or tuna cans set in a cake tin; baby food jars set in a sponge; heavy, lidded plastic containers; paper or plastic plates)
- ❏ Short-handled brushes
- ❏ Small house-painting brushes (several widths)
- ❏ Brush alternatives (scrub brushes, dish-washing mops, feathers, sticks, cotton balls, sponges)
- ❏ Crayons
- ❏ Nontoxic water-based markers (such as Bingo markers)
- ❏ Chalk
- ❏ Small squeeze bottles of dribble salt (equal parts flour, salt, water, with a few drops of paint)

Paper

- ❏ Newspaper, newsprint
- ❏ Roll of white butcher paper
- ❏ Kraft or construction paper
- ❏ Tissue paper
- ❏ Cellophane

Dough and clay materials

- ❏ Play dough
- ❏ Clay
- ❏ Poking and sticking materials (wooden pegs, Popsicle sticks, shells, stones, jar lids, bottle caps, corks, rubber stoppers, golf balls, metal keys)
- ❏ Airtight containers for dough and clay

Furnishings

- ❏ Sink or water supply
- ❏ Buckets, clear boxes, or racks to store brushes
- ❏ Holder for colored markers
- ❏ Labeled containers for crayons, chalk, similar items
- ❏ Bucket for transporting paintbrushes to sink
- ❏ Low shelves with wheels, low supply cart
- ❏ Paper storage rack
- ❏ Upright or horizontal holder for paper roll
- ❏ Table(s)
- ❏ Easel, freestanding or wall-mounted
- ❏ Plastic or vinyl smocks, wooden pegs to hang them on

What Caregivers Need for the Toddlers' Block Area

Blocks

- ❑ Large plastic, foam, or cardboard "brick" blocks (at least 20)
- ❑ Wooden unit blocks (including half units, basic units, double units)

Vehicles, people, animals

- ❑ Sturdy wooden or plastic dump trucks
- ❑ Sturdy wooden or plastic bulldozers
- ❑ Small cars (easy for child to hold in one hand)
- ❑ Small vehicles that can hold peg people or animals
- ❑ Wooden, rubber, or plastic people and animal figures

Furnishings

- ❑ Low storage shelves
- ❑ Labeled baskets, bins, plastic milk crates, or clear plastic containers

What Caregivers Need for the Toddlers' House Area

Dolls and accessories
- ❏ Baby dolls (soft-bodied, reflecting the racial and ethnic identities of the children in the program)
- ❏ Simple doll clothes (with Velcro closings)
- ❏ Baby bottles
- ❏ Baby blankets
- ❏ Doll bed (large and strong enough to hold a toddler)
- ❏ Doll carriage and/or stroller (large and strong enough to hold a toddler)

Kitchen furnishings
- ❏ Toddler-sized stove
- ❏ Toddler-sized sink
- ❏ Toddler-sized refrigerator
- ❏ Toddler-sized table and chairs
- ❏ Phones (toy and/or real)

Dishes and utensils (real, not toy)
- ❏ Small pots and pans (including cooking equipment children find at home, e.g., wok, rice steamer, tortilla press, clay pot)
- ❏ Utensils: spatula, whisk, tea strainer, wooden spoons, metal measuring cups and spoons, bottle brush
- ❏ Plastic cups, bowls, plates
- ❏ Spoons
- ❏ Empty food containers (milk cartons, cereal boxes)
- ❏ Corks and shells for food

Dress-up clothes and accessories
- ❏ Hats
- ❏ Shoes
- ❏ Vests, jackets, short dresses
- ❏ Scarves, bandanas, fabric remnants
- ❏ Purses (with handles or short straps), change purses
- ❏ Briefcases
- ❏ Keys on chains
- ❏ Lunch boxes
- ❏ Bangle bracelets without clasps
- ❏ Full-length mirror (unbreakable)

Nontoxic plants
- ❏ Hardy house plants (philodendron, Christmas cactus, grape ivy)
- ❏ Traditional garden plants (nasturtiums, lettuce, herbs, grass)

Storage
- ❏ Low shelves
- ❏ Large open containers, baskets, tubs, plastic milk crates
- ❏ Wooden pegs and shower curtain rings (to hang pots and pans)

What Caregivers Need for the Toddlers' Toy Area

Things to fit together and take apart

- ❏ Sturdy puzzles (three to five pieces; any knobs should be firmly attached)
- ❏ Shape sorter and shapes
- ❏ Graduated-size nesting objects: cans, tins, boxes, cups, spoons, people or animal shapes
- ❏ Large interlocking blocks (Lego, Duplos, bristle, magnetic)
- ❏ Wooden pounding bench, pegs, and mallet
- ❏ Large plastic pop-together, pull-apart beads

Off/on, open/close materials

- ❏ Flashlights (easy-to-operate switches or buttons, child-safe battery compartments)
- ❏ Zippered bags, pouches, cosmetic cases
- ❏ Wooden and metal boxes with hinged lids, easy-to-work latches or locks

Things for filling and emptying

- ❏ Small, colored wooden blocks
- ❏ Wooden counting cubes
- ❏ Large wooden beads, short lengths of lacing or plastic-coated wire
- ❏ Short lengths of metal chain
- ❏ Large pegs and pegboards
- ❏ Collections of strong shells, smooth stones; pine cones; wooden peg-style clothespins, spools, balls/blocks; fabric pieces
- ❏ Containers to fill and empty (oatmeal boxes, tins, baskets)

Things for pretend play

- ❏ Small people figures
- ❏ Small animal figures
- ❏ Small, sturdy vehicles: cars, trucks, buses, campers
- ❏ Simple train
- ❏ Small, soft puppets, toddler-sized

Furnishings

- ❏ Low storage shelf
- ❏ Open baskets and containers (labeled) for small items

What Caregivers Need in the Outdoor Play Yard for Infants and Toddlers

Natural features
- ❑ Shade trees
- ❑ Shrubs, grasses, flowers
- ❑ Raised vegetable/herb garden
- ❑ Hill
- ❑ Shallow water course
- ❑ Stepping stones
- ❑ Soft surfaces (sand or rubber matting) under climbers and swings

Movement materials (infants)
- ❑ Gentle slope
- ❑ Tree stump rounds
- ❑ Logs
- ❑ Railroad ties or landscape timbers
- ❑ Flat rocks
- ❑ Steps
- ❑ Large, inflated inner tube
- ❑ Low platform
- ❑ Canvas- or vinyl-covered mattress
- ❑ Bench or wagon (to pull up to stand)
- ❑ Boxes, cartons
- ❑ Tunnels
- ❑ Tents
- ❑ Infant swing seat

Things that move in the wind
- ❑ Banners, streamers
- ❑ Foil pie tins
- ❑ Wind chimes

Crawling surfaces
- ❑ Grass
- ❑ Aromatic-herb ground cover
- ❑ Sand
- ❑ Leaves
- ❑ Decking
- ❑ Pathways of flagstone, clay, concrete, wood

Water play materials (mobile infants)
- ❑ Small pails, pans for water
- ❑ Floating objects

Things to climb (toddlers)
- ❑ Toddler climbing structure (over soft surface)
- ❑ Slide

Things to get inside of (toddlers)
- ❑ Sturdy corrugated boxes, cartons
- ❑ Tunnels
- ❑ Low-hanging trees or shrubs

Things to balance on (toddlers)
- ❑ Tree stump rounds
- ❑ Flat rocks
- ❑ Planks, flat boards (1" × 12")
- ❑ Balance beam on or very close to the ground

Swings (toddlers)
- ❑ Soft-seated swings (over soft surface)
- ❑ Very low cloth hammocks (over soft surface)

What Caregivers Need in the Outdoor Play Yard for Infants and Toddlers (cont.)

Materials for sand play and water play (toddlers)

- ❏ Large sandbox
- ❏ Buckets and other containers
- ❏ Shovels, scoops, funnels, sieves
- ❏ Plastic dump trucks
- ❏ Shells, sticks, stones
- ❏ Water source

Balls (toddlers)

- ❏ Beach balls
- ❏ Rubber playground balls, 10" and 12"
- ❏ Tennis balls
- ❏ Small rubber balls toddlers can hold in one hand

Riding/rocking toys (toddlers)

- ❏ Rocking toys (rocking horse, rocking boat)
- ❏ Riding toys (to sit on, scoot with feet, no steering mechanism) for younger toddlers
- ❏ Riding toys (to sit on, scoot with feet, simple steering) for older toddlers
- ❏ Horns and bells for riding toys
- ❏ Small tricycles (10" wheels) for toddlers approaching age three

Push and pull toys (toddlers)

- ❏ Wagons
- ❏ Lightweight wheelbarrows, garden carts, shopping carts, baby buggies
- ❏ Plastic sleds

Loose materials (toddlers)

- ❏ Paints and paper
- ❏ Colored chalk
- ❏ Bubble-blowing materials
- ❏ Beanbags
- ❏ Blankets for tents
- ❏ Blankets or mats for young infants

Storage

- ❏ Shed
- ❏ Watertight storage box
- ❏ Carts/baskets, bags, wheeled luggage, buckets with handles for transporting materials from indoors

Transport vehicles (infants)

- ❏ Wagons
- ❏ Strollers

Surfaces/play space boundaries (infants)

- ❏ Blankets or mats to lie on
- ❏ Low fence or wall of wood, stone, brick
- ❏ Low shrubs
- ❏ Large bolsters (canvas- or vinyl-covered)

Enjoy your active learning environment. If you look forward to entering it each day, so will the children in your care.

5

Establishing Schedules and Routines

Routines are patterns of care that, when done repeatedly, become expected.…When routines are predictable, babies know what to expect and are able to trust their world and that their needs will be met. Routines assure a stable environment.

— Kovach & Da Ros-Voseles (2008, p. 64)

onsistent routines and dependable adult behavior contribute to children's sense of ease and comfort in their care setting. Child care patterns and routines are emotion regulators. When infants and toddlers can anticipate what is going to happen next, they learn to choose behaviors that fit with the upcoming activities, thus, their "learned behaviors contribute to systems of self-control" (Butterfield, 2002, p. 30). Such predictable patterns enable infants and toddlers to avert their anxiety about being fed or changed and focus their energy instead on exploring materials and interacting with people in the safety and security of their caregiving environment.

In an active learning program, the infants' and toddlers' day includes certain *regular daily events:* arrival and departure, one or more choice times, outside time, and (for older infants and toddlers) one or more group times. Interspersed among these daily events are *individual caregiving routines:* the supportive, child-focused adult-child interactions that occur during eating, napping, and bodily care (including diapering, using the toilet, washing, and dressing).

Organizing the Day for Active Learning

Providing a predictable daily schedule and unhurried caregiving routines in an infant-toddler care setting helps young children build trust in their own abilities to predict, anticipate, and influence what will happen next. They learn there will be many opportunities to try out their actions and ideas in interesting and safe surroundings. The following scenarios illustrate the dynamics in a center with an organized day:

> *Three older infants — Jacob, Roberto, and Eva — play on the floor at mid-morning choice time. Shannon, their primary caregiver, sits on the floor with them. Roberto crawls up and down a slightly inclined ramp. Eva, sitting in a large carton tipped on its side, explores a collection of tins and oatmeal boxes. Jacob explores two big rubber balls, several tennis balls, and a Wiffle ball. He holds them, mouths them, drops them into a hole at the top of a large plastic cube, takes them out through a hole in the side of the cube, and crawls after them as they roll across the floor. At one point, Jacob crawls to Shannon, puts his head in her lap, and rubs his eyes. "Jacob," she says while stroking his head, "you look sleepy. I'm going to pick you up." When she picks him up, Jacob nestles close, lays his head on her shoulder, and closes his eyes. "It looks like it's time for your nap," she says, gently rubbing his back. She carries Jacob to his crib, lays him down, checks to make sure he doesn't need a diaper change, and covers him with his favorite bunny blanket. "Have a nice sleep," she says as Jacob at first fights to keep his eyes open and then quickly falls asleep. Shannon returns to Roberto and Eva, who continue with their play.*

~

Six toddlers sit at a low table, eating lunch. Their caregivers, Rudy and Ann, sit with them at the table and converse with them about what happened during the morning. As the children finish, they put their cups and plates into a dish tub, leave the table, and return to the riding toys they were playing with before lunchtime. Rudy stays at the table with the children who are still eating, while Ann sits on the floor near the children who are using riding toys.

When all the children have finished eating, Rudy removes the dish tub and wipes the table. Ann then takes the children, individually or by twos, into the bathroom for the caregiving routines that precede naptime. After that, she returns them to play with the riding toys until naps. Until each child has been to the bathroom and it is time for stories and naps, Rudy takes Ann's place on the floor with the children who are using riding toys.

These scenarios typify the daily occurrences in a HighScope active learning infant-toddler program. In the first scenario, the three infants have selected materials of particular interest to play with during choice time. When Jacob shows signs of sleepiness, his caregiver responds to his cues by putting him into his crib for a nap. Eva and Roberto continue to play and, like Jacob, will nap when they are ready. The six toddlers in the second scenario are engaged in a sequence of activities — lunch, riding toys, bodily care

A consistent overall daily schedule gives children a sense of continuity and control.

routines, riding toys, stories, and naps. They move with assurance from one part of their day to the next. Using the riding toys serves as an enjoyable transition from lunch and bodily care to stories and naps. The children also experience certain predictable elements within each activity. For example, every day as they finish lunch, the toddlers put their dishes into the dish tub.

Routines are not only about *what* is done to care for infants and toddlers but

Why Caregiving Routines Are Important

- *Children learn.* Caregiving routines provide regular daily opportunities for adults to interact with infants and toddlers in a patient, alert manner so children can participate in and learn through routines.

- *Children and adults strengthen their bonds.* Building strong relationships with children and looking for ways to support their experiential learning is the driving force behind caregiving routines; efficiency is *not!*

- *Adults watch and listen to children.* Caregiving routines provide intimate, one-on-one opportunities for adults to see what infants and toddlers do and say and to scaffold (support and extend) their learning across the developmental spectrum.

- *Adults learn.* During caregiving routines, adults slow themselves down to the child's pace, look for KDIs (the knowledge and skills that infants and toddlers learn), and begin to see the experience from the child's perspective.

also about *how* these routines — eating, bathing, sleeping — are carried out (Evans & Ilfeld, 1982b). When routines are carried out in an unhurried manner with tenderness, patience, and forethought about what children experience and learn during these times of day, both adults and children benefit. Teachers see their actions as meaningful rather than laborious, and they enjoy the day more because children are happier and less irritable. Infants and toddlers enjoy the intimacy of the contact and the things they see, hear, and do at such times. (See "Why Caregiving Routines Are Important" above.)

Because caregiving routines are so important in the early years, caregivers learn and respond to each infant's or toddler's *personalized* daily schedule and, at the same time, develop an *overall* daily schedule that accommodates as closely as possible all children in the group. For

ideas on how to establish daily schedules that meet children's individual needs while accommodating the group as a whole, see "Ideas for Creating Daily Schedules" on page 285.

Coordinating multiple infants' and toddlers' schedules can be a challenge. This is one reason that infant-toddler care groups are small, and there is one caregiver for every two to four children. The complexity of dealing with multiple schedules also makes it critically important for the caregiver teams to spend time each day discussing their observations of children and planning around them. They also need to solicit input from parents to help them develop (and periodically revise) daily plans for individual children and the group as a whole.

Though it is challenging to organize a program around a number of children, the benefits to them are great. When daily

Ideas for Creating Daily Schedules

1. **Gather information about each child's day.** Have primary caregivers ask parents what their child's schedule is at home (what time they eat, sleep, are awake, etc.). Ask each primary caregiver to share her information about each child.

2. **Enter each child's information on a grid.** Enter all the information by times on a grid, (see p. 286 for a sample), using the elements of the day (e.g., arrival, departure, feeding or mealtime, naptime, choice time).

3. **Look for activities among children that occur around the same time.** Look across the filled-out schedules of all the children. Based on this information, consider the following:

- What patterns do you see emerging across all schedules?

- When might it make sense to have choice time? Outside time?

- When might it make sense to have a group time for the older children?

- How might you work out feeding and mealtimes when children end up eating at the same time?

4. **Create an overall sequence of events.** Write down what an overall daily schedule for these children might look like including arrival, departure, choice time, outside time, group time, feeding and mealtime, and naptime (see p. 287 for a sample).

schedules and caregiving routines are predictable and well coordinated rather than frequently in flux, infants and toddlers are more likely to feel safe and secure. Knowing what will happen next when they wake up from a nap, for example, helps children become attuned to the rhythm of their own body and the rhythm of the day. When the day moves along on a known course, children can signal their individual needs to eat, sleep, wash, change into dry clothes, or use the toilet, and after participating in these care routines, they can rejoin the ongoing flow of events. At the beginning of the day, if children know what they will be doing after their parents leave, separating from parents and joining caregivers and peers is easier for them. As they experience the rituals and repetitions of a consistent daily schedule, infants and toddlers gain a sense of continuity and control.

Consistent routines, thus, help children develop both emotional and behavioral self-regulation. Behaviors that are repeated each day become internalized into habits. These habits, in turn, provide a sense of control and comfort. For children, just as for adults, habitual "patterns organize our behavior, organize our thinking, and help us fit in successfully with others" (Butterfield, 2002, p. 30). Moreover, carrying out caregiving routines contributes to young children's sensory and intellectual

Grid for Recording the Daily Schedules for Eight Children

Time	Child 1	Child 2	Child 3	Child 4	Child 5	Child 6	Child 7	Child 8
6:30 a.m.								
7:00 a.m.								
7:30 a.m.								
8:00 a.m.								
8:30 a.m.								
9:00 a.m.								
9:30 a.m.								
10:00 a.m.								
10:30 a.m.								
11:00 a.m.								
11:30 a.m.								
12:00 p.m.								
12:30 p.m.								
1:00 p.m.								
1:30 p.m.								
2:00 p.m.								
2:30 p.m.								
3:00 p.m.								
3:30 p.m.								
4:00 p.m.								
4:30 p.m.								
5:00 p.m.								
5:30 p.m.								
6:00 p.m.								

An Overall Daily Schedule for Eight Children

Elements of the Day	Approximate Times (Optional, will vary from day to day)

development. For example, NAEYC's guidelines on developmentally appropriate practice emphasize that eating not only meets a basic physical need but "it is also a rich sensory and emotional experience" (Copple & Bredekamp, 2009, p. 85). Likewise, the regularity of routines suits the mental development of toddlers who are "cognitively ready to learn sequences of events and feel more secure when they know what will happen next in their day" (p. 101).

Guidelines for Organizing Daily Schedules and Caregiving Routines

This chapter deals with specific ways to establish and carry out daily events and caregiving routines in an active learning setting. It begins with a discussion of these two basic guidelines:

- Create an overall daily schedule that is *predictable yet flexible.*

- Incorporate *active learning, including adult support,* into each event and caregiving routine.

Create an overall daily schedule that is predictable yet flexible

Infant-toddler caregiver teams strive for an overall daily schedule that is predictable — organized and consistent — and still flexible enough to accommodate the needs of individual children. Caregivers and children alike need the reassurance of knowing the general shape of the day (what event will happen next) and

of having the ability to bend the overall schedule of events to suit various sleeping, eating, and bodily care needs. So, while predictability and flexibility may seem contradictory, in fact, in an infant-toddler center, they go hand-in-hand to create an unhurried, child-centered day. (See "Benefits of a Predictable Yet Flexible Daily Schedule" on p. 289.) Some strategies for combining predictability and flexibility are these:

Organize the day around regular daily events and caregiving routines

Depending on the age of the children, this will include the daily events of arrival/departure; choice and outside time; and group time; and the routines of eating, sleeping, and diapering or using the toilet.

Follow the overall daily schedule consistently

In a typical caregiver team's group of children, each child has a daily schedule based on his or her particular needs. This means that a number of individualized daily schedules occur simultaneously, calling for both flexibility and organization on the part of caregiving staff. Fortunately, there are common elements among infants' and toddlers' individual daily schedules that often overlap. This overlap makes it possible for caregivers to create an overall daily schedule that is stable and yet responsive to individual children. For samples of three individualized daily schedules (for Bobby, Carlos, and Latisha) and the overall schedule that evolved from

Benefits of a Predictable Yet Flexible Daily Schedule

- Children learn to trust their teachers who listen and acknowledge children's individual needs, pace, and way of doing things.

- Children trust themselves and their own abilities to predict, anticipate, and influence what will happen next.

- Children gain a sense of ease and comfort when the schedule is suited to their individual temperaments and learning abilities.

- Teachers enjoy the day more because children are happier and less irritable.

Coordinating children's personal schedules can be a challenge. That's why infant-toddler care groups are small, with one caregiver for every two to four children.

One task of the caregiving team is to arrange the elements of the day in an order that makes sense for them and their children. For example,

(1) arrival,

(2) breakfast,

(3) choice time,

(5) group time,

(6) lunch,

(4) outside time,

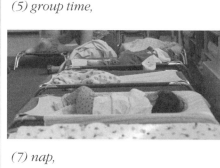

(7) nap,

(8) group time,

(9) choice time,

and (10) departure.

them, see "Sample Daily Schedules for an Infant-Toddler Program," pp. 292–293.

One task of the caregiver team is to arrange the elements of the day in an order that makes sense for them and their children. For example, in the sample daily schedules shown on pages 292–293, caregivers Yvonne, Kim, and Leanne have organized the events of their center's day into the following sequence: arrival, choice time, breakfast, choice time, group time, outside time, lunch, nap, group time, snack, outside time, choice time, and departure. Whereas they consistently follow this schedule with most of the children on most days, they integrate each child's personal caregiving routines — eating, bodily care, napping — into this overall schedule as needed.

Young infant Bobby, for example, generally naps through part or all of the morning and afternoon group times and through most of the afternoon outside time, although he often has his bottle outdoors, when he wakes up from his afternoon nap. Carlos and Latisha, both toddlers, participate in the entire sequence of morning events and then lie down for naps after lunch. Carlos tends to sleep soundly and sometimes naps through afternoon group time. Latisha generally plays on her cot and is always up and ready for afternoon group time! By creating a consistent overall schedule, caregivers enable children to drop in and out of various events according to their personal needs and to still be able to anticipate what happens next. Bobby, Carlos, and Latisha do not know that

lunchtime occurs at noon every day, but they do know that every day after morning outside time they have lunch and that after lunch come naps. (See "Using Photos of the Daily Events," p. 294.) While the daily overall schedule remains the same, the duration of any given event may change from day to day. On the day the children play on the new climber, for example, they are extra tired and nap a little longer than usual, so caregivers shorten afternoon choice time.

Accommodate children's natural rhythms and temperaments

As caregivers spend time with children, they begin to see the day through the children's eyes. With a comfortable overall daily schedule in place, they can approach it in an unhurried manner, giving children time to deal with daily events and caregiving routines according to individual temperament as shown in the following examples.

At choice time, Travis, an older infant, takes one thing after another out of a basket of household objects. He examines each object briefly and then discards it for something new. On the other side of the basket, Damian, also an older infant, selects one wooden spoon, which he mouths and explores with great interest, often pausing to watch Travis, and then turns his full attention again to the spoon. After 20 minutes or so, Damian rubs his eyes, yawns, and looks drowsy. He readily goes to sleep when his caregiver

Sample Daily Schedules for an Infant-Toddler Program

Overall	Bobby (Young Infant)	Carlos (Young Toddler)	Latisha (Older Toddler)
Arrival (7:30– 8:30 a.m.)	7:45 a.m. Bobby's mom holds him as she talks with Yvonne, his primary caregiver. Mom gives Bobby to Yvonne. He smiles from Yvonne's arms as his mom leaves.	8:05 a.m. Carlos leans against Leanne, one of his secondary caregivers, and waves to his mom from the window as she walks to her car.	7:35 a.m. Latisha says "Bye-bye" to her dad as she sits in Yvonne's lap (Yvonne is her secondary caregiver). Latisha shows Yvonne her new hat.
Choice time	Bobby lies on a blanket, exploring balls and scarves with his whole body.	In the house area, Carlos plays with corks, shells, pots, and pans.	In the house area, Latisha puts on bangle bracelets and wraps baby dolls in scarves.
Breakfast	Bobby drinks from a bottle while Yvonne holds him. Bobby gazes, smiles, and coos with Yvonne as she changes his diaper.	Carlos eats toast and cereal, drinks juice from a spouted cup, pausing often to watch other children at the table. He greets Kim, his primary caregiver, when she arrives. Carlos climbs up the steps to the changing table. He gives Kim the dry diaper.	Latisha eats toast and cereal. She pours her own and Carlos's juice. She hugs Kim, her primary caregiver, when Kim arrives. Latisha uses the toilet and washes her hands by herself. "I do it!" she tells Kim.
Choice time	Bobby stretches and rolls. He reaches for, grasps, and explores a rattle, a small tin, a cloth bear, and a small paper bag. Bobby cries and rubs his eyes. Yvonne puts him in his crib for a nap.	Carlos carries and stacks blocks. He brings a book to Kim for her to look at with him.	Latisha loads blocks into the doll buggy, wheels them to the dolls, builds an enclosure, and puts the dolls inside it. She wheels the blocks back to the block shelf at the end of choice time. She and Kim put blocks back on the shelf.
Group time Today caregivers Yvonne and Kim have planned an experience around exploring rhythm instruments.	When Bobby wakes, Yvonne takes him to the changing table. Bobby sucks his thumb and places his other hand on Yvonne's hand as she changes his diaper. Bobby drinks briefly from his bottle while Yvonne holds him. He watches children at group time shaking bells.	Carlos shakes bells with his caregivers and the other children and then returns to the book area and looks at books by himself.	Latisha shakes bells and then plays the drum with her caregivers and the other children.
Outside time	Bobby lies on a blanket, wiggles, stretches, and watches children on the climber.	Carrying a book, Carlos climbs up the steps to the changing table. He looks at the book while Kim changes his diaper. Carlos uses a shovel and a rake in the sandbox.	Latisha rolls balls down the slide and also under the climber. She brings a ball to Bobby. Latisha uses the toilet and washes her hands. She plays for a bit with the stream of water from the faucet.
Lunch (begins at noon)	Bobby coos as Yvonne talks to him about how she is changing his diaper. 12:30 Bobby drinks from his bottle in Yvonne's arms.	Noon. At Kim's table, Carlos eats spaghetti with a spoon and with his fingers.	Noon. Latisha eats spaghetti and pours her own milk. After lunch she wipes off the lunch table with a cloth. "I do it!" she tells Kim.

Sample Daily Schedules for an Infant-Toddler Program (cont.)

Overall	Bobby (Young Infant)	Carlos (Young Toddler)	Latisha (Older Toddler)
Nap	Bobby rolls, stretches, and explores balls on the mattress next to the window. Bobby holds a dry diaper as Yvonne changes him. Bobby gurgles to Yvonne as she settles him in his crib for a nap.	Carlos climbs up to the changing table. He looks out the window and shows Kim a dog he sees outside. Carlos brings a rubber dog and a picture book to naptime. Kim tucks his blanket around him. Carlos climbs up to the changing table. He is still a bit groggy from his nap.	Latisha takes books to her cot. Kim tucks a blanket around her. After looking at books, she sleeps briefly.
Group time Today, Kim and Yvonne have planned an opportunity for children to explore and play with containers, paintbrushes, stones, and a tub of water.	Bobby sleeps in his crib.	With Kim and the other children in his group, Carlos fills and empties containers with water.	With Kim, Carlos, and the other child in her group, Latisha uses water and a paintbrush to "paint" stones. Latisha uses the toilet, washes her hands and her stones. "Clean," she tells Kim.
Snack	Bobby plays peekaboo with his secondary caregiver, Kim, as she changes his diaper after his nap.	Carlos smooshes some banana pieces and licks them off his fingers. Carlos brings a diaper from his cubby when Kim asks him to.	Latisha tells Kim, "I do it" and peels her own banana half.
Outside time	Since the other children are outside, Bobby has his bottle outdoors in Yvonne's arms. When he is finished, he lies on a blanket, watching and kicking at dandelions. Bobby continues to kick his legs as Yvonne changes his diaper.	Carlos rides a wheeled toy, pushes a small grocery cart, and fills it with balls and leaves.	Latisha puts her stones in a wagon and pulls it about looking for "more stones."
Choice time	Bobby plays peekaboo with Kim. He lies on a blanket on the floor and babbles to Mallory, another infant, lying next to him.	Carlos looks at books. He brings Kim over to the bookrack and tells her to "sit" and "read." Carlos climbs up to the changing table. He looks out the window for the dog.	Latisha washes her stones, puts them in her cubby, and rides a wheeled toy. Latisha uses the toilet, washes her hands, and then changes into a clean pair of socks.
Departure (4:00–5:00 p.m.)	3:35 p.m. Bobby's aunt arrives. Bobby wiggles all over with pleasure. His aunt holds Bobby, snuggles him, and chats with Yvonne about Bobby's day. Then they leave for home.	4:40 p.m. Giving Kim a hug, Carlos leaves with his grandmother after taking her to the window and saying "doggy."	4:15 p.m. Latisha's mom arrives. Latisha shows her mom her stones, gives Kim a hug, and leaves with her mom.

Using Photos of the Daily Events

Older infants and toddlers enjoy looking at themselves in photos. To give children a sense of their daily schedule, caregivers take a series of photos of children involved in regular daily events and caregiving routines and mount the photos in order along a wall at children's eye level or in a small album with sturdy pages (like board books) that young children can grasp and turn. Over a period of time, caregivers will have enough photos to assemble a personal daily-event photo sequence featuring each child. Providing and looking at these photos with children is one way caregivers help them begin to identify and talk about the parts of their day at the center. The photos also provide a good way to share the children's daily experiences with their parents and are updated periodically as children get older and expand their involvement in each part of the day.

This caregiver uses laminated pictures of the daily events to share with the children what is happening that day.

places him in his crib. Travis, however, continues to explore the objects in the basket throughout choice time. Next, he joins the group singing activity and then heads out the door when it is outside time. He skips his morning nap altogether, even though yesterday he napped through group time and most of outside time.

Because Damian's caregivers understand temperamental differences, they see his fairly calm and persistent play and predictable sleeping patterns, as well as Travis's high-energy play and irregular sleeping habits, as normal variations within the boys' daily schedules.

At the end of afternoon naptime in a toddler program, Matt takes great pleasure and care in putting on his socks and shoes. By the time he has completed the task, however, the other children have finished snack and are on their way to outside time. Instead of attempting to hurry Matt with his shoes so he can eat with the other children, Matt's caregivers take his snack outside. He eats it while sitting on the steps and then looks for a tricycle to ride.

Matt's caregivers recognize his persistence at problem solving, a trait he regularly shows as he works with materials and masters motor skills throughout the day. It may also be the reason that he takes a long time with his shoes after nap because, after a very sociable morning, he is not yet ready to be sociable at snacktime. Other children, they notice, sometimes choose to watch rather than join group singing and movement experiences, or they choose to leave the group to spend time by themselves sitting under the climber or in the pillows with a book. Because Matt's caregivers understand that children in group care need time alone, they are flexible in anticipating and supporting the choices children make about watching, joining, or leaving the group experiences embedded in the overall daily schedule.

Flexibility was also the key in another toddler program in which children routinely fussed before the morning outside time. When their caregivers discovered that some of the children were hungry at this time, they made the midmorning snack available before instead of after

outside time as part of the overall daily schedule. With their energy restored, the children were ready to begin outside time with enthusiasm.

Provide a smooth flow from one interesting experience to the next

While some children handle transitions more easily than others, any shift in tempo or focus can be stressful on bodies and minds already deeply engrossed with everything around them. Therefore, caregivers minimize the number of transitions by dividing the day into large blocks of time. They also try to ease children's transitions from one major part of the day to the next. One way they do this is through

As individual children finish breakfast, they leave the table and begin choice time while other children continue to eat. In this way, regular daily events overlap somewhat to accommodate children's personal rhythms and allow less whole-group waiting.

Guidelines to Successful Smooth Transitions

- Reduce the number of transitions.

- Do not transition the whole group at once. Begin the next event with children who are ready, while other children complete the earlier activity.

- Eliminate waiting time by having one activity start as soon as another finishes or by having the end of one activity overlap with the beginning of another.

- Provide a consistent yet flexible routine.

- Provide time for transitions.

- Take cues from children about the beginning and end of events.

- When needed, offer children choices during a transition: "You can come inside for lunch by walking or hopping like a rabbit."

- Provide short, predictable transitional activities (e.g., use brief movement and music activities to capture children's attention).

- Predict for children what is coming next (e.g., give warnings, use pictorial daily routine).

short, predictable transitional activities. A typical transitional activity is planned carefully to avoid disrupting children's chosen exploration and play, and it is consistent from day to day so children know what to expect. To help children retain a sense of control, the transitional activity is simple and active — for example, toddlers regularly using riding toys between lunch and bodily care. Giving toddlers some choices about the coming activity is another way to ease a transition (e.g., "What would you like to bring to naptime?"). Caregivers also help children to anticipate what will happen next (e.g., "Stories and nap are next").

It is important for caregivers to avoid having children line up or sit waiting for the next event without anything to do. Whole-group transitions do not work for infants and toddlers because they each move at their own pace; when forced to stop or move on to keep up with peers

or adults, they may become anxious and find themselves in a power struggle with adults. Adults, therefore, need to take cues from children (rather than from the clock) about the beginnings and endings of events. To prevent having a whole group of children waiting, caregivers overlap activities by beginning the next event with some children who are ready while the other children are still engaged in or completing an earlier activity. When, for example, toddler Cassie wakes up early from her nap and begins to play with her doll, her caregiver gets a doll and plays along next to her. As other children wake up, they watch or come over with their dolls. Gradually naptime ends, and group time begins. In the process, the dolls and the children get their diapers changed!

In general, caregivers provide time and support for children as they shift gears to move from one regular daily event to another. Even when children must leave the child care home or center at the end of the day but are reluctant to stop what they are doing, caregivers give children choices along with the reason for stopping: "We have to leave the sandbox, Martin, because your mommy's here. You can get in the wagon for a ride to the gate, or you can pull the wagon to the gate." (See "Guidelines to Successful Smooth Transitions" on p. 296.)

Incorporate active learning, including adult support, into each event and caregiving routine

Instead of setting aside a special time of the day for active learning, caregivers in a HighScope infant-toddler setting include the ingredients of active learning in each daily event and caregiving routine. This means that throughout the day, they support and interact with children as they work with materials, make choices, and communicate or talk, and that they interpret and build on children's actions and communications in terms of the KDIs. The specific strategies caregivers use include these:

Be patient with children's intense interest in things around them

Infants and toddlers are curious about anything that moves, makes a noise, smells, or touches their skin or mouth — an ant, a blade of grass, a person's hand, a ticking clock, a stick, a piece of newspaper. Materials adults may view as commonplace and uninteresting can fascinate young children. Running water and even the water faucets themselves, for example, may fascinate a toddler washing up before lunch. Though

caregivers might wish that toddlers would spend less time at the sink, they are patient. They understand that for toddlers, hand washing is not the mundane experience it is for adults. It is also a time for discovery and learning.

Value children's need for sensory-motor manipulation and exploration in each event and routine

Throughout the day, infants and toddlers manipulate and mouth materials. At snack- and mealtimes, many children explore their food as they eat, because food to them is simply another irresistibly attractive material. They do not yet make distinctions between materials to play with, materials to eat, and materials to look at but not touch. Therefore, caregivers in active learning settings assume that some

For these toddlers, washing their hands is not only about getting clean. It is also a time to discover how water feels on their hands and how the faucets make water start and stop, gush and dribble, and go fast and slow.

exploration is part of children's eating, and they plan accordingly. As another example, interacting with a baby in a game of peekaboo with the clean diaper adds to the time it takes to change a diaper. At the same time, it does lend interest and thus often enhances the child's willingness to take part in this inescapable caregiving routine. Further, playing simple peekaboo and hiding games helps a very young child understand that something or someone still exists when out of sight, which is known as *object permanence.*

Share control of the day with children by giving them choices

Infants and toddlers in child care settings have no choice about being there. However, by giving children choices throughout the day, caregivers lessen conflicts and power struggles. Each part of the day, thus, presents opportunities for choices and decisions children *can* make: They can choose, for example, what, how much, and how to eat; what to hold, look at, or put on during diaper changes; whether to use the potty or the toilet; whether, how, and how long to participate in an activity; what child to sit next to at group time; and, for older infants and toddlers, what comfort items and quiet toys to take along to naptime. Making these choices and decisions on a daily basis and being able to change their mind from one day to the next tends to give children a sense of control over their day. It also makes them aware of the characteristics of the objects or actions they are choosing

between, an awareness that will eventually help them form internalized mental representations later in the course of their development.

Be alert to children's communications and talk throughout the day

Each part of the day is ripe for communication and language from children. A bottle-feeding infant, for example, may communicate with a caregiver by steadily maintaining eye contact, smiling, playing games with the bottle, turning away, and pausing to watch other children. A hungry toddler may give full attention to eating and turn to conversation only later, when he or she feels full and satisfied. A toddler may talk or sing to a favorite stuffed animal at naptime, recalling an experience or telling a story. Children often communicate very little when they are thoroughly engaged with materials. When this occurs, caregivers wait and observe for a natural way to enter their play before conversing with them. Other times they have a lot to communicate and say when least expected — while walking outdoors, while sitting on the toilet, or while wiping the table after lunch.

Work as a team to provide ongoing support to each child during the day

Adult support should remain constant from the time a child enters the program setting until the child leaves. The members of a caregiver team do not have the option of switching from having supportive interactions with a child at choice time, for example, to having directive interactions

For young children, food is just another material to feel, smell, squish, and, eventually, eat!

with that child at group time, to letting that child cry in his crib at naptime. They instead work together to acknowledge children's feelings and maintain a problem-solving approach to conflict throughout the entire day. This includes not taking a punitive approach to biting, not sending children away from the lunch table when they play with food, and not telling children they can't play with toys when they tussle over them in the sandbox. Throughout the day, caregivers use the support strategies discussed in Chapter 3 to build a sense of a community where children can feel safe, secure, and free to explore and to enjoy the company of their peers.

Look at children's actions and communications through the lens of the KDIs

Caregivers in a HighScope active learning setting watch and listen to whatever children are doing and use these observations to plan ways to support each child's development throughout the day. They gather information about children's interests, strengths, and development by relating these observations to the KDIs for infants and toddlers. These scenarios, for example, all involve KDIs:

> *At lunch, Michael swats at his spouted cup to make it rock back and forth.*

Guidelines for Organizing Daily Schedules and Caregiving Routines: A Summary

Create an overall daily schedule that is predictable yet flexible.

❏ Organize the day around regular daily events and caregiving routines.

❏ Follow the overall daily schedule consistently.

❏ Accommodate children's natural rhythms and temperaments.

❏ Provide a smooth flow from one interesting experience to the next.

Incorporate active learning, including adult support, into each event and caregiving routine.

❏ Be patient with children's intense interest in things around them.

❏ Value children's need for sensory-motor manipulation and exploration in each event and routine.

❏ Share control of the day with children by giving them choices.

❏ Be alert to children's communications and talk throughout the day.

❏ Work as a team to provide ongoing support to each child throughout the day.

❏ Look at children's actions and communications through the lens of KDIs.

When it stops rocking, he says "Again!" and gives it another push. (Cognitive development KDI: 35. Cause and effect.)

~

At choice time, Emma sits on the floor, holding and rocking a doll, and then lays the doll in the cradle. When Malek, another child, approaches, Emma holds her finger to her mouth and says "Shhh!" (Creative arts KDI: 36. Imitating and pretending.)

~

At group time, Evan stands up and spins around in circles. Periodically

he says "Down" and plops to the floor on his bottom. (Physical development and health KDI: 13. Moving the whole body.)

~

At outside time, Seanna sits in her caregiver's lap and fills one plastic bottle with small rocks and another plastic bottle with small sticks and grass. She shakes both bottles and then gives the stick-and-grass-filled bottle to her caregiver, indicating that she wants the caregiver to shake it. (Cognitive development KDIs: 24. Exploring same and different; 29. Filling and emptying.)

As she assembles a puzzle, this toddler engages in approaches to learning KDI 2. Problem solving *and cognitive development KDI* 30. Taking apart and putting together.

Using the KDIs to interpret children's communications and actions serves as the basis for the next day's plans and provides caregivers with a daily bank of detailed stories and anecdotes to share with parents and guardians. Each daily event and caregiving routine thus provides an opportunity to enjoy, learn about, and understand individual children.

Understanding Arrival and Departure

"Good morning, Martha and Monique," says Chantal, a caregiver, to Monique and her mom. Monique, a young nonmobile infant, has been coming to the child care center for five weeks. She arrives in her mother's

Warm, leisurely greetings from caregivers assure children and their parents that the care setting is a safe and friendly home-away-from-home.

arms and smiles at Chantal, who is her primary caregiver. After her mom and Chantal chat for a bit about Monique's new interest in watching and laughing at the family cat, Monique's mom snuggles and kisses her and then gives her to Chantal, who hugs her, smiles, and says, "It's nice to see you, Monique!" They walk with Monique's mom to the door. "Bye, bye, Monique," says her mom. "I'll be back this afternoon." "Bye, bye, Mommy — see you later," Chantal says for Monique.

At the end of the day, Monique lies on her back on a quilt next to Sasha, another infant. Monique holds and mouths a wooden ball. When she hears her mom arriving and greeting Chantal, Monique drops her ball, smiles, and wiggles all over in anticipation. Her mom sits down next to her, and after picking her up for a kiss, a hug, and a snuggle, she holds her close and says, "You've been playing next to Sasha again!" Monique smiles and coos in her mom's arms as her mom walks over to Chantal to catch up on the day's events and round up Monique's bottles and supplies. At the end of their chat, Chantal strokes Monique's arm and says, "Bye, Monique! See you tomorrow!" Monique and her mom depart.

～

Evan, a young toddler, arrives with Veana, his mom, for his third day at the center. "Good morning, Veana and Evan," says Chantal. Evan holds his mom's hand and watches another toddler, Athi, at the sand table while Mom and Chantal exchange information about the day. Observing Evan's tight grip on his mom and his focus on the sand play, Chantal joins Athi at the sand table with the thought that Evan might come there, enabling her to gradually make contact with him through a mutual interest in sand toys. She doesn't address or approach Evan at this point, because he is so clearly avoiding her.

Eventually, Evan and his mom make their way to the sand table. When his mom squats down by the table, Evan stands between her knees and scoops up sand with his hands. From her place on the other side of the sand table, next to Athi, Chantal moves a bucket and shovel within Evan's reach. He takes the shovel and begins to fill the bucket. Chantal, continuing to interact with Athi, says gently, "Athi, you're digging a pretty big hole!" — whereupon Athi gives her a spoon so she can dig a hole like his.

Throughout this time, Chantal talks now and then with Evan's mom but continues to wait for a cue from Evan that he is ready for her to interact with him. Eventually, when she sees Evan eyeing her spoon, she gives it to him, saying "Maybe you would like a spoon too, Evan." He takes the spoon and begins to dig. As he enlarges his hole, he leaves the safety of his mom's knees and moves to the end of the sand table, between his mom and Chantal. When Athi begins to drive a dump truck around the sand table, Chantal backs away from the table so Athi and his truck can drive in front of her. When Athi gets to where Evan is playing in the sand, Evan puts his hand on the truck and Athi stops. "Looks like Evan wants your truck to back up!" Chantal says. Athi laughs at this idea and begins backing his truck around the table. Looking up at Chantal briefly, Evan smiles and then returns to his play.

When it's time for Evan's mom to leave, she gives him a hug and tells him she'll be back after nap. He watches her sadly as she walks toward the door but remains at the sand table with Chantal and Athi. "Mommy go," he says to Chantal pressing himself against her side. "It's sad for you to see Mommy go — she'll come back after nap," Chantal says, slipping her arm around his shoulders.

At the end of the day, Evan is just waking up from his nap when he sees his mom come through the door. He runs into her arms, and as she talks with Chantal, he strokes his mom's face. After gathering Evan's things, his mom says good-bye to Chantal. Lightly touching Evan's back, Chantal tells him, "See you tomorrow!" He smiles at her from the safety of his mom's arms.

Arrivals and departures like the ones in these scenarios involve the rituals that set the tone for the child's away-from-home experience. At arrival time, warm, leisurely greetings from caregivers help to assure infants and toddlers that even though their parents must leave, they are in the hands of trustworthy people who will respect them and keep them safe until their parents return. At departure time, the caregivers' pleasant, friendly good-byes and warm wishes for return allow children to reunite with their parents; they are relieved to see their parents and, at the same time, know that the adults saying good-bye care about them and they feel comfortable with

Older infants and toddlers are more likely to be apprehensive and to cling to their parents during departure time.

returning to the center the next day. In the short run, learning to deal with the daily greetings and good-byes at arrival and departure times allows children to enlarge the scope of their trust from parents and family at home to caregivers and peers at the center. In the long run, coping successfully at these times gives children a solid basis for coping with the comings and goings of relatives and friends for the rest of their lives.

Even when a child care setting has a greeting area, there is no definite place where greetings and good-byes must take place. Where they occur depends on the needs and preferences of the child and parent. One mom may sit in a comfortable chair, nurse her infant, chat with the caregiver, and give her child to the caregiver without ever leaving the greeting area. Other parents will come into the play space and say their good-bye or hello wherever their child is comfortable that day — at the sand table, on the mattress next to the books, or outside in the play yard. At one center, when Nolan grew to be an older toddler and had been going to the same center for two years, he and his mom developed a fairly elaborate good-bye ritual that took him to the top of the indoor climber. He would first give his mom a good-bye kiss near the door and then hurry across the room and climb rapidly up to what everyone called the crow's-nest. When he got to the top, he would say "Okay, mommy!" to signal that it was okay for his mom to go out the door. Once outside, she turned

and waved at him, and from his high perch, he waved back at her through the window.

As infants and toddlers separate from their parents to join the child care community at the beginning of the day, they typically engage in a variety of behaviors. These may range from crying, screaming, flailing, clinging, thumb sucking, avoiding eye contact, or simply ignoring the parent or caregiver involved to smiling, cooing, picking up an interesting plaything, watching other children with interest, waving good-bye to the parent, or joining an activity in progress. Their responses to rejoining a parent at the end of the day may vary just as widely, including delight at being reunited, renewed anger at having been abandoned earlier in the day, or a reluctance to stop the ongoing activity and go home. Furthermore, these responses may change from day to day and from one stage of development to the next, with islands of predictability in between!

Nonmobile (very young) infants generally respond to separations and reunions with relative ease. At this age, an infant is apt to greet a familiar primary caregiver with a smile, settle peacefully into her arms, and gaze into her face. At the end of the day, the infant will often alert to the sound and sight of a returning parent and begin to wiggle, smile, and vocalize with pleasure.

As they learn to creep and crawl, infants develop a sense of themselves as separate beings distinct from their parents. Realizing that parents can disappear, they fear they may not return! At arrival time, therefore, it is not uncommon for these mobile infants to cling to their parents, cry, avoid eye contact with the caregiver, and head for (maybe even try to open) the door through which their parents have just taken leave.

Young toddlers enjoy their newfound walking ability and the freedom it allows them to explore and carry all kinds of interesting objects. While they remain concerned about losing sight of their parents, they are usually irresistibly drawn to examine whatever they can get their hands on. They may still protest when a parent leaves, but they can also make connections with caregivers and peers through objects and playthings of particular interest. At the end of the day, young toddlers may simply continue their explorations and play when their parents arrive, or they may throw themselves into their parents' arms and cry with relief!

Older toddlers are developing the ability to hold in mind mental images of absent people and past events. They remember their parents leaving them at the center on previous mornings and anticipate that it will happen again today. At the same time, they are developing a strong sense of independence and initiative and an increasing ability to communicate with such powerful phrases as "Mommy stay!" and "No!" At the beginning of the day, their objections to a parent's departure can be loud and physical. They need to sense some control over how they ease

themselves into the setting and how long it takes to do so. Fortunately, they are usually increasingly interested in the people and materials in the child care setting and eager to make choices about what they are going to do after their parents leave. At the end of the day, older toddlers may resist leaving the center until they have finished a particular activity. They may be perfectly cheerful as they reunite with their parents or they may be tearful, whiny, and demanding.

How Caregivers Support Children at Arrival and Departure

During arrival and departure times, it is important for caregivers to give children and parents warm welcomes and good-byes and to support their separation and reunion processes. The following strategies can help in carrying out this caregiver role:

- Carry out greetings and good-byes calmly to reassure the child and parent.

- Acknowledge the child's and parent's feelings about separation and reunion.

- Follow the child's signals about entering and leaving the activity of the program setting.

- Communicate openly with the child about the parent's comings and goings.

- Exchange information and child observations with the parent.

Carry out greetings and good-byes calmly to reassure the child and parent

Separating and reuniting can be difficult for children and their parents. Given the potential for family distress at the beginning and end of the day, it is important that caregivers approach these times calmly and optimistically. By remaining attuned to yet outside of the emotional fray, caregivers make themselves available to offer reassurance and support. Although some caregivers may recall their own less-than-happy separations and reunions, it is important that they refrain from reliving them at these times so they can focus instead on the immediate needs of the children and parents before them. The presence of a calm, friendly caregiver can help to reassure anxious children and parents. A caregiver's calmness can also reassure the other children who are present, who have already separated from their parents for the day.

Acknowledge the child's and parent's feelings about separation and reunion

An infant or toddler may feel especially vulnerable when left by a parent in a place that is not home, with people who are not familiar. Having no conventional sense of time, the child cannot distinguish between being left for six hours and being left forever. Thus, young children's emotions at the beginning of the day in a child care setting may range from discomfort, anxiety, fear, or terror to sorrow, loneliness, grief, or despair over abandonment.

At the end of the day, it is not unusual for children to express conflicting emotions — residual anger at being left by their parent; increasing fear they may be abandoned by their parent as they watch other children being picked up before them; and, finally, joy at their parent's return and relief that at last, in their parent's arms, they can safely fall apart from the stresses and strains of their day.

When parents leave their child at the child care center or family child care home, they may feel sad about missing their child, guilty about leaving him or her in someone else's care, and anxious about getting to work on time. Later, at the end of the day, they may look forward to reclaiming their child, feel hurt and perhaps jealous when the child ignores them or resists leaving the caregiver, and feel tense about fitting in all the household tasks that they need to do before bedtime.

Caregivers can help reduce the emotional intensity of separations and reunions by gently and matter-of-factly describing the emotions they are witnessing — the point is to simply acknowledge and validate these feelings, not judge them. Here are several examples of ways a caregiver might describe a child's feelings at a parent's departure:

- "It's sad for you to see your mommy go, Terry."

- "You're crying so hard that your eyes are closed, Jamal. You don't like to see Mommy leave for work."

- "You're holding on to me so tightly, Angelina! It's scary for you to see

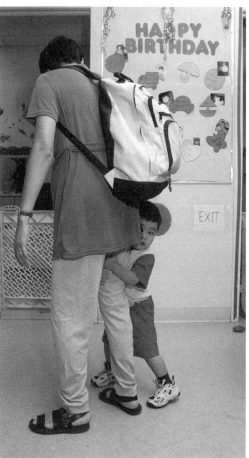

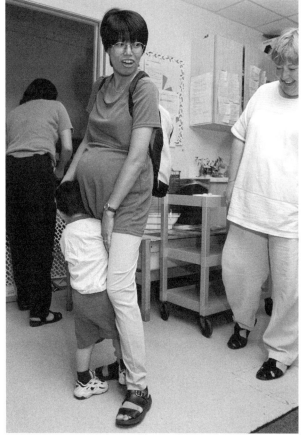

Letting go of Mommy and accepting a trusted caregiver in her place for the day takes time, courage, and lots of support.

Mommy go, isn't it? Let's sit in the cozy chair together."

Caregivers might also try to describe a parent's feelings. Here are some examples:

- "It looks like you want to stay with Verdell and leave in time for work, Ms. Smith. It's hard to be pulled in opposite directions."

- "It must be upsetting to have Mickey cry when you're so glad to see him, David. Maybe it's his way of telling you how relieved he is to see you at the end of the day. Now he really feels free to express himself."

When caregivers let children and parents know that they recognize and are trying to understand their feelings, it actually helps children (and parents) begin to regain emotional balance. By putting nonjudgmental words to children's and parents' feelings, caregivers help children's and parents' emotions to recede, clearing the way for them to think about moving on to the next part of the day.

Occasionally a child seems inconsolable when a parent leaves. The child may be new to the center, returning from a long absence, tired, coming down with an illness, or entering a new stage of self-awareness. There may be events at home that disturb the child's equilibrium, such as the arrival of a new sibling, the loss of a job, or friction between the parents. At these times, it is important for the caregiver who always greets the child to remain calm, to describe the child's feelings, and to stay with the child to provide comfort and physical contact (holding, stroking, rocking, carrying) until the child recovers.

Sometimes, as they prepare to leave their child, parents have more difficulty with separation than their children have. Again, caregivers can support anxious parents by remaining calm, acknowledging their feelings, and encouraging them to take plenty of time and stay at the center as long as they are able to. Eventually, over time, with caregivers displaying patience and giving attention to the feelings involved, both children and parents will gain trust in the center staff and confidence in themselves and will be able to enter and leave the center with a sense of hope and ease.

Follow the child's signals about entering and leaving the activities of the program setting

Parents, of course, make the decision about placing their infant or toddler in a particular child care setting. However, when adults follow the child's signals or cues about how he or she prefers to enter or leave the activities of that setting each day, the child then has as much control as possible in the larger situation of having to be in that setting. Each child copes with making the transition from home to care setting and back again in a particular and personal way. One way many infants and toddlers soothe themselves during this emotional time is by clinging to some item that connects them in a tangible way to home — a special blanket, a doll or stuffed animal, a pacifier, or a photo of a family member (see p. 194). If a child hangs on

After saying good-bye to Mommy, this toddler needs some time to himself, which his caregiver respects by being available while giving him plenty of space until he is ready to join in.

to such a comfort item during arrival and departure, it is important for caregivers to respect this choice as an assertion of self and an important step in the development of self-help skills. Attempts to take away comfort items — claiming a child is getting "too big" for them or should "be over" the separation by now — overlook the child's resourcefulness in using these items. The child will give them up voluntarily when he or she is ready.

Older infants and toddlers who can move about on their own may cope with the transition from home to care setting in a variety of ways. For example, they may at first cling to their parent and then turn to a toy or select some plaything and come back to their parent, showing no desire for physical or eye contact with any caregiver. When ready, however, such children will gradually ease their way into caregiver contact in the presence of their parent or after the parent departs.

For example, when Evan (p. 302) arrives with his mom for his third day at the center, Chantal (his caregiver) respects Evan's initial avoidance of her, knowing that he will make contact with her when *he* is ready. She also knows that if she imposes herself on him, she will only heighten his concerns about his new setting. Instead, she makes herself available for gradual approach by kneeling down on the far side of the sand table, using the table both as a buffer against too much contact too quickly and as something mutually interesting that they can both play at without direct interaction.

Communicate openly with the child about the parent's comings and goings

To foster trust and communication, caregivers let children know when their parents leave and return to the center. Although occasionally a parent may wish to leave quickly and quietly while his or her child is engaged in play, it is important for the child to know where the parent is, rather than to look up and discover that Daddy or Mommy has left without saying good-bye. In the long run, for the child, the pain of hearing a parent's "Good-bye, see you after nap" is less than the pain of actually feeling betrayed by a parent who leaves with no notice.

One way to make the parent's comings and goings no mystery is to encourage the child and parent to establish a ritual for separation and reunion. It is important for parent(s) to establish a morning ritual to help ease a child's separation from home and into the child care setting. Caregivers can help parents understand that the circumstances surrounding dropoff time can affect a child's emotional well-being and behavior throughout the day. A quick good-bye and departure does not help children adjust to the separation or ease into the program's routine. By contrast, establishing a consistent ritual that children can depend on gives them a sense of security and lets them separate from a parent as they begin their day. Knowing how important this process is, parents (or whoever routinely drops off the child) can adjust their morning schedules to allow time for this reassuring ritual.

The scenarios presented on pages 301–303 contain several examples of these types of rituals. In these examples, each time a parent says good-bye, she also lets the child know when she will be coming back. Although very young children may not comprehend what such statements actually mean or precisely how long it will be until Mom or Dad returns, at some level, the children understand and are comforted by the parent's reassuring promise of reunion.

Parent-child separations and reunions have a relationship to the endless games of peekaboo and hide-and-seek that caregivers play with infants and toddlers. Hiding behind the sofa and then popping out, or hiding the stuffed bunny under the blanket and then revealing the bunny with a flourish and an exclamation of "peekaboo," is a way for children to act out and begin to understand that people come and go (that parents leave in the morning and return at the end of the day) and is one of the important concepts that children learn in their first year of life.

Exchange information and child observations with the parent

Seeing parents at arrival and departure times provides an opportunity for caregivers to exchange important information about the child's life at the center and at home. Caregivers can fill parents in on children's actions, communications, and care at the center: "Today, Evan spent all of choice time with Athi at the sand table, digging holes and driving dump trucks"; "Landon ate all of his food and drank a full bottle before his nap today." Parents can let caregivers know what children did at home: "I couldn't believe my eyes this morning. Monique was standing up holding on to the side of her crib. She's never done that before!"; "Gabrielle didn't sleep very well. She is teething and was fussy most of the night." This type of information exchange is helpful in planning for children's development as well as planning for their caregiving routines or any special adjustments that need to be made during the day.

Understanding Feeding and Mealtime

Molly, a young infant, lies cradled in her caregiver's arms and drinks from a bottle. When Molly stops sucking for a moment, her caregiver says, "My, Molly, you sure are hungry today!" Molly gazes intently at her caregiver's face for several seconds and then returns to her bottle and resumes sucking.

~

Mingyu, an older infant, sits on the floor, eating at a small tray table. She holds a cracker in one hand as she tries with her other hand to eat with a spoon. After several attempts to get some green beans onto the spoon, she drops the spoon and eats the beans, one at a time, with her fingers, still holding the cracker in her other hand.

At snacktime, toddler Steven accidentally bumps his arm into his spouted cup, tipping it over on the table. He watches a little milk dribble out, then picks up the cup, takes a drink, and sets the cup upright again. After a slight pause, he purposely repeats this action sequence a few more times before drinking the rest of his milk.

In George and Nanette's family child care program, each toddler brings lunch from home. Just before lunch, while Nanette plays with the children and helps them put toys away, George gets the lunches and finishes any necessary preparations, such as warming, cutting, or combining ingredients. When George begins to bring the food to the table, Nanette gets the children started with hand washing. Once the

Even for toddlers, mealtimes are social interludes based around eating and enjoying food.

Young children do not refrain from active learning as they eat; they simply transfer their attention and actions to things edible!

too sometimes likes to dip fruit into her yogurt. Throughout the meal, children and caregivers continue to eat and converse together about topics raised by the children, such as drinking with straws and cups and dipping things in yogurt.

Babies' feedings and children's mealtimes go beyond fulfilling a basic need for nourishing food. For infants, these times provide close physical contact with an attentive adult. When a young infant's cries of hunger are met with a full bottle and the comforting arms of a pleasant caregiver, that child is able to grow and thrive because he or she learns to trust the world as a place where people recognize and respond to an infant's needs. For the older infant, mealtime is a time to eat but also to explore new tastes, smells, and textures and to try self-feeding with fingers, a spoon, or a cup.

For the toddler, mealtime becomes increasingly sociable. As toddlers eat, they usually enjoy interacting with others and being part of the mealtime conversation. They also continue to explore and try new foods and gain skill at feeding themselves. According to Mangione (1990), "young children are in the process of developing lifelong attitudes toward food and the experience of eating. In a relaxed setting they form positive attitudes and learn vital social skills" (p. 11). In short, feedings and mealtimes are social interludes based around eating and enjoying food.

children sit down around a small table with their lunches, George and Nanette get out their lunches and join the children's table as the children are comparing the drinks they brought from home with one another. Toddler Sarah takes a spoonful of a cup of yogurt and then decides to put her grapes in the yogurt before continuing to eat it. Nanette comments that she

Where a feeding or a mealtime takes place depends on the stage of the child involved. A primary caregiver of young infants lovingly holds each child and attends to his or her bottle-feeding while sitting in some comfortable place. Some infants, content with this close contact and attention, focus intently on their bottle and caregiver, with little or no regard for where they are and whatever is going on around them. Other infants, who are easily distracted and continually turning away from the bottle to watch other children and adults, may best be fed in a fairly secluded place.

As discussed in detail in Chapter 4, infants who are sitting and beginning to try solid foods are generally propped up in some way while the caregiver offers food on a spoon. Older infants who are interested in picking up finger foods, guiding the spoon to their mouth, and exploring food with their hands usually sit on low chairs or on the floor to eat at low one-person tables. Toddlers eat together with their caregivers in small groups at low tables. Both infants and toddlers can enjoy mealtimes outdoors in pleasant weather.

The scenarios at the beginning of this section illustrate typical behaviors very young children engage in during feeding or mealtime. Molly, in the first scenario, is like many young infants in that she enjoys her bottle, satisfies her hunger, and pauses from time to time to gaze at something that catches her attention — her caregiver's face, another child, the movement of a curtain. In the security of their caregiver's arms, bottle-feeding infants are free to set their own pace, dividing their energies

between drinking and examining the world through their eyes.

Older infants, like Mingyu, bring new physical skills to eating. They can sit unassisted, so they have greater control of their arms and hands and can easily put things in their mouths. Mingyu enjoys figuring out the best way to get the green beans into her mouth. When the spoon doesn't work, she uses her fingers to feed herself. Just as she explores materials during the rest of the day — fitting blocks into a shape sorter, nesting graduated cups inside one another, or putting a bottle into a baby doll's mouth — Mingyu uses mealtime for problem solving, exploring, and developing physical skills.

Toddlers continue to explore food and materials during mealtime. For several minutes, Steven, for example, is more interested in the reactions of his cup and milk than in eating. *What happens to the milk in the spouted cup when it tips over? Why doesn't more of the milk spill out? Is there any more milk left in the cup?* We don't know for sure if these or similar questions are going through his mind as he experiments with his cup, but we can observe his fascination with tipping and dribbling. Toddlers also tend to enjoy socializing and interacting with others as they eat.

As caregivers become accustomed to the exploratory feeding and mealtime practices of infants and toddlers, they find, much to their relief, that most children also do actually *eat* their food — in adequate quantities and at a pace that meets their personal needs — and thus they receive the benefits of good nutrition. Studies show that children often make up for a small meal or a missed meal at the next mealtime, and that as long as children have plenty of energy and are growing normally, their sometimes erratic eating habits are nothing for parents or caregivers to be concerned about (American Academy of Family Physicians, 2010).

At the same time, teachers and caregivers know that fingering food and dribbling milk are normal behaviors at feeding or mealtime in an infant-toddler care setting. Infants and toddlers do not refrain from active learning as they eat; they simply transfer their attention and actions to things edible! While they are not yet ready to practice formal table manners, they do engage in an experience that eventually leads to manners — the pleasure of eating and conversing in a warm, supportive setting.

How Caregivers Support Children During Feeding and Mealtime

During feeding or mealtime, caregivers provide a pleasant, relaxed atmosphere so children can eat and enjoy their food in the company of others. The following strategies help them carry out this role:

- Hold and pay close attention to the bottle-feeding infant.

- Support the older infant's interest in feeding him- or herself.

- Join toddlers at the table during meals.

- Include older toddlers in mealtime setup and cleanup.

Hold and pay close attention to the bottle-feeding infant

Because bottle-feeding babies cannot feed themselves, they depend entirely on caregivers to hold and feed them when they are hungry. A caregiver establishes a special connection with an infant while holding her and feeding a bottle.

By holding bottle-feeding babies, caregivers try to re-create the familiar closeness and security infants feel in their parents' arms when they are nursing or drinking from a bottle at home. We also know from recent brain research that touch during bottle-feeding increases infants' digestive abilities and decreases stress (Schiller, 2008). Babies who are stroked and held while they eat have healthier blood-sugar levels and are better able to maintain body temperature (Carlson, 2006). Thus, touching and holding babies at feeding time provides both social-emotional and physiological benefits.

During the feeding, the caregiver gives her major attention to the infant. Though she does not disturb the child's active engagement with the bottle, she is ready to interact whenever the baby shows an interest in doing so. For example, during pauses when the child takes a rest from sucking, the caregiver may smile, make faces, chat softly, or stroke the infant's head; the infant may grasp the caregiver's fingers, face, hands, or clothing. Through these exchanges, the caregiver and baby build a personal relationship through which the child learns, on a very basic level, that he or she can rely on this non-parental adult for physical and emotional needs.

Propping babies up to drink from their bottles unattended may be efficient, especially in a group-care setting. However, we know from the work of Rene Spitz (see Chapter 1, p. 29) that children fed consistently in this manner fail to thrive not from a lack of food but from the absence of loving human attention and physical contact. Fortunately, holding bottle-feeding babies comes quite naturally to most caregivers! Also, when each primary caregiver is responsible for at most three infants, there *are* enough arms to hold babies while they eat.

Support the older infant's interest in feeding him- or herself

As children learn to creep and crawl and sit by themselves, they generally become interested in the eating habits of older children and adults. They watch "big" people eat crackers, use spoons, and drink from cups or glasses, and they attempt to imitate these actions. While caregivers take pleasure in holding and feeding infants, it is important to allow infants to change and grow and to be alert to the signals that they are ready to take over parts of the meal themselves. Children generally begin self-feeding by using their fingers, because this is easier for them than using a spoon — they are already adept at putting their fingers in their mouth. It will

This caregiver gives all of her attention to the baby she is feeding.

take them more time to master the use of a simple utensil, like a spoon, to convey food from a plate or bowl to their mouth. Understanding these facts of child development, caregivers give older infants some foods they can easily pick up and eat with their fingers along with some runny foods (applesauce, yogurt, cooked cereal) that work better with a spoon.

Using fingers to eat has these two distinct advantages for the very young active learners: It gives children (1) control over when they eat without having to wait for their caregiver's assistance and (2)

 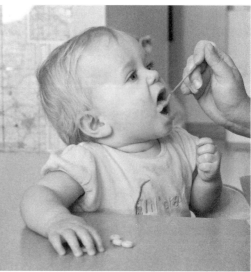

This older infant eats cereal that she can easily feed to herself while her caregiver feeds her applesauce with a spoon.

experience feeling and touching different substances, such as a hard carrot stick and soft, mushy rice pudding (Goldschmied & Jackson, 1994). While young children are interested in how food feels in their hands, they are also interested in learning how to eat like "big people" — with utensils, such as a spoon. Before a child gains skill with a spoon, the caregiver provides one spoon for the child and another for herself so that the child can practice using the spoon, along with his or her fingers, and the caregiver can help with feeding without taking away the child's spoon. The message in this is "that we acknowledge that later on he will handle the spoon for himself" (p. 77).

Just as older infants mix finger and spoon use, so they might drink some milk from a spouted cup and some milk from their bottle. When a bottle-feeding child begins to show interest in drinking from a cup, caregivers share this observation with parents so they can coordinate their approaches to cup versus bottle use. If, for example, the parents are gradually cutting back on bottles at home as the child uses a cup more and more often, caregivers take a similar approach at the center. This way, children's dual needs — for milk and for practicing self-help — are acknowledged in a consistent way throughout the day. Again, during the time infants drink from both cups and bottles, caregivers should not leave them to drink from their bottle unattended.

Caregivers should remember, too, that children's abilities to feed themselves can change abruptly. For example, one day Amanda drops her spoon over and over again, not getting any food to her mouth, and the next, she is scooping spoonful after spoonful of applesauce into her mouth with great gusto!

Join toddlers at the table during meals

In the scenario on pages 313–314, George and Nanette join their toddlers for lunch to create a pleasant setting in which to enjoy food and one another's company. Caregivers in HighScope programs approach mealtimes as daily opportunities to build relationships with children by supporting their conversation, exploration, and repetition and by providing assistance as needed as children continue their journey toward independent eating within a social context. By taking part in meals with children, caregivers send a positive message not only about eating but also about social relationships at the child care center: *We can do all sorts of enjoyable things together — play, take walks, read books, talk, and share food and food experiences!*

Toddler-initiated mealtime conversation tends to focus around children's observations and musings about the materials at hand — "Who make [lunch]?" "You like eggs?" "Oranges at our house too!" "Look! Bread broke!" "Dripping!" "More milky!" "No 'nanas. No!" "Dog cookie!" "He gots more!" Because caregivers come to know each child, they can help carry on the conversation by filling in the missing parts of children's often very brief statements, as the following example shows.

Conversations at mealtime occur during the pauses, when children take a break from eating.

Zach: (Addresses Rachel.) *Who make?*

Caregiver: *Rachel, Zach is wondering who made your lunch.*

Rachel: *Daddy.*

Zach: (He watches Rachel take a bite of her sandwich.) *Daddy make.* (He picks up his own sandwich.) *Mommy make. Make Todd's.*

Caregiver: *I understand, Zach. Your mommy made your sandwich, and she made your brother Todd's sandwich too.*

Zach: (Chewing a bite of his sandwich, nods his head and smiles.)

At the table with George and Nanette (p. 314), where Sarah has added her grapes to her yogurt, and Nanette has commented that she sometimes does the same thing, this is what ensues:

> *Watching Sarah and hearing Nanette's comment, Elijah holds a cracker in his hand and looks around for something he can dip it into. The closest thing he can see is Henry's yogurt, but when he dips his cracker into it, Henry says "No!" and pushes his hand away. Nanette says, "You want something to dip your cracker into, Elijah, but Henry doesn't want you to dip into his yogurt. Let's get you some yogurt from the refrigerator." Elijah's face clears, and he nods yes. Nanette brings a large container of yogurt, a serving spoon, and a small bowl. Elijah serves himself some dipping yogurt and begins to dip.*

For snack, Denise, a caregiver, has given her four toddlers each a half of a banana with the peel still on (she knows her children like to do the peeling themselves):

> *Leon removes his peel entirely and flaps it about with one hand as he holds and eats his banana half with the other. Minyon peels her banana, puts it on her napkin, and breaks it into bits with her spoon. She lifts each banana piece to her mouth with her fingers. Clea watches Minyon, then peels her banana half, mashes it with her spoon, and spoons it up to her mouth. Max peels his banana half, squeezes it in his hand, and then licks it off his hand.*

Although Denise prefers to eat her banana in a more conventional manner, she understands that the children's explorations are a normal part of their ongoing curiosity about objects and how their actions affect them.

Caregivers eating with toddlers can also support their need for the repetition that allows them to eventually master a variety of self-help skills — pulling out the stool or chair to sit on and pushing it in again at the end of the meal, unwrapping a sandwich, peeling a banana, spooning yogurt into a bowl, pouring a cup of milk, and wiping up their spills.

Include older toddlers in mealtime setup and cleanup

Mealtimes present routine tasks older toddlers can easily carry out and take great satisfaction from — passing out plates, bowls, cups, and napkins; pouring their own juice and milk from small pitchers;

Mealtimes present tasks older toddlers can easily carry out and take great satisfaction from, including serving themselves food using a measuring cup and pouring their own milk from a small pitcher.

serving themselves food from plates and serving dishes; throwing napkins into the wastebasket; scraping leftover food from plates; putting used dishes in dish tubs for clearing; and wiping the table with soapy water and a sponge. As Goldschmied and Jackson (1994) have stated,

> *Involving the older children in tidying and cleaning up can mean more effort for the staff as it is usually quicker for the adults to do it themselves. But if we look on everything that happens in the nursery as part of the children's learning, this [preference for doing it quickly] is a short-sighted approach.*

There will be some occasions when time pressure is too great, but it is usually possible to organize some of the helping so that both adults and children enjoy it and feel a sense of achievement. (p. 24)

Understanding Time for Bodily Care

Josh, a young infant, intently watches his caregiver, Isobel, as she changes his diaper and sings these words to the tune of "Here We Go 'Round the Mulberry Bush": "Josh is getting his diaper changed, his diaper changed, his diaper changed. Josh is getting his diaper changed, early in the morning."

~

Xavier, an older infant, wiggles his toes and kicks his legs as Melissa, his caregiver, changes his diaper. At one point, he holds one foot with both hands and guides his foot into his mouth. "Oh, Xavier," says Melissa, pausing to admire his flexibility, "you've put your 'toesies' into your mouth!" She tickles his free foot. He then lets go of the foot he already has in his mouth, grabs his other foot, and puts that into his mouth. "Now you've put your other toesies into your mouth!" says Melissa. He and Melissa repeat this game several times before completing his diaper change.

~

Maria, a young toddler, reaches for the washcloth that Toni, her caregiver, is about to use on Maria's face. "So, Maria," says Toni, "you want to wash your own face!" Maria takes the washcloth from Toni and uses it to pat her cheeks. "You really know how to wash your cheeks, Maria!" says Toni. "Let's see if you can wipe your mouth too." Maria moves her hand toward her mouth and then rubs the cloth back and forth across her lips.

~

Zar, a toddler, notices a bunch of balloons suspended from the ceiling above him while Annie, his caregiver, changes his diaper. "Balloon?" he says. "Yes, you see balloons, Zar," says Annie, "lots of balloons!" Zar repeats the word "balloon" over and over again. After each repetition, he pauses and looks at Annie, who repeats "Lots of balloons!" and laughs.

~

After lunch, Joan and Pam's six toddlers look at books and work with puzzles before they take their nap. As they play, Pam tells them, "You have time for a few more books and puzzles. Then I'm going to help you change diapers." While Joan remains on the floor with the children, looking at books and helping with puzzles, Pam approaches and speaks to Aura, who is holding a book in her lap and rubbing her eyes: "You're looking at the book about farm animals, Aura," (Aura nods) "and you're rubbing your eyes!" Aura replies, "Sleepy." "Come with me for a diaper change, then nap," says Pam, leading her to the changing table. As Pam changes Aura's diaper, Aura wipes her own hands and face with a warm, moist paper towel that Pam has handed her. After changing Aura's diaper, Pam approaches each of the remaining children in a similar manner — commenting on their play; taking them to the changing table; offering them a warm, moist towel; and continuing the conversation with children who are not too sleepy. Two of the older toddlers, Jason and Misty, are in the process of

Through the gentle, one-on-one interactions involved in bodily care, caregivers take the opportunity to build trusting relationships with children.

learning to use the toilet. She asks them, in turn, if they need to sit on the potty. Jason says no, but Misty says yes and takes a turn on the potty before getting her fresh diaper.

~

Misha, an older toddler, is learning to use the potty chair. His caregiver,

Carla, and his parents are working together to support this new interest. Today when Misha gets up from his nap, Carla checks his diaper. "Your diaper is still dry, Misha!" she says. "Would you like to sit on the potty chair?" He sleepily rubs his eyes and shakes his head no. The other children are not awake yet, so Carla holds

Misha in her lap in the rocking chair and reads him a storybook. When they're finished, Carla asks again if he'd like to use the potty chair. This time he says yes and removes his own diaper. "You took off your own diaper, Misha," says Carla. Misha heads for the potty chair.

For infants and toddlers, the brief routines of bodily care — diaper changes, dressing, washing, and using the potty or toilet — occur frequently and fairly regularly throughout the day. This means whenever children are wet or soiled and before and/or after eating and napping — generally every hour or so, depending on the age, health, and habits of the child. At the most basic level, these routines promote cleanliness, physical comfort, and health by minimizing children's exposure to infection and diaper rash, but they can also contribute to children's emotional well-being. Through the gentle, one-to-one interactions involved in bodily care, children have an opportunity to build trusting relationships with caregivers and gain a sense of security in the care setting. Also, during the process of washing, diapering, dressing, and undressing, infants and toddlers begin to sense how their own bodies can bend and move.

Infants eventually use this knowledge to accomplish such self-help tasks as holding and handing over their diaper or washcloth or pulling up and pulling down their own pants. They use these opportunities to experience a variety of sensations, observe their surroundings,

and communicate with their caregivers. They also learn that while the inevitable care routines often interrupt their other exploration and play, they can almost always return fairly quickly to the situation they left.

In a child care setting, bodily care consistently takes place in the diapering and dressing areas and the child-oriented bathrooms described in some detail in Chapter 4 on pages 214–218. In short, the diapering and dressing areas and bathrooms should be easily cleaned, reasonably located, convenient for adults, and pleasant for children. To support the development of children's self-help skills and their "me do it" approach to life, sinks and toilets need to be low; faucets, as well as soap and towel dispensers, need to be child friendly. For toddlers, there should be steps leading up to the changing table and they should be able to access clean clothes themselves.

As adults help younger children with their bodily care routines, the children will continue to explore, play, fuss, babble, laugh, wiggle, drop things on the floor, ask questions, put things in their mouth, cry, and smile. In other words, they remain sensory-motor learners even when engaged in an activity that is largely adult controlled. As they grow from infants to toddlers, however, children can begin to take an increasingly active role in their own care routines.

Nonmobile infants are apt to lie fairly still for the diapering and washing process. As they lie there, they are often content to simply gaze at their caregiver's face or some nearby interesting object. They may also smile; imitate simple sounds the caregiver makes; grasp her finger; or hold some easily grasped object, such as a rattle or a small wooden spoon. Infants, like Josh (p. 321), enjoy hearing a simple diaper-changing song about themselves.

Enjoying their newfound mobility, older infants tend to move around a lot during their bodily care routines. They may roll back and forth, kick their legs, or put their toes in their mouth as Xavier does (p. 322). They may reach for and try to grasp their caregiver's hair, glasses, or shirt — or any appealing thing within reach. Given a clean washcloth or a clean diaper to hold, an older infant may drop it over his or her own face, then pull it away, initiating a game of peekaboo. During diapering and washing, children at this stage also take great pleasure in interacting with their caregiver in other simple games, such as playing "This little piggy…" on the toes, tickling, dropping the diaper or any other handy object, or pointing to body parts ("Where's Xavier's nose? There it is!").

By the time they can walk, young toddlers often actively resist the idea of lying still on their back for any length of time, especially just for a diaper change! Climbing up and down the steps of the changing table seems to make up for some of this temporary constraint. To have *some* control over their own diapering-washing-dressing process, young toddlers need to take as much action on their own behalf as possible — using their own washcloth

or towel and picking out which diaper or clean clothing to wear. They enjoy communicating in a give-and-take manner, as Zar does when he and his caregiver take turns saying "Balloon!" and "lots of balloons!" and playing hiding games (p. 322). As a further example, during Zar's diaper change on another day, he holds a baby wipe tightly in his fist and says "Gone" to caregiver Annie. "Oh, dear," Annie replies, "Zar's wipe is all gone!" Zar opens his fist and, with a big smile, reveals the missing baby wipe. "There it is!" exclaims Annie. Again, Zar closes his fist around the wipe, and they repeat the same action sequence and interchange several more times.

Older toddlers are quite involved in their own bodily care routines and often refuse help: "Me do it!" They can take off their own diapers, shoes, socks, pants, and shirt; wash their own hands and face by themselves at the sink; and fetch their own clean clothes and diapers. Toward the end of their second year, many older toddlers, like Misha and Misty (pp. 322–323), take an interest in sitting on the potty or toilet and passing the time there with an interesting picture book or magazine.

How Caregivers Support Children During Bodily Care Routines

While going through the routines of children's bodily care, caregivers try to share control with children as much as possible by following child cues and finding ways for the infant or toddler to take an active part in the task at hand. Being mindful of the following specific strategies is helpful in carrying out this role:

- Fit bodily care around the child's exploration and play.

- Focus on the child at hand during the care routine.

- Give the child choices about parts of the routine.

- Encourage the child to do things for her- or himself.

Fit bodily care around the child's exploration and play

In an active learning setting, caregivers approach bodily care routines from a child's perspective. This means, first of all, respecting whatever the child is already doing at the time bodily care becomes necessary. Instead of swooping down and briskly carrying a child off to the changing table for an efficient diaper change and hand washing, for example, caregivers first try to enter the child's current experience. Although bodily care will disrupt that experience, it is possible to lessen the impact of this disruption by giving children some advance indication of their need for a diaper change or potty break and then giving them some time to come to a stopping point in their play.

Young infants busily exploring materials may not understand what caregivers are saying to them about an upcoming diaper change, but how they act and speak may make a difference:

"Josh, I see you holding that silk scarf and watching it move," says caregiver

Isobel. She watches him wave the scarf and follow it with his eyes. "I'm going to take your scarf so I can pick you up," she says, to let him know what is going to happen next. "Then we'll go to the changing table for a diaper change." Although Josh is reluctant to give up his scarf, he nestles comfortably into Isobel's arms, reassured by her interest in his actions, warm tone of voice, and gentle touch. After his diaper change, Isobel brings Josh back to his blanket on the floor. "Here you are with a clean diaper, and there's your scarf," Isobel says as Josh reaches for the scarf.

Older infants and toddlers at play begin to understand what you are saying:

"Zar, I can see that you are stacking up the blocks," says Annie as she watches him balance a column of small, colored wooden blocks. "After a few more blocks, we need to go to the changing table to change your diaper." Zar looks up toward the changing table and back to his blocks. "You can come back to the blocks after your diaper change," she reassures him. Zar adds several more blocks to his stack, then, while holding a block in one hand, he reaches for Annie's hand with the other and heads with her to the changing table. After Zar, still holding his block, climbs down from the changing table in his clean diaper, Annie says, "There you go, Zar, back to the blocks!"

Gradually, children begin to fully realize that although they have to interrupt their play, they can play a bit more before stopping, and after their care routines, they can return to what they were doing. Some children, like Zar with his block, carry a toy along to the changing table as a solid reminder of the play they wish to continue.

Focus on the child at hand during the care routine

Although infants and toddlers cannot read words, they can read people. They distinguish between caregivers who regard bodily care as distasteful and those who take pleasure in interacting with them during bodily care. When caregivers understand the impact of their interactions with children, they give their major attention to the child they are diapering, dressing, washing, or assisting in the bathroom. They know that this genuine interest in the child strengthens the child-caregiver bond and the child's feelings of trust and security.

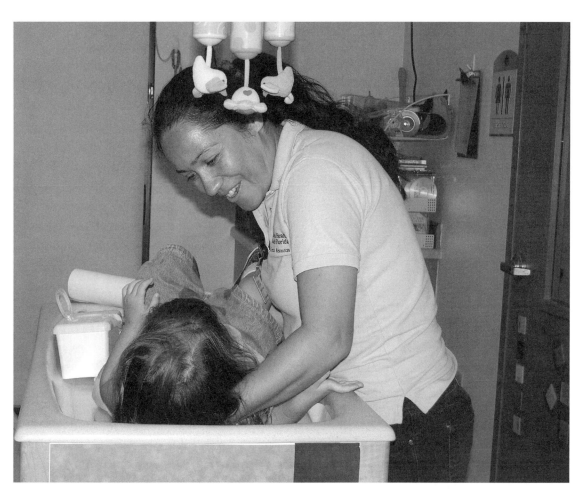

This caregiver is making lots of eye contact and enjoying her interactions with the child she is diapering, which helps strengthen their bond.

One way to focus on the child during bodily care is for the caregiver to *make a lot of eye contact* with the child. This allows the caregiver to make sense of what the child is communicating through every expression, action, or gesture. It also lets the child see and read the caregiver's face and have the sense of commanding and holding her attention. When Xavier puts his toes in his mouth, he is aware that caregiver Melissa sees him do it (p. 322). She watches his actions closely instead of continually gazing out over the rest of the room as her hands go through the motions of diapering. Because she watches and responds to his actions, Xavier knows he has her attention and energetically plays "This little piggy…" with her during his diaper change.

Focusing on the child includes *responding to child cues*. Infants and toddlers rely greatly on nonverbal communication and depend on caregivers to understand what they are saying, as caregiver Melissa does in this scenario:

One morning during his diaper change, Xavier feels like playing the game of putting toes in the mouth and having his other foot tickled by Melissa. Later that day, however, he is really sleepy and lies quietly with his hand on Melissa's as she changes his diaper. Even though they both enjoyed playing the "toesie" game earlier in the day, Melissa sees that Xavier's mood has changed and that what he really wants now is to fall asleep in his crib. As she changes his diaper, she softly sings him a lullaby.

A similar example would be this one involving Zar who, on one day (see p. 322), plays the balloon game with Annie, his caregiver, as she changes his diaper:

The next day, Zar lets Annie know that he really wants to get back to the sand table as quickly as possible. He wiggles around so he can see the sand table, points in that direction, and says "Down! Down!" "Let's get this diaper changed quickly," Annie says as she removes his soiled diaper, "so you can get back to the sand!"

And in another example, some days, Misha (p. 323), who is learning to use the potty, lets caregiver Carla know that he wants her to stay near him in the bathroom. Other days he tells her, "Go there!" — so she moves away from him to stand in the bathroom doorway. (See "When Toddlers Use the Potty or Toilet: Tips for Caregivers, p. 329.)

Focusing on the child also involves *talking about what the caregiver and child are doing*. Caregivers can comment on what they see and understand about the child they are changing, washing, or dressing ("Oh, Xavier, you've put your 'toesies' in your mouth!" "You really know how to wash your cheeks, Maria!" "You took off your own diaper, Misha!"). Older children understand these comments and know that their caregivers are interested in them. Very young children may not understand exactly what their caregiver is saying, but they know that her actions and words are concerned with them.

When Toddlers Use the Potty or Toilet: Tips for Caregivers

1. **Follow children's cues.** Children will let you know by their words and actions when they are interested in sitting on the potty or toilet or trying to wear underpants in place of diapers. Be alert to each individual child so you can support his or her efforts when the time is right.

2. **Coordinate with parents.** When you see that a child is interested in using the bathroom, share your observations with parents. Together, come up with a way to proceed that is as consistent as possible between the home and the child care setting.

3. **Be patient with children.** Children take their time learning any new skill, and using the toilet is a fairly complex one. Remember that each child will learn this skill at a personally comfortable pace. Pressure from adults can actually slow down the whole process. When accidental soiling occurs, treat it matter-of-factly, as you would any other problem children encounter during the day: "Looks like your pants are wet, Jacob. Let's go find your dry ones to put on."

Give the child choices about parts of the routine

With the help of supportive caregivers, children can make choices within each bodily care routine. For example, a child can choose which type of protective pants to use or hold a clean diaper in each hand and decide which one to give to the caregiver to put on. Children can choose which washcloth to use or whether they want to use a cloth or a disposable wipe on their face and hands. Older toddlers can decide whether or not to sit on the potty or whether to sit on the potty or the toilet. Such simple decisions may seem insignificant to adults, but they involve infants and toddlers as active players and give them a sense of being in charge of their own bodily care.

Another way to give children choices during bodily care is through the learning environment. How caregivers set up the dressing and diapering area and bathroom determines what choices children have about what to look at or watch during bodily care. A strategically located mirror, a window, a mobile, or a rotating display of family photographs, pictures, art reproductions, plants, or weavings, for example, can provide children with a range of choices about what to look at when they are not gazing at their caregiver or putting their toes in their mouth. For example,

Sean, a young infant, lies on his back on the changing table, sees his reflection in the mirror on the wall next him, and makes cooing noises at his own image. "There you are in the mirror,

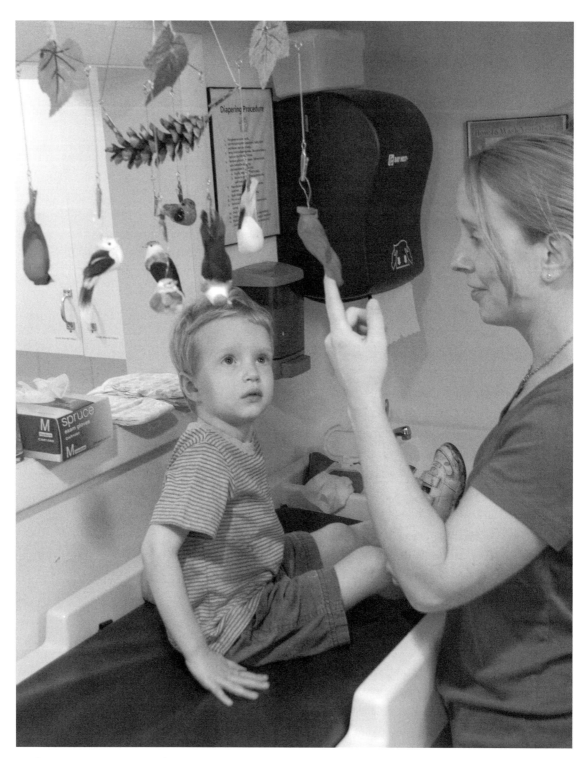

In this center, caregivers take turns making and rotating mobiles above the changing table. This gives the children something to look at during diaper changes and also is a natural conversation starter.

Sean," his caregiver says during a pause between coos, "getting your diaper changed!"

Since infants and toddlers are sensory-motor learners, even during bodily care routines they like to have something in their hands to see up close, feel, mouth, smell, or listen to. Caregivers provide infants with some choice about what to hold: They might offer a choice between holding a clean diaper or a small clean washcloth, for example, or provide a basket of small objects to choose from (a set of metal measuring spoons, a rubber squeaker toy, a rattle, a small cloth book). The objects should be compact so children can hold on to them with one hand without putting them in contact with bodily waste. If contact does occur, however, caregivers should simply put the object aside for a thorough sanitizing before returning it to the basket. Caregivers can also provide these same kinds of choices for toddlers, though they may also decide to bring some toy from their play along with them to the changing table. As they are making their selection of an item to bring with them, caregivers help them find something that is not too big and will not easily be soiled. The small block Zar brings to the changing table, for example, fits in his one hand. And on the potty, Misha reads a book he can easily hold by himself. Remember, too, that the objects children see and hold during bodily care may spark conversation:

"Twee," says Jill, pointing to a picture on the wall during her diaper change. "You see a tree in the picture," replies

Shannon, her caregiver. "Birdy," continues Jill. "There's a birdy in the tree," comments Shannon.

Encourage the child to do things for her- or himself

As they move toward independence, children assert their desire to do things for themselves. While their early attempts at bodily care are time consuming and inefficient by adult standards, caregivers patiently support these attempts, just as they patiently support children in learning to feed themselves, stack their own blocks, and walk unassisted.

Bodily care routines provide ongoing opportunities for infants and toddlers to try out and practice self-help skills. Older infants can hold their clean diapers, washcloths, and small articles of clothing for the caregiver. Young toddlers enjoy using a washcloth to wipe their face and hands and climbing up the steps to the changing table. Many older toddlers will naturally insist on washing their own face and hands, brushing their teeth, pulling their own pants down and up again when they use the potty, putting their own arms in sleeves and legs in pants, getting their own clean clothes from their cubby or tub, and zipping their own zippers (with a little help in getting them started).

As children do more and more things for themselves, caregivers are freer to watch them in action and to appreciate and comment on their emerging skills: "I see you pushed your hand all the way through your coat sleeve, Misha" says his caregiver, Carla, as she holds his coat for him.

As children do more and more things for themselves, caregivers are freer to watch them in action and to appreciate and comment on their emerging skills.

Understanding Naptime

Sue and Rosie's eight toddlers are busily engaged in their personal before-nap rituals: Lydia and Sam each pull off their socks, put them carefully under their cot, and then lie down, where-upon caregiver Sue sits down between their cots and lightly rubs each child's

back. Sam sucks his thumb, and Lydia clasps her favorite stuffed bunny — both lie quietly on their cots. Jonah gets his pacifier from his cubbie, puts it in his mouth, and curls up on his cot for sleep. Colin lies holding his stuffed monkey and singing quietly to himself "Monkey, monkey, mon-kee! Monkey, monkey, mon-kee!" Colleen and Ida search the room for their "dollies." When they find them in their cubbies, they return with them to their cots. Colleen covers her-self with her blanket, keeping her doll outside the blanket. Ida asks caregiver Rosie's help in covering herself and her doll. Lex, lying on his side, drives a small truck across his pillow. Teresa brings a basket of books to her cot and selects one to look at. Ten minutes later, all the toddlers are asleep but Teresa — she lies on her cot looking at books.

～

Shawna, an older infant, rubs her eyes after midmorning snack and looks very sleepy. Pam, her caregiver, puts Shawna in her crib for a nap even though recently she hasn't been taking a morning nap. On this particular day, however, Pam is alert to Shawna's signs of tiredness, because Shawna has just returned to the center after a few days at home with a bad cold.

～

This is Lamont's first day in caregiver Bonnie's group at the child care center. An older toddler, he plays energetically until midmorning, when he falls asleep on the floor in the block area. Although the other toddlers in the group no longer take a morning nap, Bonnie sets up a cot close to where Lamont is sleeping and gently lifts him onto it. There he sleeps soundly for about 45 minutes while the rest of the children continue to play around him. "Why he sleeping?" another toddler, Malika, asks Bonnie, pointing to Lamont on his cot. "This is Lamont's first day," she says, "and he's worn out!" "Night, night," says Malika, patting him softly on the back. Lamont does not stir. After lunch, Lamont naps again along with the rest of his peers.

~

It is midafternoon. Four of the six young infants in Jenna and Barbara's care are still napping in their cribs. Lena, one of the infants awake, is having a bottle in caregiver Barbara's arms. As Hannah, one of the sleeping infants, begins to wake up, she catches the eye of her caregiver, Jenna, who smiles back at her and hands Hannah her favorite "blankie." Hannah quickly covers her face with her blankie and then pulls it away. "Peekaboo," says Jenna every time Hannah's smiling face emerges from under the blanket. After several rounds of peekaboo, Jenna says to Hannah, "Okay, one more peekaboo, and then it's time for a diaper change and a bottle!"

In the meantime, Lena finishes her bottle, and Barbara settles her on a blanket spread out on the floor and

offers her a basket of interesting things to play with. Just then Zeke wakes up and starts crying furiously in his crib. Leaving Lena, who has chosen a wooden clothespin from her basket, Barbara moves to pick up Zeke and hold him in her arms, saying "I bet you're ready for your bottle right now!" She takes his bottle from the warmer, and he eagerly takes it with both hands and begins to suck on it.

Naptime in an infant-toddler program occurs both on demand, when children tire, and as a regularly scheduled part of the day. Naps provide the sleep and rest that are necessary for children's growth and development. Like adults, tired children are often cranky and irritable; sleep helps restore their good nature. It also provides a quiet retreat from the intensely social demands of the child care setting. In short, napping allows children to reenergize physically and emotionally for the next part of the day.

In addition to its restorative nature, sleep may also serve an important structural and physiological function in the brain. While the connection between sleep and brain development is only beginning to be understood, scientists hypothesize that the stimulation that occurs during REM (rapid eye movement) sleep helps to strengthen neural connections. The growth of these connections as the brain matures, known as "plasticity," underlies the brain's ability to control behavior, including learning and memory (National Center on Sleep Disorders Research, 2003).

Napping provides a quiet retreat from the intensely social demands of the child care center.

Although an infant or toddler may fall asleep anywhere in the center — in a caregiver's arms, in a cozy armchair, under the climber — caregivers usually move the child to continue and complete the nap in a cradle, basket, crib, or cot. This practice frees caregivers to attend to other wakeful children; protects the sleeping child from being stepped on by peers at play; and consistently provides each child with a personal, familiar sleeping place.

Toddlers, as they gain a stronger sense of self and a familiarity with the care setting, often express a particular preference about where to sleep. For example,

a toddler may wish his cot to be close to a light source (for looking at books), near a particular caregiver, or alongside the cot of a special friend. Caregivers may also decide to use one area of the room for the cots of the children who tend to sleep longer and another area of the room for the cots of those who wake up first. The "early risers" might sleep closer, for example, to the bathroom, the book area, or the exit to outdoors.

For the most part, children in an infant-toddler program fall asleep at naptime. And if they do not sleep, they rest. Most infants take from two to three sleeping naps a day, whereas for older toddlers, one nap after lunch generally is enough. While most toddlers take either a long or a short sleeping nap, some get the rest they need by lying awake on their cots for some or all of their naptime, looking at books or busying themselves quietly with some chosen plaything.

How Caregivers Support Children During Naptime

Caregivers respect and accommodate each child's need to sleep or rest when tired and to wake up on his or her own when rested. They use these specific strategies in doing so:

- Schedule naptime around each child's individual needs.

- Help children settle down to nap.

- Provide quiet alternatives for nonsleepers.

- Provide for children's various styles of waking up.

Schedule naptime around each child's individual needs

When children are involved throughout the morning in interesting and vigorous exploration both indoors and out, it makes sense to schedule an after-lunch naptime as part of the overall daily routine. However, with this predictable naptime in place, it is also very important to accommodate children's personal napping schedules, recognizing that a child's need for naps changes with age and personal circumstances. For example, when Shawna (p. 332) returns to the center after an illness, her caregivers anticipate her continued need for extra sleep, and Pam is not surprised to see Shawna rubbing her eyes in the middle of the morning. "You're still working on getting over that cold," she says to Shawna. "I'm going to tuck you into your crib for a nap so you'll feel better." Nor is Bonnie (pp. 332–333) surprised that Lamont, though one of the older toddlers, falls asleep before lunch on his first day at the center. Instead of expecting him to conform to the routine that works for the other toddlers, she accepts his tiredness as an indication of the energy he is pouring into his new venture.

Caregivers talk with and listen to parents when they arrive with their children so they know when to anticipate a change in children's sleep patterns: "Ola was up late last night with his cousins. He may need an extra nap today!" "Seraya fussed all through the night. I think it's her teeth." "I had a hard time getting Lukas up this morning. He wanted to stay asleep, and then he fell asleep in the car on the way here."

Help children settle down to nap

Once it is clear to them that it is naptime, infants and toddlers develop their own rituals for falling asleep. Some infants fall asleep as soon as they are in their own familiar crib or cradle. Some fuss, and to settle into sleep, they may need their caregiver to rock, stroke, or pat them and perhaps sing them a little song. Other infants suck their thumb or pacifier or wiggle and squirm until they find

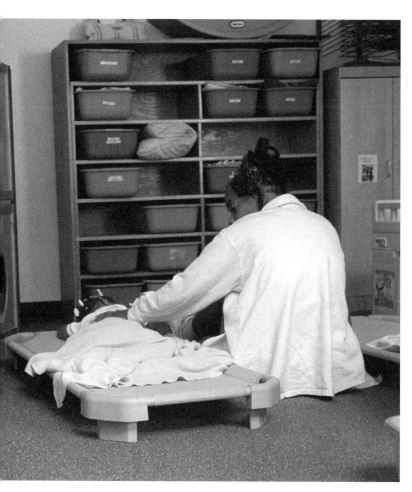

Some toddlers like a back rub before they settle down for a nap.

Provide quiet alternatives for nonsleepers

During their regularly scheduled after-lunch naptime, some toddlers may occasionally or routinely remain awake for some or all of the time. This presents another opportunity for choice. Caregivers Sue and Rosie, for example, expect their toddlers to rest on their cots during the naptime, but they can choose a book or a toy to use as they rest. On the day described on page 332, each of the toddlers except Sam has brought something to bed — a favorite stuffed bunny, a pacifier, a stuffed monkey, a "dolly," a small truck, a basket of books. After 10 minutes, all the children are asleep except Teresa, who looks at books. And on some days, even Teresa sleeps.

In another center, caregivers Lynne and Elba have four toddlers who routinely sleep for about two hours and four who rest or sleep for only an hour or less. Upon waking, the four "short nappers" have the choice of playing in the book area, the toy area, or the art area — all areas of quiet activity, located the farthest away from the "long nappers." And on some days, after all the short nappers are awake, they go outdoors with one of the caregivers.

Provide for children's various styles of waking up

Some children awake from a nap happy and ready to get on with their day. Some are fussy, unsure of where they are, and in need of physical contact and comfort — being rocked in the rocking chair or taking a trip in a caregiver's arms to look out the

a comfortable sleeping position. Toddlers continue to need personal attention as they settle down for naps. Some toddlers may request a back rub or a song. Others may need help or simply acknowledgment as they choose a book to look at on their cot, locate the special blanket or toy they want to sleep with, or get a drink of water. Over time, through observation, trial and error, and tips from parents, caregivers can discover how to help each child settle down to nap.

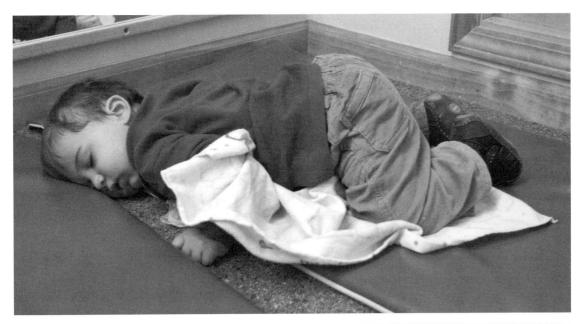

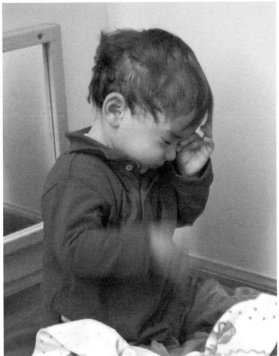

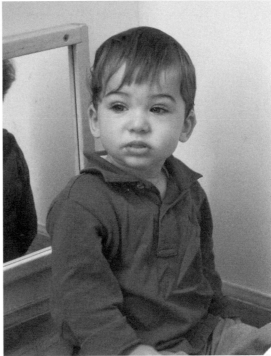

Different children have different ways of waking up. This child wakes slowly and is content to sit on the mat before reorienting himself to his surroundings.

window. Others wake slowly and are content to lie on their cot or in their crib for a few minutes, just watching the afternoon unfold and reorienting themselves to their surroundings.

Caregivers provide comfort and contact as needed, interact with children during after-nap bodily care, and begin the next part of the day — snack, outside time, choice time, for example — in such a way that children are free to join in gradually as they awake and feel ready.

Understanding Choice Time

Ike, a young nonmobile infant, lies on his back on a blanket. He kicks his legs and waves his arms and then reaches for a small cloth ball that lies near him. He grasps the ball, chews on it for a bit, and lets it go. He sees a wooden spoon on his blanket, grasps it in his hand, and then lets it go. He turns his head back toward the ball, which has rolled just out of his reach, and reaches toward it. El, his caregiver, is seated near him on the floor and gently pushes the ball in his direction. Ike grasps it and brings it to his mouth. He turns for several minutes to watch Aisha, the baby on the blanket next to his and then turns back to his ball.

∼

At choice time, Shelley and Nick, two infants in the creeper-crawler stage, sit on the floor on either side of a basket. Nick pulls out a ball of yarn from the basket, drops it, watches it roll away from him, and then crawls after it. Shelley dips a length of chain in and out of a measuring cup and then tries the same thing with the chain and the oatmeal box.

∼

During choice time, T.C., an older infant, crawls toward a "platform" that is a low carton covered in red paper. As T.C. crawls along, the small wooden block he holds in one hand makes a bumping sound each time it hits the carpet. When he reaches the red platform, he crawls onto it, and with a big smile on his face, bangs his wooden block against the box-platform to make a hollow thumping sound. "You're banging the box with your block, T.C.!" says Anne, his caregiver. T.C. laughs and keeps banging. She moves three similar blocks over next to his platform so they are within his reach. "Maybe you would like to have a block for your other hand," she comments. T.C. pauses, looks at the additional blocks, selects one, and bangs both blocks on the platform.

∼

At the water table, two young toddlers, Sarah and Micah, stand side by side dropping stones and shells into sieves. Sandy, a caregiver, joins the children at the table. Kneeling down, she too begins to drop objects into a sieve, selecting only shells and looking at each shell carefully as she does so. "Shell!" Micah says, handing a shell to

Sandy. "Thanks for the shell, Micah!" she says, adding it to the others in her sieve. Observing this interaction, Sarah digs down into the shells at the bottom of the table, comes up with one, and offers it to Sandy, saying "S'ell." "Thanks for the shell, Sarah," says Sandy.

~

Matt, a toddler, and Joan, his caregiver, sit on the floor facing each other. Matt rolls three balls toward Joan, who rolls them back to him. After 10 minutes or so, Matt leaves the balls and heads for the dress-up clothes in the house area. He selects a shirt and takes it to Joan for help with putting it on. As Joan holds the shirt while Matt slips his arms into the sleeves, she asks, "Where you are going in your shirt, Matt?" In reply, Matt goes to the water table, where toddlers Sarah and Micah (from the preceding scenario) are playing with shells. He watches them and then puts a shell in Micah's sieve. Micah takes it out of the sieve, looks at it, puts it back, and then looks up and smiles at Matt.

~

During choice time, Magali sits on the floor in sight of Sharelle, Kevin, Maurice, and Dierdre, the four toddlers in her care. Sharelle scrambles up the ladder climber and scoots back down again. Then she calls out Magali's name ("Gali"), climbs up the ladder again, and turns at the top to make sure Magali sees what she is doing.

"Sharelle, you climbed up the ladder, and now you're at the top!" Magali observes. Over in the book corner, Kevin looks at the big book about cars and trucks. Maurice, who is at the table in the art area, scribbles with a red crayon on a big sheet of paper. Dierdre takes all the food out of the house area's refrigerator and arranges it on the table and then sits on a stool beside the table and pretends to eat. In the meantime, Kevin brings his book over to Magali, plops down in her lap, and says "Read!" As Magali reads, Dierdre leaves the house area and also climbs onto Magali's lap to hear the story. "So, you want to hear the story too, Dierdre!" says Magali.

Choice time is a sustained block of time when infants and toddlers can investigate and explore materials and actions and interact with their peers and caregivers. In a supportive and safe environment that affords interesting materials and opportunities as well as open space to move freely in various ways, each child chooses what to do based on personal interests, inclinations, and level of development and ability. Choice time provides children with a virtually uninterrupted period of exploration and play.

A great deal of learning occurs at choice time. Through their self-chosen sensory-motor explorations, infants and toddlers engage in experiences that support learning in all the KDI content areas. They fill and empty, put in and take out, discover that objects still exist when out

Choice time provides young children a sustained period of time to explore and play with what they choose.

of sight, repeat an action to make something happen again, and so forth. As they interact with people and materials, children practice skills and begin to construct knowledge in all the areas of the KDIs: approaches to learning; social and emotional development; physical development and health; communication, language, and literacy; cognitive development; and creative arts. Choice time takes place within a rich social context, so children have the opportunity to watch others at exploration and play, imitate their actions, and build relationships with others. They can also communicate their frustrations and triumphs to attentive, interactive caregivers.

Caregivers familiar with the HighScope Preschool Curriculum may recognize choice time as the infant-toddler version of work time, when HighScope preschoolers pursue activities of their own choosing.

Unlike the preschool work time, choice time for infants and young toddlers is not preceded by planning time and followed by recall time. However, older toddlers may begin to plan and recall once they are able to hold mental images and thus think about what they want to do or have done. In a very basic way, choice time promotes infants' and toddlers' sense of themselves as doers, decision makers, and problem solvers. By carrying out their own initiatives, they learn how to make things happen. They discover they can choose where to crawl; what to climb; what to mouth, stack, or carry; and whose hand to hold. This time of being fully in charge of these decisions forms the heart of the infant's or toddler's day in a HighScope program.

Choice time takes place in the thoughtfully equipped and arranged infant and toddler indoor play spaces. In these play spaces, children move freely and have easy access to ample and diverse materials appropriate to their developmental and ability levels. (As we discuss later in this chapter, outside time is also a children's choice time, but in an outdoor setting.)

Throughout choice time, infants and toddlers move about, explore materials and actions, and play near and with peers and caregivers. They do all of this at their own pace, according to their individual interests and abilities. What they do is truly their choice. Adults do not impose their own ideas about what infants and toddlers should be doing and learning. Rather, they follow the children's initiatives while being aware of the opportunities for learning (the KDIs) and supporting the children's intentions.

Nonmobile infants make their choices from an array of appealing materials caregivers place within their reach. They grasp, wave, mouth, drop, coo, or babble at whatever they have chosen — a wooden rattle, a woolen ball, a silk scarf. They try out and explore such physical actions as stretching, kicking, rolling, turning over, and looking at themselves in a mirror. They also sometimes stop to watch other infants and older children and to perhaps babble or gesture toward them or cry (if, for example, they see another child crying).

The choices and possibilities for exploration and play are greater for mobile infants. They may sit next to and explore a treasure basket containing commonplace objects (e.g., a lemon, a wooden spoon,

metal keys on a ring, a tennis ball; see Treasure Baskets in Chapter 4). They may crawl or creep to a shelf of books or toys and choose one to examine. They may carry things in their mouth or hand as they crawl, or they might sit beside a shallow pan and dabble in water or pat sand. They may decide to crawl up and down a gently sloping ramp or to pull up to a standing position by taking hold of various fixtures or furnishings. As they move about the play space, they may seek another child to play beside. They might choose to interact with a caregiver in a simple game of peekaboo, drop the spool, or bang the blocks.

Toddlers engage in increasingly complex exploration and play. For example, they look at books and identify familiar people, animals, and objects in pictures; stack, topple, and carry blocks; maneuver toy trucks, cars, motorcycles, and animals; work with puzzles and pegboards; scribble, tear, and paint; dress up, play house, and push their baby dolls in buggies or carts; and throw balls, climb, slide, and crawl into cartons and tunnels.

As they grow in awareness of themselves and others, younger toddlers begin to initiate social behaviors, such as hugging and patting another child to show affection, bringing a toy or comfort item to another child, or playing a game of peeking at another child through the window in the climber. Older toddlers can address one another by name and make simple requests of peers: "Ben, me [want] car." They try out the actions of a child playing

During choice time,

a nonmobile infant makes his choice from an array of appealing materials in his reach,

a mobile infant watches the older toddlers use the sensory table through a glass partition,

a younger toddler maneuvers toy trucks across the floor,

and an older toddler draws with crayons.

nearby. For example, when Marie fits pegs in a pegboard, Alana joins her with another pegboard. As Alana starts to sing "Row, Row, Row Your Boat" while putting pegs into *her* board, Marie sings along with her. The two girls enjoy doing things together — going down adjacent slides, playing together in the rocking boat, scaling the climber side by side, painting next to each other, and using phones together. As they begin to have a strong sense of "me" and "mine," toddlers also tend to engage in social conflict. And, as they begin to be able to hold mental images, some toddlers may, when asked, indicate what they plan to do: They may point to the art area when they want to explore with play dough, for example, or say "balls" before they run to find some balls to play with.

How Caregivers Support Children During Choice Time

During children's choice time, caregivers make themselves physically and emotionally available to observe and interact with them. At the same time, they respect children's need to explore and play at their own pace with people and materials of particular interest to them. The following strategies are all part of this balanced role:

- Pay close attention to children as they explore and play.

- Tailor actions and responses to follow children's leads and ideas.

- Engage in communication give and take with children.

- Support children's interactions with peers.

- Use a problem-solving approach to children's social conflicts.

- Offer older toddlers opportunities to plan and recall.

- Encourage toddlers to put materials away after choice time.

Pay close attention to children as they explore and play

As they venture out to explore the physical and social world, infants and toddlers depend on teachers and caregivers to see and understand what they are doing and to provide the support, encouragement, and assurance they need. A caregiver's attentive, responsive presence during choice time assures infants and toddlers of the immediate availability of a known and trusted adult. Caregivers also benefit when they pay attention to children. It allows them to enter the child's world; see each child's strengths, interests, and temperament; attune themselves to each child's pace and interests; and collect anecdotal information that guides the way they support, plan, and advocate for the children in their care.

Literally joining children at their level in the play space lends an important physical dimension to paying them "close attention." In active learning settings, caregivers find themselves crawling along on hands and knees with the creeper-crawler, lying on the floor near the baby who is stretched out on a blanket, or squatting next to toddlers playing at the sand table.

Joining the children at their level in the play space allows this caregiver to enter their world so that she can see and better understand her children's strengths, interests, and temperaments.

A caregiver might sit on the floor with a lapful of children, sit on a small chair at a low table as children scribble and mold play dough, or serve as a leaning post for a child who is learning to sit or stand or cruise.

If caregivers assume vantage points such as these, they will find that they can readily see, hear, and touch the children in their care. Once a caregiver is down on the floor and physically close to children, she watches and listens carefully in an attempt to understand what individual children are doing and communicating and carefully considers each child's choices and intentions so she can interact and respond in a meaningful way. This is better than swooping down on a child with new and possibly unrelated ideas, which may actually be disruptive to what the child is doing. Anne (p. 338), for example, watches T.C. crawl and climb onto the platform with his block in hand, but she doesn't understand what he has in mind until he proudly starts to bang the hollow platform with his block.

Caregivers who are observing play at the children's level are ready and available when children need comfort and contact. The caregiver provides a "home base" children can come back to before heading out again on their own. As very young children explore and play at choice time, they may momentarily lose their nerve and may search out a touch, hug, or cuddle or a lap to sit on before returning to their chosen activity. For example, a creeper-crawler may climb into his or her caregiver's lap for refuge when a loud toddler pushing a big truck huffs by. Or consider this scenario of a child in need of contact and reassurance before he risks trying a new material or working alongside his peers:

> *Jason, a toddler, is sucking his thumb, his other arm wrapped around his caregiver's leg. He is watching two children molding clay at the art table. His caregiver kneels down, slips her arm around him, and says, "Jason, it looks like you're watching the kids with the clay." He nods in agreement. "Shall we go to the art table and work with some clay too?" she asks. He nods yes, takes her hand, and leads her to the art table.*

Tailor actions and responses to follow children's leads and ideas

Throughout choice time, children make a series of spontaneous choices and decisions. By tailoring their actions and responses to follow children's cues, caregivers acknowledge and respect children's intentions, which shift and change over the course of their explorations and play. When their caregivers heed, respond to, and build on children's communications and actions — instead of ignoring or overriding them — children retain a sense of control over what is happening. By taking this nondirective but participatory approach, they also have the opportunity to gain insight into children's thinking and reasoning and are better able to scaffold their learning.

Often, the cues infants and toddlers offer are expressed not in words, but in actions, gestures, or facial expressions. For example, when nonmobile infant Ike's ball rolls away from him (p. 338), he is too young to crawl after it or to say "Hey, I want my ball back!" Instead, he conveys this message to El, his caregiver, by turning his head and reaching toward the ball. From her attentive position next to him, El reads his gestures (This is how Ike *expresses initiative* [approaches to learning KDI]), gets the message, and rolls the ball back within his reach. By still letting Ike reach for the ball, instead of giving it to him, El is also supporting the KDI that children *do things for themselves.*

In another situation, caregiver Sandy joins toddlers Sarah and Micah at the

This caregiver follows the child's interest in the spider and the magnifying glass by using the magnifying glass herself and describing what she sees.

water table (p. 338). Watching the children put rocks and shells into their sieves, Sandy follows their lead by imitating their actions — with a slight variation. When Sandy begins to select *only shells* for her sieve, the toddlers find this of interest and spontaneously begin to say "shell" each time they offer her another shell. Sarah

and Micah continue their play and include Sandy in it, because instead of attempting to redirect or restructure their play, Sandy follows their idea and builds on what they are already doing. At the same time, Sandy learns about Sarah's and Micah's ability to distinguish shells from stones and to name objects they have chosen. She recognizes this ability as a cognitive development KDI: *Exploring same and different*.

Older toddlers often indicate that they want to do things for themselves. At choice time, it is not unusual for them to push away a helping hand or to say "Me do it!" as they try to take the top off a container, fit shapes into a sorting box, or try to climb into a low carton and get stuck with one leg hanging over the side. In these situations, caregivers respect children's initiatives and their desire to figure things out on their own. They simply remain attentively present and offer the children encouragement by describing what they see ("You're turning that block a lot of different ways to try to fit it in the slot, Chris"). If the child is becoming too frustrated, the teacher might offer a suggestion ("Sometimes when I wrap a baby doll, I put her on the floor") or might offer some physical support, for example, holding a bottle still while the child unscrews its cap. Although toddlers' problem-solving attempts are often awkward, time consuming, and difficult for caregivers to witness, it is clear that most children take great pleasure in solving these toddler-sized problems on their own with a minimum of help.

Following children's leads and ideas requires caregivers to be observant, patient, flexible, and open to the child's viewpoint. They also need to resist the urge to jump in with a set agenda based on preconceived ideas of what an infant or toddler of a specific age should be doing. On the other hand, this approach does not

Following a young child's lead and ideas requires a caregiver to be observant, patient, and flexible.

mean the caregiver is passive. To the contrary, the more the caregiver knows about child development and how to support early learning (using the KDIs as a guide), the more the caregiver can actively support children's active learning.

Engage in communication give and take with children

At choice time, caregivers in a HighScope active learning setting communicate in an even give-and-take manner with infants and toddlers in both conversation and play. This means encouraging the child to set the pace and to freely contribute to each interchange, and it means matching, not ignoring or overriding, the child's contributions. This allows them to share control with the children and to model the partnership of everyday social exchange.

Before they learn to talk, infants and toddlers keep up their end of the conversation with sounds, gestures, and actions. Caregivers, in turn, incorporate children's nonverbal contributions into their part of the conversation. The following examples illustrate some exchanges between caregivers and nonverbal children at choice time:

> *Aneesha, a young infant, lies on her back, touching her stuffed lamb and cooing to it. Still touching her lamb, she turns to smile at Elba, her caregiver, and then smacks her lips at Elba. In return, Elba smiles at Aneesha; imitates her lip smacking; and says, "I see you, Aneesha!" Aneesha wiggles and smacks her lips again. Elba, in turn, smacks*
> *her own lips and says to Aneesha, "You like to smack your lips! Aneesha wiggles and then turns her attention back to her lamb.*

~

> *Bryce sits on the floor, dropping chestnuts into one of two empty tin buckets. At one point he stops and, catching the eye of Cora, his caregiver, drops another chestnut into the bucket with a clatter; then he laughs. In return, Cora picks up a chestnut and drops it into the other bucket. They repeat this chestnut-dropping exchange until Bryce finally turns away from Cora and focuses his attention on patting down his bucket full of chestnuts.*

~

> *From his perch at the top of the climber, toddler Ethan drops a rubber ball over the rail. He watches where the ball finally comes to rest on the floor, then climbs down to retrieve it, and scrambles back up the climber with it. He then throws it down again, this time looking at caregiver Brandon and making the sound "ffwiiisssss" as he throws it. "Ffwiissss," says Brandon, "there goes the ball!" They repeat this exchange several times as Ethan goes through the same action sequence over and over again until he finally tires.*

Older toddlers like Sarah and Micah (pp. 338–339) incorporate words into their exchanges. Note that each time Sarah or Micah says the single word "shell," Sandy, their caregiver, makes a reply that is relatively short as well ("Thanks for the shell"). By making a short reply, Sandy matches the child's contribution instead of burying Sarah or Micah in a barrage of words. Consider another situation at choice time:

> *Caregiver Sylvia watches Jamie paint on a large sheet of paper on the art area table. Jamie stabs his brush at the paper over and over again. As he pauses to examine the resulting splotches of color, he says "Feets!" "It looks like you made feet on your paper," observes Sylvia. "More feets!" Jamie says, as he selects a new brush and a new color and resumes making splotches. "You're making more feet," says Sylvia. Jamie is too engrossed in painting to respond to this second observation, and Sylvia does not press him to do so.*

While these conversational exchanges may seem brief and mundane, they are examples of how adults respect the style and pace of the children involved. Notice that Jamie's caregiver does not try to press her point or prolong the conversation with such questions as "Do you like playing with paint?," "Are you having fun?," and "What color are you using?" Toddlers need time to find the language that fits with their actions. Questions often pressure children to respond to subjects they may not be inclined toward at the moment and tend to disrupt children's actions or thought processes. Consequently, when questioned by an adult, children many times ignore the question or even leave

what they are doing (perhaps to get away from the questions and the questioner). Caregiver questions can thus interfere with communication, whereas caregiver comments, observations, and acknowledgments tend to keep conversational exchanges going. (For more information on appropriate questioning strategies with young children, see Hohmann, Weikart, & Epstein, 2008.) By contrast, when teachers quietly work alongside children (e.g., using art materials in the same way), children remain engaged in their play for

Toddlers need time to find the language that fits with their actions, so caregivers spend a lot of time patiently listening — in this case, the conversation is about pigs!

extended periods of time and use materials in more complex ways (Kindler, 1995).

Support children's interactions with peers

In child care settings, choice time takes place within a social context. Though infants and toddlers often choose to engage in solitary pursuits, they also take the opportunity to observe, play alongside, and imitate their peers. By thoughtfully supporting these early bids at social interaction, caregivers can help children to form positive peer relationships and to see themselves and others as members of a community.

Caregivers in infant-toddler settings find that given the opportunity, even children as young as two months old may exhibit interest in one another. For example, putting a pair of nonmobile infants on their back close together on the floor at choice time allows them to enjoy each other's company. The two infants will often communicate their interest in each other through wiggling; turning their heads toward each other; and exchanging gazes, smiles, coos, and babbles. If one cries, the other cries. One of the pair may become less animated or even sad when his or her special "blanket-mate" is out of sight or at home for the day. As caregivers pay close attention to certain pairs of infants, they gently comment on the social interactions they see: "Meagan, you're watching Lu." "I'll bet you miss Rabb today, Jack. He's home with a cold."

Caregivers continue to watch for and acknowledge peer preferences as infants begin to creep and crawl and to pull themselves up to stand. At choice time, these infants will often use their newfound mobility to seek the company of a particular child, as in this scenario:

> *Toddler James deliberately chooses to sit on the floor and explore materials next to another toddler, Tab, and he even makes a friendly but unsuccessful attempt to touch the wire whisk Tab is examining with his hands and mouth. When Tab finally gives up his whisk, crawls over to the sofa, and pulls himself up to a standing position, James abandons his basket of household items, crawls after Tab, and pulls himself up to stand at the other end of the sofa. After a struggle, Tab climbs onto the sofa. James works very hard to climb onto the sofa too. During a moment of rest, he looks over his shoulder at his caregiver, Marsha. "James," she says, recognizing his action and its social implications, "you're working very hard to climb onto the sofa with Tab."*

Caregivers support toddlers' peer interactions by providing equipment that allows children to play side by side: wide slides, climbers, and stairs; lots of table, floor, and easel space; rocking boats; cozy chairs and nooks with room for two. They provide two or more similar wheeled toys, shovels, and buckets, so children can play with such toys together and try out one another's actions with the toys. Finally, they provide play materials that two or three toddlers can gather around and still

Caregivers support toddlers' peer interactions by thoughtfully describing children's intentions to help facilitate their attempts at social play.

Here caregiver Julie asked Marco where he was going. He replied, "Tain…Cogo."

"What do you need for your train trip?" Julie asked.

"Oney," Marco said.

"So Marco needs money for this train trip to Chicago. I wonder where he will get it," Julie said.

The "train" made a quick stop at the dress-up area, where Eliza got a purse with money and shared it with Marco.

retain individual control of, such as play dough, sand and water, and finger paints.

When a toddler's attempt to connect with a peer goes unnoticed by the other child, an attentive caregiver can help bridge the gap by describing the child's attempt, as this scenario with toddlers Sasha and Max illustrates:

> *Sasha is stacking the large cardboard blocks. Max sees what Sasha is doing, gets two more blocks from the shelf, and puts them down in front of Sasha. When Sasha does not notice the blocks, caregiver Mona comments, "Max, you brought some blocks for Sasha to use." At this, Sasha looks up, sees the blocks, and adds them to his stack. Max goes back to the shelf for two more blocks. This time, as Max approaches Sasha, he says "Blocks," puts them down, and adds one to the stack himself. Sasha looks up and adds the remaining block to the stack.*

By thoughtfully describing children's intentions toward their peers, caregivers can help to facilitate toddlers' attempts at social play.

Use a problem-solving approach to children's social conflicts

Toddlers are primed for social conflict! They are strong, mobile, and adept. They have a growing sense of possession ("Mine!") and a fixed belief in their own point of view. During the most peaceful choice time in a well-stocked setting, toddlers, with their gusto, emerging communication skills, and social inexperience,

are bound to engage in disputes with peers over claims to space, materials, and even caregivers. At the same time, with adult support, they are usually capable of quickly settling their own disputes — possibly because they are so focused on the immediate present. Conflicts and disputes at choice time are opportunities to help toddlers find sociable alternatives to such negative behaviors as biting and grabbing. As described in Chapter 3, teachers can use the following six steps to help toddlers resolve disputes: calmly approach toddlers in conflict, stopping hurtful actions; acknowledge children's feelings; gather information; restate the problem; engage toddlers in describing the problem and finding a solution; and offer follow-up support. Here is an example of these problem-solving strategies in action:

> *Colin and Justin, two older toddlers, stand in the block area. Colin holds a plastic figure of a firefighter that Justin is trying to take away from him. They struggle, becoming increasingly upset. Nancy, their caregiver, approaches calmly and kneels on the floor beside them. They stop struggling to look at her. "You look upset!" she says to the two children, stroking each one gently. Colin nods in agreement. **"I angry!"** Justin announces loudly. "So, you're angry," Nancy says to Justin. "And you're upset," she says to Colin. "You both want the firefighter," she continues, stating the problem as she sees it. Colin and Justin nod yes. "Let me hold the firefighter," she says to Colin, who*

This caregiver calmly works through the problem-solving approach with two children who want the same plastic giraffe. In the end, the children decide on taking turns, with the young boy having it first.

then opens his hand, releasing his grip on the figure. Nancy takes it gently from him and holds it in her hand so both children can concentrate on the problem rather than the toy itself. "What can we do about this?" she asks the boys, seeking their ideas rather than offering her own. She wants them to think, and she knows that they will be far more interested in carrying out their own idea, rather than hers, for a solution. At first they look at her blankly, but after a minute or so, Colin says "Bambulance ban!" and heads off toward the toy shelf. He returns shortly with a figure of an ambulance driver (belonging to the same toy set as the firefighter). He hands his "ambulance man" to Justin, who takes it with a smile. "So now Justin has the ambulance man," states Nancy. "I can give the firefighter back to Colin." Neither child disputes this. She hands the firefighter to Colin, and the two boys toddle off in different directions, each clutching his own toy figure. With their caregiver as mediator, they have solved the problem themselves.

Offer older toddlers opportunities to plan and recall

Planning (thinking about what you are going to do before you do it) and recalling (remembering and reflecting on what you did after you did it) are intellectual processes that depend on the ability to imagine, to form mental images of materials, places, people, or actions. From

HighScope's work with older children, we know that three-, four-, and five-year-olds are increasingly able to plan and recall — to think about their own future and past doings and to talk about and describe these thoughts. As older toddlers approach age two-and-a-half to three, they are beginning to develop these same capacities. They communicate these intentions and recollections through a streamlined combination of gestures, actions, and key words.

Simple, brief times of planning and recalling individually with older toddlers

One way to support older toddlers who may be starting to plan and recall is to briefly describe what you see them doing — "You're putting dinosaurs on blocks!"

help them to call up mental pictures of what they would like to do or what they did, to connect their ideas with these actions, to communicate their intentions to others, and to begin to organize their past actions into a simple narrative. (*Note:* Preschoolers plan and recall in small groups at fixed times in the daily routine as well as during individual adult-child interactions at opportune moments. Planning and recalling with toddlers takes place in one-on-one exchanges with caregivers, at whatever point during the day the adult senses an opening and the child's readiness.) This planning before children have started their exploration or play and recalling when they have come to a stopping point gives caregivers a chance to support children's emerging ability to think about future and past events. Planning and recalling are the hallmarks of *executive function,* two of the higher-order abilities that will later allow children to organize and complete tasks.

Caregivers using the support strategies for choice time that are listed on page 343 are already supporting toddlers' planning and recalling as they describe what they see and hear children doing:

- "You're banging the box with your block, T.C.!"

- "Sharelle, you climbed up the ladder, and now you're at the top!"

- "You're turning that block a lot of different ways to try to fit it in the slot, Chris!"

- "Meagan, you're watching Lu."

- "James, you're working very hard to climb onto the sofa with Tab."

These descriptive statements help toddlers build the language to refer to their own actions and playthings. Eventually, with his caregiver providing a wide array of climbing choices and patiently describing what he is doing when he climbs, James, for example, as an older infant, begins to understand what it means to "climb." By the time he reaches later toddlerhood, based on his broad range of experiences, James may well be able to picture himself climbing something before actually doing so. When his caregiver says at the beginning of choice time, "James, show me what you will play with at choice time today," he may point to the climber and say "Cwimb!" before heading off to put this simple, toddler-appropriate plan into action.

Caregivers plan and recall with individual toddlers when they see some signs that a child might be ready for and interested in this process. One sign is the child's ability to form mental images. In an active learning setting, infants and young toddlers accumulate a wealth of sensory-motor experience. Eventually, as older toddlers, they begin to be able to hold in mind pictures of these experiences. For example, Teri, a toddler, realizes when settling down for naptime that she does not have her favorite blanket with her. From her position lying on her cot, she cannot see the blanket, but she has a mental picture of it lying on the floor between the couch and the wall in the book area, where she last used it at choice time. Seeing that Teri can retrieve an unseen object by remembering its location,[1] Teri's caregiver knows that the toddler can hold an experience in mind and therefore may be ready to indicate a simple plan before going into action at choice time.

Other signs that a toddler may be ready to plan are the child's spontaneous actions and pronouncements. In the anecdote on page 339, for example, Kevin brings his caregiver a book he has selected, plops down in her lap, and says "Read!" Through his actions and words, he lets her know that he has a pretty clear picture of what he (and she!) are about to do. In another situation, Jamie (p. 349) pauses to look at his painting, names his splotches "feets," and then declares "more feets" before continuing to work on his idea with a new brush and new color. Saying "more feets" (and selecting a new brush and color) is his toddler shorthand for *Now I'm going to make some more feet using a different color.*

When a toddler like Teri, Kevin, or Jamie seems ready to plan, a caregiver can ask that child at the beginning of choice time (or perhaps during choice time — at the point of an activity change) a simple question about his or her intentions. It should be a question the child can answer with an action, gesture, or word. Here are examples of ways to begin:

"What will you play with, Jody?" Jody leans against her caregiver and looks around. "Can you show me something you'd like to play with?" asks her caregiver. Jody goes to the doll buggy, grabs the handle, and looks back at her caregiver, who nods and says, "You're going to play with the buggy." Jody pushes the buggy toward the house area.

~

"Can you show me where you will play, Amir?" Amir points toward the block area. "Oh, you're going to play in the block area," says his caregiver. Amir nods and heads for the shelf of wooden unit blocks.

~

"What will you do at choice time, Mimi?" Mimi sits in her caregiver's lap, removes her thumb from her mouth, points to a child drawing with markers on a large sheet of white paper, and says, "Do that!" "Oh, you're going to draw with markers, like Elana," interprets her caregiver. Mimi nods and repeats, "Do that!" "That's what you're going to do," affirms her caregiver. Mimi heads for the art area, selects a sheet of paper and a marker, and begins.

Note that planning with toddlers is a brief, intimate, one-to-one interaction. The caregiver kneels or sits on the floor next to the child, often putting an arm around the child or in some way offering comfortable

---

[1]See the Child Observation Record for Infants and Toddlers (HighScope, 2002a), item AA, level 4: "Child retrieves an object not seen for a while."

physical contact. The child communicates a plan by using actions (pointing, nodding, looking at, or going to an object or place) and sometimes by saying a key word or two (naming a material, action, or possibly a peer already engaged in that activity or with whom he or she wants to play). When the caregiver translates the toddler's plan into a short verbal statement, it is a way of checking to make sure the child's intentions are understood. It's a good idea for caregivers to ask toddlers about their plans for choice time when they are in a relatively open part of the play space, where it is easy for them to look around to see what their choices are.

Recalling with toddlers often begins quite spontaneously, like this, as children share home stories with their caregivers:

> *When he arrives in the morning, Kamari runs to his caregiver, saying "Puppy, puppy!" "Oh, Kamari," exclaims his caregiver, "you saw a puppy?" "Puppy Nama's," he explains. His mom nods, backing up his story. "You saw a puppy at your Nama's house?" asks his caregiver. "Lick me!" says Kamari. "And the puppy licked you!" responds his caregiver.*

This puppy story illustrates how recalling occurs because children, like adults, want to share the important things that happen to them with the important people in their lives. The recalling about a toddler's activity might occur *during* choice time, as Jody leaves playing with the doll buggy to play with puzzles, for example.

Like planning, recalling is a brief, intimate caregiver-toddler exchange. "Something happened!" comments the caregiver. "Popped!" says the toddler to her caregiver, pointing to the pop-up toy.

Or the recalling might occur *at the end of* choice time, as Amir is putting away some blocks. A caregiver may encourage a child to recall with a simple statement or question:

> *"I saw you pushing this doll buggy over to the climber, Jody," says her caregiver. She has joined Jody, who is now standing next to the buggy but gazing across the room. Jody nods. "What did you do with the buggy?" asks her caregiver. "Babies," says Jody patting the babies in the buggy. "You put babies in the buggy?" asks her caregiver. Jody nods yes. Then Jody takes her caregiver's hand, leads her across*

the room to the puzzle shelf, and says "Puzzles!" She is announcing her next plan. "Oh, so now you plan to play with puzzles," her caregiver says, interpreting Jody's new plan. Jody dumps out the three-piece duck puzzle and begins to move the pieces about.

～

"What did you do with the blocks, Amir?" *his caregiver asks, as she and Amir stack the blocks on the shelf at the end of choice time. Amir raises his arm over his head and says "Up." "You stacked the blocks up. I remember — I saw you!" interprets his caregiver. "Up, up, up!" says Amir. "You stacked the blocks up, up, up!" his caregiver affirms.*

Like planning, recalling is a brief, intimate caregiver-toddler exchange. Either one — planning or recalling — may occur at almost any time of the day. At naptime, for example, Mimi sits on her cot, taking off her shoes and socks. She looks up and sees her drawing hanging on the wall. "Me do!" she says. When her caregiver sees what Mimi is looking at, she tries filling in the context for her story: "That's the picture you drew in the art area today." "Me draw!" agrees Mimi, making drawing motions with her arm. "You moved your arm back and forth to draw," comments her caregiver.

The idea behind planning and recalling with older toddlers is to provide them the opportunity to think about what they are going to do and what they have done

and to express these thoughts in their own particular blend of actions and words. To do so, each child needs individual support from an attentive caregiver and freedom to get started on his or her plan right away. Although as noted above, planning and recalling generally take place one-on-one, for some toddlers who are approaching three years of age and playing in small groups, these processes might take place with a group of two or three. (See "Strategies for Planning and Recalling With Older Toddlers" on pp. 360–361.) This initiation into small-group planning and recall time provides an early experience in listening and sharing (communication, language, and literacy) and develops a sense of participation in group routines (social and emotional development).

Encourage toddlers to put materials away after choice time

Toddlers exhibit a number of developmental characteristics that enable them to participate in the process of putting things away at the end of choice time. Because they like water and are interested in imitating adults and using adult tools, they see washing the paint off the art table as an enjoyable activity, not a chore. Also, toddlers like to fill and empty containers, so putting balls back into the ball tub or shells into the shell basket is as satisfying as taking them out! Because toddlers notice similarities and differences, they can see that the books on the couch belong back on the rack with the other books, whereas the blocks on the couch belong back on the shelf with the other blocks. At the same time, toddlers have no need to be thorough, efficient, or exact. Even in a well-organized and labeled play space, toddlers participate in putting toys away in their own particular manner ("Me do it!") and at their own pace, as the following anecdotes illustrate:

> *At the end of choice time, Mario's caregiver suggests, "Let's put these books back on the shelf, Mario." Mario picks up an armload of books from the pile of cushions where he and several other children have been looking at them, carries them over to the low bookshelf, and places the whole armful in a pile on the shelf.*

> ∼

> *John picks up the empty food containers, plates, and utensils he has spread out on the table in the house area; puts them into the wooden refrigerator; closes the door; and looks with satisfaction at the now empty table. "Aw gone!" he says.*

> ∼

> *Lydia stands at the sink with several paintbrushes. She holds each brush under the running water for quite some time, watches the colors swirl down the drain, and then "paints" the counter next to the sink with water.*

> ∼

> *Blake loads some blocks he has been playing with into a wagon, pulls the wagon to the block shelf, turns over the wagon, dumps out the blocks next to the shelf, rights the wagon, and heads back to load some more blocks into his wagon.*

Putting toys away works best when caregivers put toys away along with the children and are willing to accept toddlers' ideas about how to do things. Caregivers should remain calm and positive and not expect toddlers to handle the cleanup process all on their own or even to completely pick up any one area or group of items. With patient support and encouragement, toddlers can participate in the *process* of cleanup and enjoy the contact, interaction, and satisfaction it affords. After a good effort on everyone's part, caregivers move on to the next part of the day. After all, they can always complete cleanup while children nap or after they have left for the day.

Understanding Outside Time

> *At outside time, two nonmobile infants, Tabor and Lizzy, are wiggling and cooing as they lie on a blanket. Sheila, their caregiver, sits next to them on the grass holding a third infant, Kaylee, who is sucking her thumb and gazing at Tabor and Lizzy. "Here we are outside, looking all around," Sheila sings to all three babies as she gently rocks Kaylee.*

> ∼

Strategies for Planning and Recalling With Older Toddlers

When adults see signs that older toddlers can participate in more formal planning and recalling, they can begin to do this in very concrete ways. This may play out in two different ways.

- **Option 1** — If it is at the beginning of the year and adults are working with a group of children that are mostly young toddlers, they can use planning and recall language as noted in this chapter (e.g., "What will you play with?," "What did you do with the blocks?"). Over time, adults read the toddlers' cues and see that they are beginning to understand what is being asked and can participate in these conversations. Adults can then change the routine to regularly include planning and recall times and begin to plan with the children more formally in concrete ways (see below).

- **Option 2** — If the children are of mixed ages, adults can do formal planning and recalling with the older toddlers in one area of the room while the other children are involved in choice time or other parts of the day. As adults read the younger toddlers' cues (as in option 1 above), they can be added to the group and included in the concrete planning and recall strategies.

The following is a list of concrete strategies for planning and/or recall that can be used with individual children and/or with a small group of children. Concrete means that children see and often touch the materials while they plan and the materials are also in front of them when they recall. Adults should *not* use strategies that are more appropriate for preschoolers, such as providing abstract props (e.g., area signs), encouraging children to elaborate on their ideas, or using verbal strategies alone.

1. **Nonverbal pointing or touching (Planning and/or recall)**
   - Children point to an area. Adult models planning (or recall) language by describing where the children are pointing.
   - Children point to or touch an object in an area. Adult models planning (or recall) language by describing what children are pointing to.

2. **Get a toy (Planning and/or recall)**
   - Children bring something they plan to (or did) play with to the table. Each child tells what he or she plans to (or did) do with the object.

3. **Purse (Planning and/or recall)**
   - Children use a purse to collect something they want to (or did) play with.

4. **Riding toy (Planning and/or recall)**
   - Children drive a toy to the area they want to (or did) play in.

5. **"Feelie" box (Recall)**
   - Adult places objects that children used during work time in a box. Children take turns guessing objects by how they feel, naming the object, and recalling what they did with it.

6. **Boxes (Planning)**
   - Adult sets out boxes of different sizes. Each child finds an object from the interest area where he or she is planning to play that fits in one of the boxes.

Strategies for Planning and Recalling With Older Toddlers (cont.)

7. Ball (Planning and/or recall)
   - Children roll or bounce the ball into the area they want to (or did) play in.

8. Objects from areas (Planning and/or recall)
   - Adult gets items that represent each area, and children choose the area they want to (or did) play in.

9. Train (Planning)
   - Children line up behind adult and pretend to be a train. Train moves around to each area where adults and children talk about the materials in the area. If a child plans to play in that area, he or she "gets off" the train. Then the train goes to the next area.
   - *Variation:* Instead of a train, the children pretend to move around the room on a boat, car, or truck, or they crawl or jump from one area to the next.

10. Rope (Planning and/or recall)
    - Children and adult grasp the rope and move about the room like a train; each child "gets off" at the area in which he or she wants to (or did) play.

11. Paper towel tube (Planning and/or recall)
    - I spy — Child looks through the "spy glass" at the area he or she is going to (or did) play in.
    - *Variation:* Children use real binoculars.

12. Camera (Planning and/or recall)
    - With a pretend camera, children point and take a picture of the area where they want to (or did) play and talk about what they will (or did) do there.

13. Flashlight (Planning and/or recall)
    - Children spotlight the area they want to (or did) play in.

14. Tape measure (Planning and/or recall)
    - As the adult holds one end of the tape measure, children take turns pulling the end of the tape to the area(s) they are going to (or did) play in.

15. Tape (Planning and/or recall)
    - Children put a piece of tape on the object or area where they want to (or did) play.

16. Hats (Planning and/or recall)
    - Children take turns pulling objects (that they have brought from different areas of the classroom) out of a hat. As children identify the area an object comes from, the adult asks who brought that particular object and what they will (or did) do with it.

17. Mystery bag (Recall)
    - Adult gathers items that children played with, and children say what they did with them.

Outside time allows infants and toddlers to extend their exploration and play to an outdoor setting.

Hans and Thomas, who are both at the creeper-crawler stage, sit on a blanket spread under a tree on the playground. From a basket of objects beside them, Hans chooses a large pine cone to hold, and Thomas picks out two hand-sized rocks to hold and bang together. Sandy, their caregiver, sits next to them, watching as they explore. She also watches Emma, a nonmobile infant who is lying on the blanket and looking up at the leaves on a low-hanging branch.

"You see the leaves, Emma," she says softly. Emma waves her arms and kicks her legs.

~

Sarah, an older infant, crawls over to the chainlink fence that surrounds the play yard. She sits next to it, grasps one of the links, and wiggles the fence back and forth as she watches the preschool children playing in the tree house in the adjacent play yard. In the meantime, infant Amanda crawls to Robin, her caregiver; sits in Robin's lap; and watches Sarah at the fence. Looking up at Robin, Amanda points in Sarah's direction. "You see Sarah over at the fence," Robin comments. Amanda leaves Robin's lap to crawl across the grass toward Sarah. Close by, Alejandro, another infant, crawls up the two low steps of the deck, sits on the deck for a bit, crawls back down the steps, and crawls back up again. As he pauses again on the deck, Robin says, "Alejandro, you've been crawling up and down the steps!"

~

At outside time, Tessa, a young toddler, throws balls into an empty plastic wading pool. When all the balls are in the pool, she climbs into the pool with the balls, sits down, and throws the balls out. She bangs on the empty pool with her hands and her heels, climbs out, retrieves each ball, and throws it into the pool again.

~

At the sandbox, Riley, a young toddler, scoops handfuls of sand into a bucket while Carole, his caregiver, holds the bucket steady. When Carole puts one hand into the bucket, Riley laughs as he pours sand over her hand. Joel, an older toddler, sits on the edge of the sandbox near Carole, shoveling sand into a small bucket he has placed between his feet. When the bucket is full, he dumps out the sand and starts over again.

~

Crane and L.J., two toddlers, travel back and forth between the foot of the beech tree, where they have discovered some stones, and Carole, their caregiver, who is perched on the edge of the sandbox holding Riley's bucket. On each of their trips, they bring Carole a stone. "Big," says Crane, handing her a stone. "This **is** a big stone," Carole agrees. "My big," says L.J. "Your stone is big too, L.J.," she says. The children pile their stones in front of Carole and then head back to the beech tree for more.

~

Toddlers Maria and Samuel each climb into one of the two child-sized cartons they have helped their caregiver carry outside. They laugh as they first squat down in their carton, jump up, and then climb out. They repeat the same action sequence several more times.

~

Nanette, a caregiver, and two of her toddlers, Lindy and Peter, spread out a long sheet of white butcher paper on the grass. Nanette puts a rock at each corner of the paper to help hold it in place. Then Peter pulls the "paint wagon" over to a spot near the paper (the wagon contains some containers of tempera paint, a bucket of water, and several kinds of brushes). Peter and Lindy each select a brush, dip it into one of the paint containers, squat next to the paper on either side of the paint wagon, and paint. They use whole-arm motions to make large painting strokes.

Outside time allows infants and toddlers to extend their exploration and play to an outdoor setting. As at choice time indoors, children make choices about what to do outdoors. Children find the outdoors rich in sensory-motor experiences for constructing new knowledge. At outside time, infants and toddlers begin to gain a sense of distance as they experience what is up close — spiders, worms, grass — and what is far away — the treetops, the house next door, the clouds. They have the rare opportunity to be big compared to ants, grasshoppers, birds, squirrels, and dandelions. They can freely move, throw things, and play in water and snow. They gather and collect leaves, twigs, rocks, walnuts, and seed pods. In the sunlight, they soak up the vitamin D they need to absorb calcium for strong bones and teeth.

Overall, spending daily time outdoors in all seasons positively affects the way even very young children eat, sleep, and feel. Properly dressed, they need to spend time outside every day in all but the most extreme weather conditions. Whether a child care program is in a cold, hot, or moderate climate, caregivers can find an appropriate time each day to take the children outdoors. Where this time period occurs in program's daily routine may shift with the change in seasons. Midday, when the sun is at its height, might work best when it is cold, while early morning may be most comfortable in climates where the heat builds up later in the day. Some programs have outside time at the very beginning and/or end of the program day to minimize the number of times children

have to get (un)dressed in outdoor gear. Caregivers ask families to provide adequate outdoor clothing to keep children dry as they slosh through a puddle, protect their heads from the sun as they splash about in a wading pool, or keep them insulated as they roll around in a mound of soft snow. Caregivers should also have adequate outerwear so that concerns about their own comfort do not overrule their judgments about what is best for young children.

Outdoor play spaces appropriately designed and equipped for infants' and toddlers' outside time were described in Chapter 4. To sum up, for infants the play space includes materials and equipment that encourage movement, things that flutter in the wind, a variety of crawling surfaces, water-play materials, and things that are visually interesting. For toddlers the play space includes natural features like hills and boulders; things to climb and swing on; things to get inside of, crawl through, and balance on; sand and water; toys to rock, ride, push, and pull; and items such as balls, beanbags, chalk, and painting materials. Occasionally at outside time, caregivers, infants, and toddlers take a walk around the block, to a nearby park, a neighbor's garden, or a local shop.

During outside time, infants and toddlers observe, explore, and play on their own or with others at their own pace and level of interest and development. Depending on temperament, some children cautiously approach outdoor sounds, textures, sights, and sensations, while

You never know what excitement you'll encounter during outside time! These toddlers love to watch and hear the nearby construction workers and trucks behind the safety of a fence.

others take to outdoor play with energy and curiosity about every new creature and experience.

Nonmobile infants like Tabor, Lizzy, Kaylee, and Emma (p. 359 and p. 362) spend most of their outside time lying on their backs while gazing at nearby sights, wiggling, stretching, and reaching for or grasping at objects. They enjoy feeling the warmth of the sun and the movement of

the air. They also move from place to place in their caregiver's arms or in a stroller.

Mobile infants like Hans, Thomas, Sarah, and Alejandro (pp. 362–363) sit and explore objects or materials and examine growing things. They crawl across the grass, up and down steps, over small hills, and into large boxes. They pull themselves up to stand by holding on to a low bench, a picnic table, or the edge of the sandbox.

During outside time,

a nonmobile infant lies on her back and moves her arms and legs while looking at the sky,

older (and more mobile) infants are gently pushed in a swing,

a young toddler discovers a bug, and

an older toddler rides a tricycle.

With help, they swing in a swing or go for gentle wagon rides.

Young toddlers use the clear expanses of the outdoor play area for walking, carrying, pushing, climbing, throwing, and exploring. While their movements may be awkward, outside they have lots of space for maneuvering, falling down, and picking themselves up. Older toddlers, who have become pretty steady on their feet, take advantage of the outdoor space to run, ride, climb, swing, slide, throw, dig, paint, play in water, fill and empty, collect stones, make up simple games, and grapple with problems — how to cover the picnic table with a sheet to make a house, how to get the riding toy back up the hill, and what to do when two toddlers want to fill the same dump truck with walnuts.

How Caregivers Support Children at Outside Time

Caregivers pay close attention to children's outdoor exploration and play, offer children physical and emotional support, and interact with children in enjoying all the features of the outdoor environment. The following specific strategies help them carry out this role:

- Provide loose materials for children's comfort and play.

- Provide a variety of experiences for nonmobile infants.

- Use the same general support strategies used at choice time.

- Observe nature with children.

- Bring outside time to a gentle close.

Provide loose materials for children's comfort and play

Nonmobile infants spend most of their time outdoors lying on blankets spread on the ground, so caregivers keep some clean blankets in a basket or diaper bag that they can easily grab on their way out to the play yard. Because some older, mobile infants may at first be hesitant to crawl or cruise around outdoors, they often appreciate being given a basket of interesting objects to explore while sitting on a blanket, until they work up their courage to move across the grass, up the steps, or over the stone walkway to find their own things to explore.

The baskets of playthings for mobile infants can be kept ready by the door to the play yard. Caregivers can place other loose playthings or materials in wagons so toddlers at the "Me do it!" stage can help to transport them outside, as Peter does when he pulls the paint wagon outside (p. 363). Caregivers can also provide small buckets, baskets, or cloth bags with handles, and toddlers can use these to carry out their sand toys, tennis balls, streamers, bubble-blowing equipment, and playground chalk.

Provide a variety of experiences for nonmobile infants

While mobile infants and toddlers generally find lots of things to explore and play with outside in the presence of their trusted caregivers, nonmobile infants depend on caregivers to put them in some location where they can easily stretch and wiggle and watch interesting things.

During outside time, caregivers use the same strategies they used for supporting children at choice time. They pay close attention to what the children do, engage in conversational give and take with them, and encourage them to help put away playthings at the end of outdoor time.

This means putting infants down in a safe place and varying that place from time to time. Then they can see a variety of sights — blooming flowers, tree bark, dried leaves on the lawn, branches overhead, sky and clouds, children crawling, stems of grass, stones, and banners waving. On warm days, caregivers place babies near the edge of a blanket so they can feel the grass with their feet or hands. As caregivers carry babies outside and back inside again, they stop so the babies can have an up-close look at the pine tree, the toddlers playing next door, or the rabbit in his cage. If caregivers occasionally wheel infants in strollers, they choose a route that provides interesting things for the children to see, hear, and feel against their skin and vary the route to diversify the experiences.

Use the same general support strategies used at choice time

In many ways, outside time is choice time moved outdoors. Therefore, once caregivers have moved infants and toddlers and their materials safely outdoors, they use the strategies described on pages 343–359 for supporting children at choice time: They pay close attention to children as they explore and play, follow their leads and ideas, engage in play and conversational give and take with them, support their peer interactions, help them take a problem-solving approach to any social conflicts, and listen for older toddlers to talk about their intentions and about what they have done (their planning and recalling). And at the end of outside time, caregivers encourage toddlers to help put away playthings and carry materials back indoors.

Observe nature with children

One of the special pleasures of being outside with very young children is witnessing their wonderment as they roll in snow, splash in puddles, squat to watch ants move a crumb toward their anthill, find an intricate spider web on the fence, point to birds flying overhead, or gather their own pile of stones. Even though infants and toddlers say relatively little during these experiences ("Big," "My big"), they are gaining an essential understanding of the natural world through their actions and senses.

Caregivers do not need to overwhelm very young children with a barrage of words and lengthy explanations about what they are seeing and doing, but they do need to appreciate children's actions and interests; comment on or acknowledge them when it is natural to do so; and allow children plenty of time to stop and smell the flowers, watch the worms in the dirt, shuffle through the leaves, and pick up yet another stick. Teachers should also be aware of any aversion they have to the outdoors so as *not* to pass along fears or disgust to children. If teachers and caregivers acknowledge and appreciate children's open-minded sense of wonder at the natural world, they may find that seeing bugs and slime through their eyes helps them change their attitudes too.

One of the great pleasures of being with children is witnessing their wonderment about what they find, including a crawling bug!

Bring outside time to a gentle close

Five minutes or so before the end of outside time, caregivers tell children that the time outdoors is almost over. Nanette, for example, going from child to child, sings, "Five more minutes of outside time, then we'll go inside for lunch." Even though children may not know exactly what an adult is saying or singing, eventually they associate the same ritual phrase or song with rounding up the toys and going back inside, going home, or whatever happens next in the routine. Even with infants, it is important to let them know why you are picking them up, folding up their blanket, and carrying them inside. "I'm going to pick you up, Emma," says Sandy, her caregiver. "It's time for us to go back inside."

Understanding Group Time

At group time, caregiver Sonja places a dishpan on the floor between Maggie and Sean, mobile infants. The dishpan contains about an inch of water and some yellow rubber ducks. "Here are some water and some ducks," Sonja says to the children, joining them on the floor. Maggie leans over and splashes her hands in the water. Sean pushes a duck along and then picks it up by the head and brings it to his mouth. Watching him, Maggie puts the fingers of one hand into her mouth, makes a face, and then returns to splashing.

$\sim$

At group time, toddlers Conner, Nick, Cher, and Jo and their caregiver Jenna spread newspapers on the art table. When the table is covered, Jenna sets down a tray of small plastic squeeze bottles that the children have been using at the water table. "Here are some bottles of dribble salt (p. 239) for you to squeeze," she says to the

children. Conner selects a bottle, shakes it, turns it upside down, and squeezes it with both hands. Jenna tries the same actions with a bottle she selects, and Nick watches Conner. Noticing Nick watching him, Conner takes another bottle, sets it down in front of Nick, and says "Bottle?" Nick simply looks at the bottle. "Nick, it looks like Conner is giving you a bottle to squeeze," Jenna interprets. Taking the bottle, Nick squeezes it as Conner did, then sticks a finger into the resulting pool of dribble, licks his finger, and makes a face. Jenna follows suit, sticking her finger into the dribble she has squeezed out and then tasting it. She comments to Nick, "It tastes salty."

Cher and Jo dribble salt from their bottles while moving their arms back and forth. Jenna tries moving her arms the same way. As Conner and Nick continue to squeeze their bottles and muck about, Cher and Jo leave the table, wash their hands at the sink, and then take their empty squeeze bottles to the house area. Jenna, Conner, and Nick continue to dribble salt. When Conner and Nick have emptied all the squeeze bottles and have saturated the newspaper, they help Jenna push the sodden newspaper into the wastebasket. "Aw gone!" says Conner.

$\sim$

Debbie, a caregiver, and her four toddlers, Miranda, Timmy, Sean, and Sarah, sit on the floor in the toy area. Set out between them are three containers of red, yellow, and blue plastic stacking pegs, one container for each color. Each person has a peg-board. "Here are some new pegs and pegboards," Debbie says. "Let's see what we can do with them!" Sean imme-diately selects one peg after another and pushes them into the holes on his pegboard. After watching Sean, Timmy also puts a few pegs in his board and then fits a peg on top of one that is already in the board. "Oh, Timmy," comments Debbie, "you're stacking one peg on top of another! I think I'll try that," and she does. Sean tries out Timmy's stacking idea and laughs as some of his stacks tumble over. In the meantime, Miranda and Sarah, ignor-ing the pegboards, make chains by fastening several pegs together in a line on the floor. At one point, Sarah dumps out the container of red pegs and picks out several red pegs that she adds to the end of her chain. Then she goes to the book area, selects a book, and looks at the pictures, talking softly to herself.

~

Mike and Shawna, a caregiver team for eight toddlers, have a morning group time for all their children fol-lowing outside time. As Mike helps children remove and hang up their coats, Shawna begins to play a CD of lively recorded instrumental music she knows the children like[2] and puts

a basket of rhythm instruments on the floor in the movement area. Shawna sits down next to the basket, selects a set of sand blocks, and begins to play her blocks along with the music. As the children (and eventually Mike also) join her in the movement area, they begin to select other instruments and also play along with the music. Tod-dlers Rene and Eddie, however, simply watch the instrument players for a bit and then settle down in the toy area to play with some toy cars and animals. Shawna and Mike use their instru-ments to try out actions they see the children using. When the first musical selection ends, Shawna selects another, slower piece of music. When that piece ends, Shawna sings, "Time to put your instruments away, your instruments away. Time to put your instruments away, and wash your hands for lunch." The children drop their instru-ments back into the basket and head for the low sinks in the bathroom. Mike, in the meantime, wheels the lunch cart to the eating area.

Group times are caregiver-initiated parts of the day that include opportunities for children to engage in active learning. *Caregiver-initiated* means the caregiver has an idea for the activity and plans what might happen based on mobile infants' and toddlers' interests and development. The purpose of group time is *not* to

---

[2]For examples of recordings suitable for a toddlers' movement activity like this one, see the musical recordings and related resources available at HighScope's online store (www.highscope.org).

During this group time, these three children and their caregiver gather around the table to make cheesy biscuits.

Each child who wants to gets a chance to pour and mix the ingredients.

instruct children in some area of knowledge or have them practice a skill, nor is it intended to enforce social interaction. Rather, group time allows children who are interested to explore materials and actions, and if they choose, to observe, imitate, or play alongside others. A child's participation in group time is wholly voluntary.

Group times generally focus on either exploring and using materials or enjoying songs, nursery rhymes, and movement and music activities. During a typical group time, one or two caregivers gather with the older infants and toddlers. The group is small — generally with no more than four children per caregiver and no more than eight children altogether. The adult gets the activity started and encourages children to use materials or move their bodies in their own way.

Typically, smaller groups engage in exploring materials while larger groups join in a music or movement activity. However, there are no hard and fast rules. There may even be as few as two children in a group, depending on how many choose to participate. This small group size makes it easier for even quiet or withdrawn children to join in, enables children to have close physical contact with their caregiver, and allows the caregiver to pay close attention to each child while monitoring the tenor of the group as a whole. It is a daily opportunity for children and caregivers to communicate in an intimate social setting as they share or use common materials or enjoy moving together to music.

Caregivers gather the group together and introduce the materials or activity for group time, but children are the doers and choice makers, actively shaping what happens as the group time unfolds. Children also determine the length of group time. (See "Ways to Make Group Times More Flexible and Responsive to Children" on p. 374.) Some children, for example, may squeeze dribble salt for 10 minutes, whereas others may spend several minutes watching the activity and then turn to play with other materials around the room. Likewise, some may move to the music, others may watch from the sidelines, and the rest may get involved in unrelated activities in nearby areas. To suit the nature of older infants and toddlers, group times are fluid and dynamic, varying in length and content, depending on the actions, ideas, and interests of the children involved.

Group times help children build a repertoire of shared experiences they can turn to in their play and in communication give and take at other times of the day. Caregivers will notice that, over time, children grow in their ability to communicate and interact with one another during group time; also, the time they remain together in common pursuits gradually increases.

Group time can also serve as a time when children check in for reassurance and support from others after venturing out into the play space during choice time and outside time. For caregivers, group time serves as a unique opportunity to offer children materials and challenges

Ways to Make Group Times More Flexible and Responsive to Children

- Keep the group size small. Typical group size is up to four children with one caregiver and up to eight children with two caregivers. Groups may be smaller but should not be larger.

- Stop or change the activity if no one is participating.

- Attend to children's cues, leads, and communications (e.g., use the same materials they are interested in; imitate their actions and sounds; comment on their choices, gestures, and expressions; interpret their communications to one another).

- Help children exit the group as needed (to change a diaper, locate a co-caregiver, put a tired child to bed), and facilitate continuity for those who remain (recommence activity around the object that was interesting to the remaining children).

- Include choices for children (e.g., books, materials/objects for each toddler).

- Schedule group time when children may be most inclined to do something (e.g., after outside time, after nap).

- Anticipate that children will come and go from the group.

that reflect the KDIs and to observe the various ways different children think of using the materials or solving any problems they meet along the way.

Group time need not occur at the same place every day. Where the group gathers depends on the materials called for and the nature of the activity. In the scenarios beginning on page 370, for example, group time takes place in the infants' play space, in the art area, in the toy area, and in the movement area. At other times, the group might gather for their activity in a tent, on the deck of the climber, around the sand and water table, on the steps, under the low-hanging branches of a pine tree, or in the garden. Children and their caregiver might sit on the floor, on the ground, at a table — wherever the chosen activity dictates. Group times involving

singing and movement generally take place in the movement area or outdoors, where there is plenty of space for children to move freely.

Caregivers do not plan group times for the youngest, nonmobile infants. In settings with mixed-age groups, however, these very young infants, when awake, may watch the group activity of the older children from a safe vantage point (as Bobby does while drinking from his bottle, p. 292). Watching allows infants to be part of the communal action, and they often will be eager to join group time once they can sit up and use both hands for exploration.

Older infants and toddlers explore and play with materials at group time much as they do at choice time (see p. 371). Mobile infants, like Maggie and Sean

(p. 370), enjoy very simple group experiences, such as splashing in water. During music and movement activities with older children, they are apt to watch from a distance or from the safety of a caregiver's lap. Young toddlers may drift in and out of group time, while older toddlers, with their increasing sociability and sense of self, are both likely to engage in social conflict *and* likely to sense the needs of their peers as they go about a group-time activity.

How Caregivers Support Children During Group Time

During group time, caregivers present children with a specific set of materials or some experience that may be new or of particular interest to them. Caregivers then support the choices children make as they explore, try out their own ideas, and solve problems in connection with the materials or experience presented. The following strategies contribute to carrying out this role:

- Plan ahead and provide active group experiences.

- Gather materials and offer them to children.

- Respect children's choices and ideas about using the materials.

- Comment briefly and specifically on what children are doing.

- Interpret children's actions and communications for other children.

- Let children's actions signal when group time should end.

Group time does not have to occur in the same place every day. This group time takes place outside, where the children and teacher are using bubble-blowing materials.

Plan ahead and provide active group experiences

In a HighScope active learning infant-toddler program, the caregiver team meets daily for planning (see p. 63 in Chapter 2). This is when they think ahead about what they will present in the way of materials or experiences at a future group time. Building on the KDIs and reflecting on what they know about the children in their care help them to think of group-time experiences that the children will enjoy, find challenging, and be able to master. They might decide to build group time around *some materials and simple actions that will be new to the children,* around *some favorite and familiar materials or actions,* or around *opportunities for movement and music.* Knowing the originating ideas and the children's diverse abilities and developmental levels helps caregivers plan how to scaffold (support and extend) and follow up the individual and group learning that occurs. (See "Planning for Group Times With Materials" and "Planning for Group Times With Movement and Music" on pp. 377–378).

It is important that group time be an *active* time for children rather than a school-like "lesson," because infants and toddlers are geared for movement and learning through sensory exploration; they are not likely to submit passively to adult instruction. When group-time experiences are planned *ahead of time,* children do not have to wait as caregivers gather materials, group time can begin and end smoothly, and the daily routine can flow, for example, from outside time to group time to lunch.

Building group time around new materials and actions

Planning group times around materials new to the children is one way to introduce and add materials to the play space that children can then explore or play with at choice time. Caregiver Debbie, for example, plans a toddlers' group time around some new plastic stacking pegs and pegboards she thinks they are ready to

*This family child care provider planned a group activity with a new material — shaving cream — that older toddlers **and** preschoolers could enjoy exploring.*

Planning for Group Times With Materials

Originating idea

- Think about the children's interests and abilities.

- Plan a group experience around one of the following:

    – New materials and actions,

    – Favorite materials and actions, or

    – KDIs

Materials

- Specify what is needed.

- Gather enough materials for each child and adult(s) ahead of time.

- Prepare backup material(s) (alternative but related materials if children lose interest and/or want to expand their explorations), if needed.

Possible KDIs: Anticipate KDIs that might be observed.

Beginning: Begin with a simple opening statement that describes the materials or gives the children an open-ended idea to get started. Choose only one way to begin the activity:

- Describe the materials,

- Connect the materials to children's previous play, or

- Tell a short, open-ended story connected to the materials.

Middle: Think about how children will use materials and how adults will scaffold children at different developmental and ability levels.

What children might do: How might children use the materials according to their developmental or ability levels? How might they communicate? How long will each child stay with the activity?

How adults scaffold children's learning:

- Offer materials: "What can you do with ___?"

- Respect children's choices and ideas.

- Move from child to child.

- Watch what individual children do with the materials.

- Listen to what children say.

- Interpret children's actions and language.

- Using own set of materials, imitate or copy what children are doing.

- Comment briefly, specifically on children's actions.

- Bring out backup material(s) as needed.

End

- Let children's actions and interest levels signal when group time should end.

- Use a choice-time approach to cleanup.

Follow up

- Think about how children can use the materials at other times of the day.

- Say where materials will be placed for children to find, if applicable.

Planning for Group Times With Movement and Music

Originating idea
- Think about the children's interests and abilities.

- Plan a group time around one of the following:

    – New or favorite music experience,

    – New or favorite movement experience, or

    – KDIs

Materials
- Specify what is needed.

- Gather enough materials for each child and adult(s) ahead of time, if applicable.

Possible KDIs: Anticipate KDIs that might be observed.

Beginning:
- Begin with a simple song, rhyme, or movement activity to get children's attention to come and join.

- Start right away. Don't wait for all children to join before beginning.

Middle: Think about what the children will do and how adults will scaffold children at different developmental and ability levels.

What might children do: How might children move their bodies freely? How might individual children communicate their ideas (e.g., gestures, pointing, speaking)?

How adults scaffold children's learning:
- Participate on the children's level.

- Give children choices about songs and movements.

- Give children time to interact and respond in their own way.

- Keep the group time active (apply the ingredients of active learning).

- Encourage children's efforts.

- Watch and listen to children's cues.

End
- Let children's actions signal when group time should end.

- Plan for a smooth transition to the next activity.

Follow up
- Think about how you can use the ideas from the children for another group time.

---

handle (p. 371). These later become part of the toy area. In a similar way, a group-time activity can be an initiation for new blocks, large shells, push vehicles, picture books, paintbrushes, finger paints, cartons, musical instruments, or climbing equipment.

Group time can also be a chance for children to explore the properties of materials and try out such actions as splashing or squeezing. (See Sonja's group time and Jenna's group time on p. 370.) Other actions to try out at group time might be tearing or crumpling paper, pouring water or sand, mixing sand and water, balancing blocks, pushing golf tees into blocks of Styrofoam, spreading finger paint, smooshing dough or clay, washing baby dolls, climbing up and down the climber, opening and closing the hinged lids of boxes, responding with one's body to music, or exploring the different sounds one's voice can make.

Caregivers should remember two things while planning a group time around new materials and actions: First, the overall idea should be simple; the caregiver should be able to introduce the experience to children in one short sentence ("Here are some new blocks to try") or with a simple action (standing one block on top of another). Second, the caregiver should focus on *doing* rather than *making*. Jenna, for example, plans an opportunity for her toddlers to squeeze dribble salt on paper, and this they do with gusto. She does not expect them to make dribble salt pictures to hang up or take home. (See "Sample Plan for Group Time: Finger Paints" on p. 380 and "Sample Plan for Group Time: Filling and Emptying" on p. 381.)

Building group time around favorite, familiar materials and actions

Planning group time around materials or actions children are already used to and particularly enjoy might be done for several reasons: to support children's interests, to allow them to gain a sense of mastery, or to encourage them to extend their knowledge by trying out slight variations on what they already know. Caregiver

Joanne, for example, knows her children like to crumble their bread and crackers at mealtime. She plans a group time around crumbling stale bread for the birds to provide children with the opportunity to crumble bread in a slightly different context. In another setting, a caregiver notices that her children often ask her to read them the book *Goodnight Moon* (by

This caregiver noticed that the children often ask her to read the same picture book, so she reads this book to them at group time near the book area.

Sample Plan for Group Time: Finger Paints

Originating idea
New material: Introduce the children to finger painting.

Materials
- White butcher paper to cover the art table
- Pieces of masking tape to fasten the edges of the paper to the table
- Red finger paint emptied into a flat cake pan
- Painting smocks

Possible KDIs
A. **Approaches to learning 3. Self-help:** Children do things for themselves.

E. **Cognitive development 22. Exploring objects:** Children explore objects with their hands, feet, mouth, eyes, ears, and nose.

F. **Creative arts 37. Exploring art materials:** Children explore building and art materials.

Beginning (Opening statement or action)
Gather in the art area, and say "We need to put on smocks so we can paint." Be ready to help with smocks and long sleeves.

Middle (Support children's ideas and initiatives)

What children might do: Children may put on their own smocks, spread butcher paper on the table, and tape down the edges. They may dip their fingers or hand in the finger paint or watch others before doing it themselves. Children may spread paint on their hands or smear it across the paper. Some children may taste the paint (which is nontoxic). They may use sponges and towels to help wipe the paint off the table and probably take longer than usual washing their hands (may notice or comment on the "red soap").

How adults scaffold children's learning: Ask the children for help spreading the paper: "Now we'll spread the paper on the table so we can finger-paint on it." Show children how to tape down the edges, and provide them with tape pieces. Place the cake pan of finger paint in the middle of the table, and say "This is finger paint. Let's put our hands in it and spread the paint on the paper." Watch to see what each child does. If no child approaches the finger paint, try dipping your own fingers in the paint, to give them an idea of what to do. Once children begin exploring the paint in various ways, try out and comment on children's various actions. Listen for children's observations. Be ready to add another layer of butcher paper if children want a clean work surface. As a backup material, have sponges ready for children who do not want to put their hands in the paint.

End (Transition to the next part of the routine)
As children finish, have them go to the sink and wash their hands. Leave the paper on the table to dry, or roll it up and discard it. As needed, remind children what the next part of the routine is.

Follow up
Store a day's supply of red finger paint in a flat, plastic container with a tight lid to keep it from drying out. Add this container of finger paint to the art area for children to use at choice time. During choice time, be ready to help children spread out some paper, or skip the paper and have them use the tabletop as a finger-painting surface. (When children are finished, provide them with sponges and buckets of warm soapy water for cleaning the paint off the table.)

Sample Plan for Group Time: Filling and Emptying

Originating idea
New and favorite actions: Children enjoy emptying containers of toys. What happens when they start with empty containers they can fill?

Materials
- Sandbox and sand
- Small buckets, shovels
- Scoops
- Empty food containers
- Wagon next to sandbox

Possible KDIs
E. Cognitive development 22. Exploring objects: Children explore objects with their hands, feet, mouth, eyes, ears, and nose; 29. Filling and emptying: Children fill and empty, put in and take out.

Beginning (Opening statement or action)
Let children know where group time will be. Say, for example, "Today, we're going outside to the sandbox for group time." Get into the sandbox with the children.

Middle (Support children's ideas and initiatives)

What children might do: Children may sit or squat in the sand, scoop sand with their hands, try out shovels and scoops, put sand in containers, dump sand out of containers, use containers as scoops, pat sand, empty sand on the grass outside the sandbox, carry buckets of sand, and use buckets to fill the wagon with sand.

How adults scaffold children's learning:
Watch to see which materials the children use and how they use them. Listen for children's words and ideas. Describe children's actions and try them out. For example, you might say, "You're scooping sand into the bucket, Jackson. I'm going to scoop sand too." You might attempt a slight variation on a child's actions if the child seems open to trying something new.

End (Transition to the next part of the routine)
As the activity ends, remind children what the next part of the routine is. Gather the sand toys in a basket or wagon to put in their usual storage place; children may want to help.

Follow up
Watch to see if children carry out similar actions at choice time at the sand table. Imitate and comment on their actions. Encourage them to choose a toy from the sand table to bring with them at outside time.

Margaret Wise Brown), so she plans to read this favorite story to them at group time in a cozy setting on the pillows in the book area.

Caregivers can plan group times around any of their children's favorite equipment or materials: steps and ramps, tennis balls, rubber or plastic animal or people figures, small photo albums, puzzles, interlocking blocks, quart-size milk cartons and shells, markers and paper, play dough, riding toys. Depending on the particular children involved, favorite actions might include twisting off jar

Deciding to focus on KDI 29. Filling and emptying, this caregiver has a group time around the water table, with lots of cups and scoops.

lids, washing furniture with sponges and warm water, tearing paper bags, filling and emptying buckets at the sand table, rolling balls toward each other, rolling dough or clay, or filling and shaking tins filled with corks. Again, for very young children, it makes sense for caregivers to plan group experiences that are simple, can be introduced briefly and simply, and incorporate materials and actions related to what adults see children enjoying at other parts of the day. (See "Sample Plan for Group Time: Steps, Ramps, and Boards" on p. 383.)

Building group time around the KDIs or the Infant-Toddler COR

Referring to the KDIs and the Infant-Toddler COR can help caregivers keep all aspects of infant-toddler development in mind as they plan meaningful experiences and generate ideas to scaffold young children's learning. These tools guide adults as they choose the materials or the movement and music experiences that will be the focus of group times. The KDIs and Infant-Toddler COR allow teachers not only to think about areas of learning that build on children's current interests but also identify new experiences that older infants and toddlers might not choose on their own.

For example, a caregiver may want to focus on KDI 30. *Taking apart and putting together* (cognitive development). During group time, the caregiver can introduce a new material that supports this KDI, such as cans with different-sized holes cut out of the lids and different-sized objects to fit into the holes and take back out. In

Sample Plan for Group Time: Steps, Ramps, and Boards

Originating idea
Favorite materials and actions: The children like climbing up and down steps and ramps and walking along the edge of the sandbox.

Materials
- Rocking boat turned step-side-up
- Vinyl-covered wedges and cubes
- Ramps made from the hollow blocks and boards

Possible KDIs
C. Physical development and health 13. Moving the whole body: Children move the whole body (rolling, crawling, cruising, walking, running, balancing).

E. Cognitive development 31. Seeing from different viewpoints: Children observe people and things from various perspectives.

Beginning (Opening statement or action)
Gather children in the movement area for group time, and say "Let's see how many things we can do on the steps, ramps, and boards."

Middle (Support children's ideas and initiatives)
What children might do: Children may concentrate on walking up and down steps, walking or running up and down ramps, or balancing on boards, or they may try each action. They may rearrange the boards and ramps. A child may climb up to sit on top of the rocking-boat steps or on top of a vinyl cube and watch the others from there.

How adults scaffold children's learning: Sit or kneel on the floor. Watch how children balance and pick themselves up if they fall. Be ready to offer comfort and contact as needed. Comment on children's actions, using simple words to describe their actions and positions. You might say, for example, "Josh, you're crawling up the ramp" or "Celia, you're stepping down off the block." Assist as needed with rearrangements if children decide to move equipment.

End (Transition to the next part of the routine)
As the activity ends, remind children what the next part of the routine is. Put away the materials in the area(s) where they are usually stored. Children may want to help.

Follow up
Bring the boards outdoors at outside time for children to walk on and use for making low bridges that they can cross. Place the boards near the steps to the deck.

addition to the general adult-child interaction strategies discussed in Chapter 2, the caregiver can plan to use language specific to this KDI (e.g., "You're fitting the block in the hole," "I see you pushing the sponge into the can and now you are taking it out"). As backup and follow-up materials, the caregiver can make sure the children also have access to stacking pegs, Duplos, and tubes of different widths.

The Infant-Toddler COR also inspires caregivers to focus on one or more specific areas of early development. For example, if a teacher sees that several children never or rarely engage in *problem solving* (KDI 2) during play, she can provide a range

Group times can be planned around simple children's songs and rhymes. In this group time, the caregiver leads the group in singing and making hand motions to "If You're Happy and You Know It."

of puzzles for the group to work with. During group time, the caregiver uses a variety of adult-child interaction strategies, paying close attention to how the toddlers are using the puzzles and assembling the pieces. As children encounter problems fitting the puzzle pieces into the correct places, she allows them to try different ways, patiently waiting to see if they request help or offering help if she sees signs of frustration. By observing and jotting down anecdotes, the caregiver notices each child's level of ability in solving problems with materials, uses this information to complete the Infant-Toddler COR, and then plans ways to individually support the child's problem-solving efforts throughout the day.

Building group time around movement and music experiences

Singing and moving with children at group time gives them opportunities to explore movement, to build a common repertoire of songs and rhymes, and to experience steady beat.[3] Mike and Shawna, for example, plan a group time in which their toddlers select and play rhythm instruments to fast and slow recorded music. In one infant-toddler program, caregivers planned a group time in which children walked (and enjoyed falling down) on the "bumpety bump" (which was the children's name for a lumpy surface made from two full-sized bed sheets sewn together and stuffed with fist-sized scraps of foam rubber). For a variation, caregivers also covered the bumpety bump with mats before children walked on it. (Caregivers got the idea for this activity from the book on movement exploration by Molly Sullivan [1982].)

Group times can be planned around simple children's songs and rhymes, such as the following:

- *Nursery rhymes* — Diddle, Diddle, Dumpling; Hey Diddle, Diddle; Hickory, Dickory, Dock; Humpty Dumpty; Jack Be Nimble; One, Two, Buckle My Shoe; Pat-a-Cake; To Market, to Market; Pease Porridge Hot; Ride a Cock-Horse; This Little Piggy Went to Market; Two Little Dicky Birds

- *Children's songs* — Are You Sleeping?; The Muffin Man; Happy Birthday; I'm a Little Teapot; Jingle Bells; London Bridge; Open, Shut Them; Rain, Rain, Go Away; Ring Around the Rosy; Rock-a-bye, Baby; Row, Row, Row Your Boat; The Bear Went Over the Mountain; Twinkle, Twinkle, Little Star; Where Is Thumbkin?

In addition to these traditional songs and rhymes from Mother Goose, caregivers should include traditional songs and rhymes from the cultures of the children and families in their setting and ask parents to teach the songs to them, or, if possible, to join the children at group time.

Young children often want to sing or chant their favorite songs and rhymes not only in group time but also after group time, and even then, they ask for them "Again!" throughout the day. They may ask for a song or rhyme, then listen while others sing or chant it, and join in on only a few favorite words or phrases. Some caregivers make a picture card for each song or rhyme the children know (e.g., a drawing of Humpty Dumpty on a wall might be used for "Humpty Dumpty," and a picture of rain falling on children standing under an umbrella for "Rain, Rain, Go Away"). Some children then use the cards to indicate their choice of a song or rhyme to sing or chant. Other children refer to their song or rhyme choice by saying a key word like "Dumpty" or "Rain."

Many times caregivers will sing and chant songs and rhymes unaccompanied by recorded music. Using their own voice (which infants and toddlers will love even if the caregivers believe they can't sing) and perhaps accompanying themselves on a keyboard, guitar, or autoharp allows caregivers to set the pitch within the

---

[3]For more about young children and steady beat, see *Round the Circle* (Weikart, 2000).

These caregivers planned this movement experience for group time. Together, they built a ramp on which children climbed and then took turns jumping into a soft pillow.

children's singing range and to adjust the tempo of the song to the children's pace. It also frees children to add their own ideas. On a very windy day, for example, the children in one program decided to sing "wind, wind go away" to the tune of "Rain, Rain, Go Away." Another day, the children substituted their own names in "The Bear Went Over the Mountain," singing, for example, "Jason went over the mountain...." Later in the year, this version turned into a song to sing at cleanup, while putting toys away: "Jason's putting the blocks on the shelf, Jason's putting the blocks on the shelf...."

Some movement experiences caregivers might plan for children at group time include these: walking to music; waving scarves to music; patting or moving various body parts to music; crawling through tunnels of different lengths and widths; rolling on mats or up and down ramp-shaped cushions; playing with rubber playground balls; playing in cartons; tossing balls into large cartons; running around the climber (a tree, or an easy chair) while singing "Run around, run around, run around the climber" to the tune of "Jingle Bells." (See "Sample Plan for Group Time: Moving to Music With Scarves" below.)

Gather materials and offer them to children

Before the children arrive in the morning, or while they are napping in the afternoon, caregivers gather the materials

---

Sample Plan for Group Time: Moving to Music With Scarves

Originating idea
Movement and music experiences: The children enjoy moving to music. What might they do with scarves?

Materials
- Music player
- Recordings of musical selections, both fast and slow
- Scarf for each child and adult

Possible KDIs
F. Creative arts 40. Responding to music: Children respond to music.

C. Physical development and health 14. Moving with objects: Children move with objects.

E. Cognitive development 34. Speed: Children experience "fast" and "slow."

Beginning (Opening statement or action)
Put the basket of scarves in the middle of the movement area, and say "Here are some scarves you might like to use for dancing."

Middle (Support children's ideas and initiatives)

What children might do: Children may select a scarf, stay in one place and move the scarf, move from place to place holding their scarves, watch one another, and try out one another's movement ideas. Some children will continue moving the same way when the music changes; others will pause and listen and then move a different way.

How adults scaffold children's learning: As children select scarves, put on the first musical selection and watch to see what children do. Describe and imitate their actions. Watch to see how children move with the second musical selection. Comment on how their movements have changed, for example, "You're moving faster to this music."

End (Transition to the next part of the routine)
End with a slow selection, and ask children to put their scarves back in the basket. As needed, remind children what the next part of the routine is.

Follow up
Add the basket of scarves to the movement area for children to use at choice time.

that will be used for group time and place them close to where they will be using them. They make sure to have some materials for each child to use. These preparations allow the group time to begin immediately so children do not have to wait while adults prepare things and so the materials, songs, or actions involved help to draw children to group time. In presenting the materials to children, caregivers keep their introduction brief and to the point (e.g., "What can you do with these blocks?," "Choose an instrument you want to play").

Generally, children themselves will begin to handle and explore the materials as soon as they are close enough to reach them. On the rare occasion when children hesitate or show no interest in the materials adults have selected, caregivers can use the materials themselves, for example, dipping their fingers in the paint and smearing them on the page or filling and emptying a bucket of sand. If their actions do not inspire children, they set the materials aside for another day and offer children instead small cars, blocks, animal figures, puzzles, or whatever it is they know the children currently enjoy. Some children who are not initially interested in the new materials may try them out later during group time after watching their peers explore them.

Respect children's choices and ideas about using the materials

As active learners, children make a variety of choices at group time. For example, they decide whether or not to participate, how long to stay, what to do with materials, what materials to add, and how to vary actions and words to songs. Caregivers strive to provide interesting materials and experiences children will want to explore and try out at group time. Then they support children's choices and ideas, because they understand children's need to learn in their own way and in a hands-on manner.

Caregivers respect children's group-time choices and ideas by putting themselves at the physical level of the children, watching what they are doing, and listening to what they say. Following children's leads by imitating their actions and repeating their words both indicates to children that the caregiver sees and hears what they are doing; this also helps the caregiver understand what children are thinking and learning. During Jenna's group time (p. 370), it may be that Conner and Nick feel free to squeeze all the bottles dry because Jenna, their caregiver, has joined them in a companionable manner, takes her cues from them, and dribbles salt just as they do.

Comment briefly and specifically on what children are doing

Another way caregivers let children know they see and appreciate what they are doing is to describe their actions. "You're stacking one peg on top of another!" caregiver Debbie comments to Timmy (p. 371). Such comments open the door to further observations from children without pressuring them to respond. Brief, factual comments also help children recognize that their actions can be described in words. Being on the child's physical level, looking for a momentary pause in the action, and catching the child's eye are ways to address these comments to the child in a way that is personally meaningful. In contrast, nonstop talk from the caregivers, however well-intentioned, may distract children from what they are doing or serve as background noise children filter out as they explore and play; it may even discourage them from talking.

Interpret children's actions and communications for other children

Infants and toddlers communicate in their own personal "languages," using a combination of words and gestures. Sometimes they understand one another, and sometimes they need "translation." At group time, as several children work in the same general area using the same materials, they have many opportunities for give-and-take communication with peers, but they may need caregivers to help them out from time to time. When Conner (p. 370) says "Bottle?" as he places a bottle of dribble salt in front of Nick, for example, Nick simply looks at the bottle. Aware of Conner's gesture and Nick's apparent confusion, caregiver Jenna offers an interpretation of Conner's words and gesture: "Nick," she says, "it looks like Conner is giving you a bottle to squeeze." This appears to make sense to Nick, because he reaches for the bottle and starts squeezing.

Unhurried by her caregiver at group time, this child takes on a toddler-sized challenge — balancing one cylindrical block on top of another.

Sometimes caregivers will be confused about what children mean. At one point as he stacks pegs, for example, Timmy knocks one of his stacks over and says "Bo!" Debbie, his caregiver, has no idea what he means, but she knocks her stack over and says, "Bo!" Whatever it means, this becomes a turn-taking game Debbie and Timmy play for several rounds. Later, when Timmy says "Mo eg," Debbie responds with, "Timmy, I don't understand. Can you show me what you mean?" Timmy gets up, walks around her to a container of pegs, picks one up with each

How Caregivers Support Children Throughout Daily Events and Caregiving Routines: A Summary

Daily Events:

Arrival and departure
- ❏ Carry out greetings and good-byes calmly to reassure the child and parent.
- ❏ Acknowledge the child's and parent's feelings about separation and reunion.
- ❏ Follow the child's signals about entering and leaving the activities of the program setting.
- ❏ Communicate openly with the child about the parent's comings and goings.
- ❏ Exchange information and child observations with the parent.

Choice time
- ❏ Pay close attention to children as they explore and play.
- ❏ Tailor actions and responses to follow children's leads and ideas.
- ❏ Engage in communication give and take with children.
- ❏ Support children's interactions with peers.
- ❏ Use a problem-solving approach to children's social conflicts.
- ❏ Offer older toddlers opportunities to plan and recall.
- ❏ Encourage toddlers to put materials away after choice time.

Outside time
- ❏ Provide loose materials for children's comfort and play.
- ❏ Provide a variety of experiences for nonmobile infants.
- ❏ Use the same general support strategies used at choice time.
- ❏ Observe nature with children.
- ❏ Bring outside time to a gentle close.

Group time
- ❏ Plan ahead and provide active group experiences.
  - ❏ Introduce new materials and actions.
  - ❏ Revisit favorite, familiar materials and actions.
  - ❏ Plan around the KDIs or Infant-Toddler COR.
  - ❏ Provide movement and music experiences.
- ❏ Gather materials and offer them to children.
- ❏ Respect children's choices and ideas about using materials.
- ❏ Comment briefly and specifically on what children are doing.
- ❏ Interpret children's actions and communications for other children.
- ❏ Let children's actions signal when group time should end.

Caregiving Routines:

Feeding and mealtime
- ❏ Hold and pay close attention to the bottle-feeding infant.
- ❏ Support the older infant's interest in feeding him- or herself.
- ❏ Join toddlers at the table.
- ❏ Include older toddlers in mealtime setup and cleanup.

How Caregivers Support Children Throughout Daily Events and Caregiving Routines: A Summary (cont.)

Bodily care routines

❑ Fit bodily care around the child's exploration and play.

❑ Focus on the child at hand during the care routine.

❑ Give the child choices about parts of the routine.

❑ Encourage the child to do things for her- or himself.

Naptime

❑ Schedule naptimes around each child's individual needs.

❑ Help children settle down to nap.

❑ Provide quiet alternatives for nonsleepers.

❑ Provide for children's various styles of waking up.

---

hand, and takes them back to his peg stacks. "Oh," says Debbie, "I see — you want more pegs." She moves the container within his reach. Timmy has the satisfaction of knowing he has communicated successfully with Debbie. He also benefits from hearing her elaborate on his use of language.

Let children's actions signal when group time should end

The length of group time varies from day to day. It may last 3 minutes or 10, depending on the children's involvement. Some days, the children will want to sing one song and no more. Other days, they will want to sing every song they know — and to sing some more than once. At each group time, however, caregivers know when group time is at an end by the signals children send them. For example,

caregivers know group time is at an end when all the children are at the sink washing their hands; when all the children have left the movement area to play with the dolls, zoom cars, or sit at the lunch table; or when the children have rolled up all the newspaper covered with dribble salt and stuffed it into the wastebasket.

On the occasions when, for example, children in their group are still finger-painting or splashing in water when the lunch tray is arriving, caregivers warn children so they have time to come to a stopping point (e.g., "In three more minutes we will have to stop for lunch"). As group time comes to an end, children may choose to help the caregiver put away the materials. Sometimes cleanup, such as sponging the paint off the table, is as much or more fun than the group-time activity itself!

6

Child and Program Assessment

Assessment can be used to ensure that individual children's needs are met and that each child benefits from educational experiences; unfortunately, assessment can also be used to harm children — to label, track, or deny children opportunities. Similarly, assessment can be used to inform and enhance curriculum or to narrow and limit curriculum. Assessment has the potential to improve teaching or to impoverish it.

— Bredekamp & Rosegrant (1992, p. 6)

In the NAEYC position statement on the previous page, Sue Bredekamp and Teresa Rosegrant recognize both the potentials and risks of assessing children and the programs that serve them. For child assessment and program evaluation to have a positive rather than a negative effect, Sam Meisels (2001) advises us to "bear in mind the root word of 'evaluation' — value" and to think about how the process we are using to assess young children corresponds "to the values by which we try to lead our professional lives or manage our professional activities" (p. 5).

How do we, then, describe child assessment and program evaluation in a way that corresponds to the values we uphold? Bredekamp and Rosegrant (1992) define child assessment as "the process of observing, recording, and otherwise documenting the work children do and how they do it, as a basis for a variety of educational decisions that affect the child" (p. 10). They say program evaluation and accountability addresses the question of whether the program, as implemented, meets its goals and objectives for children and families. In sum, when done appropriately, programs measure how much young children grow and learn and how well teachers support that development. Staff use the results of this ongoing assessment to continue what is working and improve what is not, for example, to expand children's experiences or provide caregivers with additional training.

HighScope has two comprehensive assessment tools to carry out this systematic review and enhancement process. The Child Observation Record for Infants and Toddlers (Infant-Toddler COR; HighScope, 2002a) assesses early learning in six child development domains. When completing the Infant-Toddler COR, caregivers write daily anecdotes that objectively describe children's behavior, use these notes to rate their development, and then plan activities to help individual children as well as the group have positive learning experiences. (See Chapter 2 for how caregiving teams carry out this process.) The Infant-Toddler Program Quality Assessment (Infant-Toddler PQA; HighScope, 2011) evaluates whether caregivers and agencies are using the most effective teaching and program management practices. Using the Infant-Toddler PQA, an evaluator rates a set of essential program components to identify strengths and areas for improvement.[1] Because both of these HighScope instruments reflect basic child development principles and research and are consistent with national standards and best practices, they are also suitable for use in all developmentally based programs, not just those using the HighScope Infant-Toddler Curriculum.

---

[1]HighScope has also developed and validated comprehensive assessment tools for other developmental levels and program settings, including the Preschool Child Observation Record (HighScope, 2003a), Preschool Program Quality Assessment (HighScope, 2003b), Family Child Care Program Quality Assessment (HighScope, 2009), Youth Program Quality Assessment (HighScope, 2003c), and Ready Schools Assessment (HighScope, 2006). Information about child and program assessments is available on the HighScope website at www.highscope.org.

In HighScope programs, caregivers measure children's development with authentic assessments, which include

observations of children as they interact with materials, peers, and caregivers;

portfolios of children's work; and

input from parents at conferences on what they have seen their child doing at home.

Assessment is most effective when it is a dynamic process, involves multiple contributors, and uses data collected in different situations over several time points. Information gathered this way is *authentic;* that is, it produces valid results that can help us evaluate how well programs serve children and families. Conducting valid assessment takes time and money. It requires obtaining the instruments, training caregivers and supervisors to use them, collecting and interpreting data, applying results to make changes, and reevaluating their impact. Why, then, should early childhood programs invest their limited resources in this way?

In response, child development professors Virginia Buysse and Lisa Boyce (2003) answer that professionals "are motivated by a genuine desire to understand how our work affects young children, families, and the programs that serve them.... Program evaluation is a worthwhile investment when information obtained through systematic data collection leads to more effective ways of identifying children and families who need services or of designing interventions that are more acceptable and effective" (p. 4). In HighScope infant and toddler caregiving settings, assessment is conducted with these goals for children and programs in mind.

This chapter on child and program assessment begins with an overview of authentic assessment of children, followed by a brief description of the content and administration of the Infant-Toddler COR. It then presents a discussion of effective program quality measures and a brief

description of the content and administration of the Infant-Toddler PQA.

Authentic Assessment of Children

Educators assess young children to see how they are developing and how child care programs contribute to their growth. Traditional testing — measuring performance on predefined skills with "correct" standards for performance — is one way to gauge learning. But this type of assessment provides limited information and does not allow us to see the whole child. It does not tell us how children initiate their own learning, engage with materials and people, or solve problems. Moreover, it only shows how young children behave in the testing situation, not how they act in their natural environments. Given how variable infants and toddlers can be from one moment to the next — depending, for example, on whether they are dry or fed — testing is likely to yield an unreliable and invalid picture of their development (Hills, 1992).

Another way to measure children's development is with *authentic assessments*. These include objective observations, portfolios of children's work, and teacher and parent ratings of children's behavior (Jablon, Dombro, & Dichtelmiller, 2007). Because these authentic assessments take place in familiar and comfortable settings, they "provide a more accurate picture of what children normally do and reflect their true capabilities" (Epstein, 2007, p. 195).

Advantages of Authentic Assessment

Authentic assessment

- Is based on the real performance of the child, rather than an artificial testing situation

- Focuses on a broad range of developmental areas

- Assesses thinking and problem-solving abilities, not just factual knowledge

- Produces a profile of change and development over time

- Helps adults develop objective observational skills

- Helps adults become more knowledgeable about child development

- Encourages programs to become more child-oriented (view learning from child's perspective)

- Provides child-focused information adults can use to plan activities

- Makes adults pay attention to the "invisible" child

- Does not add to program time or cost if done as part of regular ongoing activities

- Can be done by all staff, including aides and assistants, with proper training

- Provides feedback to program administration and funding agencies

- Provides valuable and meaningful information for staff and parents to share

— Epstein (2007, p. 195)

Assessments based on objective observations of infants and toddlers in their typical day-to-day settings, as they interact with familiar materials and caregivers, are valid and authentic. Measures based on observation are not biased; they respect and accommodate children's cultural, ethnic, and linguistic differences. Moreover, authentic assessments help teachers and caregivers understand very early development and plan purposeful interactions and appropriate activities that support infants and toddlers on a daily basis. Comprehensive measures of early development are also more open ended and look at a broader range of behavior than tests, which tend to focus on a single domain of learning (Shepard, Kagan, & Wurtz, 1998). Finally, when authentic measures assess children over time, the results are not distorted by how children feel or their willingness to "perform" on a particular day. (See "Advantages of Authentic Assessment" above.)

Assessing Children: The Infant-Toddler COR

Overview

The Infant-Toddler COR is an observational instrument that provides "well-rounded, systematic assessment in programs serving children from the ages

Before using the Infant-Toddler COR to assess and score children's development, this caregiver takes daily anecdotes of her observations of children over a period of time.

COR, that enable us to "arrive at a meaningful portrait that can guide us in supporting that child's growth and learning.…Without a child development framework and a system for collecting and interpreting observations, these glimpses of child behavior provide only a superficial picture" (Lockhart, 2005b, p. 299).

The Infant-Toddler COR provides the naturalistic and comprehensive profile that is the hallmark of authentic assessment. It is *developmentally appropriate* because it is based on observations that occur during the course of a normal day and assesses all the domains of early growth. The measure is *reliable* and *valid,* as documented in the research reported in the User Guide (HighScope, 2002c). Finally, the instrument is *user friendly.* It can be reliably administered by trained staff. In addition, caregivers' collection of anecdotal notes on children does not disrupt the program's daily routine.

Components

The Infant-Toddler COR assessment kit includes these components:

- The User Guide, which describes how to use the Infant-Toddler COR[2]

- A detailed guide to the Infant-Toddler COR items

- Forms for recording anecdotes, summarizing and storing information about each child and the group as a whole,

of 6 weeks to 3 years" (HighScope, 2002c, p. 2). The Infant-Toddler COR utilizes the daily anecdotes collected by caregivers to periodically assess and score children's development in all the appropriate content areas of a developmentally based curriculum. It is the daily anecdotes, which are organized according to a child development framework in the Infant-Toddler

---

[2]The description of how to administer the Infant-Toddler COR in the User Guide does not take the place of the two-day training workshop. For information on training, visit the HighScope website at www.highscope.org.

and creating reports for parents about their child

- A booklet for parents explaining what the Infant-Toddler COR is and posters for quick reference to all the key elements of the Infant-Toddler COR

- *What's Next: Planning Strategies and Activities Around Infant-Toddler COR Observations* (HighScope, 2004), which is a guide caregivers can use as a follow-up to their children's Infant-Toddler COR results

As an alternative to using the print version of the Infant-Toddler COR, programs can complete the assessment using the online version, which has many additional features to support scoring, interpretation, reporting, and follow-up. For more information on Infant-Toddler COR options, support materials, and training, visit the HighScope website at www.highscope.org.

Content

The Infant-Toddler COR is organized into six categories addressing the knowledge and skills that very young children acquire and develop. There are a total of 28 items on the Infant-Toddler COR. Under each of the items are five developmental levels that describe behavior ranging from (1) simple to (5) more complex. For an example, see "Infant-Toddler COR Item With Anecdote Examples" on pages 400–401.

Collecting anecdotes

Using the Infant-Toddler COR is a continuous process. Caregivers record objective anecdotal notes on infants and toddlers daily, throughout the year, and use them to score the COR items at periodic intervals. (See sample anecdotes in Chapter 2.) Staff periodically review their anecdotes to make sure each child's development is documented in each of the Infant-Toddler COR categories, and, if necessary, fill in gaps in their observations over the next few days.

Recording objective anecdotes on children takes training and practice, but the effort pays off in several ways. It not only results in valid Infant-Toddler COR scores but also helps caregivers better understand early development and plan ways to effectively scaffold young children's growth. Here are some guidelines caregivers can follow in recording anecdotal notes:

- Date each and every anecdote.

- Identify when, where, and with whom the activity took place.

- Describe what the child did and said. Use quotes to document the child's language (if any).

- Be factual in creating a snapshot of what actually occurred. Describe, rather than interpret, what happened.

- Keep the entries short, providing enough detail to help remember and elaborate on them later when there is time. Focus on the content, not the style, of the writing.

- Be realistic in setting the number of anecdotes gathered each day.

For more information on recording objective anecdotes, see the User Guide (HighScope, 2002c). For more information

Infant-Toddler COR Item With Anecdote Examples

J. Playing with others

Level 1. Child watches another child play.
At this level the child expresses interest in social play by watching other children.

- *Ashley was lying on a mat where several other children were playing. She turned and looked at Takiya when she heard her playing the small keyboard.[3]*

- *While Hakeem was having his diaper changed, he turned his head to watch Julie and Emily play "firefighter."*

Level 2. Child shows pleasure in peekaboo, "This Little Piggy," or other simple games.
The simple social games that engage a child at this level are usually very repetitive. The child's partner in the game, usually an adult or an older child, is expected to continue the game until the child tires of it.

- *During diapering Kaylee started smiling and wiggling when Ryba (a caregiver) played "This Little Piggy" with her toes.*

- *During the afternoon snack Gareth, a school-aged child, held up Orlando's bib in front of his face and then quickly took it away. Orlando laughed out loud.*

Level 3. Child seeks the company of another child and plays alongside.
At this level the child shows a distinct preference for the company of a particular child or children.

- *During choice time Colton was playing with a basket of different kinds of brushes. Seeing this, Akito brought over his basket of small balls and played alongside Colton.*

- *After finishing her snack, Merritt went to the block area, where Rosalva was stacking the cardboard blocks. Merritt sat down nearby with some of the smaller wooden blocks and started playing with them.*

Level 4. Child hides an object for another person to find or runs away from another person in order to be caught.
In these earliest forms of hide-and-seek and tag, the child experiments with the excitement of anticipation — being caught or found by a play partner. The child also begins to initiate peekaboo games with others and enjoys games that involve pointing to different parts of the body.

- *Rod (a caregiver) was wearing his favorite baseball cap. Giggling, Emilia snuck up behind him as he knelt down to tie Leandro's shoe. She took the cap and hid it behind the aquarium.*

- *During outside time Tal played a chase game with Anna and Rene (a caregiver). Tal and Anna chased Rene until Rene fell on the ground, then the two children piled on top of her, giggling.*

Level 5. Child watches and tries out some of the actions of a child playing nearby.
At this level the child sees something interesting another child is doing (for example, squeezing and patting clay, walking along a row of wooden blocks, throwing balls from the top of the climber), and chooses to attempt some aspect of that play on his or her own.

---

[3]When completing the COR, the date of each observation is marked. See Collecting anecdotes on page 399.

Infant-Toddler COR Item With Anecdote Examples (cont.)

Level 5 (cont.)

- *During choice time Alexandra started taking off her shirt. Dee (a caregiver) asked her what she was doing. Alex replied, "Dee, I going swimming!" Jenny, watching this exchange, began to take off her clothes too.*

- *During choice time in the toy area, Miguel dumped out the pieces of a puzzle. Seeing this, Rosa got a puzzle of her own and dumped the pieces out.*

  — HighScope (2002b, p. 13)

---

on how caregiving teams observe, record, and use anecdotal notes, see Chapter 2.

Scoring

At least twice a year, caregivers use their anecdotal notes to rate each Infant-Toddler COR item on a scale of 1 to 5 to reflect each child's current level of development. As noted previously, the examples in the Infant-Toddler COR Observation Items (HighScope, 2002b) help caregivers choose the appropriate level for each child in each category.

Completing forms

After the Infant-Toddler COR is scored for each child, programs may also complete the summary forms to look at individual change over time and/or create a picture for the whole group. Group profiles help programs meet their accountability requirements. Caregivers can also enter selected child anecdotes on the parent forms to share at scheduled conferences.

Additional uses

In addition to providing caregivers with the basis of daily planning and parents with information on their child's program experience, a program's director can share anecdotal records and Infant-Toddler COR scores with other audiences as well.[4] Administrators can use Infant-Toddler COR results to monitor their programs and identify areas for staff inservice training. In addition, policymakers and funders, interested in holding programs accountable for their effectiveness, can rely on Infant-Toddler COR data to provide accurate and objective information about how children are learning and developing.

Effective Measures of Program Quality

While attention to the importance of program quality in early care and education has increased in recent years, much of this focus has been at the preschool level (*Education Week*, 2009). Yet longitudinal studies, such as those conducted

---

[4]Programs use ID numbers and aggregate data, as appropriate, to protect confidentiality.

After observing Miguel in the toy area, his caregiver wrote this anecdote: "10/27/10 After putting the wooden circles in the open coffee can, Miguel tried to fit them through the hole in the coffee can with a lid."

by the Early Child Care Research Network (NICHD, 2010), conclusively demonstrate that the quality of care received by infants and toddlers is critical to their subsequent social-emotional and cognitive health. Professional organizations such as NAEYC (2007) and Zero to Three (2008) and public agencies such as the Administration for Children and Families (2002), which funds Early Head Start, have issued standards defining high-quality program practices for children from birth to age three.

These recommendations are an essential first step in improving child care quality, particularly since they go beyond the minimal requirements that typically characterize licensing regulations. However, a necessary second step is assessing whether these higher standards are in fact being implemented in settings serving infants and toddlers. This systematic assessment is the role of program evaluation, and it requires valid measures that address all components of child care quality — nurturing adult-child relationships with continuity of care, consistent and supportive caregiving routines, diverse and appropriate equipment and materials, and respectful and sensitive interactions among caregivers and between the caregiving team and families.

The primary role of program evaluation is to answer the question "Does it work?" That is, does the program meet the outcomes or goals providers hope to achieve with children and their families? In designing an informative evaluation, program developers are forced to consider whether these are the "right" goals, whether the goals are realistic and the outcomes are attainable, and how the achievement of these goals should be defined and measured (Gilliam & Leiter, 2003).

Effective program quality measures thoughtfully address how programs are implemented and what they do to support the young children and families they serve. Epstein (2007) says useful assessments define quality along a continuum. They permit more than just a "yes" or "no" judgment about the presence of each program component and instead acknowledge that quality is achieved in stages. Effective measures also provide specific examples or indicators along this continuum so staff members can see where they are currently and the ideal they are striving for. They acknowledge that program development,

like child development, is an ongoing process. Similar to child measures, good program assessments are comprehensive. Developers validate them to see whether the dimensions chosen are indeed related to program *inputs* (such as staff training) and participant *outputs* (such as children's developmental progress and parents' satisfaction).

Program quality assessments are most often used as accountability measures (NAEYC & National Association of Early Childhood Specialists in State Departments of Education, 2003). They help administrators and policymakers decide whether and how to invest resources in program operations. However, valid and informative program evaluations can also be used in other ways. For example, they can identify professional development needs for staff as a whole.

Supervisors can also use quality measures to observe individual teachers and caregivers and provide constructive feedback on specific teaching practices. Because both the observer and the observed know how the measure defines high levels of quality, there is no hidden agenda. They can work together to achieve the highest level, defined by descriptive examples at the upper end of the scale.

Finally, effective program assessments can address many audiences. They can be used in research to study the components of high quality that other early childhood settings should emulate. The descriptions of quality help those without

Effective Program Quality Measures

Have the following characteristics:

- Define quality along a continuum, not just "yes" or "no"

- Provide users with many examples

- Are comprehensive

- Have been field-tested and validated

Can be used in the following ways:

- To support the curriculum implementation of teaching teams

- To plan and carry out a program of staff development

- To carry out research and program evaluation

- To communicate to many audiences

— Epstein (2007, p. 207)

formal training in child development — policymakers, parents, and community members — understand what is at stake in the quest for program quality. (See "Effective Program Quality Measures" above.)

Assessing Programs: The Infant-Toddler PQA

Overview

The Infant-Toddler PQA: Form A, Beta Version,[5] (HighScope, 2011) measures four domains of curriculum implementation and program operations:

1. Learning environment

2. Schedules and routines

3. Adult-child interaction

4. Curriculum planning and child observation

Within each domain is a series of items addressing the essential program components and best practices needed to support the development of infants and toddlers. In addition to the High-Scope practices discussed in this book, other sources used to define and describe quality in the Infant-Toddler PQA include NAEYC developmentally appropriate practices and accreditation criteria, Zero to Three early learning guidelines, Early Head Start Program Performance Standards, and the recommendations of the AAP. State licensing and program standards were also referenced, although these generally define only "minimum" levels of quality.

The Infant-Toddler PQA is designed to meet the criteria described above for effective program measures. The instrument uses anecdotal notes based on classroom observations, staff interviews, and documentation of program records to score items on a 5-point scale from lower to higher levels of quality. Each item

---

[5]Another component of this assessment instrument, Form B, deals with agency-level items and is in development.

Supervisors and caregivers can use informative program evaluations to work together to reach the highest level of care for the children in their program.

contains descriptors that anchor the scoring decision and make it clear what types of caregiving practices, classroom materials, and agency policies contribute to a high-quality setting. Because the Infant-Toddler PQA documents caregivers and young children engaged in typical behaviors throughout the program day, it is an authentic assessment of the setting.

To validate the Infant-Toddler PQA, HighScope conducted a pilot test in 2001–2002 with 75 diverse infant and toddler program settings. Descriptive statistics and a factor analysis based on the ratings completed by HighScope staff and field consultants were used to revise the tool to the current beta version.

Content, data collection, and scoring

The first 25 items on the Infant-Toddler PQA are organized according to four domains described on page 404. Each item contains "indicators" describing program quality at three levels of implementation, which are then combined to create one overall rating for the entire item on a five-point continuum ranging from low (1) to high (5). (See "Sample Item From the Infant-Toddler PQA: Form A" on p. 406.)

As with the Infant-Toddler COR, data used to score the Infant-Toddler PQA are collected by taking objective anecdotal notes during program observations. Additional data (e.g., about the use of

Sample Item From the Infant-Toddler PQA: Form A

III-B. Children form trusting relationships with their caregivers.

Level 1 Indicators

❑ Children are not touched, held, and/or spoken to, or are touched, held, and/or spoken to in a rough, rushed, or disinterested manner.

❑ Children do not show pleasure in their interactions with caregivers.

❑ Children do not receive caregiver attention when they demand, signal, or request it.

❑ Children do not initiate interactions with caregivers.

❑ Children and caregivers do not interact at the children's pace (e.g., caregivers hurry children through each part of the routine).

❑ Children hear only negative comments from caregivers about themselves and others (e.g., "Sam, you're making a mess — Sam always makes a mess"; "Mimi is a biter").

Level 3 Indicators

❑ Sometimes children are touched, held, and spoken to in an attentive, unhurried manner.

❑ Sometimes children show pleasure in their interactions with caregivers.

❑ Sometimes children receive caregiver attention when they demand, signal, or request it.

❑ Sometimes children initiate interactions with caregivers.

❑ Sometimes children and caregivers interact at the children's pace.

❑ Children hear some positive comments from caregivers about themselves and others.

Level 5 Indicators

❑ Throughout the day children are touched, held, and spoken to in a warm, attentive, leisurely manner.

❑ Throughout the day children show pleasure in their interactions with caregivers.

❑ Throughout the day children receive caregiver attention when they demand, signal, or request it and when they pause in exploration and play.

❑ Throughout the day children initiate interactions with caregivers (e.g., during arrival time, Wendy crawls over and sits in Hilda's lap; at outside time, Jerome brings a ball to Alicia and says, "We play?").

❑ Throughout the day children and caregivers interact at the children's pace (e.g., while going outside, caregivers lets children walk and crawl at their own pace down the hallway and down stairs to the playground).

❑ Throughout the day children hear only positive comments from caregivers about themselves and others (e.g., "Sam and Kari like paint"; "Mimi, chewing on the teether makes your gums feel better").

— HighScope (2011, p. 30)

Child and Program Assessment: A Summary

Child assessment

❑ Use a validated and authentic observation-based child assessment to measure all areas of children's development.

❑ Collect objective anecdotal notes and other documentary evidence.

❑ Use anecdotal information for daily planning for individual children's development and the group as a whole.

❑ Complete the child assessment two or three times a year to measure changes in children's development and learning.

❑ Share and discuss the results of the child assessment with families at conferences.

❑ Share the results of the child assessment with program administrators and funding agencies.

❑ Use child assessment results for professional development.

Program assessment

❑ Use a validated and authentic program assessment to measure all areas of curriculum implementation and program management along a continuum of quality.

❑ Use the program assessment to collect objective anecdotal data and other documentary evidence.

❑ Complete the program assessment one or two times a year to monitor program quality, recognize areas of strength, and identify areas for improvement.

❑ Use the results of the program assessment to create a plan for staff development.

❑ Share and discuss the results of the program assessment among the caregiving staff.

❑ Share the results of the program assessment with program administrators and funding agencies.

---

a curriculum model or planning based on child observations) may be obtained through interviews and documentation of records and procedures. Anecdotal evidence may be collected by trained outside observers, program supervisors, and/ or staff members reflecting on their own caregiving practices. Following the instrument's scoring procedures, these anecdotal data are then used to rate program quality on each item. Composite scores can also be calculated on each of the four dimensions, as well as for the instrument as a whole.

∼

Meisels (2001) reminds us that the act of conducting valid assessment on children's progress and program delivery is only the first step in acquiring useful information. Ongoing interaction with children and families should continue to inform our knowledge base about what is and is not meeting their needs. Likewise, continuous program monitoring and reflection are needed to honestly evaluate what we are doing well and where and how we can improve curriculum implementation, support services, and program operations. Finally, valid assessment calls for examining the consequences that follow from using the data. We must constantly re-assess actions and outcomes to ensure that our decisions positively affect child and staff development.

With the support of caregiver teams and caregiver-parent relationships, very young children can experience both tender care and early learning. Having the opportunity for safe, secure active learning puts this little boy in the driver's seat!

Appendix: History of the HighScope Infant-Toddler Approach

HighScope has a long history of curriculum development, training, and research in the area of infant-toddler development, beginning with parent education programs and community support for families.

HighScope's First Infant-Toddler Projects

Members of the HighScope infant division, acting under the direction of Dolores Lambie and David Weikart, began their work in parent-infant education with the 1968–1971 **Ypsilanti-Carnegie Infant Education Project** (Epstein & Weikart, 1979; Lambie et al., 1974). Funded by Carnegie Corporation of New York, this project trained professional staff to work as home visitors with mothers of infants between 3 months and 11 months old. The home visitor would meet with a mother and her infant in their home once each week for 16 weeks to play infant-centered games and to discuss child development. The parent-visitor discussions focused specifically on what the infant was doing and communicating during and between visits. Research findings from this project revealed that mothers who participated in the home visits showed more verbal interaction with their infants than did mothers in the project's randomly assigned contrast and control groups; the mothers' increased verbal interaction, in turn, facilitated their children's cognitive development (Lambie et al., 1974).

Following the Infant Education Project, Carnegie funded the **HighScope Infant Videotaping Project** (1971–1973), which resulted in 270 hours of video footage of home visitors, parents, and infants engaging in informal interactions. HighScope staff used this footage to produce videotapes on home visitor training, child development, and strategies for supporting early learning. These videotapes, and the processes they documented, became the basis for HighScope's entry into the early phases of training and dissemination in the parent-infant arena.

By 1974, HighScope staff had developed the core of what was called the Parent-to-Parent Model (Reschly, 1979). Between 1975 and 1978, with funds from Lilly Endowment Incorporated and the National Institute for Mental Health, they implemented the **Parent-to-Parent Home Visit Project.** Four women who had participated as parents in one of the earlier home visit projects became home visitors themselves. This shift from using professionals to using paraprofessionals as the vehicle for service delivery reflected a then-current trend in the family-service sector. Researchers and practitioners had begun to recognize that members of the community, with some training and with supervision by trained professionals, could establish rapport with families and effectively share child development information with parents. The evolution of four program recipients into program providers enabled the process that began with the Infant Education Project to grow within the community, creating a framework for community service by and for the parents. The four parents who had become paraprofessionals were peers, not outside experts, sharing child development information with parents. By focusing on how to best support children's development, both the peer home visitors and the parents grew in their understanding of how children learn. (For more information, see Epstein & Evans [1979]).

HighScope's fourth project relating to parents and infants, the **Adolescent Parents and Infants Project**, began in 1977 with funding from the Administration for Children, Youth and Families (now called the Administration for Children and Families) in the US Department of Health and Human Services. Research staff interviewed 98 teenager mothers from diverse socioeconomic backgrounds twice — once during pregnancy and once six months after giving birth. They also videotaped these young parents interacting with their infants. The project's goals were to find out how much teenagers know (and need to know) about infant development, what their expectations and attitudes are toward becoming parents, what support systems inside and outside their family they have, and how these factors affect their interactions with their babies (Epstein, 1980a).

The research documented that adolescent parents' expectations for their infants' development were "too little, too late" and emphasized the need for programs to help young parents become better observers and supporters of their babies' growth. Moreover, family and community support was vital to allow the young mother to continue her own development so that she, in turn, could facilitate the development of her child. For further details on the research results, see Epstein (1980b).

HighScope's Parent-to-Parent and Parent-Infant Projects

The fifth and largest initiative, the **Parent-to-Parent Dissemination Project** (HighScope, n.d.), was supported by a grant from the Bernard van Leer Foundation and ran from 1978 to 1984. Members of HighScope's family programs division, working under the direction of Judith Evans, trained people in seven diverse communities across the United States to set up their own local parent-to-parent programs. By 1981 three communities had each developed a Regional Parent-to-Parent Training and Dissemination Center. Staff at these centers provided parent-to-parent training for their regions, helped other communities start parent-to-parent programs, and acted as community resources for other programs serving families and infants. "This is the first time in my life I've ever been treated like a person and not like a case," a parent receiving home visits reported (p. 30).

HighScope conducted a case-study follow-up of participants in the Parent-to-Parent Dissemination Project at four of the project sites from 1997–1999. The original project and the results of this qualitative follow-up were published in *Supporting Families With Young Children: The HighScope Parent-to-Parent Dissemination*

Parent-to-Parent Dissemination Project

HighScope conducted the Parent-to-Parent Dissemination Project in two phases. In the first phase (1978–1984), staff looked at whether the model program, which had been successfully implemented locally, could be effectively disseminated to seven other diverse communities. Evaluators found that the model program could indeed be transferred to other communities with the same level of success as the model program (Epstein et al., 2002).

In the second phase (1997–1999), staff conducted follow-up interviews with agencies and participants in four of these communities

to obtain information that would be of interest to program planners and policymakers, including what services in a parent-to-parent program should be delivered, how they should be delivered, who should deliver them, and how programs should be funded (Epstein et al., 2002). Evaluators found that services work best if they are coordinated in a central location and delivered by professionals and paraprofessionals working in partnership, promote parent involvement, and have stable and sustainable funding.

Project (Epstein, Montie, & Weikart, 2002). The initiative revealed important lessons about the factors that allow for successful program dissemination, including both the content of the curriculum and the system for funding and delivering services. (See "Parent-to-Parent Dissemination Project" above for a summary of the findings.)

A sixth parent-infant project occurred during the 1980s, when HighScope received funding to evaluate the Ford Foundation's multisite **Child Survival/Fair Start Project**. This project worked with low-income parents and their infants in diverse agency settings and communities around the United States (Larner, Halpern, & Harkavy, 1992). In addition to funding HighScope's evaluation of its project, the Ford Foundation provided funding that enabled HighScope to consolidate the lessons learned in the Parent-to-Parent

Dissemination Project and Child Survival/Fair Start. This subsequent multisite analysis resulted in publication of *A Guide to Developing Community-Based Family Support Programs* (Epstein, Larner, & Halpern, 1995), which contains guidelines for all the steps of designing, implementing, and evaluating comprehensive child development programs for families with very young children. As Epstein and her colleagues pointed out in this guide, partnerships with parents are vital: "The sustained personal relationship that develops between the family worker and the family is the key to achieving the objectives of home visiting programs" (p. 76).

The collective experiences of working with infants, parents, and community support agencies and the knowledge of child development gained through these several parent-infant projects also culminated in three HighScope curriculum-focused publications: *Supporting the Changing Family: A Guide to the Parent-to-Parent Model* (Reschly, 1979); *Good Beginnings: Parenting in the Early Years* (Evans & Ilfeld, 1982b); and *Activities for Parent-Child Interaction, Supplement to Good Beginnings* (Evans & Ilfeld, 1982a). The principles of child development and adult support described in these publications in turn have influenced both editions of *Tender Care and Early Learning*. However, as the curriculum shifted from helping parents at home with their own children to supporting practitioners in settings serving groups of children, the implementation of these principles changed accordingly.

HighScope's Infant-Toddler Curriculum Today

Since the initial publication of *Tender Care and Early Learning* in 2000, the HighScope Infant-Toddler Curriculum has continued to evolve in its content, dissemination through onsite and online training, print and audiovisual support materials, and assessment tools. The KDIs[1] — the "content" that infants and toddlers learn through active exploration of their environment — have been refined and updated based on the latest child development theory and research. HighScope staff members disseminate a comprehensive series of workshops on infant-toddler development and the caregiving strategies that support it, based on the principles

and educational practices described in this book. Implementation is further supported through a variety of publications and DVDs on topics related to infants and toddlers.

To further support the implementation and effectiveness of child care settings, HighScope has developed and validated two assessment tools, one for children and one for programs. The Infant-Toddler COR (HighScope, 2002a) uses caregivers' systematic and objective anecdotal notes to quantitatively assess young children's progress and plan for their ongoing development. The Infant-Toddler PQA (HighScope, 2011) uses observational and interview data to rate the quality of curriculum implementation and program management. Together, these assessment tools help staff monitor and plan for children's growth and create high-quality, developmentally based services.

HighScope's Focus on Child Care Settings

Throughout the 1980s, as HighScope evaluated multisite parent-infant program initiatives implemented by other agencies, funding for its own parent-to-parent dissemination activity virtually disappeared. Later on, between 1989 and 1992, the Transactional Intervention Program, under the direction of Amy Powell, merged with HighScope to become the **HighScope Program for Infants and Toddlers With Special Needs**, a three-year national

---

[1]KDIs were formerly called key experiences.

outreach training project funded by the US Education Department's Handicapped Children's Early Education Program. The purpose of this project was to help early childhood programs implement "a family-focused intervention model for special needs infants and toddlers and their families" through training and technical assistance (Powell, 1990, p. 12). The project was based on findings that children with special needs "are more actively engaged and achieve higher levels of language and cognitive functioning when their parents engage in a responsive, nondirective style of interaction — a style we call child-oriented" (p. 13). (For a summary of HighScope's infant-toddler work, see "A History of HighScope Infant-Toddler Activities" on p. 415.)

At the same time, the demand for training in the HighScope preschool approach for three- to five-year-olds accelerated, resulting in a network of HighScope-certified trainers working in early childhood settings across the nation. Over time, many of these preschool trainers assumed positions that required them to train and support staff working in settings that served infants and toddlers. Some of these trainers, on their own, adapted the HighScope active learning, constructivist approach to the infant-toddler programs they were working with. By the early 1990s, there was a clear need for HighScope to provide new infant-toddler materials directed toward center-based programs and family child care homes. In 1993, therefore, Jacalyn

Post and Mary Hohmann, the authors of the first edition of *Tender Care and Early Learning,* initiated a project to (1) gather the most accurate, up-to-date information about supporting infants and toddlers in HighScope-based programs and other active learning settings and (2) relate these findings to the earlier HighScope work represented in *Supporting the Changing Family* (Reschly, 1979) and *Good Beginnings* (Evans & Ilfeld, 1982b).

Altogether, caregivers and directors from 21 infant-toddler programs across the country completed surveys about their current practices and collected anecdotes and child observations for this book. These programs ranged from small (6 children) to large (10 rooms of 12 children each) and from serving mixed-age groups (infants and toddlers together) to serving groups separated by age (e.g., young infants together, older infants together, young toddlers together, older toddlers together). They included center-based programs, family child care homes, and a college-based drop-in child care center. In some programs, parents attended with their children for all or part of each session. Collectively, these programs served the needs of families from a wide spectrum of income levels.

Eight of the 21 programs were visited by one of the books' authors; the remaining 13 programs submitted their survey information in writing and through telephone conversations. Staff at all 21 sites answered questions about their program routines, interactions, adult teamwork, and

A History of HighScope Infant-Toddler Activities

1968–1971 Ypsilanti-Carnegie Infant Education Project: Home Teaching With Mother and Infants

1971–1973 HighScope Infant Videotaping Project

1974 Publication of *Home Teaching With Mothers and Infants*, by D. I. Lambie, J. T. Bond, and D. P. Weikart

1975–1978 Parent-to-Parent Home Visit Project

1979 Publication of *Supporting the Changing Family: A Guide to the Parent-to-Parent Model*, by B. Reschly

1979 Publication of *The Ypsilanti-Carnegie Infant Education Project: Longitudinal Follow-Up*, by A. S. Epstein and D. P. Weikart

1977–1980 Adolescent Parents and Infants Project funded by the Administration for Children, Youth, and Families, US Department of Health and Human Services

1978–1984 Bernard van Leer Parent-to-Parent Dissemination Project

1982 Publication of *Good Beginnings: Parenting in the Early Years* and its supplement, *Activities for Parent-Child Interaction*, by J. Evans and E. Ilfeld

n.d. Publication of *Community Self-Help: The Parent-to-Parent Program*

1982–1989 Evaluation of the Ford Foundation's Child Survival/Fair Start Project

1989–1992 HighScope Program for Infants and Toddlers With Special Needs funded by the US Department of Education

1995 Publication of *A Guide to Developing Community-Based Family Support Programs*, by A. S. Epstein, M. Larner, and R. Halpern

1997–1999 Case-study follow-up of the Parent-to-Parent Dissemination Project

2000 Publication of *Tender Care and Early Learning: Supporting Infants and Toddlers in Child Care Settings*, by J. Post and M. Hohmann

2002 Publication of *Supporting Families With Young Children: The HighScope Parent-to-Parent Dissemination Project* by A. S. Epstein, J. Montie, and D. P. Weikart

2002 Publication of the *Child Observation Record for Infants and Toddlers*

2011 Publication of the *Infant-Toddler Program Quality Assessment Form A, Beta Version*

2011 Publication of *Tender Care and Early Learning, Second Edition*, by J. Post, M. Hohmann, and A. S. Epstein

child observation. In addition, staff at each site received a working list of the curriculum content[2] for infants and toddlers (see "HighScope Infant-Toddler Key Developmental Indicators" on p. 33) along with anecdote-collection sheets and guidelines for collecting anecdotes through child observation. (For a discussion of observation-based anecdotes in team planning and in child assessment, see Chapters 2 and 6, respectively.) The idea was to collect data about infants and toddlers that could be used to validate the curriculum's content and observational procedures.

Staff at each site collected observations of their children over four to six months and submitted them to HighScope program developers and researchers. The results were gratifying. The ability of site staff to reliably observe and objectively document the activities of infants and toddlers was confirmed. Moreover, their anecdotes showed that very young children, with appropriate adult support, engaged in the kinds of activities captured in the curriculum's content. Many of these child observations and adult-child interactions are included in this book, along with new anecdotes contributed by the infant and toddler programs we have worked with since then.

---

[2]Curriculum content was called "key experiences" at that time but has since been renamed KDIs.

References

Administration for Children and Families, Head Start Bureau. (2002, October). *Program Performance Standards and other regulations.* Washington, DC: US Government Printing Office.

Administration for Children, Youth, and Families, Head Start Bureau. (1999). *Head Start Program Performance Standards and other regulations.* Washington, DC: US Department of Health and Human Services.

Ainsworth, M. (1963). The development of infant-mother interaction among the Ganda. In B. M. Foss (Ed.), *Determinants of infant behavior* (Vol. 2, pp. 67–104). New York: John Wiley & Sons.

Ainsworth, M., Blehar, M. D., Waters, E., & Wall, S. (1978). *Patterns of attachment: A psychological study of the strange situation.* Hillsdale, NJ: Erlbaum.

Allison, D., & Watson, J. A. (1994). The significance of adult storybook reading styles on the development of young children's emergent reading. *Reading Research and Instruction, 34,* 57–72.

American Academy of Family Physicians (2010, February). *When your toddler doesn't want to eat.* Retrieved from http://familydoctor.org/online/famdocen/home/children/parents/behavior/224.html

American Academy of Pediatrics. (2001). Children, adolescents, and television. *Pediatrics, 107*(2), 423–426. doi:10.1542/peds.107.2.423

American Academy of Pediatrics. (2005). The changing concept of sudden infant death syndrome. *Pediatrics, 116*(5), 1245–1255. doi:10.1542/peds.2005-1499

American Academy of Pediatrics, American Public Health Association, & National Resource Center for Health and Safety in Child Care. (2002). *Caring for our children: National health and safety performance standards: Guidelines for out-of-home child care programs* (2nd ed.). Elk Grove Village, IL: American Academy of Pediatrics. Retrieved from http://nrckids.org/CFOC/

Anderson, D. R., & Evans, M. K. (2001). Peril and potential of media for infants and toddlers. *Zero to Three, 22*(2), 10–16.

Aronson, S. S. (Ed.). (2002). *Healthy young children: A manual for programs* (4th ed.). Washington, DC: National Association for the Education of Young Children.

Baker, A. C., & Manfredi/Petitt, L. A. (2004). *Relationships, the heart of quality care: Creating community among adults in early care settings.* Washington, DC: National Association for the Education of Young Children.

Bales, D., & Campbell, C. (Eds.). (2002). *Better brains for babies* (2nd ed.). Athens, GA: University of Georgia College of Family and Consumer Sciences and Georgia State University School of Nursing. Retrieved from http://www.bbbgeorgia.org

Bardige, B. (2009). *Talk to me baby! How you can support young children's language development.* Baltimore, MD: Paul H. Brookes.

Bardige, B., & Bardige, M. K. (2008). Talk to me, baby! Supporting language development in the first three years. *Zero to Three, 29*(1), 4–10.

Baroody, A. J. (2000). Does mathematics instruction for three- to five-year olds really make sense? *Young Children, 55*(4), 61–67.

Belsky, J., Vandell, D. L., Burchinal, M., Clarke-Stewart, K. A., McCartney, K., Owen, M. T., & NICHD Early Child Care Research Network. (2007). Are there long-term effects of early child care? *Child Development, 78*(2), 681–701. doi:10.1111/j.1467-8624.2007.01021.x

Benoit, D. (2004). Infant-parent attachment: Definition, types, antecedents, measurement, and outcome. *Pediatric Child Health, 9*(8), 541–545.

Bergen, D., Smith, K., & O'Neill, S. (1988). Designing play environments for infants and toddlers. In D. Bergen (Ed.), *Play as a medium for learning and development: A handbook of theory and practice* (pp. 187–207). Portsmouth, NH: Heinemann.

Bloom, P. J., & Sheerer, M. (1992). The effect of leadership training on child care program quality. *Early Childhood Research Quarterly, 7*(4), 579–594. doi:10.1016/0885-2006(92)90112-C

Bowlby, J. (1973). *Separation: Anxiety and anger. Attachment and loss* (Vol. 2). New York: Basic Books.

Bowlby, J. (1980). *Loss: Sadness and depression. Attachment and loss* (Vol. 3). New York: Basic Books.

Bowlby, J. (1982). *Attachment: Attachment and loss* (Vol. 1, 2nd ed.). New York: Basic Books. (Original work published 1969)

Bowlby, J. (1988). *A secure base: Parent-child attachment and healthy human development*. New York: Basic Books.

Brannon, E. M. (2002). The development of ordinal number knowledge in infancy. *Cognition, 83*, 223–240.

Brazelton, T. B. (1983). *Infants and mothers: Differences in development* (Rev. ed.). New York: Dell.

Bredekamp, S., & Rosegrant, T. (Eds.). (1992). *Reaching potentials: Appropriate curriculum and assessment for young children* (Vol. 1). Washington, DC: National Association for the Education of Young Children.

Bretherton, I., & Munholland, K. (2008). Internal working models in attachment relationships: Elaborating a central construct in attachment theory. In J. Cassidy & P. R. Shaver (Eds.), *Handbook of attachment: Theory, research, and clinical applications* (2nd ed., pp. 102–127). New York: Guilford.

Bronfenbrenner, U. (1985). The parent/child relationship and our changing society. In E. L. Arnold (Ed.), *Parents, children, and change* (pp. 45–57). Lexington, MA: Lexington Books.

Buckleitner, W., Orr, A. C., & Wolock, E. (Eds.).(2000). Are computers harmful to kids? A response to the "Alliance for Childhood." *Children's Software Revue.* Retrieved from http://www.childrens software.com/harm.html

Buckley, S. J., Bird, G., & Sacks, B. (2006). Evidence that we can change the profile from a study of inclusive education. *Down Syndrome Research and Practice, 9*(3), 51–53. doi:10.3104/essays.294

Butterfield, P. M. (2002). Child care is rich in routines. *Zero to Three, 22*(4), 29–32.

Buysse, V., & Boyce, L. (2003). Evaluating programs that serve infants and families: The quest for quality. *Zero to Three, 23*(6), 4–5.

Campbell, F. A., Helms, R., Sparling, J. J., & Ramey, C. T. (1998). Early-childhood programs and success in school: The Abecedarian study. In W. Steven Barnett & S. S. Boocock (Eds.), *Early care and education for children in poverty: Promises, programs, and long-term results* (pp. 145–166). Albany, NY: SUNY Press.

Cantor, P. (2001). Computers and the very young. *Focus on Infants and Toddlers, 13*(4), 1–4, 7–8.

Carlson, F. M. (2006). *Essential touch: Meeting the needs of young children*. Washington, DC: National Association for the Education of Young Children.

Carlson, V. J., Feng, X., & Harwood, R. L. (2004). The "ideal" baby: A look at the intersection of temperament and culture. *Zero to Three, 24*(4), 22–28.

Center for the Child Care Workforce. (2001). *Then and now: Changes in child care staffing, 1994–2000.* Washington, DC: Author.

Chess, S., & Thomas, A. (1996). Temperament. In M. Lewis (Ed.), *Child and adolescent psychiatry: A comprehensive textbook* (2nd ed., pp. 170–181). Baltimore: Williams & Wilkins.

Computers and young children: Interviews with Douglas H. Clements and Jane Healy. (1999). *Scholastic Early Childhood Today, 14*(1), 44–47.

Copple, C., & Bredekamp, S. (2009). Developmentally appropriate practice in the infant and toddler years — Ages 0–3: Examples to consider. In C. Copple & S. Bredekamp (Eds.), *Developmentally appropriate practice in early childhood programs serving children from birth through age 8* (3rd ed., pp. 75–107). Washington, DC: National Association for the Education of Young Children.

Cordes, C., & Miller, E. (2000). *Fool's gold: A critical look at computers in childhood.* College Park, MD: Alliance for Childhood. Retrieved from http://www.alliance forchildhood.org/fools_gold

Daniels, M. (2001). *Dancing with words: Signing for hearing children's literacy.* Westport, CT: Bergin & Garvey.

Diamond, A. (2006). The early development of executive functions. In E. Bialystok & F. I. M. Craik (Eds.), *Lifespan cognition: Mechanisms of change* (pp. 70–95). New York: Oxford University Press.

Dowling, J. L., & Mitchell, T. C. (2007). *I belong: Active learning for children with special needs.* Ypsilanti, MI: HighScope Press.

Education Week. (2009). *Quality counts 2009.* Bethesda, MD: Author. Retrieved from http://www.edweek.org

Elkind, D. (1998, September/October). Computers for infants and young children. *Child Care Information Exchange, 23,* 44–46.

Emde, R. (1998). Early emotional development: New modes of thinking for research and intervention. *Pediatrics, 102*(5), 1236–1243.

Epstein, A. S. (1980a). *Assessing the child development information needed by adolescent parents with very young children* (Final project report for Grant No. 90-C-1341 submitted to the US Department of Health, Education and Welfare). Ypsilanti, MI: HighScope Educational Research Foundation.

Epstein, A. S. (1980b). New insights into the problems of adolescent parenthood. *Bulletin of the HighScope Foundation, 6*–8.

Epstein, A. S. (2007). *Essentials of active learning in preschool: Getting to know the HighScope Curriculum.* Ypsilanti, MI: HighScope Press.

Epstein, A. S. (2009). *Me, you, us: Social-emotional learning in preschool.* Ypsilanti, MI: HighScope Press.

Epstein, A. S., & Evans, J. (1979). Parent-child interaction and children's learning. In C. Silverman (Ed.), *The HighScope Report* (pp. 39–43). Ypsilanti, MI: HighScope Press.

Epstein, A. S., Larner, M., & Halpern, R. (1995). *A guide to developing community-based family support programs.* Ypsilanti, MI: HighScope Press.

Epstein, A. S., Montie, J. E., & Weikart, D. P. (2002). *Supporting families with young children: The HighScope Parent-to-Parent Dissemination Project.* Ypsilanti, MI: HighScope Press.

Epstein A. S., & Trimis, E. (2002). *Supporting young artists: The development of the visual arts in young children.* Ypsilanti, MI: HighScope Press.

Epstein, A. S., & Weikart, D. P. (1979). *The Ypsilanti-Carnegie Infant Education Project: Longitudinal follow-up.* Ypsilanti, MI: HighScope Press.

Erikson, E. (1963). *Childhood and society* (2nd ed.). New York: W. W. Norton. (Original work published 1950)

Evans, J., & Ilfeld, E. (1982a). *Activities for parent-child interaction, supplement to good beginnings.* Ypsilanti, MI: HighScope Press.

Evans, J., & Ilfeld, E. (1982b). *Good beginnings: Parenting in the early years.* Ypsilanti, MI: HighScope Press.

Falk, J. (1979). The importance of person-oriented adult-child relationships. In M. Gerber (Ed.), *The RIE manual for parents and professionals* (pp. 115–124). Los Angeles: Resources for Infant Educarers.

Fraiberg, S. (1959). *The magic years: Understanding and handling the problems of early childhood.* New York: Scribner.

French, G., & Murphy, P. (2005). *Once in a lifetime: Early childhood care and education for children from birth to three.* Dublin, Ireland: Barnardos National Children's Resource Centre.

Garcia, J. (1999). *Sign with your baby: How to communicate with infants before they can speak.* Mukilteo, WA: Northlight Communication.

Gerber, M. (Ed.). (1979). *The RIE manual for parents and professionals.* Los Angeles: Resources for Infant Educarers.

Gerber, M. (1981). What is appropriate curriculum for infants and toddlers? In B. Weissbourd & J. Musick (Eds.), *Infants: Their social environments* (pp. 77–85). Washington, DC: National Association for the Education of Young Children.

Gerber, M. (1996, November). *Understanding infants: What makes it so difficult!* Presentation at the conference of the National Association for the Education of Young Children, Dallas, TX.

Gerber, M., & Johnson, A. (1998). *Your self-confident baby: How to encourage your child's natural abilities — from the very start.* New York: John Wiley & Sons.

Gerecke, K. (1998). Classroom adaptations for children with special needs. *HighScope Extensions, 13*(2), 1–5. Available at the HighScope *Extensions* archive: http://www.highscope.org/Content.asp?ContentId=209

Gilliam, W. S., & Leiter, V. (2003). Evaluating early childhood programs: Improving quality and informing policy. *Zero to Three, 23*(6), 6–13.

Ginsburg, H. P., Inoue, N., & Seo, K-H. (1999). Young children doing mathematics: Observations of everyday activities. In J. V. Copley (Ed.), *Mathematics in the early years* (pp. 88–99). Reston, VA: National Council of Teachers of Mathematics & National Association for the Education of Young Children.

Ginsburg, K. R. (2007). The importance of play in promoting healthy child development and maintaining strong parent-child bonds. *Pediatrics, 119*(1), 182–191. doi:10.1542/peds.2006-2697

Goldschmied, E. (1989). *Infants at work: A video.* London: National Children's Bureau.

Goldschmied, E., & Jackson, S. (1994). *People under three: Young children in day care.* New York: Routledge.

Gonzalez-Mena, J. (1992). Taking a culturally sensitive approach in infant-toddler programs. *Young Children 47*(2): 4–9.

Gonzalez-Mena, J. (2008). *Diversity in early care and education: Honoring differences* (5th ed.). New York: McGraw-Hill.

Gonzalez-Mena, J., & Eyer, D. W. (1993). *Infants, toddlers, and caregivers: A curriculum of respectful, responsive care and education.* Mountain View, CA: Mayfield.

Goodman, M., & Tomasello, M. (2008). Baby steps on the road to society: Shared intentionality in the second year of life. *Zero to Three, 28*(5), 21–25.

Goodwyn, S. W., Acredolo, L. P., & Brown, C. A. (2000). Impact of symbolic gesturing on early language development. *Journal* of *Nonverbal Behavior, 24*(2), 81–103. doi:10.1023/A:1006653828895

Gopnik, A. (2009, August 16). Your baby is smarter than you think. *The New York Times,* p. WK10.

Gopnik, A., Meltzoff, A. N., & Kuhl, P. K. (2001). *The scientist in the crib: What early learning tells us about the mind.* New York: Harper Collins.

Goswami, U. (Ed.). (2002). *Blackwell handbook of child cognitive development.* Malden, MA: Blackwell.

Greenman, J. (1988). *Caring spaces, learning places: Children's environments that work.* Redmond, WA: Exchange Press.

Greenspan, S. I. (with Benderly, B. L.) (1997). *The growth of the mind and the endangered origins of intelligence.* Reading, MA: Perseus Books.

Griffin, A. (1998). Infant/toddler sleep in the child care context: Patterns, problems, and relationships. *Zero to Three, 19*(2), 24–29.

Harlow, H. (1958). The nature of love. *American Psychologist, 13*(12), pp. 673–685. doi:10.1037/h0047884

Harms, T. (1994). Humanizing infant environments for group care. *Children's Environments, 11*(2), 155–167.

Harms, T., Cryer, D., & Clifford, R. M. (2006). *Infant/Toddler Environment Rating Scale — Revised edition (ITERS-R).* New York: Teachers College Press.

Hart, B., & Risley, T. (1999). *The social world of children learning to talk.* Baltimore, MD: Brookes Publishing.

Hauser-Cram, P., Warfield, M. E., Shonkoff, J. P., & Krauss, M. W. (2001). Children with disabilities: A longitudinal study of child development and parent well-being. *Monographs of the Society for Research in Child Development, 66*(3, Serial No. 266). doi:10.1111/1540-5834.00150

Healy, J. M. (1998). *Failure to connect: How computers affect our children's minds — and what we can do about it.* New York: Simon & Schuster.

Henderson, A., Gerson, S., & Woodward, A. (2008). The birth of social intelligence. *Zero to Three, 28*(5), 13–20.

Herbstman, J. B., Sjödin, A., Kurzon, M., Lederman, S. A., Jones, R. S., Rauh, V.,…Perera, F. (2010). Prenatal exposure to PBDEs and neurodevelopment. *Environmental Health Perspectives, 118*(5), 1–8. doi:10.1289/ehp.0901340

HighScope Educational Research Foundation. (n.d.). *Community self-help: The parent-to-parent program.* Author: Ypsilanti, MI.

HighScope Educational Research Foundation. (2002a). *Child Observation Record (COR) for Infants and Toddlers.* Ypsilanti, MI: HighScope Press.

HighScope Educational Research Foundation. (2002b). *Child Observation Record (COR) for Infants and Toddlers observation items.* Ypsilanti, MI: HighScope Press.

HighScope Educational Research Foundation. (2002c). *Child Observation Record (COR) for Infants and Toddlers user guide.* Ypsilanti, MI: HighScope Press.

HighScope Educational Research Foundation. (2003a). *Preschool Child Observation Record (COR).* Ypsilanti, MI: HighScope Press.

HighScope Educational Research Foundation. (2003b). *Preschool Program Quality Assessment (PQA).* Ypsilanti, MI: HighScope Press.

HighScope Educational Research Foundation. (2003c). *Youth Program Quality Assessment (PQA).* Ypsilanti, MI: HighScope Press.

HighScope Educational Research Foundation. (2004). *What's next? Planning strategies and activities around Infant-Toddler COR observations.* Ypsilanti, MI: HighScope Press.

HighScope Educational Research Foundation. (2006). *Ready Schools Assessment.* Ypsilanti, MI: HighScope Press.

HighScope Educational Research Foundation. (2009). *Family Child Care Program Quality Assessment (PQA).* Ypsilanti, MI: HighScope Press.

HighScope Educational Research Foundation. (2011). *Infant-Toddler Program Quality Assessment (PQA): Form A — observation items, beta version.* Ypsilanti, MI.

Hills, T. W. (1992). Reaching potentials through appropriate assessment. In S. Bredekamp & T. Rosegrant (Eds.), *Reaching potentials: Appropriate curriculum and assessment for young children* (Vol. 1, pp. 43–63). Washington, DC: National Association for the Education of Young Children.

Hohmann, M., Weikart, D. P., & Epstein, A. S. (2008). *Educating young children: Active learning practices for preschool and child care programs* (3rd ed.). Ypsilanti, MI: HighScope Press.

Honig, A. (2002). *Secure relationships: Nurturing infant/toddler attachment in early care settings.* Washington, DC: National Association for the Education of Young Children.

Hyson, M. C. (1994). *The emotional development of young children: Building an emotion-centered curriculum.* New York: Teachers College Press.

Jablon, J. R., Dombro, A. L., & Dichtelmiller, M. L. (2007). *The power of observation for birth through eight* (2nd ed.). Washington, DC: National Association for the Education of Young Children.

Jacobsen, T., Edelstein, W., & Hofmann, V. (1994). A longitudinal study of the relation between representations of attachment in childhood and cognitive functioning in childhood and adolescence. *Developmental Psychology, 30*(1), 112–124. doi:10.1037/0012-1649.30.1.112

Jalongo, M. R. (2004). *Young children and picture books* (2nd ed.). Washington, DC: National Association for the Education of Young Children.

Johnston, J., Durieux-Smith, A., & Bloom, K. (2005). Teaching gestural signs to infants to advance child development: A review of the evidence. *First Language, 25*(2), 235–251. doi:10.1177/0142723705050340

Just, M. A., Cherkassky, V. L., Aryal, S., & Mitchell, T. M. (2010). A neurosemantic theory of concrete noun representation based on the underlying brain codes. *PLoS ONE, 5*(1), e8622. doi:10.1371/journal.pone.0008622

Kagan, J. (2008). Temperament and the reactions to unfamiliarity. In M. Gauvain & M. Cole (Eds.), *Readings on the development of children* (5th ed., pp. 63–68). New York: Worth Publishers.

Kagan, S. L., Moore, E., & Bredekamp, S. (Eds.). (1995). *Reconsidering children's early development and learning: Toward common views and vocabulary* (Goal 1 Technical Planning Group Report 95–03). Washington, DC: National Education Goals Panel.

Kahn, P., & Kellert, S. (2002). *Children and nature: Psychological, sociocultural, and evolutionary investigations.* Cambridge, MA: MIT Press.

Karen, R. (1990, February). Becoming attached. *The Atlantic Monthly,* 35–70.

Katz, L. G. (1993). *Self-esteem and narcissism: Implications for practice* (ED358973). Retrieved from ERIC Digests website: http://www.ericdigests.org/1993/esteem.htm

Katz, L., & McClellan, D. (1997). *Fostering children's social competence: The teacher's role.* Washington, DC: National Association for the Education of Young Children.

Kellman, P. J., & Arterberry, M. E. (2006). Infant visual perception. In W. Damon et al.

(Eds.), *Handbook of child psychology* (6th ed., Vol. 2, pp. 109–160). New York: John Wiley & Sons.

Keyser, J. (2006). *From parents to partners: Building a family-centered early childhood program.* St. Paul, MN: Redleaf Press; Washington, DC: National Association for the Education of Young Children.

Kindler, A. M. (1995). Significance of adult input in early childhood artistic development. In C. M. Thompson (Ed.), *The visual arts and early childhood learning* (pp. 52–55). Reston, VA: National Art Education Association.

Klaus, M. H., & Kennell, J. H. (1976). *Maternal-infant bonding: The impact of early separation or loss on family development.* St Louis, MO: Mosby.

Kohn, A. (1999). *Punished by rewards: The trouble with gold stars, incentive plans, A's, praise, and other bribes* (2nd ed.). New York: Houghton Mifflin.

Kovach, B., & Da Ros-Voseles, D. (2008). *Being with babies: Understanding and responding to the infants in your care.* Silver Spring, MD: Gryphon House.

Lally, J. R. (1995). The impact of child care policies and practices on infant/toddler identity formation. *Young Children, 51*(1): 58–67.

Lally, J. R. (2009). The science and psychology of infant-toddler care: How an understanding of early learning has transformed child care. *Zero to Three, 30*(2), 47–53.

Lally, J. R., & Stewart, J. (Eds.). (1990). *Infant/toddler caregiving: A guide to setting up environments.* Sacramento, CA: California Department of Education.

Lambie, D. Z., Bond, J. T., & Weikart, D. P. (1974). *Home teaching with mothers and infants.* Ypsilanti, MI: HighScope Press.

Larner, M., Halpern, R., & Harkavy, O. (1992). *Fair start for children: Lessons learned from seven demonstration projects.* New Haven, CT: Yale University Press.

Leipzig, J. (1996). Supporting the development of a scientific mind in infants and toddlers. In B. Neugebauer (Ed.), *The wonder of it: Exploring how the world works* (pp. 29–34). Redmond, WA: Exchange Press, Inc.

Lockhart, S. D. (2005a). Look, grasp, feel, paint: Art with infants and toddlers. *HighScope Extensions, 19*(5), 1–3. Available at the HighScope *Extensions* archive: http://www.highscope.org/Content. asp?ContentId=209

Lockhart, S. D. (2005b). Open your eyes with the Infant-Toddler COR. In N. A. Brickman, H. Barton, & J. Burd (Eds.), *Supporting young learners: Ideas for child care providers and teachers* (Vol. 4, pp. 299–307). Ypsilanti, MI: HighScope Press.

Main, M., & Solomon, J. (1986). Discovery of an insecure-disorganized/disoriented attachment pattern. In T. B. Brazelton & M. W. Yogman (Eds.), *Affective development in infancy* (pp. 95–124). Norwood, NJ: Ablex.

Mampe, B., Friederici, A. D., Christophe, A., & Wermke, K. (2009). Newborns' cry melody is shaped by their native language. *Current Biology, 19*(23), 1994–1997. doi:10.1016/ j.cub.2009.09.064

Mangione, P. (1990). *Child care video magazine. It's not just routine: Feeding, diapering, and napping infants and toddlers.* Sacramento, CA: California Department of Education.

Manlove, E. E., Frank, T., & Vernon-Feagans, L. (2001). Why should we care about noise in classrooms and child care settings? *Child and Youth Care Forum, 30*(1), 55–64.

Markova, G., & Legerstee, M. (2008, May). How infants come to learn about the minds of others. *Zero to Three, 28*(5), 26–31.

Maxted, A. E., Dickstein S., Miller-Loncar, C., High, P., Spritz, B., Liu, J., & Lester B. M.

(2005). Infant colic and maternal depression. *Infant Mental Health Journal, 26*(1), 56–68. doi:10.1002/imhj.20035

Maxwell, L. E., & Evans, G. W. (n.d.). *Design of child care centers and effects of noise on young children*. Retrieved from http://www.designshare.com/research/lmaxwell/noisechildren.htm

McCartney, K., Burchinal, M., Clarke-Stewart, A., Bub, K. L., Owen, M. T., & Belsky, J. (2010). Testing a series of causal propositions relating time in child care to children's externalizing behavior. *Developmental Psychology, 46*(1), 1–17. doi:10.1037/a0017886

McLendon, J., & Weinberg, G. M. (1996). Beyond blaming: Congruence in large systems development project. *IEEE Software, 13*(4), 33–42.

Meisels, S. J. (2001). Fusing assessment and intervention: Changing parents' and providers' views of young children. *Zero to Three, 21*(4), 4–10.

Melmed, M. (2009). Zero to Three reflections: We have come a long way, baby! We also have a long way to go! *Zero to Three, 30*(2), 59–60.

Meltzoff, A. N., Kuhl, P. K., Movellan, J., & Sejnowski, T. J. (2009). Foundations for a new science of learning. *Science, 325*(5938), 284–288. doi:10.1126/science.1175626

Miller, E., & Almon, J. (2009). *Crisis in the kindergarten: Why children need play in school*. College Park, MD: Alliance for Childhood.

Miller, K. (2000). *Things to do with toddlers and twos* (Rev. ed.). Chelsea, MA: Telshare.

National Association for the Education of Young Children. (1996). NAEYC position statement: Technology and young children — ages three through eight. *Young Children, 51*(5), 11–16.

National Association for the Education of Young Children. (2007). *NAEYC early childhood program standards and accreditation criteria*. Retrieved from https://oldweb.naeyc.org/academy/standards/

National Association for the Education of Young Children & National Association of Early Childhood Specialists in State Departments of Education (2003). *Early childhood curriculum, assessment, and program evaluation: Building an effective, accountable system in programs for children birth through age 8*. Washington, DC: National Association for the Education of Young Children.

National Association for Family Child Care. (2005). *Quality standards for NAFCC accreditation* (4th ed.). Boston, MA: Author.

National Center on Sleep Disorders Research. (2003, July). *2003 National Sleep Disorders research plan* (NIH Publication No. 03-5209). Retrieved from http://www.nhlbi.nih.gov/health/prof/sleep/res_plan/

National Council of Teachers of Mathematics. (2000). *Principles and standards for school mathematics*. Reston, VA: Author.

National Institute of Child Health and Human Development (NICHD) Early Child Care Research Network. (1997). The effects of infant child care on infant-mother attachment security: Results of the NICHD study of early child care. *Child Development 68*(5), 860–879.

National Institute of Child Health and Human Development (NICHD) Early Child Care Research Network. (1999). Child care and mother-child interaction in the first three years of life. *Developmental Psychology, 35*(6), 1399–1413. doi:10.1037/0012-1649.35.6.1399

National Institute of Child Health and Human Development (NICHD) Early Child Care Research Network. (2002). Early child care and children's development prior to school entry: Results from the NICHD Study of Early Child Care. *American Educational Research Journal, 39*(1), 133–164. doi: 10.3102/00028312039001133

National Institute of Child Health and Human Development (NICHD) Early Child Care Research Network. (2003). Does quality of child care affect child outcomes at age 4½? *Developmental Psychology, 39*(3), 451–469. doi:10.1037/0012-1649.39.3.451

National Institute of Child Health and Human Development (NICHD) Early Child Care Research Network. (2010). *Study overview.* Retrieved from http://www.nichd.nih.gov/research/supported/seccyd/overview.cfm

National Reading Panel. (2000). *Teaching children to read: An evidence-based assessment of the scientific research literature on reading and its implications for reading instruction.* Washington, DC: National Institute of Child Health and Human Development, National Institutes of Health.

National Research Council. (2000). *From neurons to neighborhoods: The science of early childhood development.* Washington, DC: National Academy Press.

National Scientific Council on the Developing Child. (2004). *Children's emotional development is built into the architecture of their brains: Working paper no. 2.* Retrieved from http://www.developingchild.harvard.edu

National Scientific Council on the Developing Child. (2007). *The timing and quality of early experiences combine to shape brain architecture: Working paper no. 5.* Retrieved from http://www.developingchild.harvard.edu

Neill, P. (2008). *Real science in preschool: Here, there, and everywhere.* Ypsilanti, MI: HighScope Press.

Neuman, S. B., Copple, C., & Bredekamp, S. (2000). *Learning to read and write: Developmentally appropriate practices for young children.* Washington, DC: National Association for the Education of Young Children.

Owen, M. T. (1996, November). *Symposium on early child care and attachment: Findings from the National Institute of Child Health and Human Development Study of Early Child Care. Report of the Attachment Task Force.* Annual Conference of the National Association for the Education of Young Children, Dallas, TX.

Parlakian, R. (2004). Early literacy and very young children. *Zero to Three, 25*(1), 37–44.

Philips, J. (1969). *The origins of intellect: Piaget's theory.* San Francisco: Freeman.

Piaget, J. (1952). *The origins of intelligence in children.* New York: Norton.

Piaget, J. (1966). *The psychology of intelligence.* Totowa, NJ: Littlefield, Adams.

Pica, R. (1997). Beyond physical development: Why young children need to move. *Young Children, 52*(6), 4–11.

Post, J., & Hohmann, M. (2000). *Tender care and early learning: Supporting infants and toddlers in child care settings.* Ypsilanti, MI: HighScope Press.

Powell, A. (1990). The HighScope program for infants and toddlers with special needs. *ReSource, 9*(1), 12–16.

Powell, A. (1991). Be responsive! In N. A. Brickman & L. S. Taylor (Eds.), *Supporting young learners: Ideas for preschool and day care providers* (pp. 26–34). Ypsilanti, MI: HighScope Press.

Raikes, H. H., & Edwards, C. P. (2009). *Extending the dance in infant and toddler caregiving: Enhancing attachment and relationships.* Baltimore, MD: Paul H. Brookes Publishing; Washington, DC: National Association for the Education of Young Children.

Reschly, B. (1979). *Supporting the changing family: A guide to the parent-to-parent model.* Ypsilanti, MI: HighScope Educational Research Foundation.

Richards, J., & Cronise, K. (2000). Extended visual fixation in the early years: Look duration, heart rate changes, and attentional inertia. *Child Development, 71*(3), 602–620. doi:10.1111/1467-8624.00170

Rodd, J. (1996). *Understanding young children's behavior: A guide for early childhood professionals.* New York: Teachers College Press.

Rogers, C. R. (1983). *The freedom to learn for the 80's.* Columbus, OH: Merrill.

Rosenow, N. (2008). Teaching and learning about the natural world. *Young Children, 63*(1), 10–13.

Rothbart, M. K., & Bates, J. E. (2006). Temperament. In W. Damon, R. M. Lerner, & N. Eisenberg (Eds.), *Handbook of child psychology: Social, emotional, and personality development* (6th ed., Vol. 3, pp. 99–166). New York: John Wiley & Sons.

Rothbart, M. K., & Derryberry, D. (2000, July). *Temperament in children.* Paper presented at the 26th International Congress of Psychology, Stockholm, Sweden.

Rush, K. (2011). *Ready, sign, go! Using sign language to promote preschool learning.* Ypsilanti, MI: HighScope Press.

Rushton, S. P. (2001). Applying brain research to create developmentally appropriate learning environments. *Young Children, 56*(5), 76–82.

Sanders, S. W. (2002). *Active for life: Developmentally appropriate movement programs for young children.* Washington, DC: National Association for the Education of Young Children.

Satir, V. (1988). *The new peoplemaking.* Mountain View, CA: Science and Behavior Books.

Schickedanz, J. A. (1999). *Much more than the ABCs: The early stages of reading and writing.* Washington, DC: National Association for the Education of Young Children.

Schiller, P. (2008). *Start smart: Building brain power in the early years.* Boston: Gryphon House.

Shepard, L., Kagan, S. L., & Wurtz, E. (Eds.). (1998). *Principles and recommendations for early childhood assessments.* Washington, DC: National Education Goals Panel.

Shore, R. (2003). *Rethinking the brain: New insights into early development* (Rev. ed.). Washington, DC: Families and Work Institute.

Siegel, D. J. (1999). *The developing mind: Toward a neurobiology of interpersonal experience.* New York: Guilford Press.

Signer, S. (1995, November). *Strategies for implementing continuity of care in infant/toddler programs.* Paper developed by participants at the Program for Infant/Toddler Caregivers Graduate Conference Seminar on Continuity, Sausalito, CA.

Smith, D., Goldhaber, J., & Cooper-Ellis, C. (1998, November). *Multiple perspectives on the benefits of teacher continuity and infant and toddler centers.* Paper presented at the National Association for the Education of Young Children Conference, Toronto, Canada.

Smith, L. (2002). Piaget's model. In U. Goswami (Ed.), *Blackwell handbook of child cognitive development* (pp. 515–537). Malden, MA: Blackwell Publishers.

Snow, C. E., Burns, M. S., & Griffin, P. (Eds.). (1998). *Preventing reading difficulties in young children.* Washington, DC: National Academy Press.

Soundy, C. S. (1997). Nurturing literacy with infants and toddlers in group settings. *Childhood Education, 73*(3), 149–153.

Speltz, M. L., Greenberg, M. T., & DeKlyen, M. (1990). Attachment in preschoolers with disruptive behavior: A comparison of clinic-referred and non-problem children. *Development and Psychopathology, 2,* 31–46. doi:10.1017/S0954579400000572

Spitz, R. (1945). Hospitalism: An inquiry into the genesis of psychiatric conditions in early childhood. *Psychoanalytic Study of the Child, 1,* 53–74.

Sroufe, L. A. (1988). The role of infant-caregiver attachments in development. In J. Belsky & T. Nezworski (Eds.), *Clinical implications of attachment* (pp. 18–38). Hillsdale, NJ: Erlbaum.

Stern, D. (1985). *The interpersonal world of the infant: A view from psychoanalysis and developmental psychology.* New York: Basic Books.

Sturm, L. (2004). Temperament in early childhood: A primer for the perplexed. *Zero to Three, 24*(4), 4–11.

Sullivan, M. (1982). *Feeling strong, feeling free: Movement exploration for young children.* Washington, DC: National Association for the Education of Young Children.

Talbot, M. (1998, May 24). Attachment theory: The ultimate experiment. *The New York Times Magazine,* pp. 24–30, 38, 46, 50, 54.

Teglasi, H., & Epstein, S. (1998). Temperament and personality theory: The perspective of cognitive-experiential self-theory. *School Psychology Review, 27,* 534–550.

Thomas, A., & Chess, S. (1977). *Temperament and development.* New York: Brunner/ Mazel.

Thompson, R. A. (2008). The psychologist in the baby. *Zero to Three, 28*(5), 5–12.

Thompson, R. A. (2009). Doing what *doesn't* come naturally: The development of self-regulation. *Zero to Three, 30*(2), 33–39.

Tierney, A., & Nelson, C. A. (2009). Brain development and the role of experience in the early years. *Zero to Three, 30*(2), 9–13.

Tizard, B., Mortimore, J., & Burchell, B. (1983). *Involving parents in nursery and infant school.* Ypsilanti, MI: HighScope Press.

Tomasello, M., Carpenter, M., & Liszkowski, U. (2007). A new look at infant pointing. *Child Development, 78*(3), 705–722. doi:10.1111/j.1467-8624.2007.01025.x

Torelli, L. (1992). The developmentally designed group care setting: A supportive environment for infants, toddlers, and caregivers. In E. Fenichel (Ed.), *Zero to Three child care classics: 7 articles on infant/ toddler development* (pp. 37–40). Arlington, VA: Zero to Three/National Center for Clinical Infant Programs.

Torelli, L., & Durrett, C. (1998). *Landscapes for learning: Designing group care environments for infants, toddlers, and two-year-olds.* Berkeley, CA: Torelli/ Durrett.

Torquati, J., & Barber, J. (2005). Dancing with trees: Infants and toddlers in the garden. *Young Children, 60*(3), 40–47.

Vallotton, C. (2008). Infants take self-regulation into their own hands. *Zero to Three, 29*(1), 29–34.

van IJzendoorn M. H., Schuengel, C., & Bakermans-Kranenburg, M. J. (1999). Disorganized attachment in early childhood: Meta-analysis of precursors, concomitants and sequelae. *Development and Psychopathology, 11,* 225–249. doi:10.1017/ S0954579499002035

Volterra, V., Iverson, J. M., & Castrataro, M. (2006). The development of gesture in hearing and deaf children. In B. Schick et al. (Eds.), *Sign language development* (pp. 46–70). London: Oxford University Press.

Vygotsky, L. S. (1986). *Thought and language* (Rev. ed.). Cambridge, MA: MIT Press. (Original work published 1934)

Wachs, T. W. (2004). Temperament and development: The role of context in a biologically based system. *Zero to Three, 24*(4), 12–21.

Walley, A. C. (1993). The role of vocabulary development in children's spoken word recognition and segmentation ability. *Developmental Review, 13*(3), 286–350. doi:10.1006/drev.1993.1015

Waters, E., & Cummings, E. M. (2000). A secure base from which to explore close relationships. *Child Development, 71(1),* 164–172. doi:10.1111/1467-8624.00130

Weigand, R. F. (2007). Reflective supervision in child care: The discoveries of an accidental tourist. *Zero to Three, 28*(2), 17–22.

Weikart, P. S. (2000). *Round the circle: Key experiences in movement for young children* (2nd ed.). Ypsilanti, MI: HighScope Press.

Wells, G. (1986). *The meaning makers: Children learning language and using language to learn.* Portsmouth, NH: Heinemann Educational Books.

White, B., Kaban, B., Marmor, J., & Shapiro, B. (1972). *Child-rearing practices and the development of competence: Final report* (Grant No. CO-9909 A12). Washington, DC: Office of Economic Opportunity, Head Start Division.

Williams, A. E. (2008). Exploring the natural world with infants and toddlers in an urban setting. *Young Children, 63*(1), 22–25.

Winnicott, D. W. (1987). *Babies and their mothers.* Reading, MA: Addison-Wesley.

Zahn-Waxler, C., Radke-Yarrow, M., Wagner, E., & Chapman, M. (1992). Development of concern for others. *Developmental Psychology, 28*(1), 126-136. doi:10.1037/0012-1649.28.1.126

Zero to Three. (2008). *Caring for infants and toddlers in groups: Developmentally appropriate practice* (2nd ed.). Arlington, VA: Author.

Zero to Three. (2009). The infant and toddler years. In Carol Copple & Sue Bredekamp (Eds.). *Developmentally appropriate practice in early childhood programs serving children from birth through age 8* (3rd ed., pp. 53–73). Washington, DC: National Association for the Education of Young Children.

Zero to Three and the Ounce of Prevention Fund (2000). *Starting smart: How early experiences affect brain development* (2nd ed.). Retrieved from http://www.zerotothree.org/site/DocServer/startingsmart.pdf?docID=2422

Zigler, E., & Bishop-Josef, S. J. (2009). *Play under siege: A historical overview. Zero to Three, 30*(1), 4–11.

Index